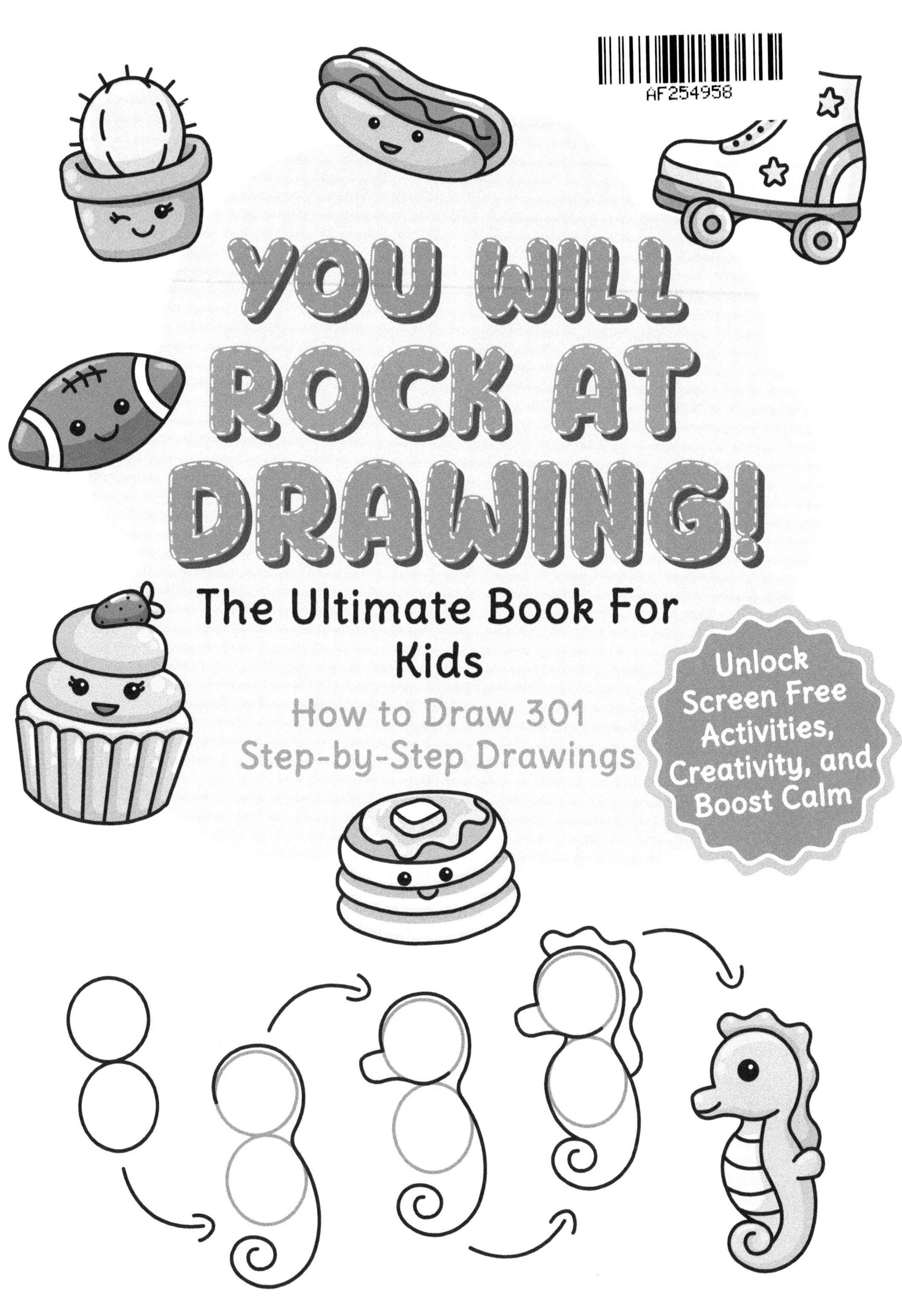
AF254958
YOU WILL ROCK AT DRAWING!
The Ultimate Book For Kids
How to Draw 301 Step-by-Step Drawings
Unlock Screen Free Activities, Creativity, and Boost Calm

HOW TO USE THIS BOOK

PENCIL & ERASER

Before you start, all you need is a pencil and an eraser. A pencil is perfect for drawing because you can:

- Make changes
- Try again
- Keep going

If you feel like adding some color later, colored pencils are a fun option. Go at your own pace. Drawing is more fun when you take your time.

HOW TO PRACTICE AS YOU DRAW

Soft lines are easy to change, and that's a good thing. Follow the arrows step by step to finish your drawing. When you're done, use the extra space to:

- Try it again
- Make it your own
- Practice just for fun

There's no wrong way to practice. The more you draw, the better you get.

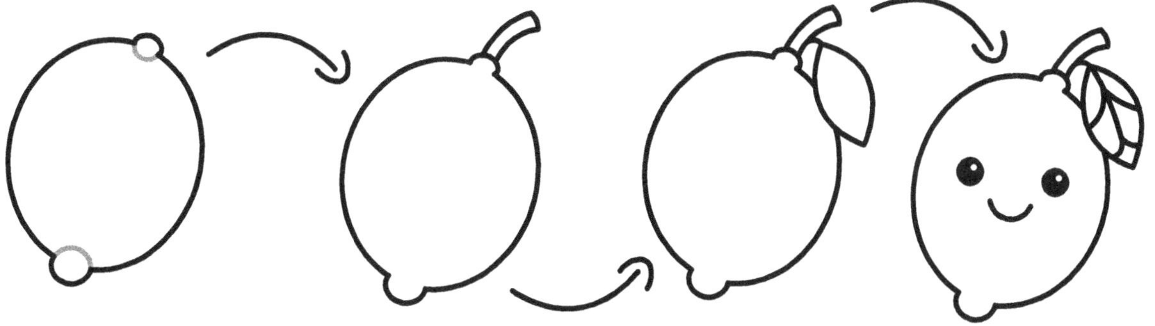

LEARNING TO DRAW LINES

Before you start, practice drawing some lines. It's a fun way to get your hand moving and ready to create.

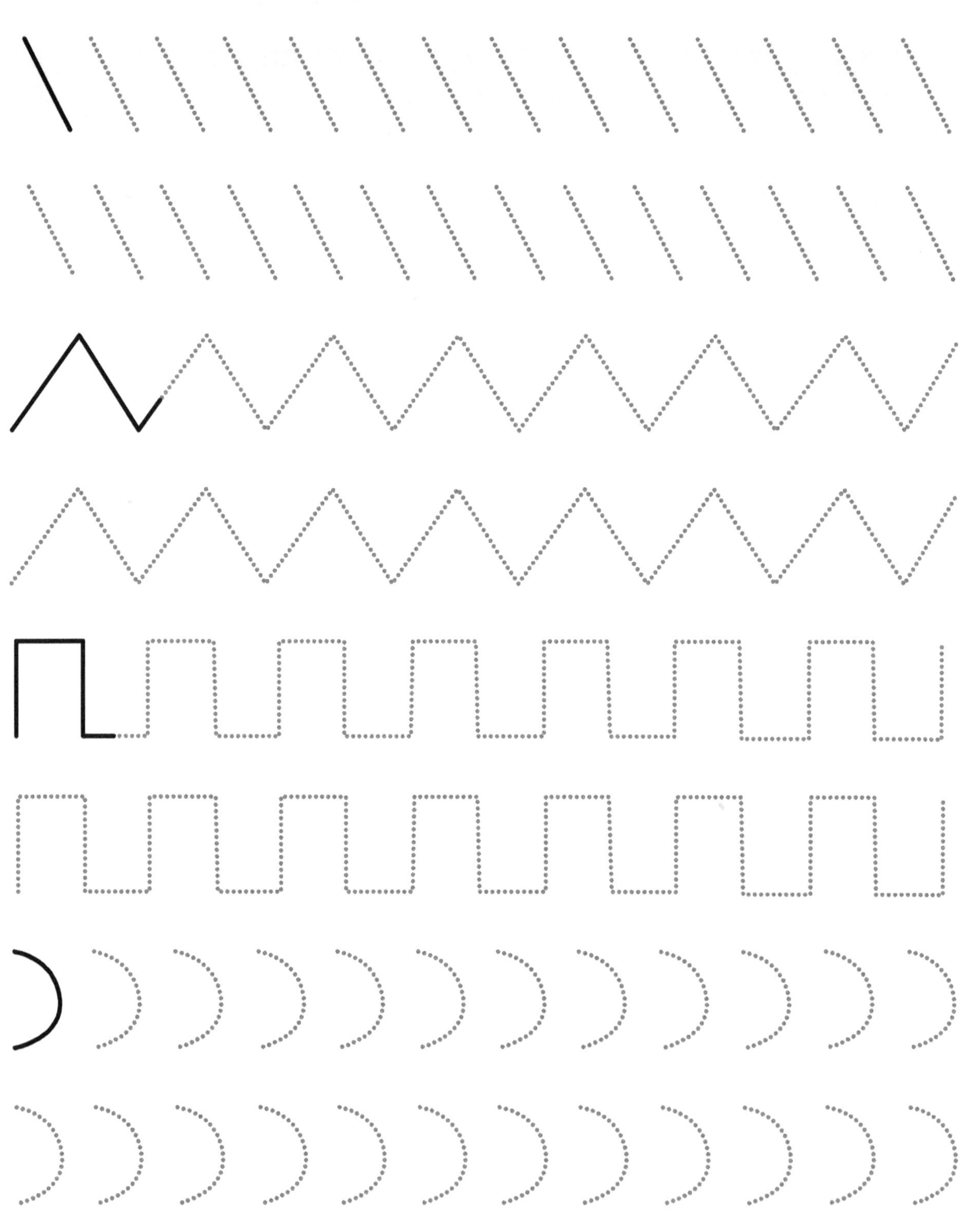

LEARNING TO DRAW LINES

Before you start, practice drawing some lines. It's a fun way to get your hand moving and ready to create.

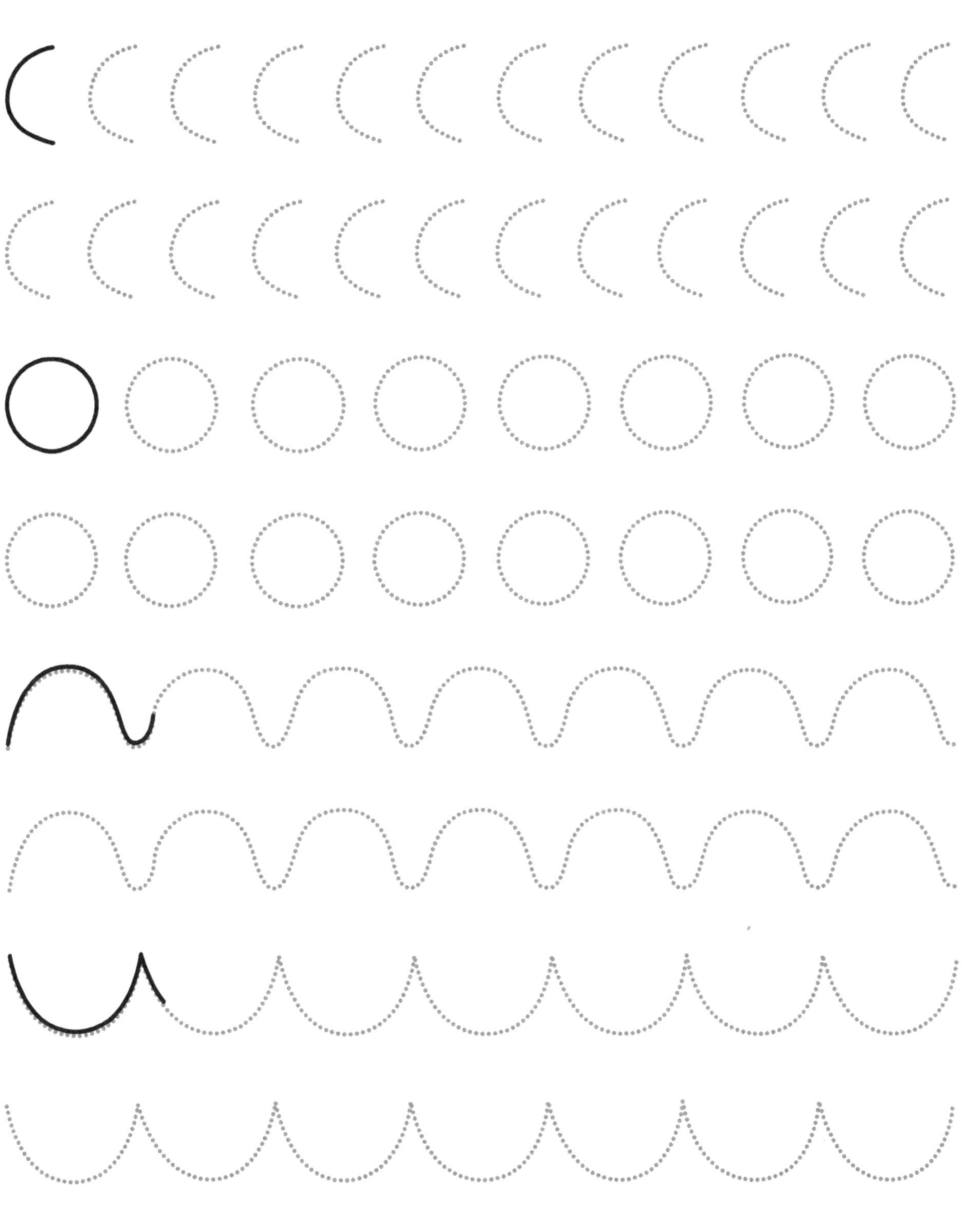

TABLE OF CONTENTS
HAPPY SNACKS & TREATS

JUNK FOODS

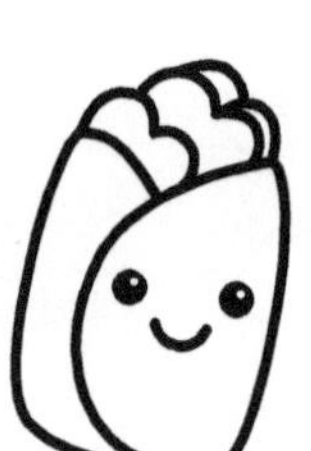

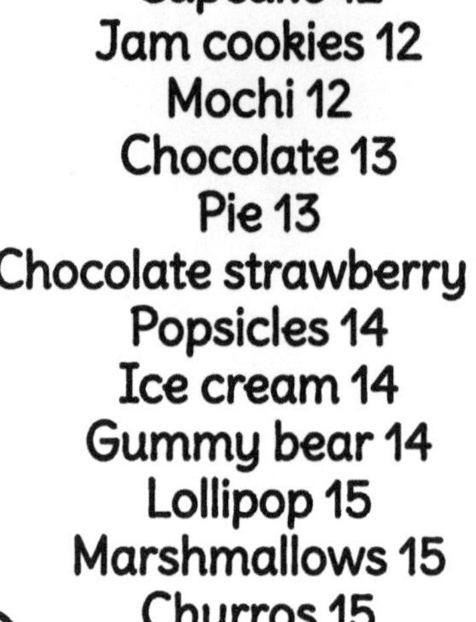

BREAKFAST BUDDIES

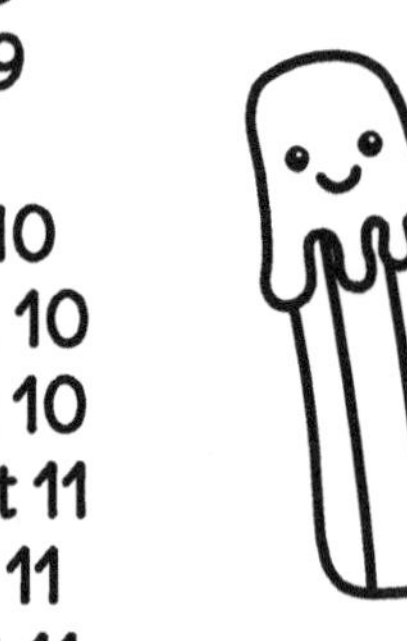

SWEETS TREATS

FRUITS & VEGGIES

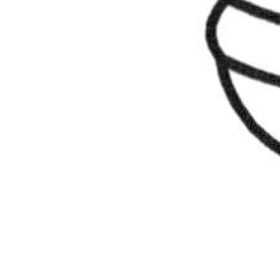

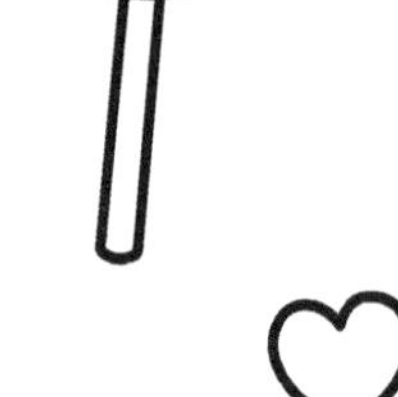

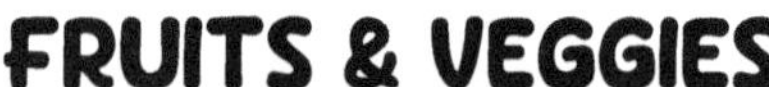

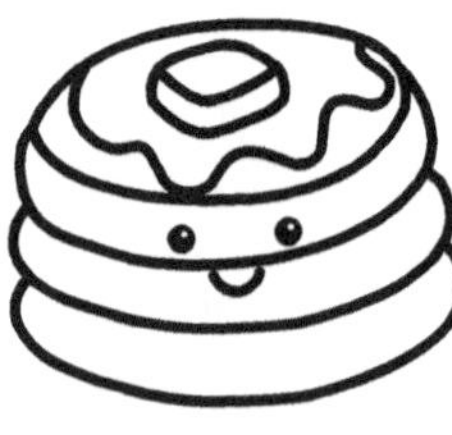

FRIENDLY CREATURES

PET FRIENDS

Cat 28
Dog 28
Piggy 28
Hamster 29
Bunny 29
Cow 29
Goat 30
Horse 30
Chinchilla 30

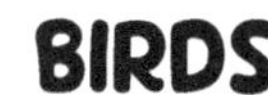

AMAZING WILD ANIMALS

Bear 31
Reindeer 31
Panda 31
Fox 32
Wolf 32
Lama 32
Hedgehog 33
Koala 33
Bat 33
Chipmunk 34
Cheetah 34
Lion 34
Tiger 35
Elephant 35
Monkey 35
Sloth 36
Giraffe 36
Zebra 36
Camel 37
Otter 37
Crocodile 37
Lizard 38
Snake 38
Turtle 38

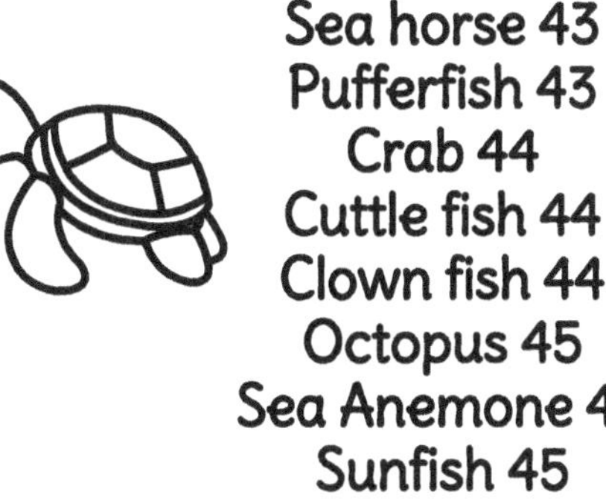

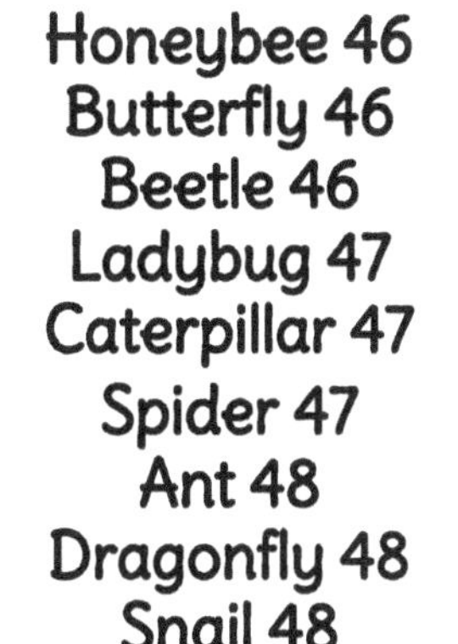

SEA ANIMALS

Eel 39
Axolotl 39
Whale 39
Shark 40
Starfish 40
Seashell 40
Ray 41
Koi fish 41
Goldfish 41
Squid 42
Whale 42
Dolphin 42
Seal 43
Sea horse 43
Pufferfish 43
Crab 44
Cuttle fish 44
Clown fish 44
Octopus 45
Sea Anemone 45
Sunfish 45
Sunfish 45

TINY INSECTS

Honeybee 46
Butterfly 46
Beetle 46
Ladybug 47
Caterpillar 47
Spider 47
Ant 48
Dragonfly 48
Snail 48

MAGICAL BEINGS

Unicorn 49

Dragon 49
T-rex 49
Mermaid 50
Griffin 50
Phoenix 50

BIRDS

Duck 51
Parrot 51
Penguin 51
Toucan 52
Rooster 52
Peacock 52
Cockatiel 53
Flamingo 53
Owl 53

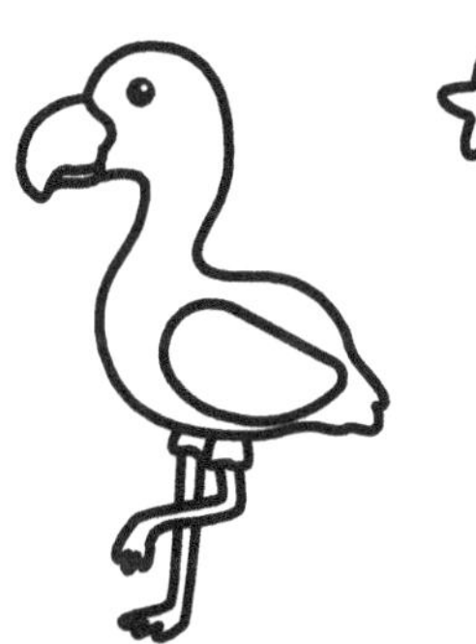

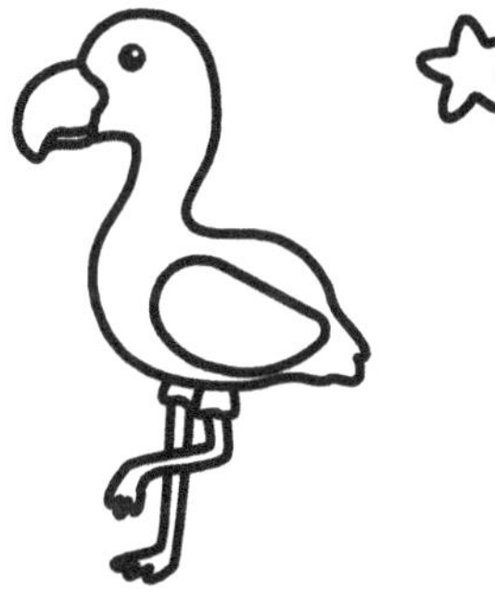

VEHICLES

Car 55
Ice cream truck 55
Tipper truck 55
Roller skates 56
Pickup truck 56
Bus 56
Boat 57
Train 57
Airplane 57
Hand scooter 58
Skateboard 58
Bicycle 58

SPORTS & GAMES

Frisbees 59
Jump ropes 59
Basketball 59
Football 60
Soccer ball 60
Baseball bat 60

Baseball glove 61
Boxing gloves 61
Hockey stick 61
Racket 62
Shuttlecock 62
Whistle 62

TOYS

Teddy bear 63
Yoyo 63
Spinner 63
Gum ball 64
Toy camera 64
Doll 64
Walkie-talkie 65
Balloon 65
Playdoh 65
Poppit 66
Robot 66
Alphabet blocks 66

Interlocking bricks 67
Dice 67
Dominoes 67
Slime jar 68
Toy phone 68
Drum 68
Bell 69
Crayons 69
Pyramid 69
Rocket 70
Binculars 70
Xylophone 70

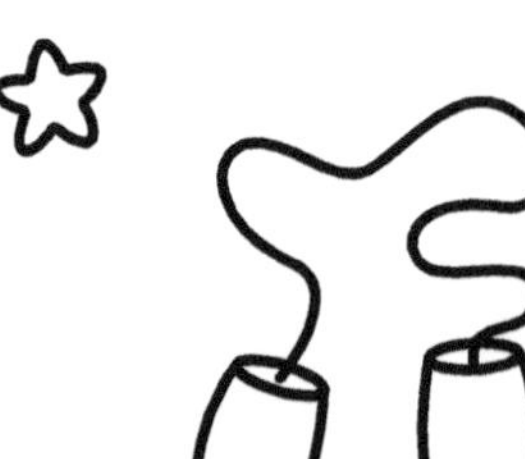

EVERYDAY WONDERS

NATURE

Sun 72
Moon 72
Star 72
Rainbow 73
Cloud 73
Rain 73
Waterdrop 74
Snowflake 74
Mountain 74
Ice 75
Wood 75

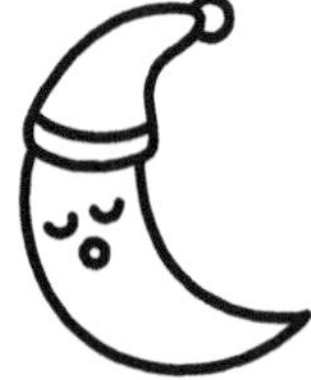

Fire 75
Earth 76
Saturn 76
Tornado 76

PLANTS

Leaf 77
Clover leaf 77
Flower 77
Mushroom 78
Cactus 78
Bonsai 78

FESTIVE

Snowman 79
Christmas tree 79
Christmas hat 79
Christmas ball 80
Wreath 80
Pumpkin basket 80
Witch hat 81
Broom 81
Ghost 81
Shull 82
Candle 82
Eyeball candy 82

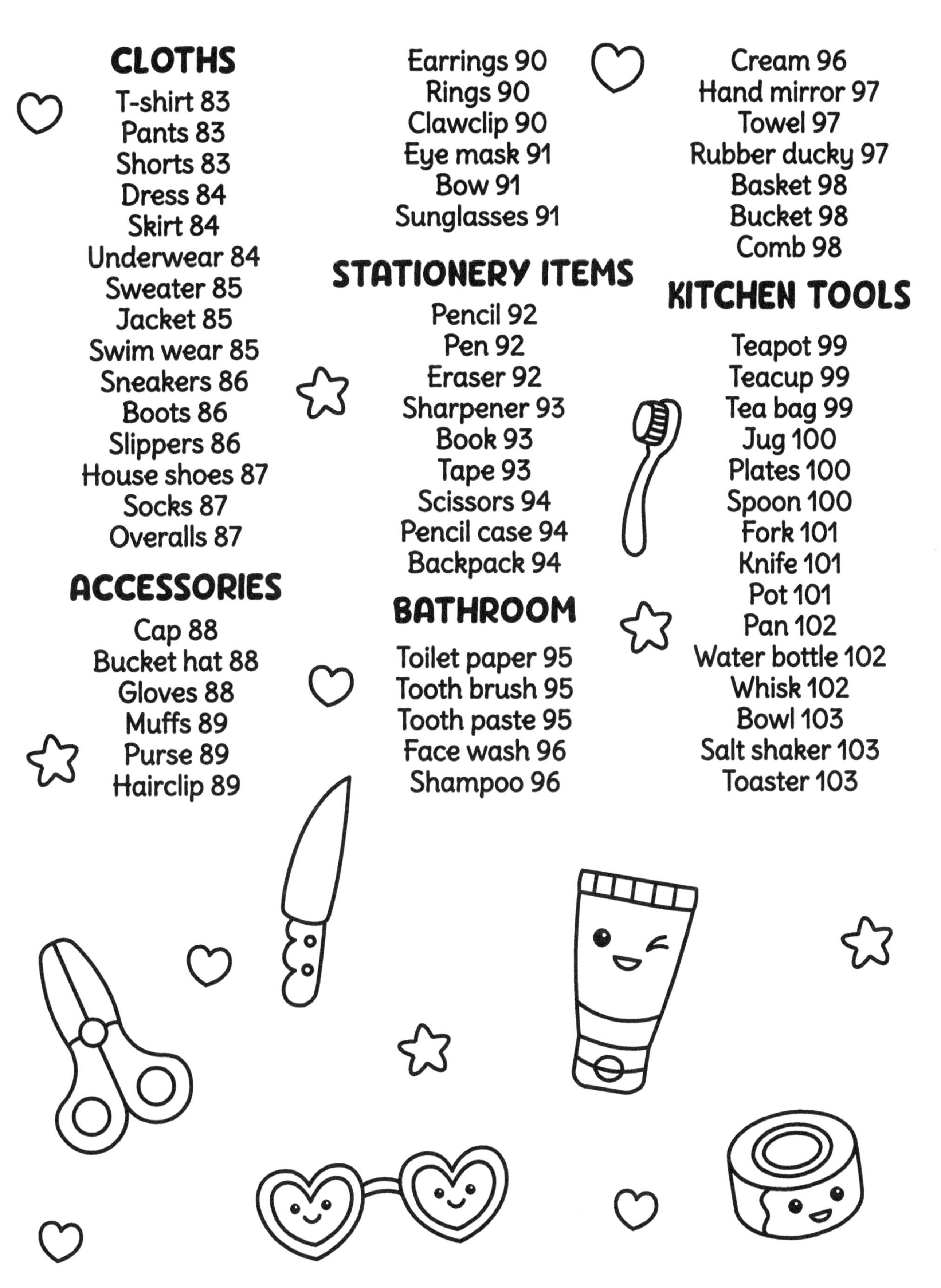

HAPPY
SNACKS
& TREATS

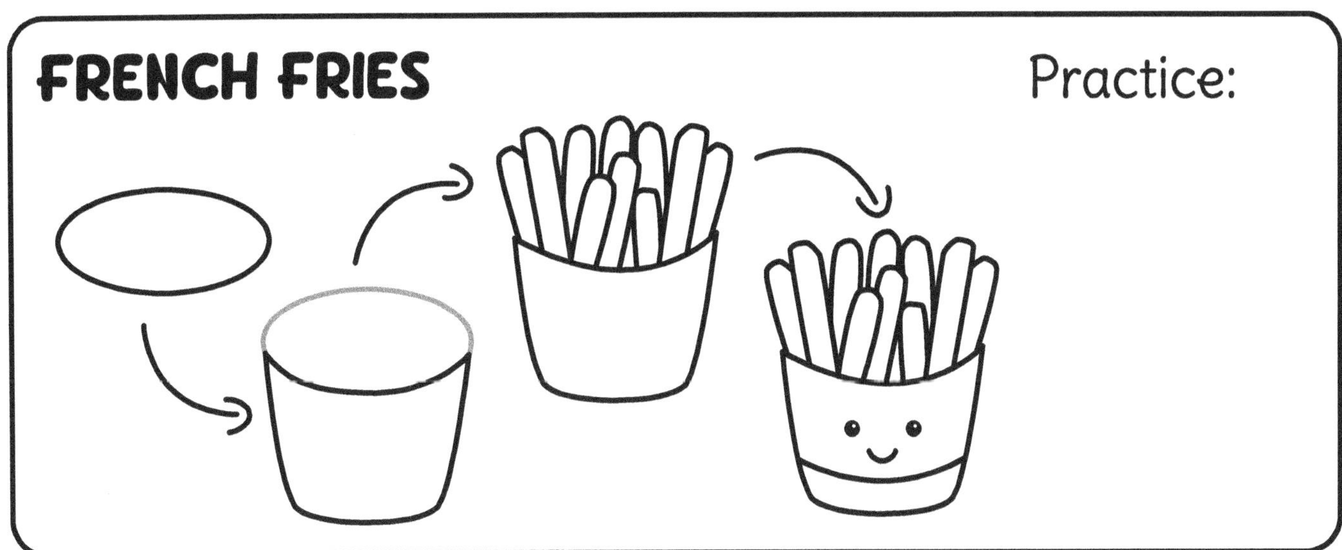

FRENCH FRIES

Practice:

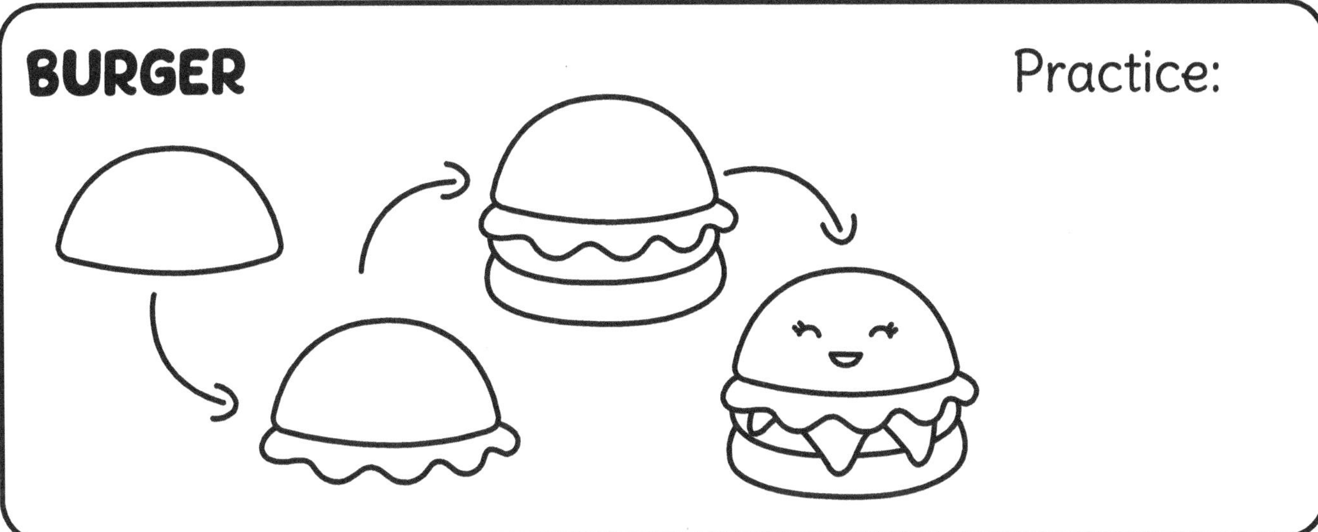

BURGER

Practice:

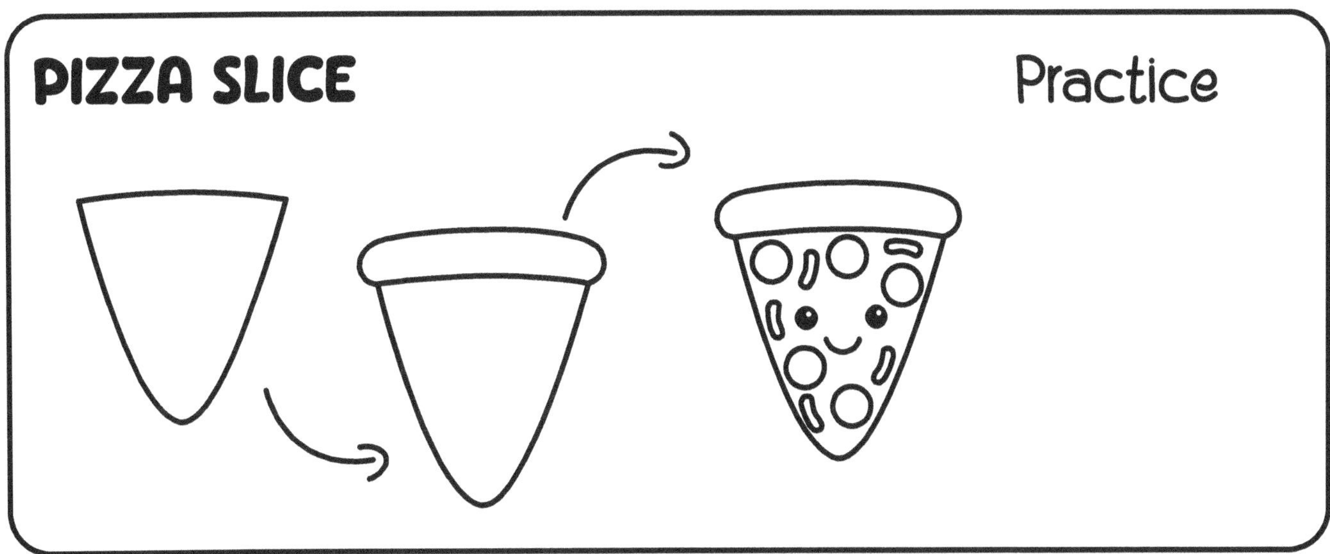

PIZZA SLICE

Practice

POPCORN

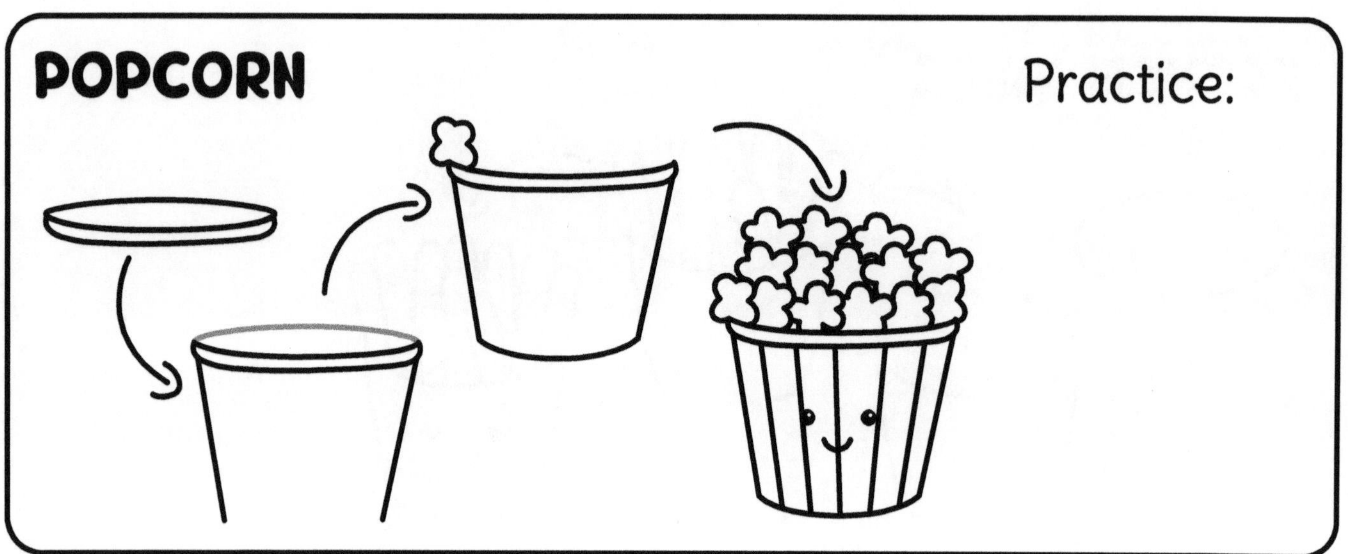

Practice:

HOTDOGS

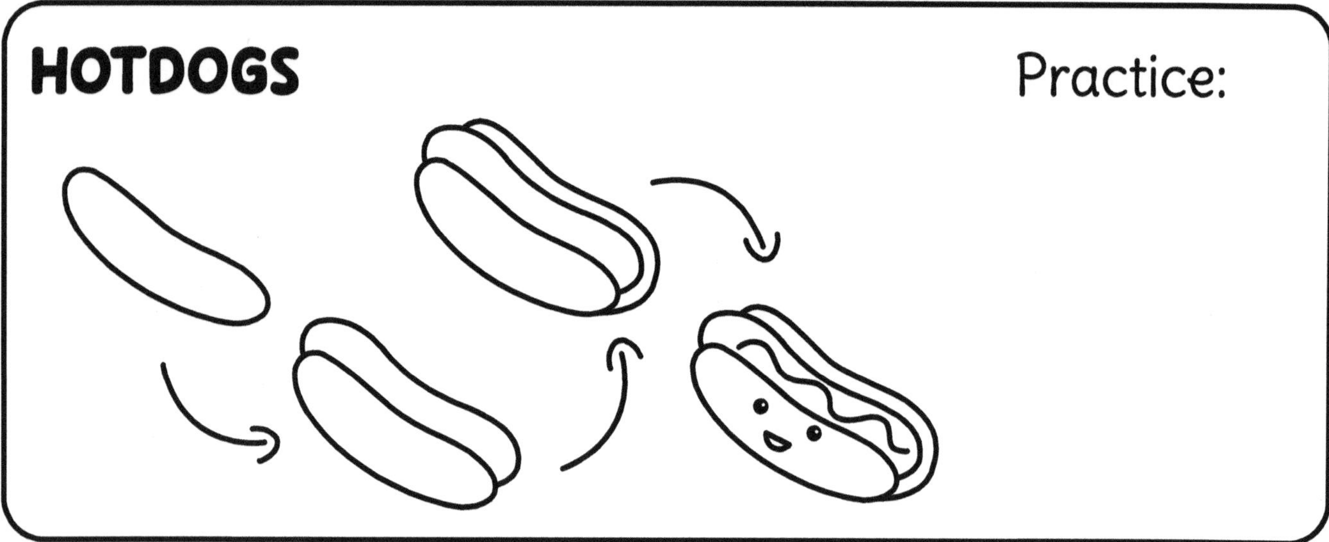

Practice:

CHICKEN LEG

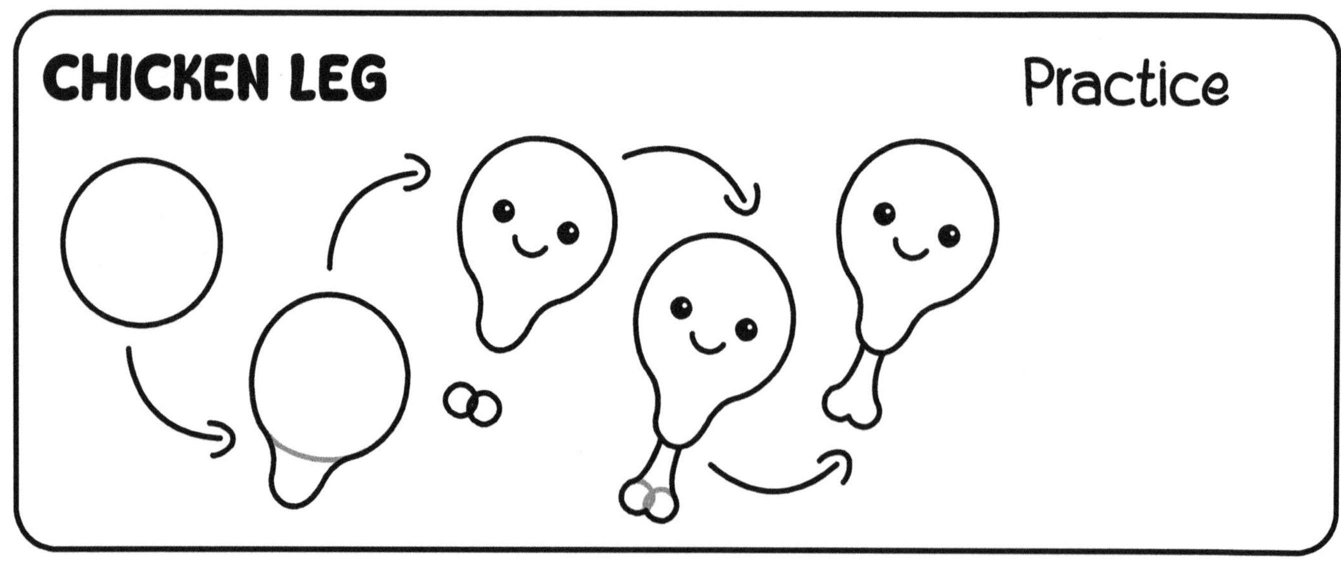

Practice

BAG OF CHIPS Practice:

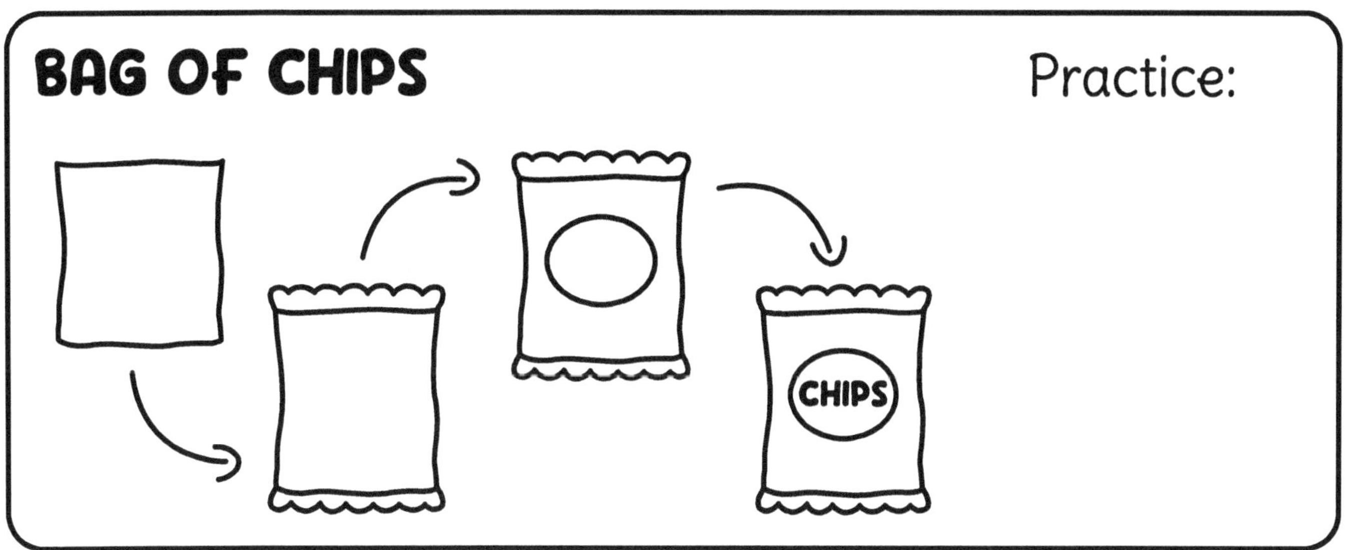

SAUSAGES Practice:

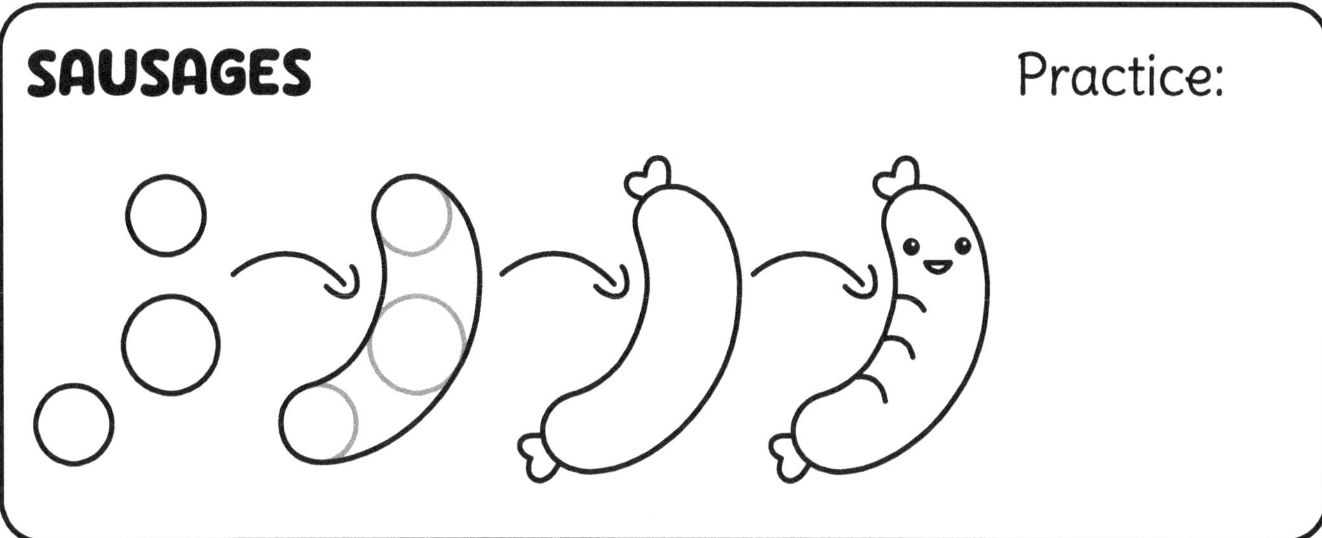

TACOS Practice

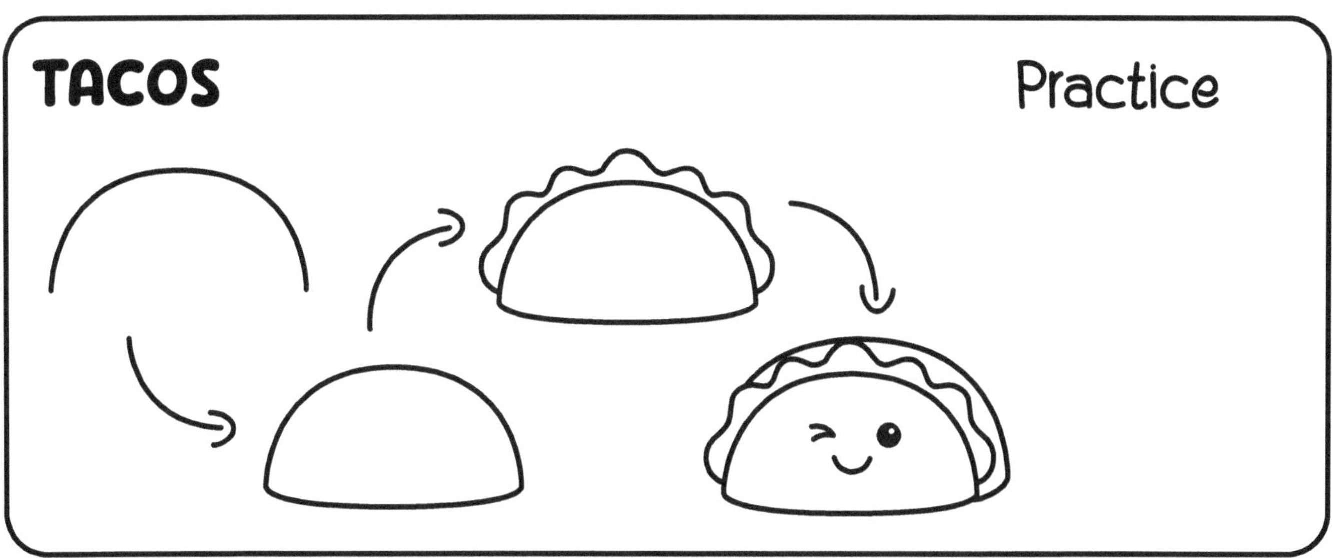

BURRITO

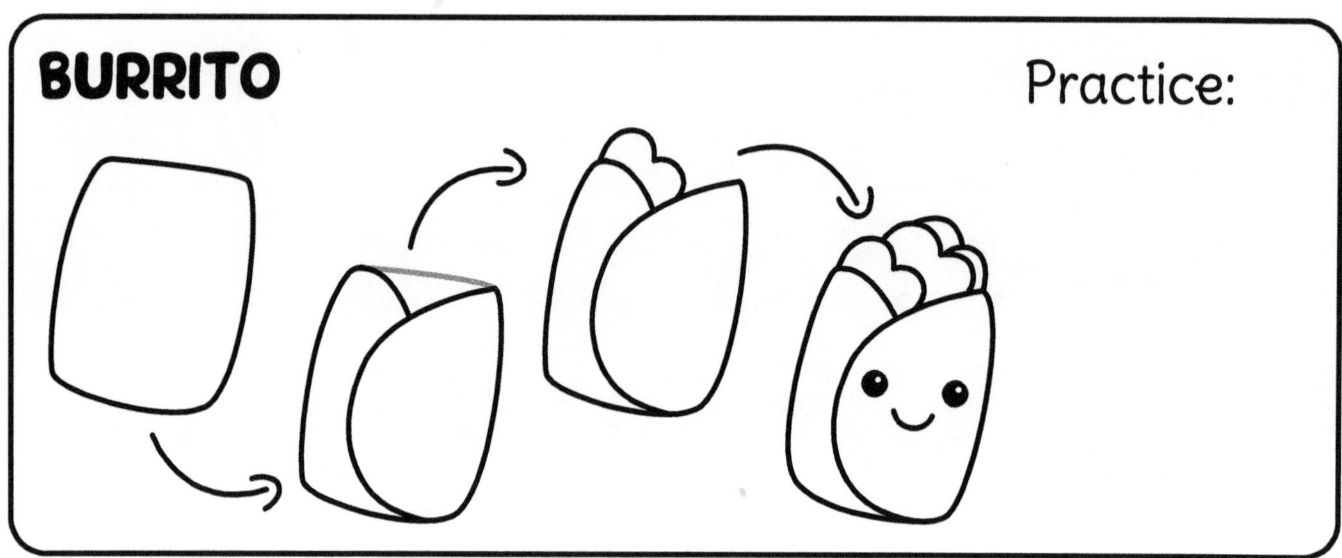

EMPANADA

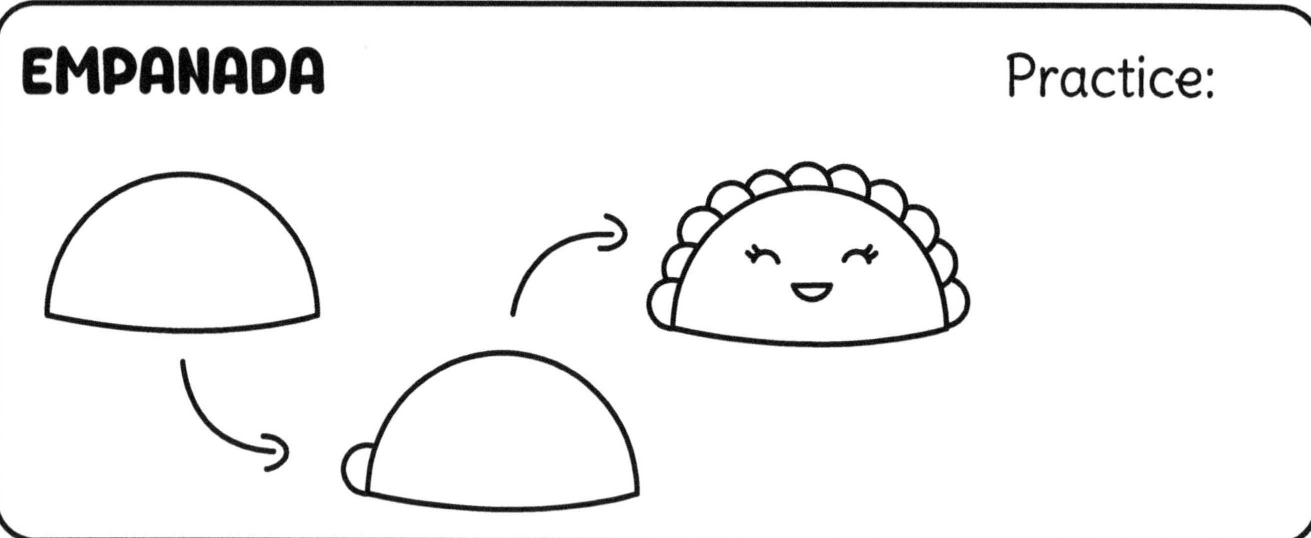

CRACKERS

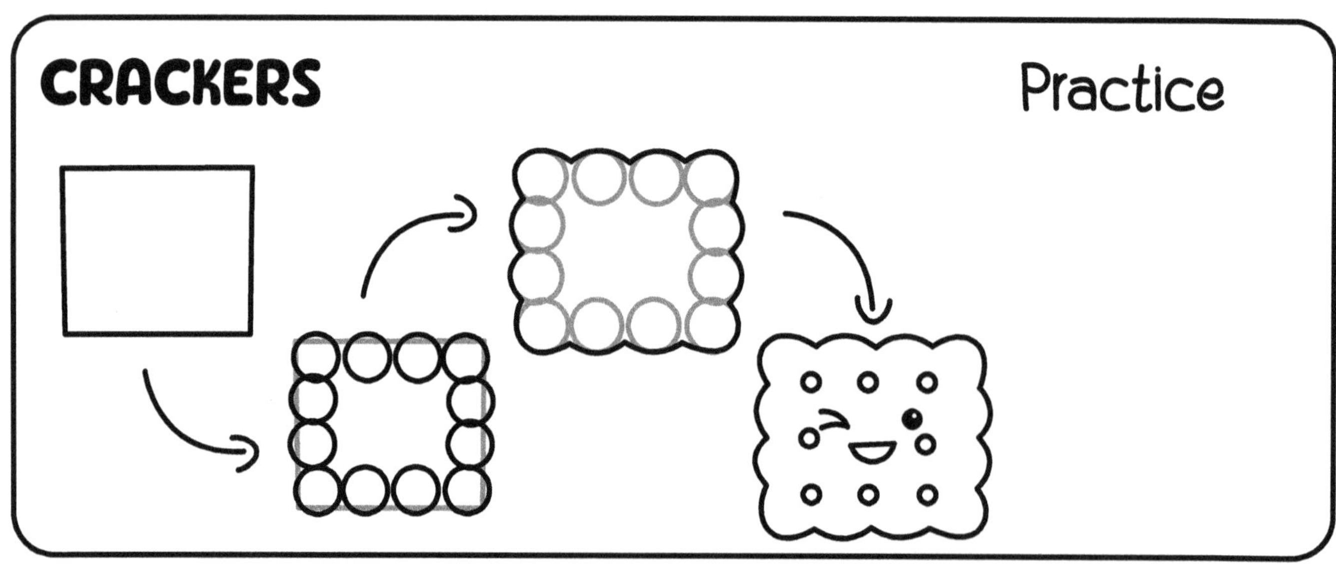

SODA CAN

Practice:

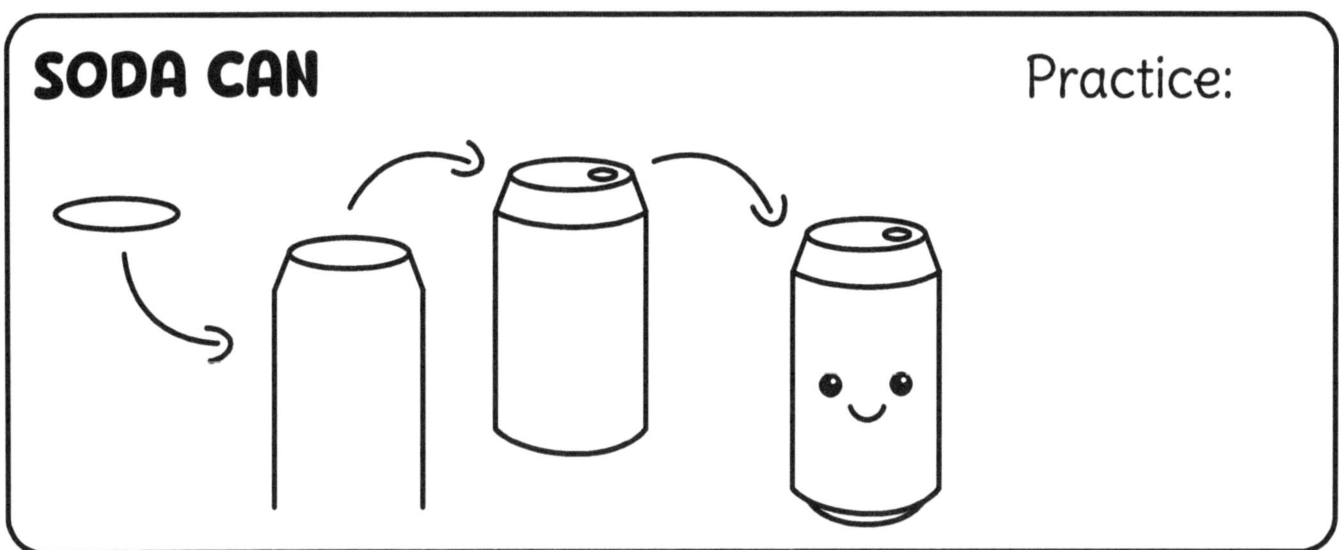

PRETZELS

Practice:

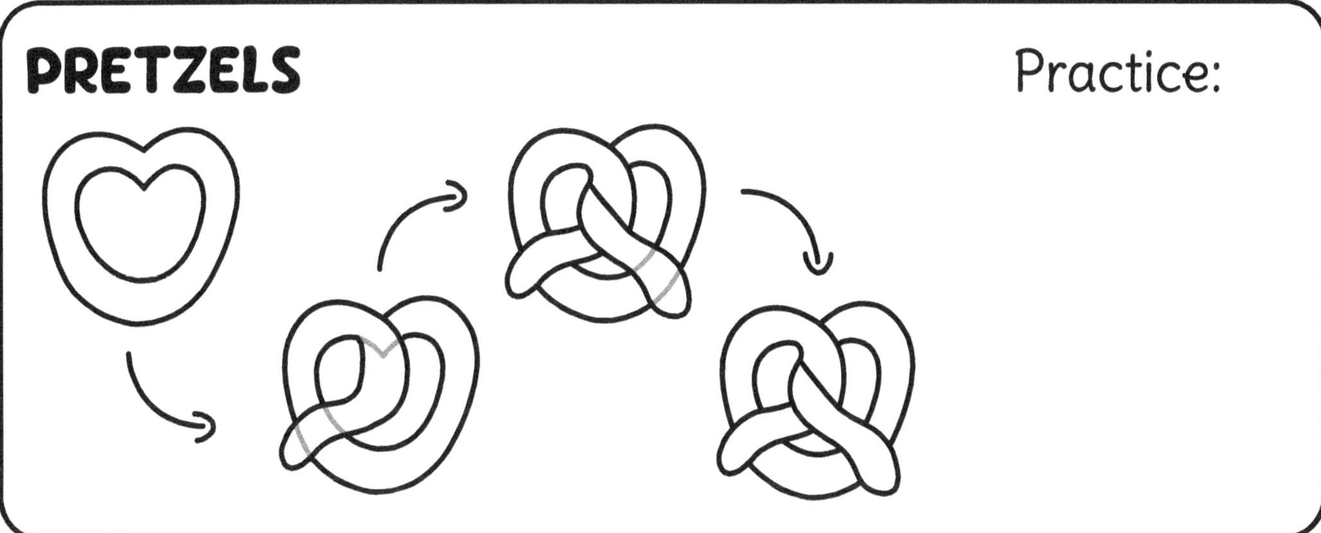

NOODLES

Practice

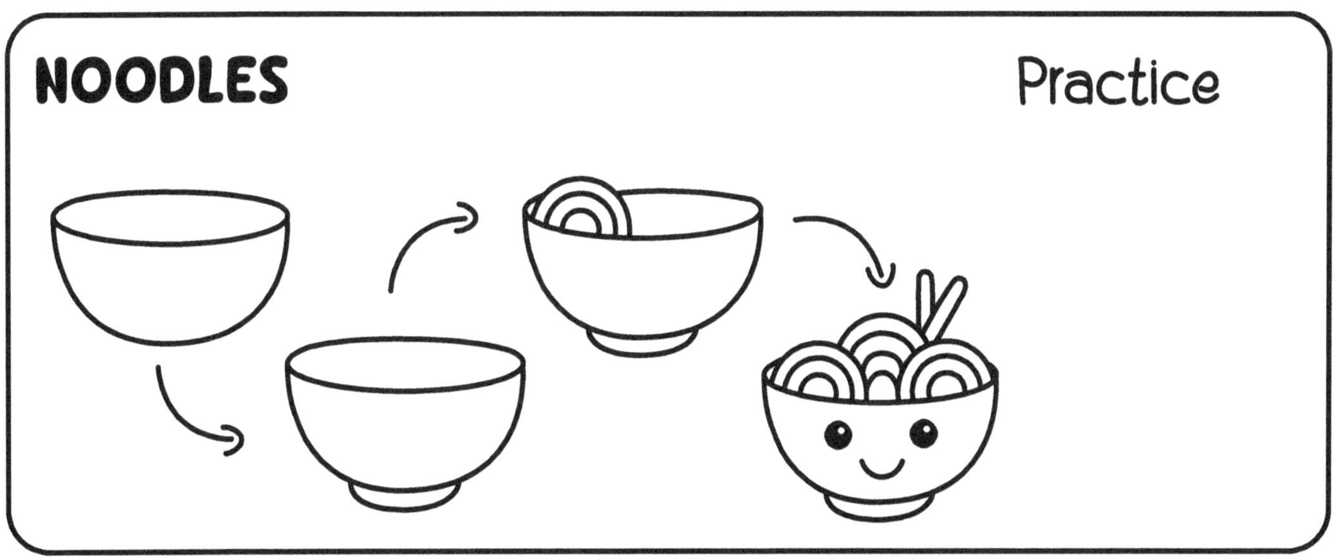

TEMPURA

Practice:

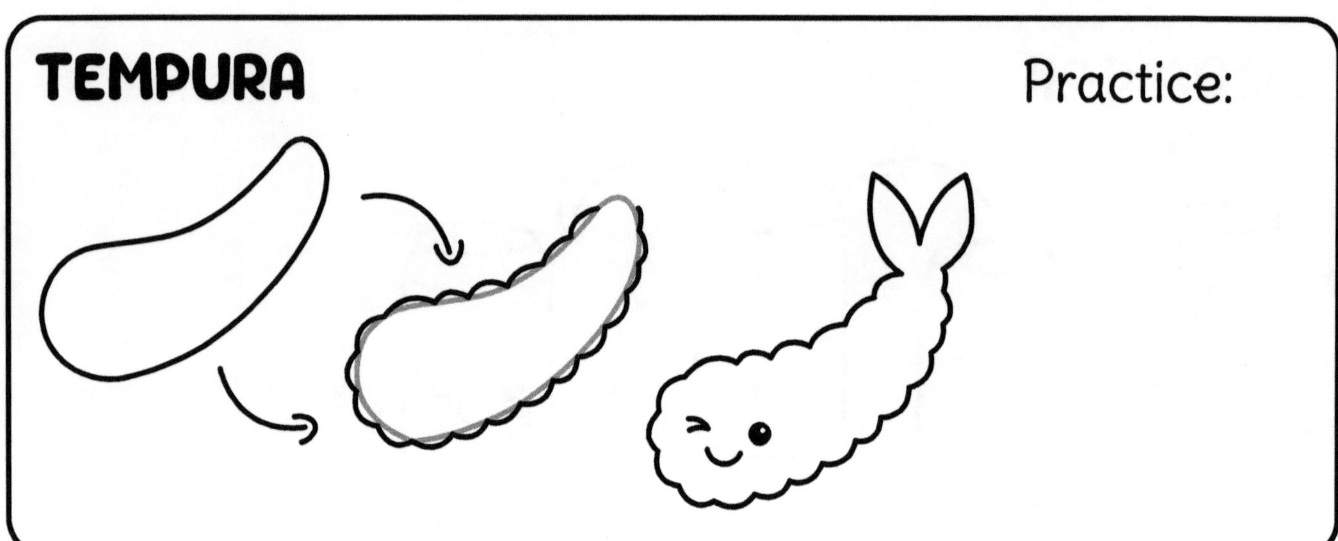

CORNDOG

Practice:

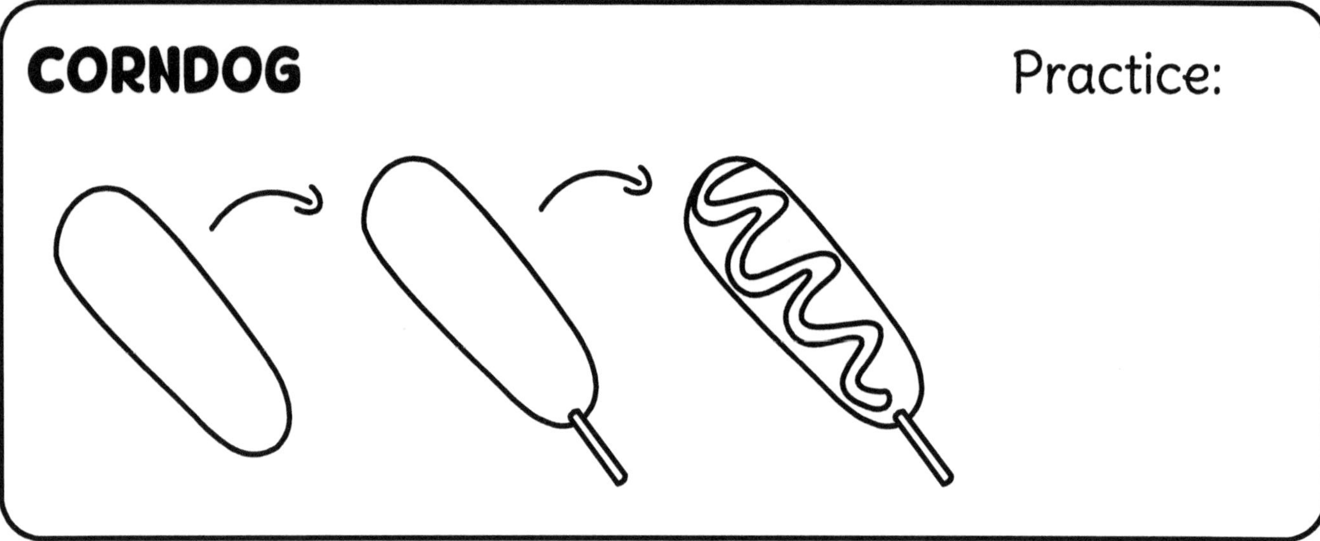

SUSHI

Practice

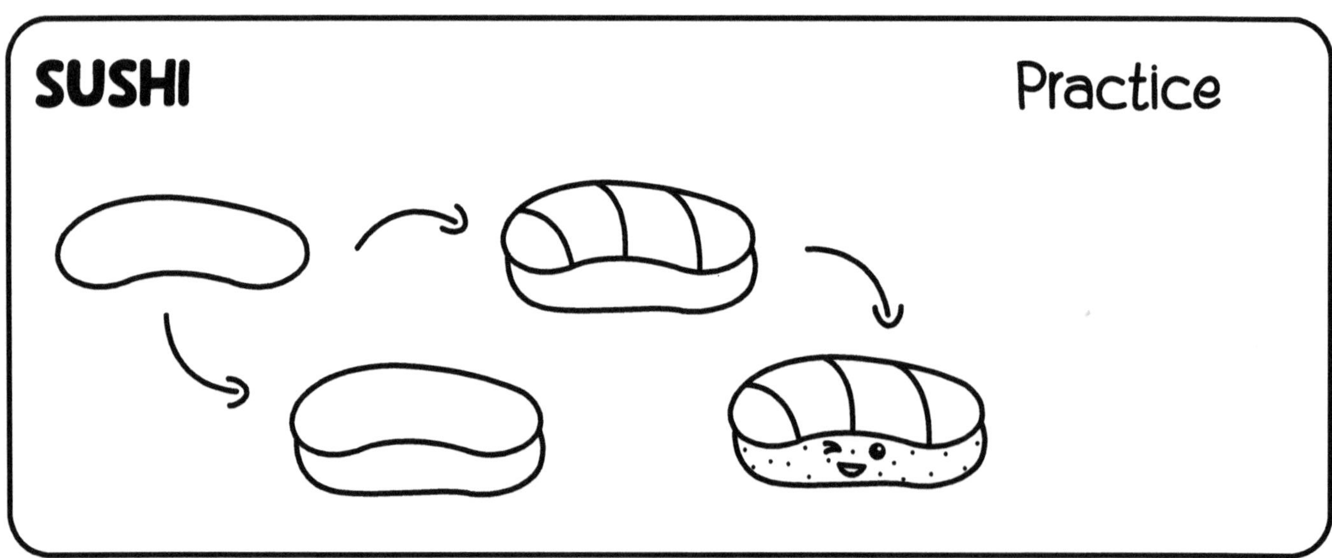

BREAKFAST BUDDIES

PANCAKES
Practice:

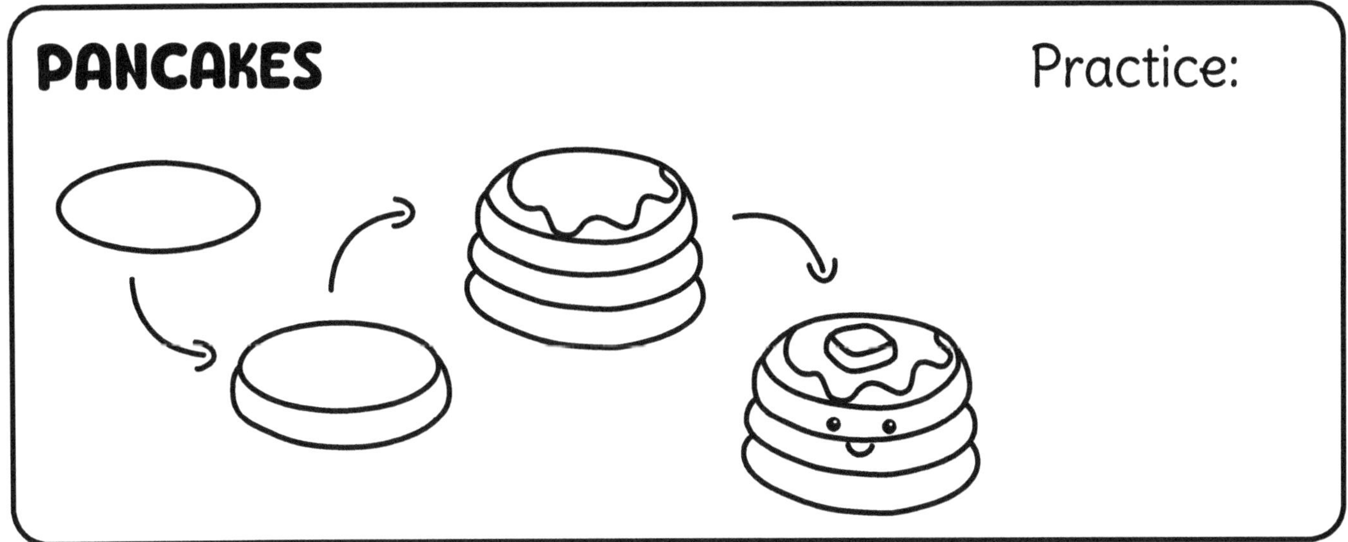

WAFFLE
Practice:

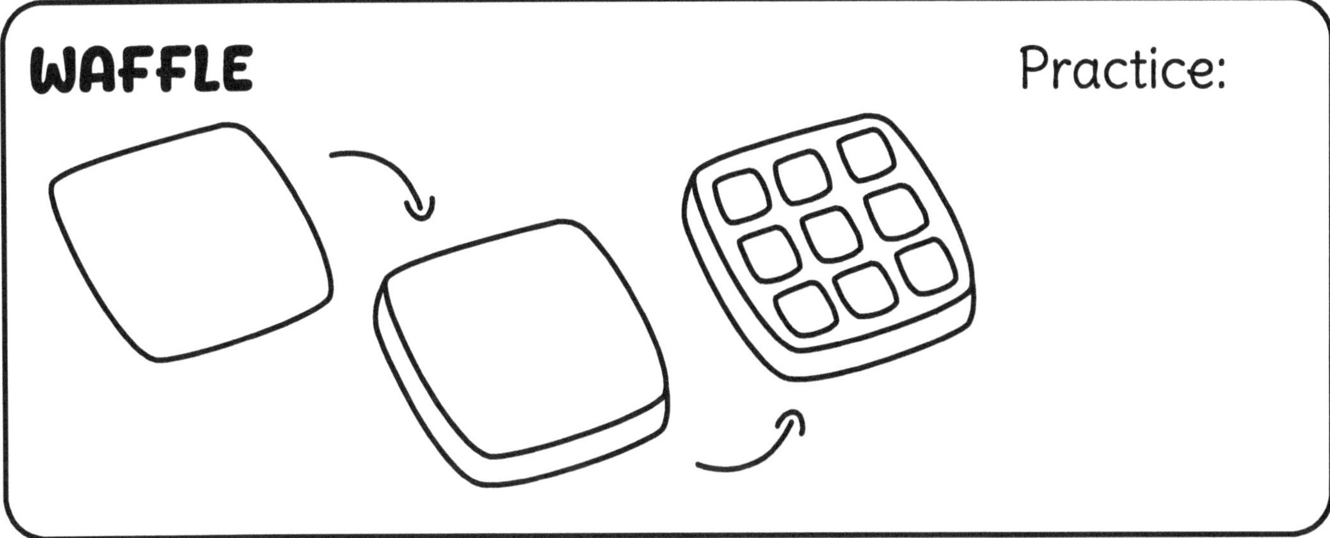

BREAD
Practice

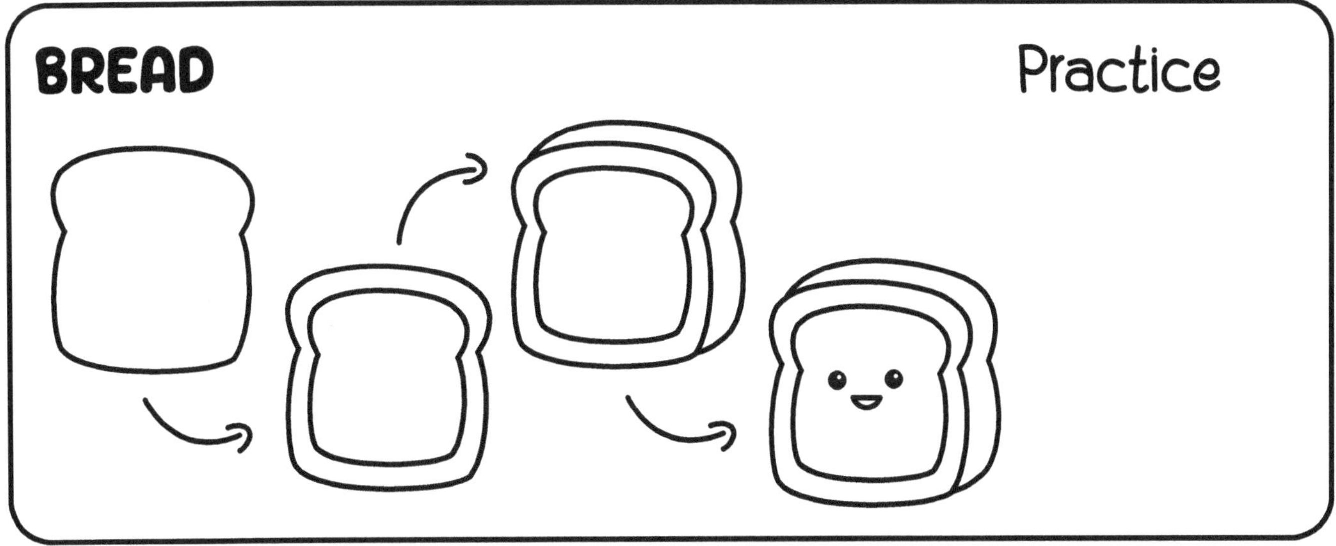

SANDWICH

Practice:

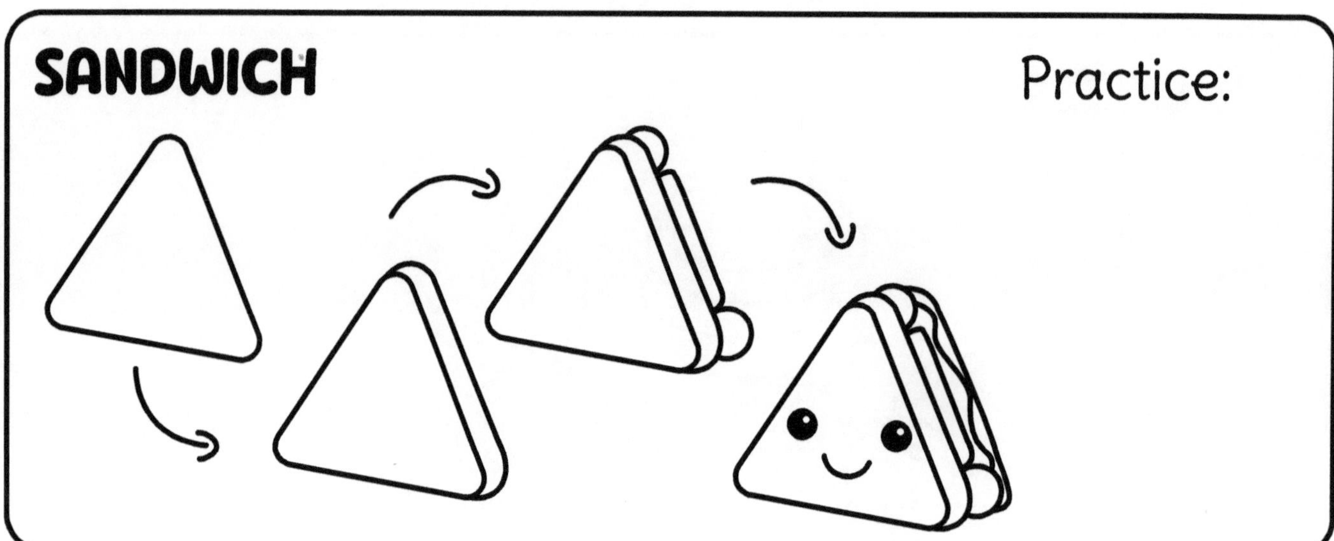

FRIED EGG

Practice:

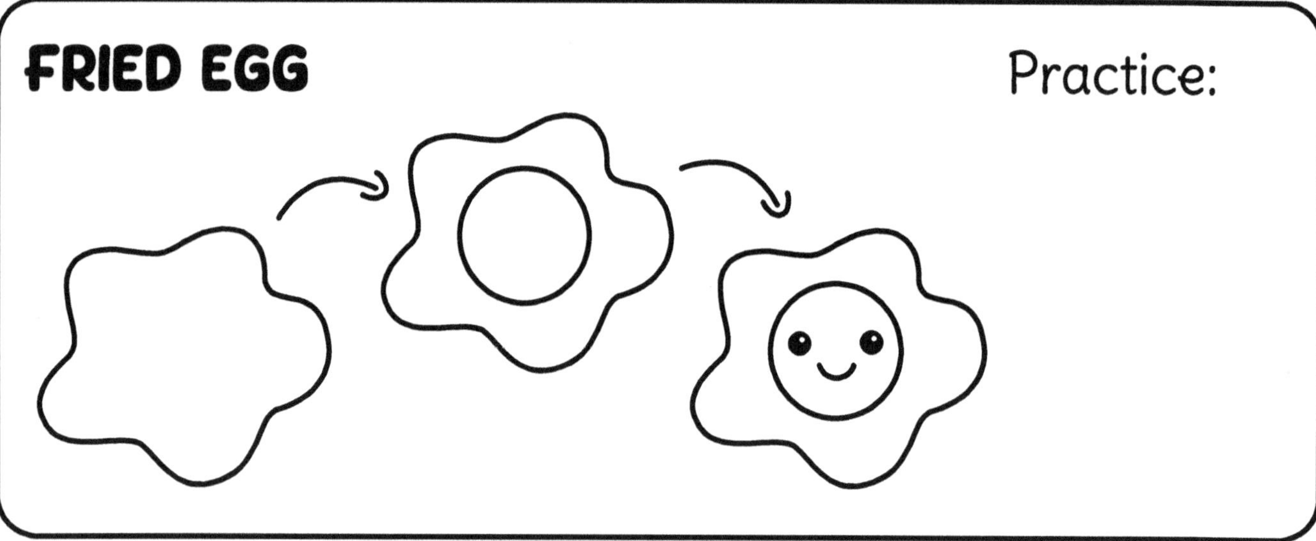

BOILED EGG

Practice

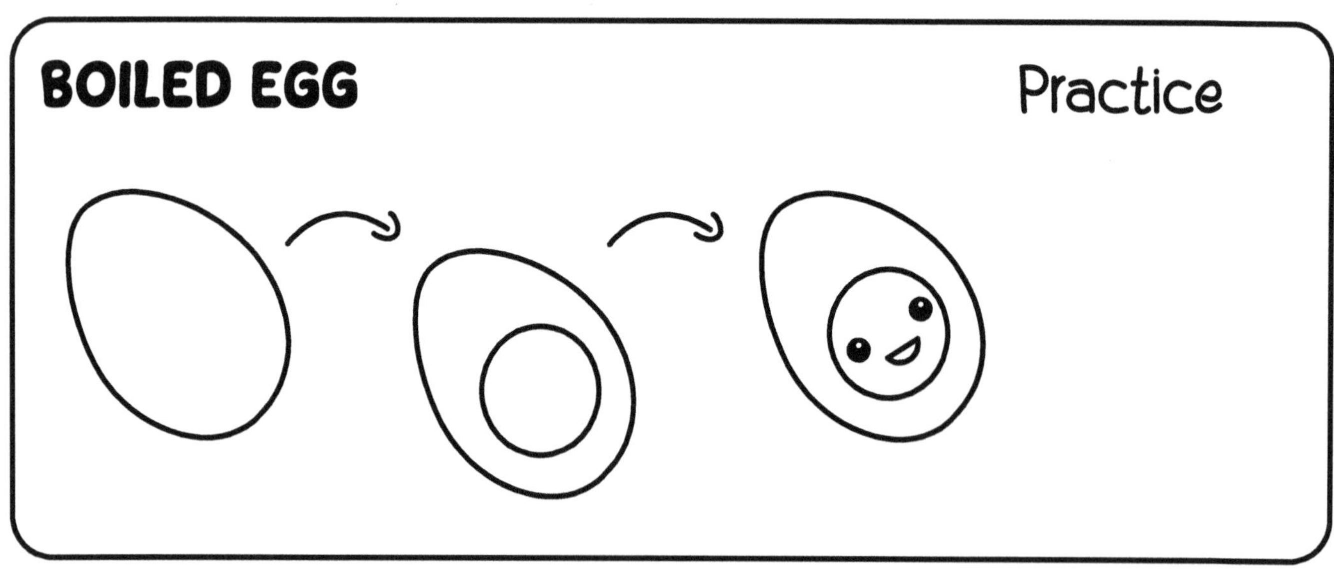

BACON

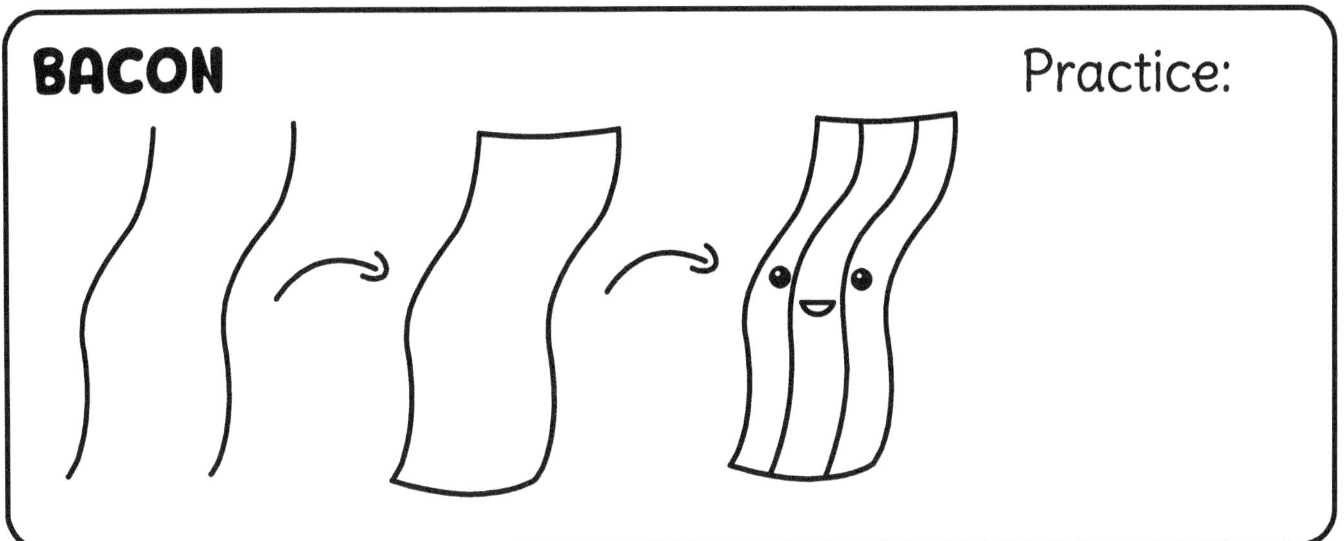

YOGURT

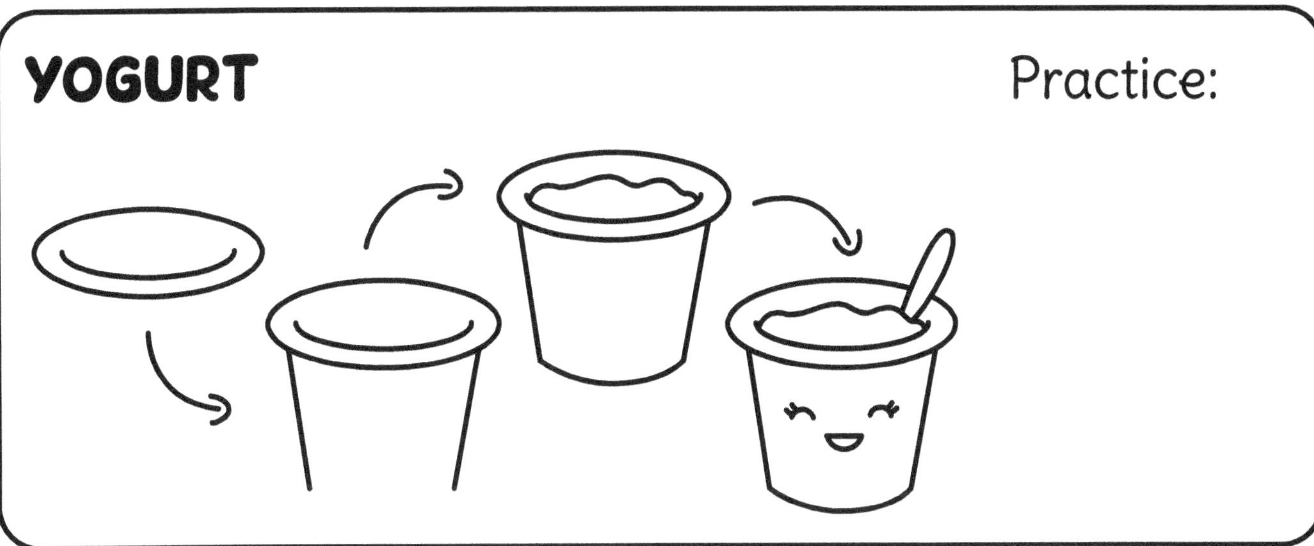

MILK

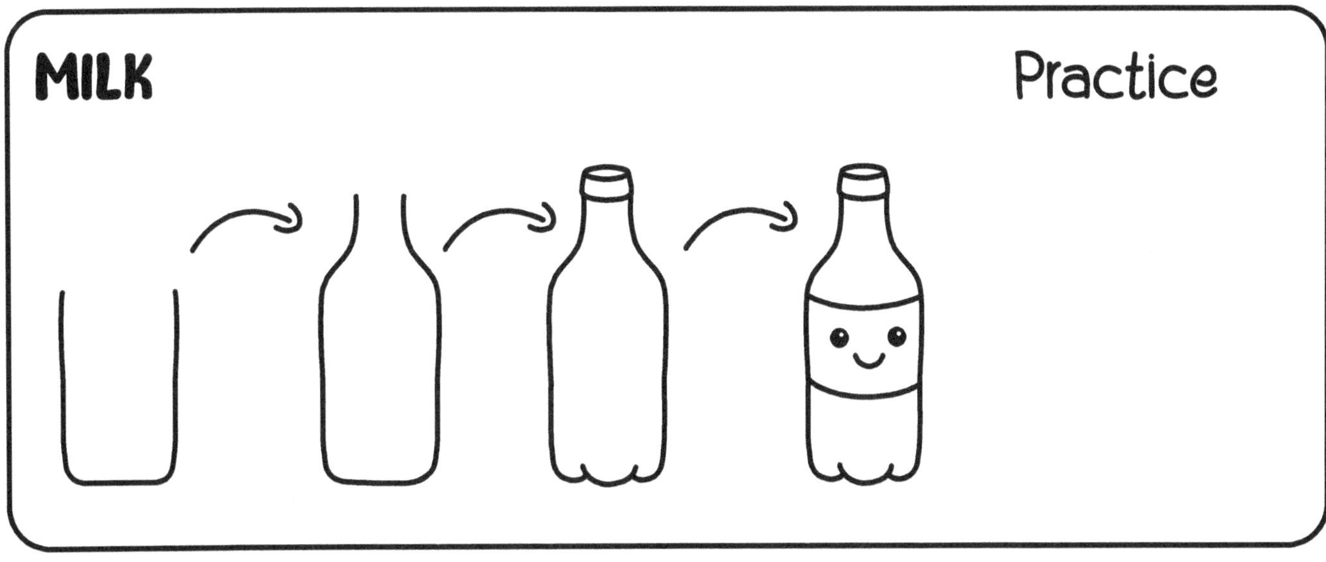

CHEESE

Practice:

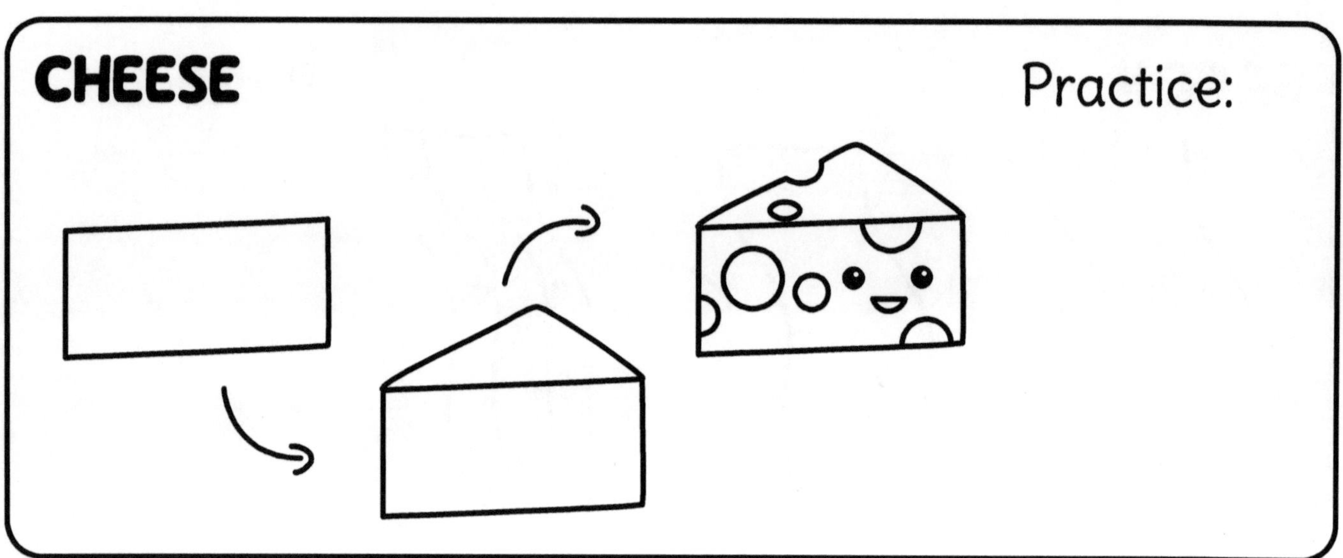

RICE CAKE

Practice:

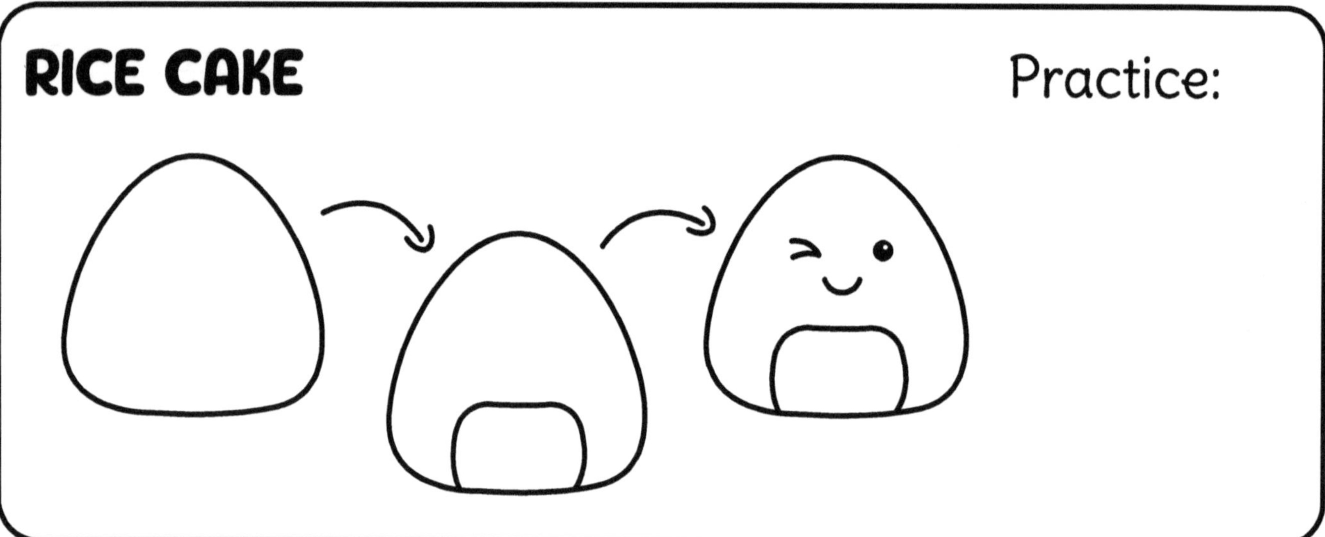

JUICE BOX

Practice

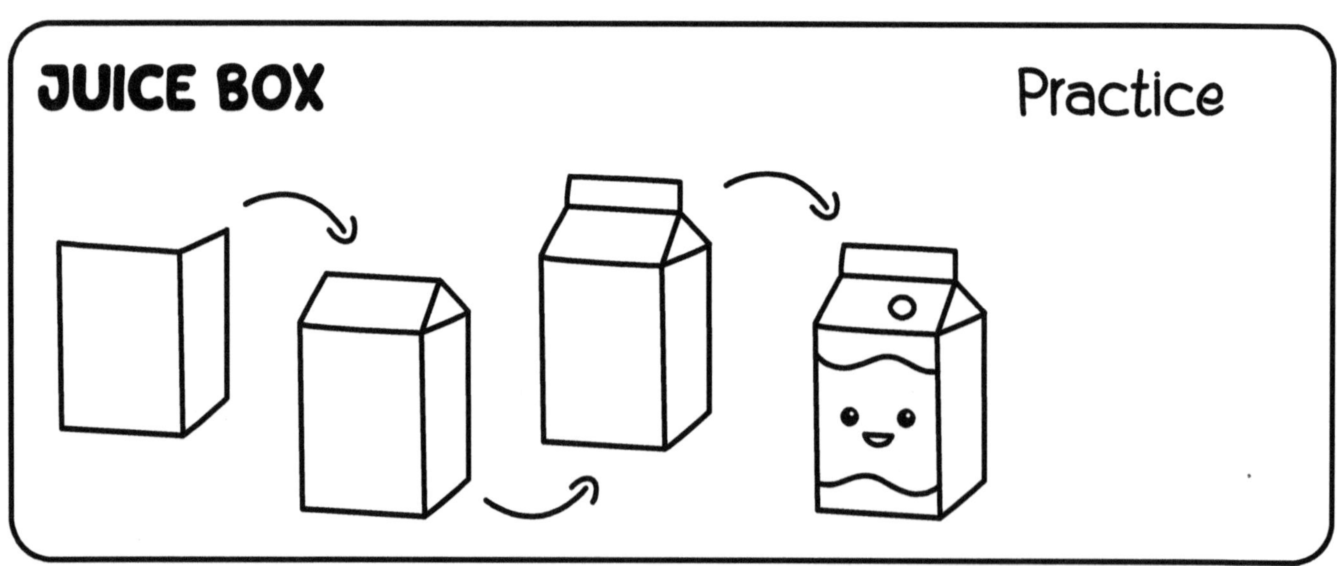

DOUGHNUT

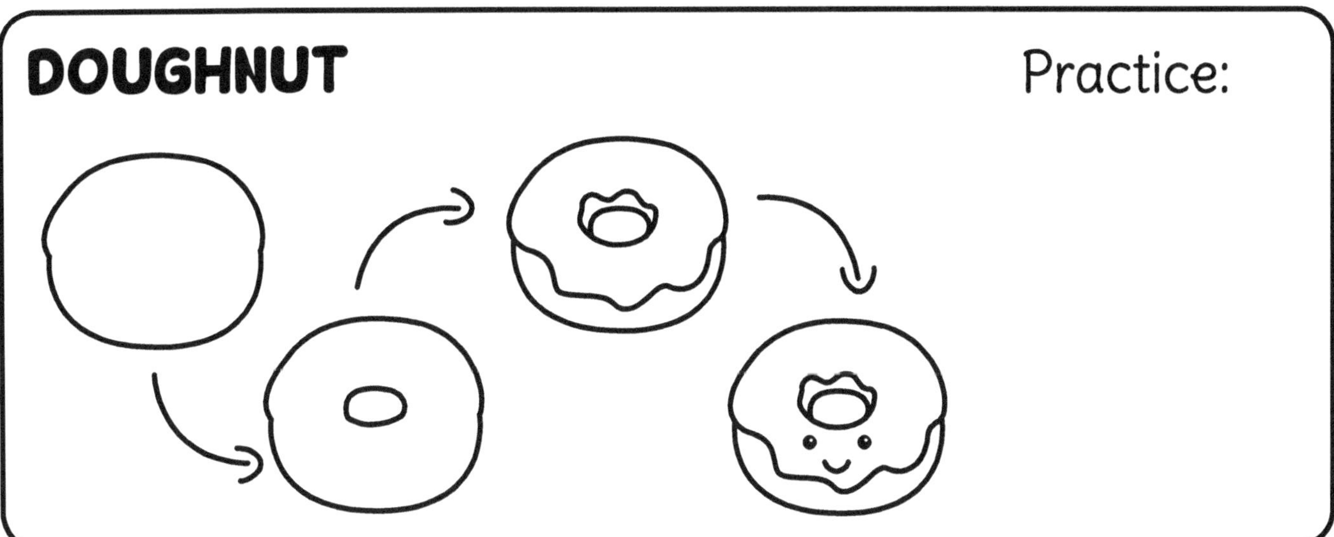

PUDDING

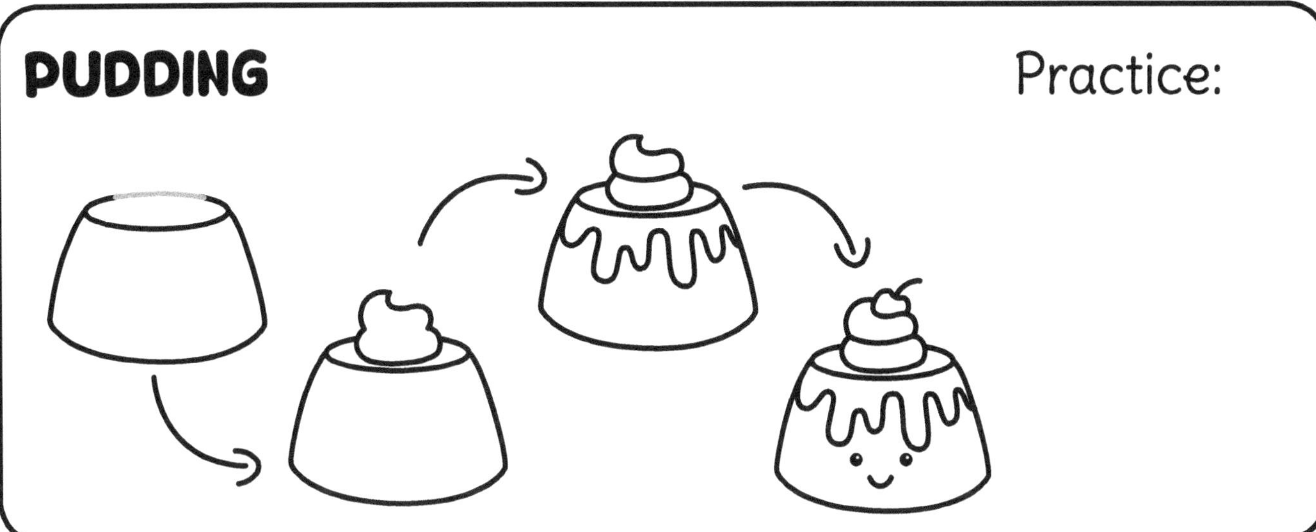

CROISSANT

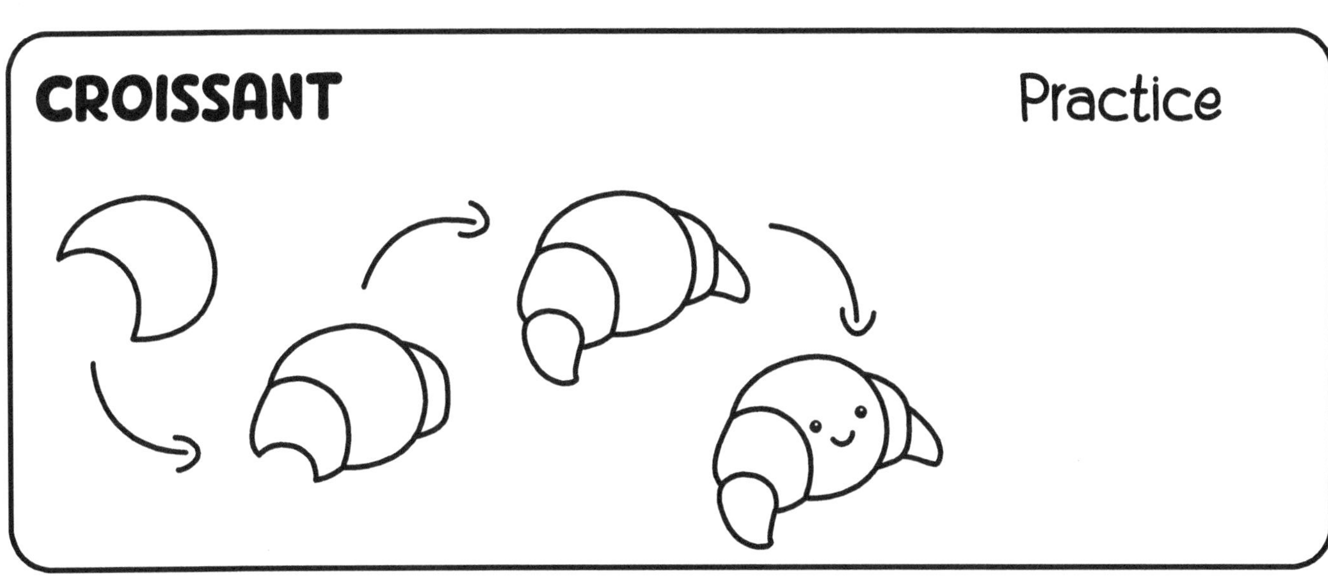

SWEETS TREATS

CUPCAKE
Practice:

JAM COOKIES
Practice:

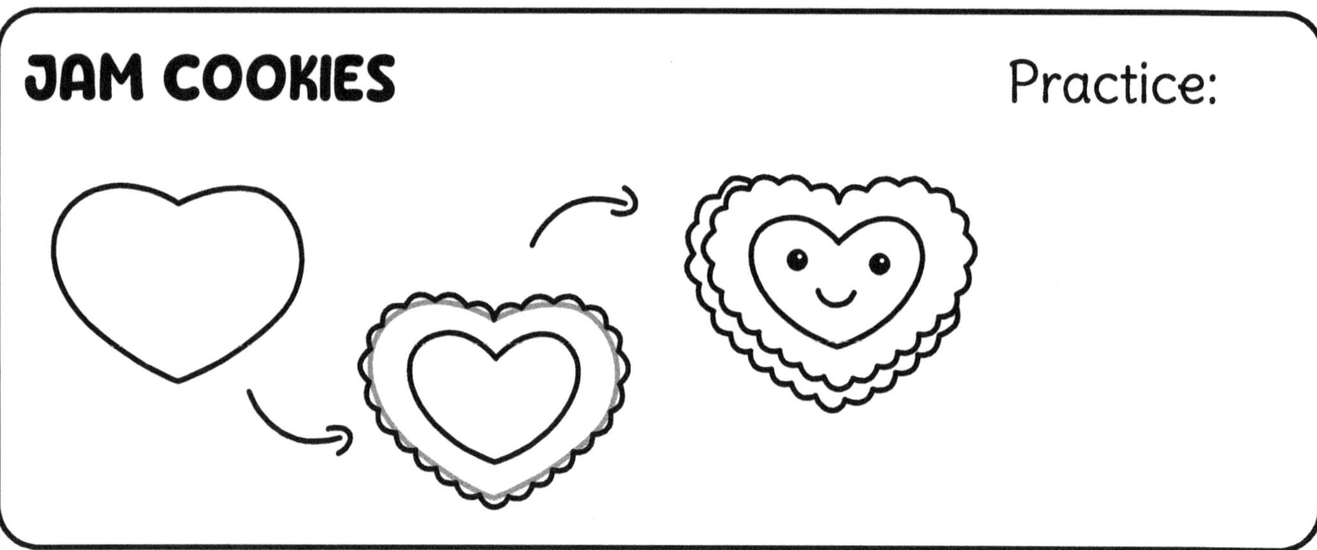

MOCHI
Practice

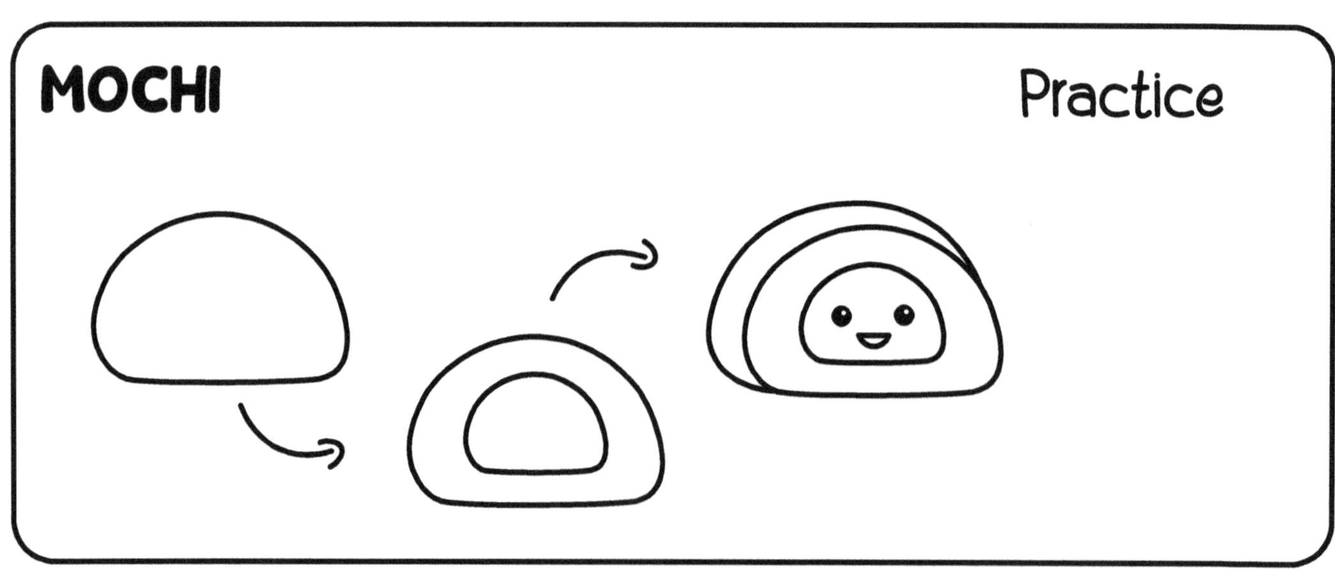

CHOCOLATE

Practice:

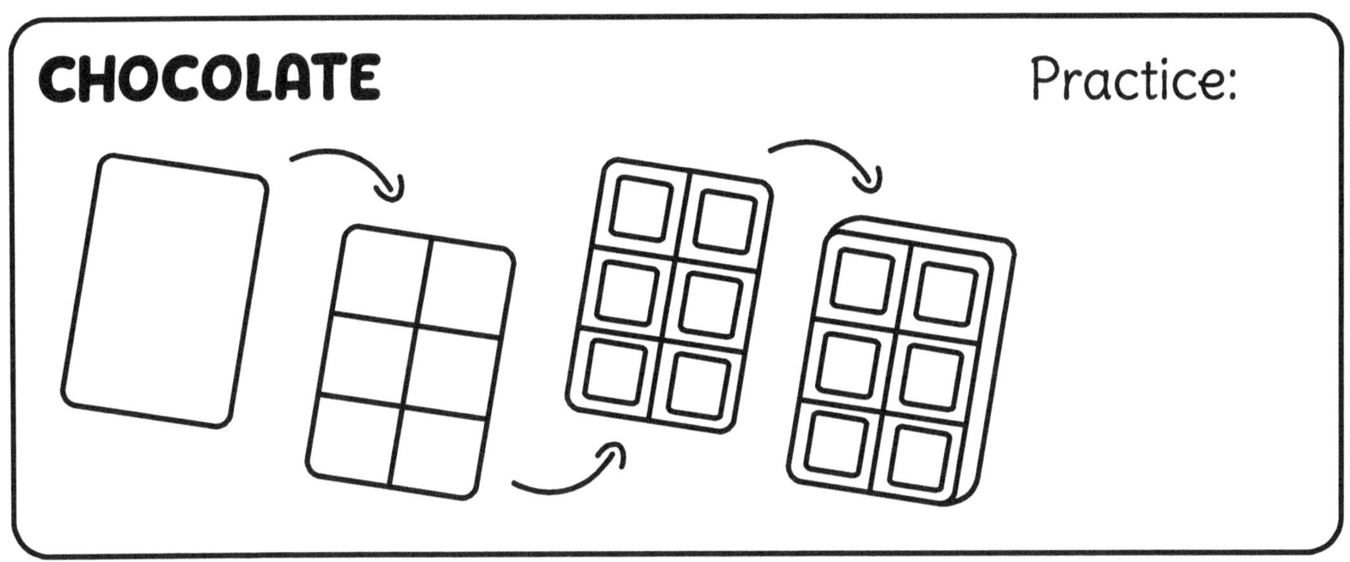

JAM PIE

Practice:

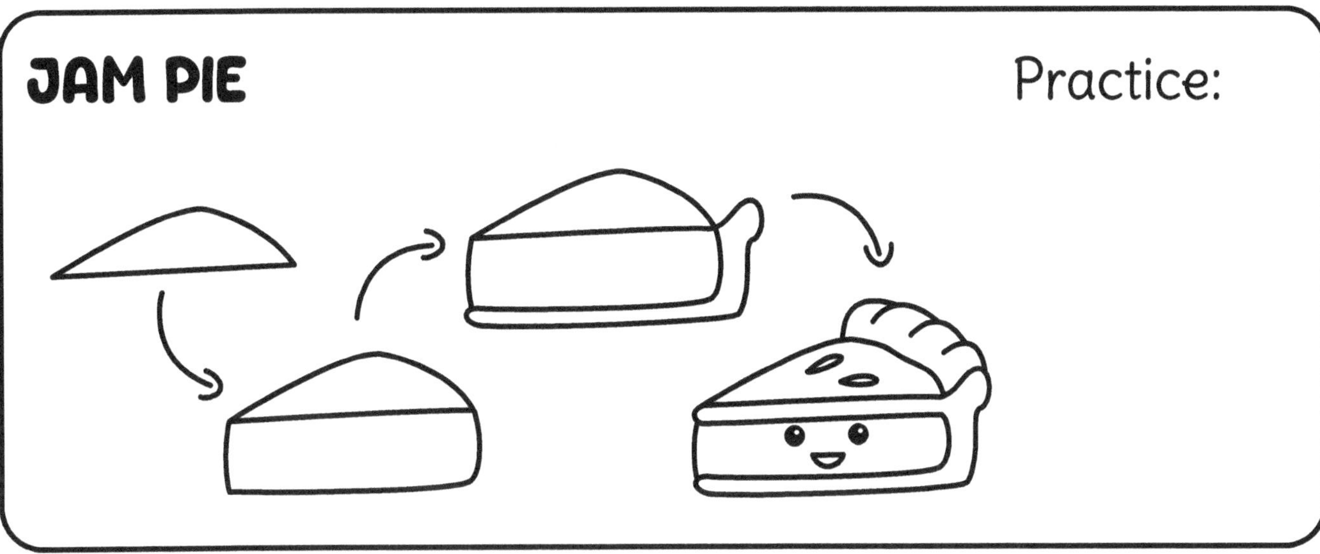

CHOCOLATE STRAWBERRY

Practice

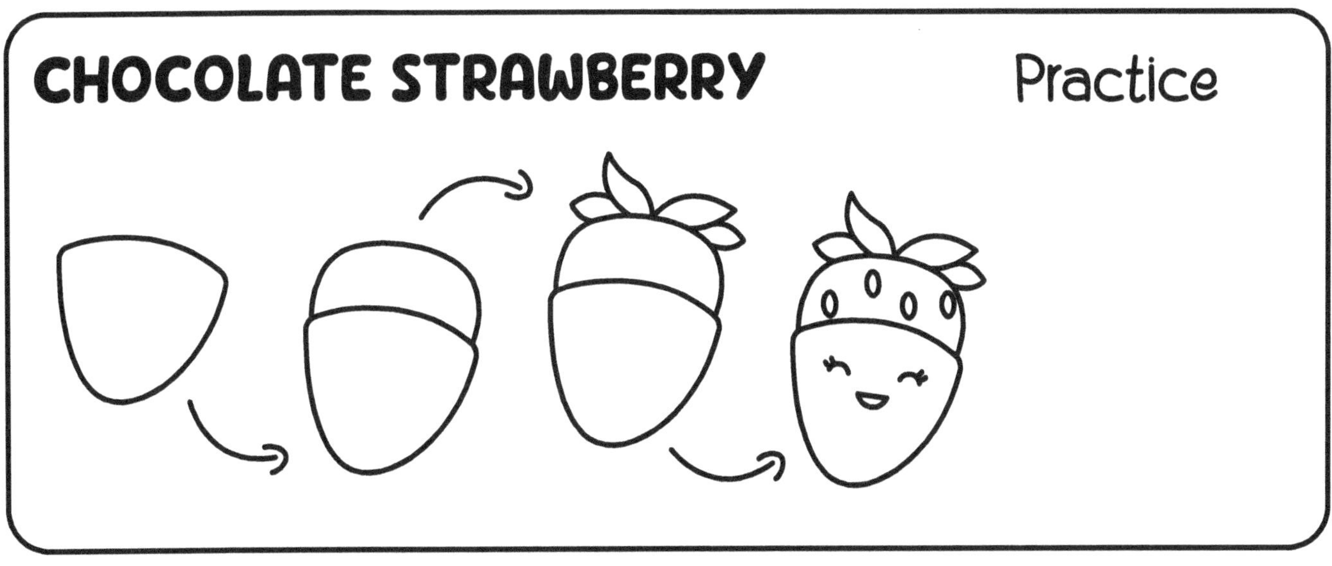

POPSICLE

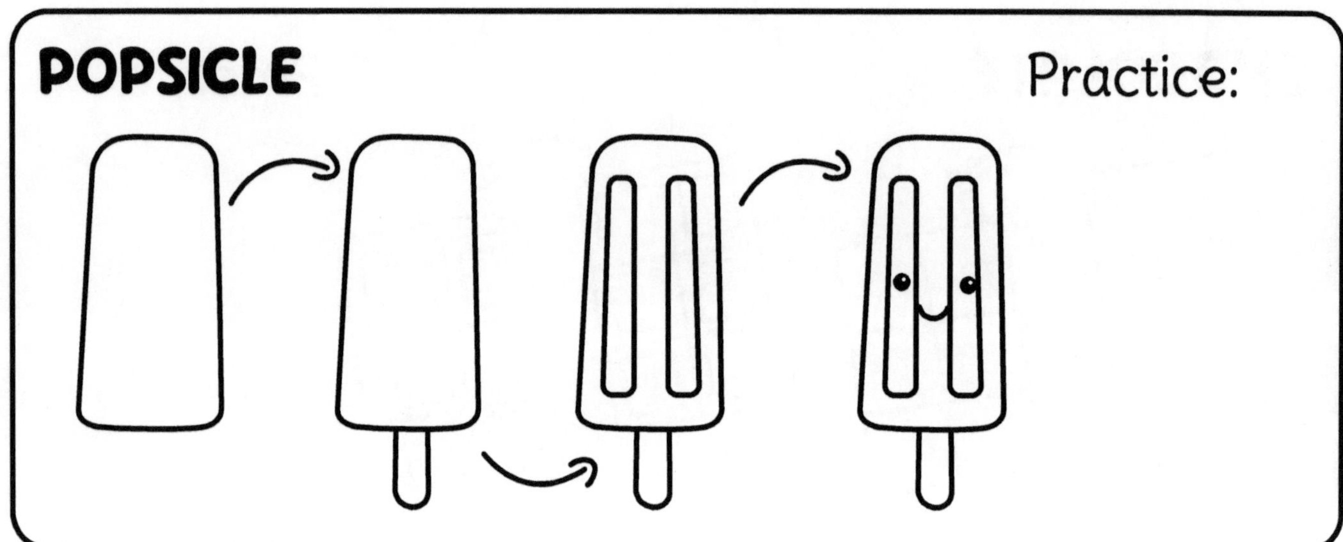

ICE CREAM

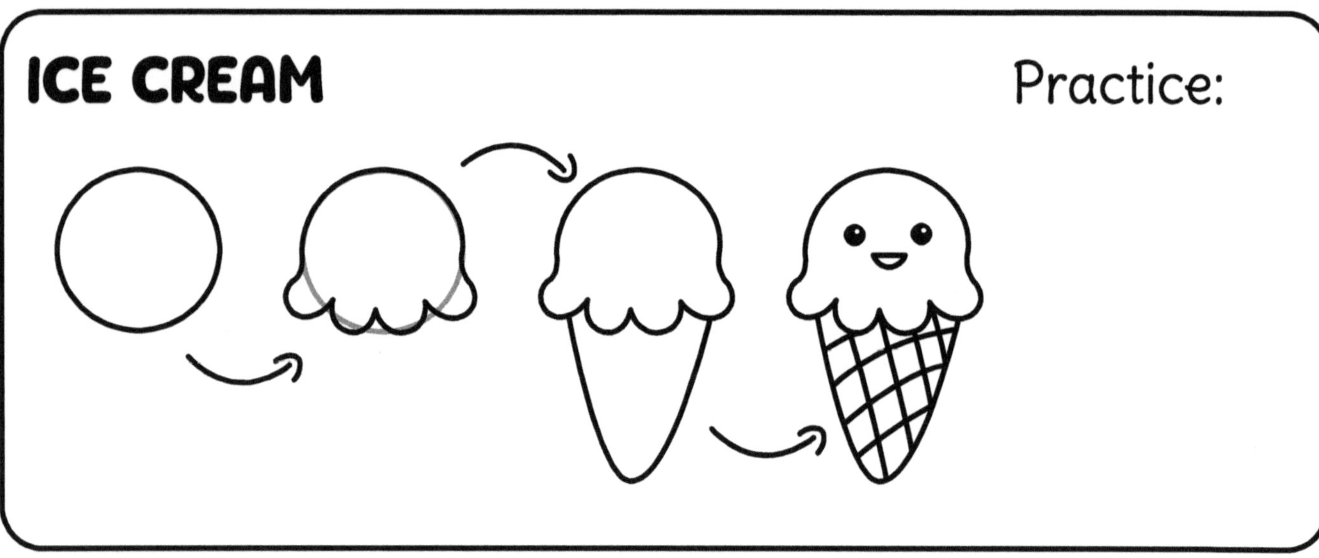

GUMMY BEAR

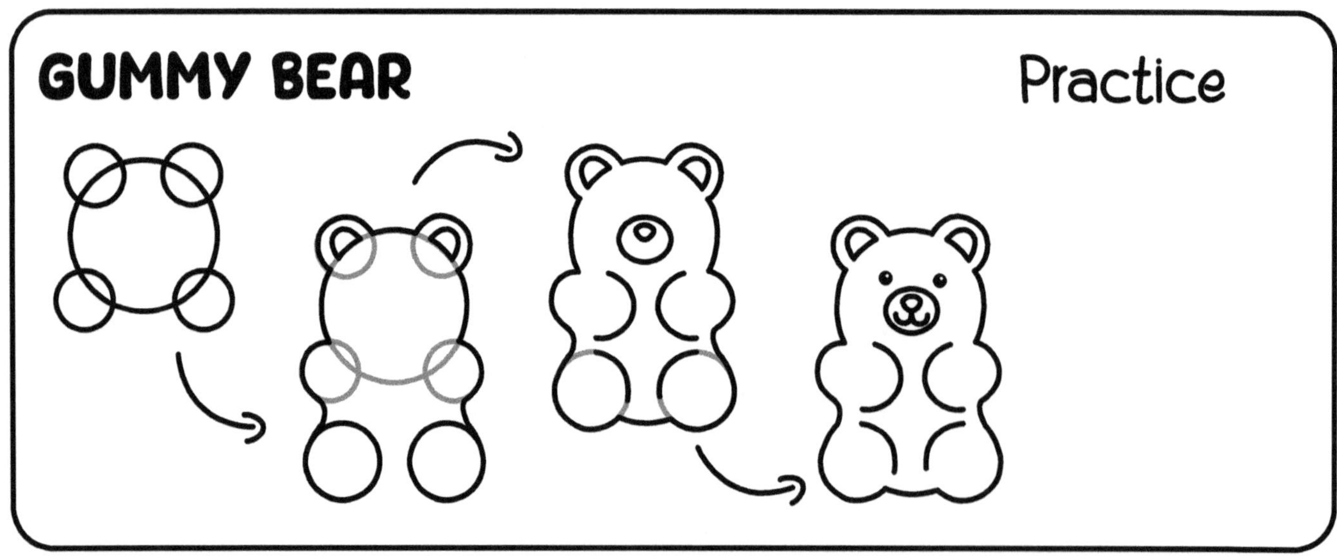

LOLLIPOP

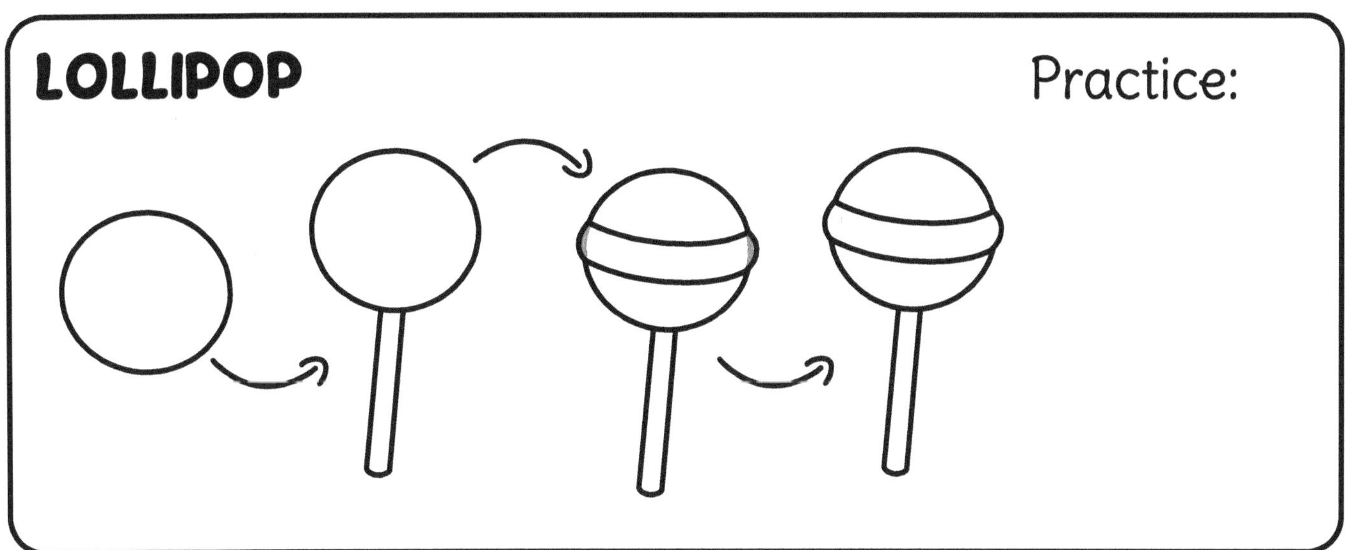

MARSHMALLOWS

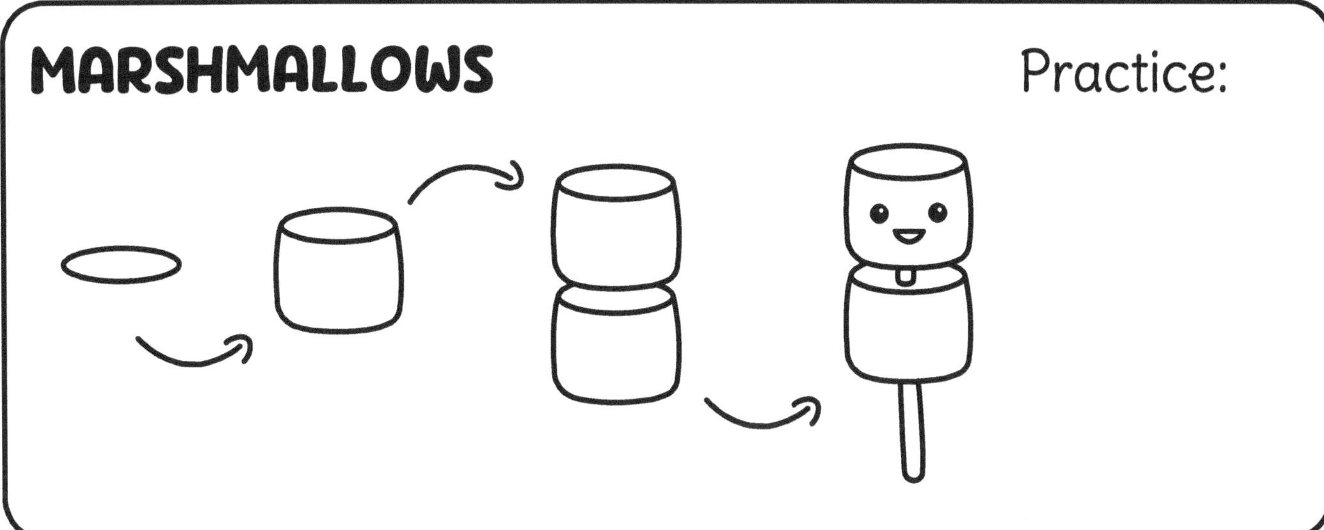

CHURROS

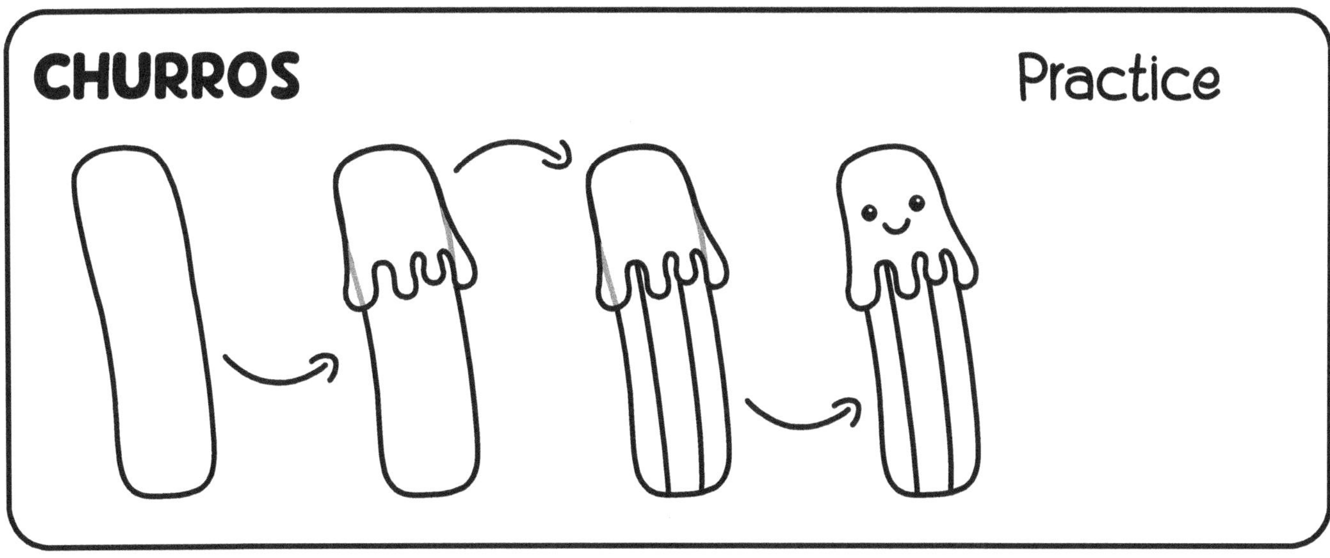

GINGERBREAD

Practice:

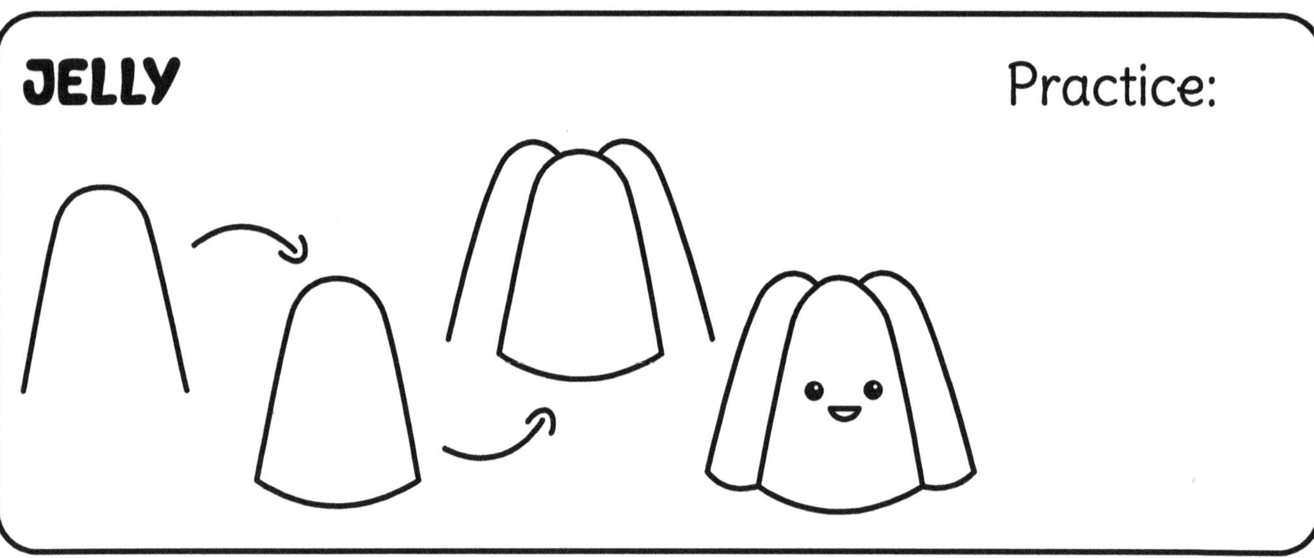

JELLY

Practice:

TANGHULU

Practice

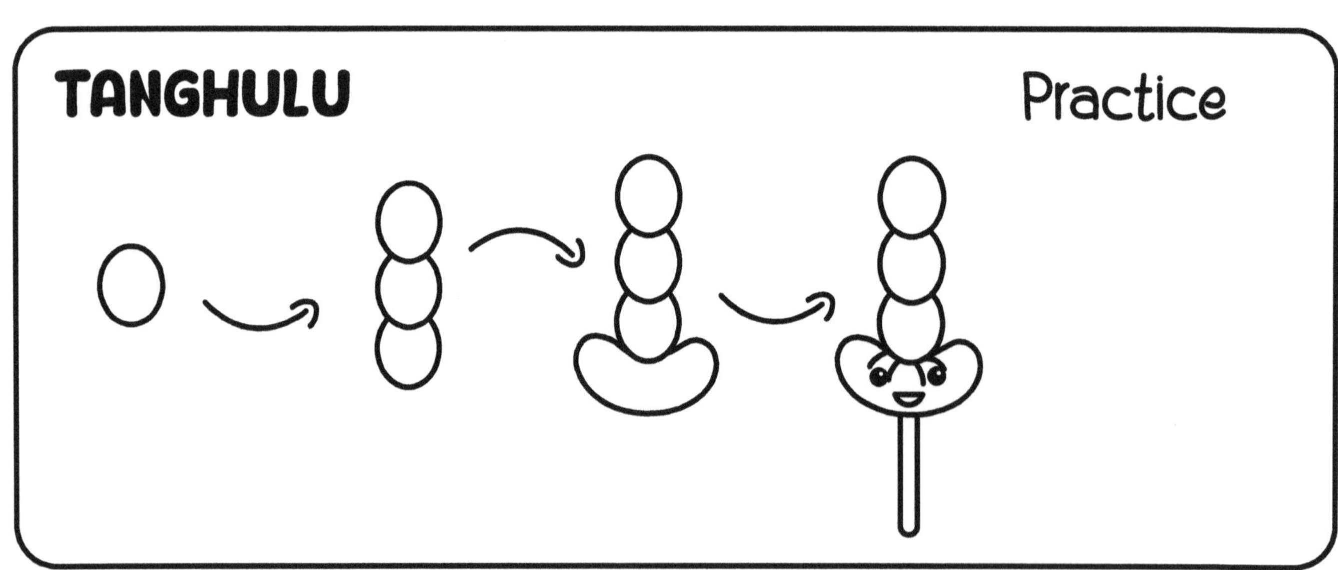

TAIYAKI

Practice:

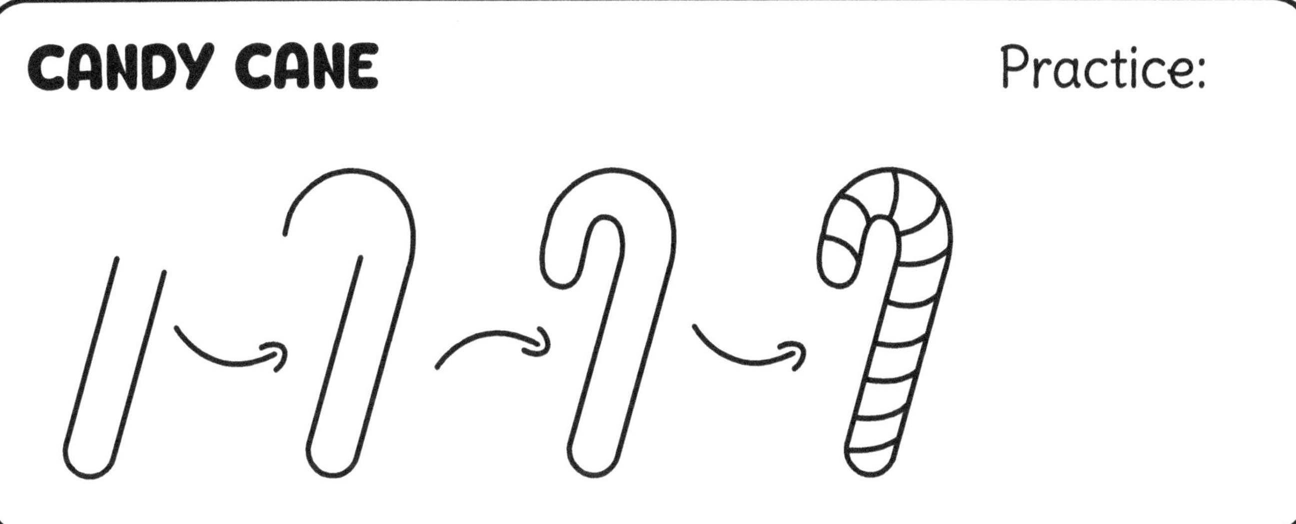

CANDY CANE

Practice:

TOFFEE

Practice

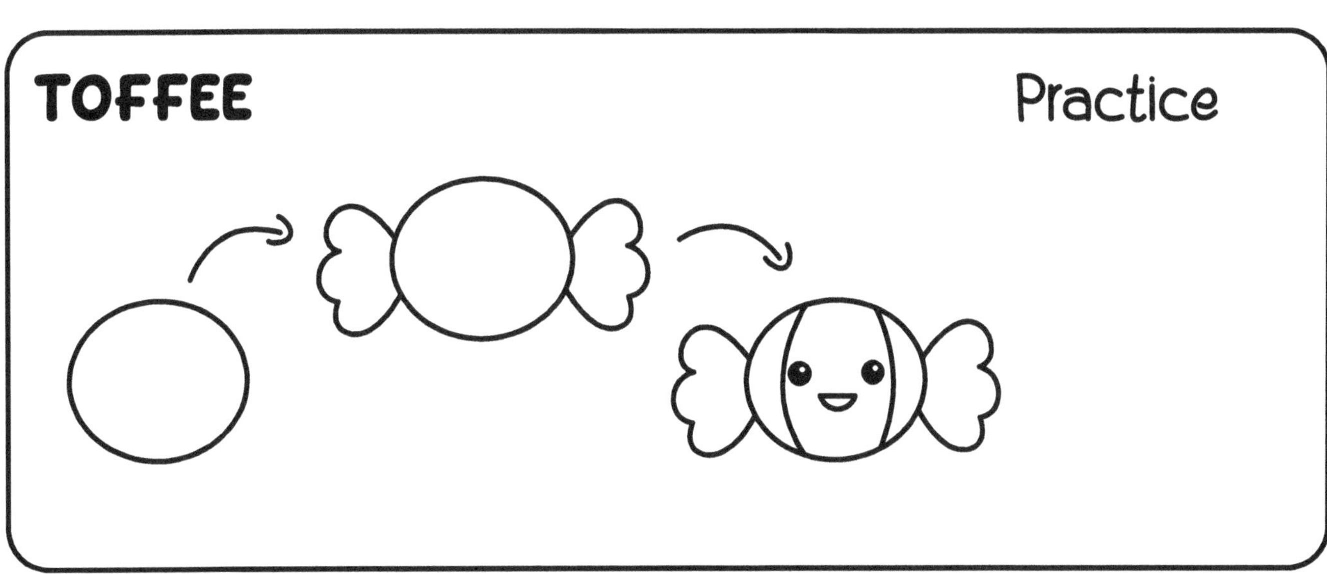

S'MORE

Practice:

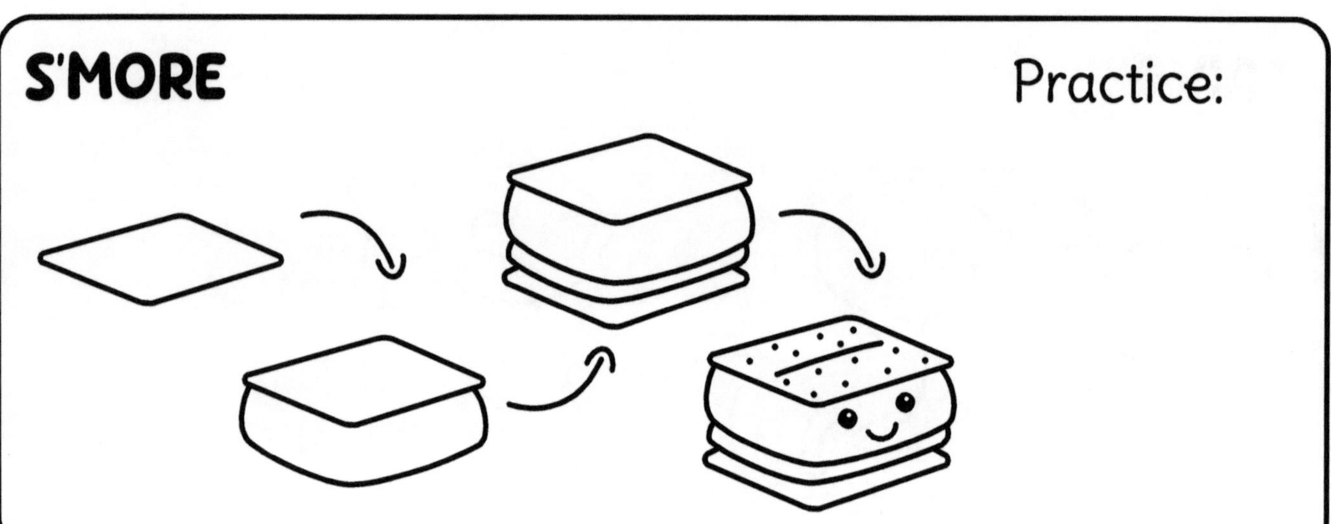

MACARON

Practice:

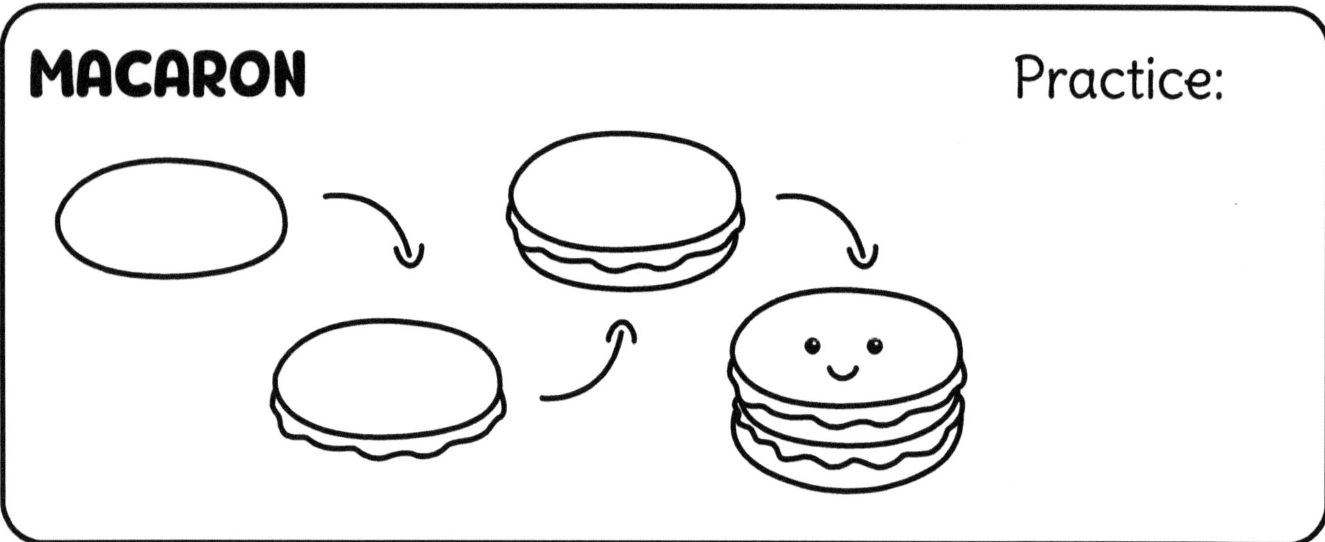

CANDY RING

Practice

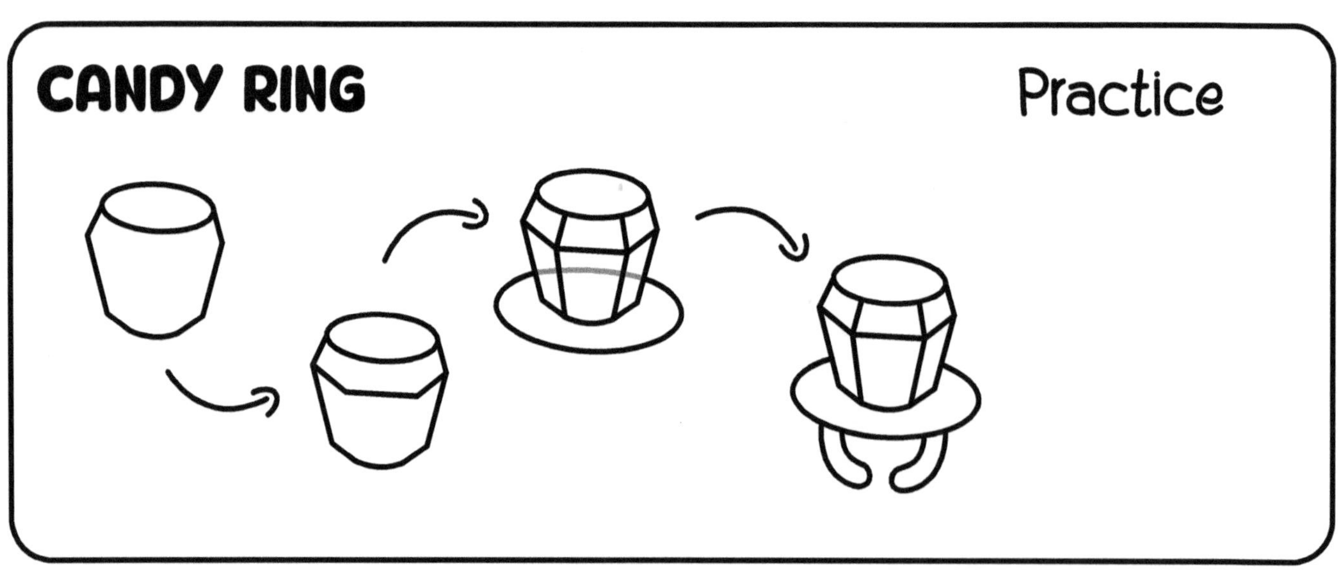

FORTUNE COOKIE

Practice:

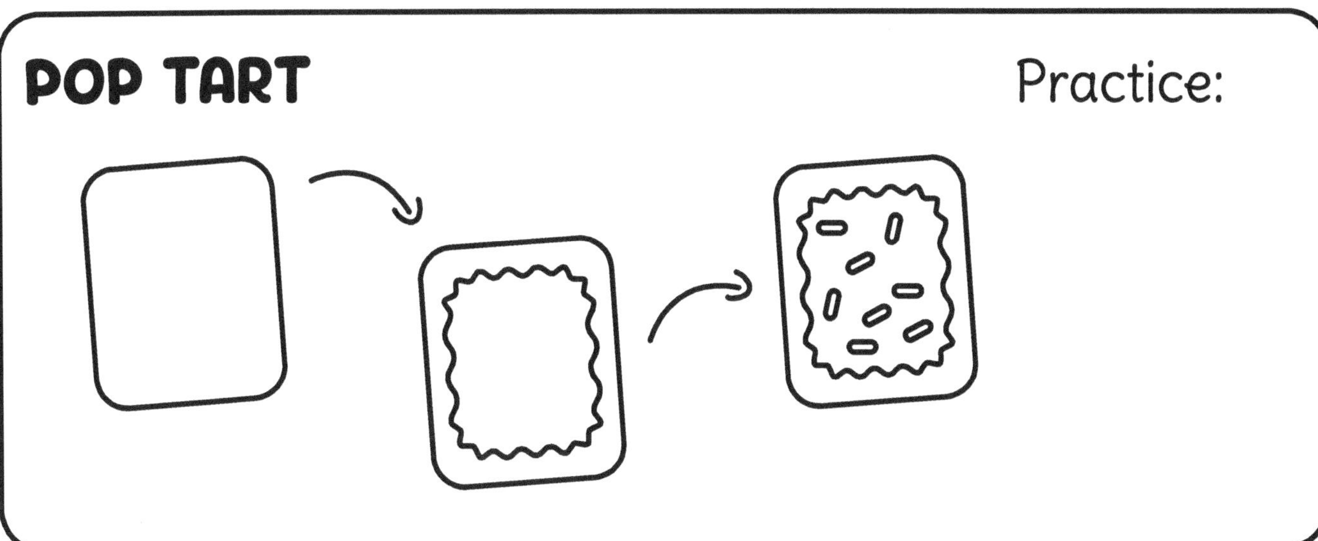

POP TART

Practice:

HONEY

Practice

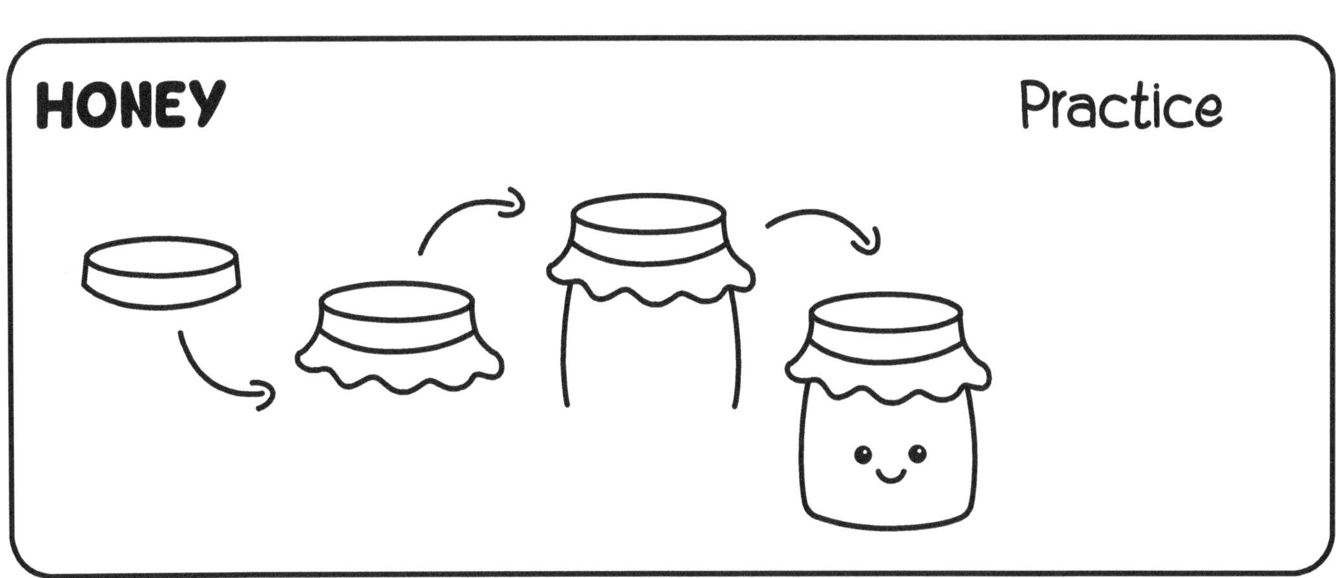

BANANA

Practice:

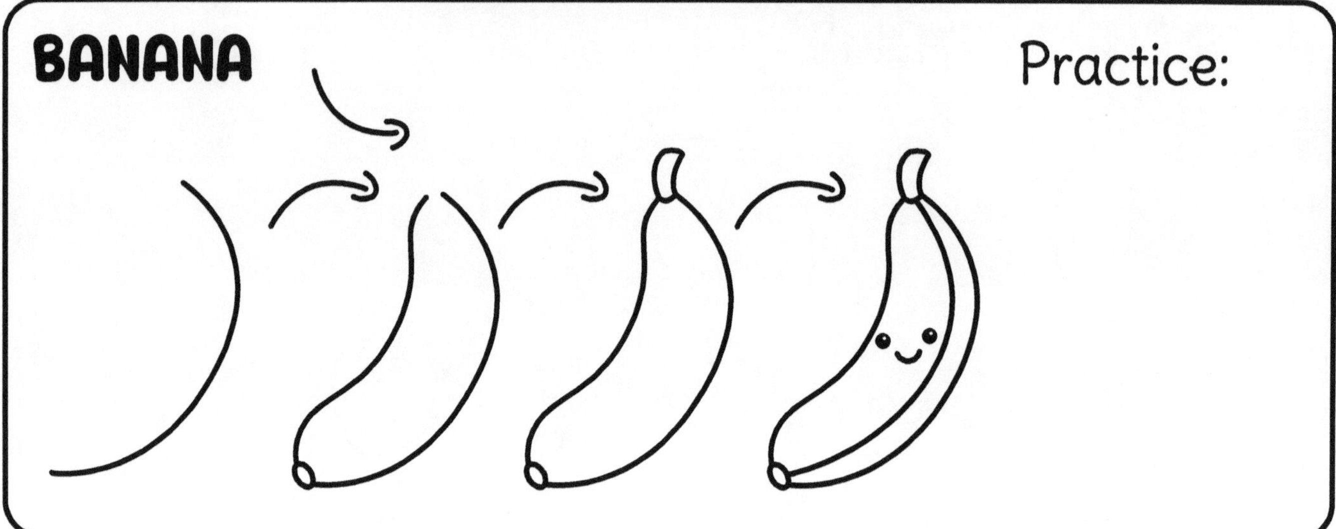

MANGO

Practice:

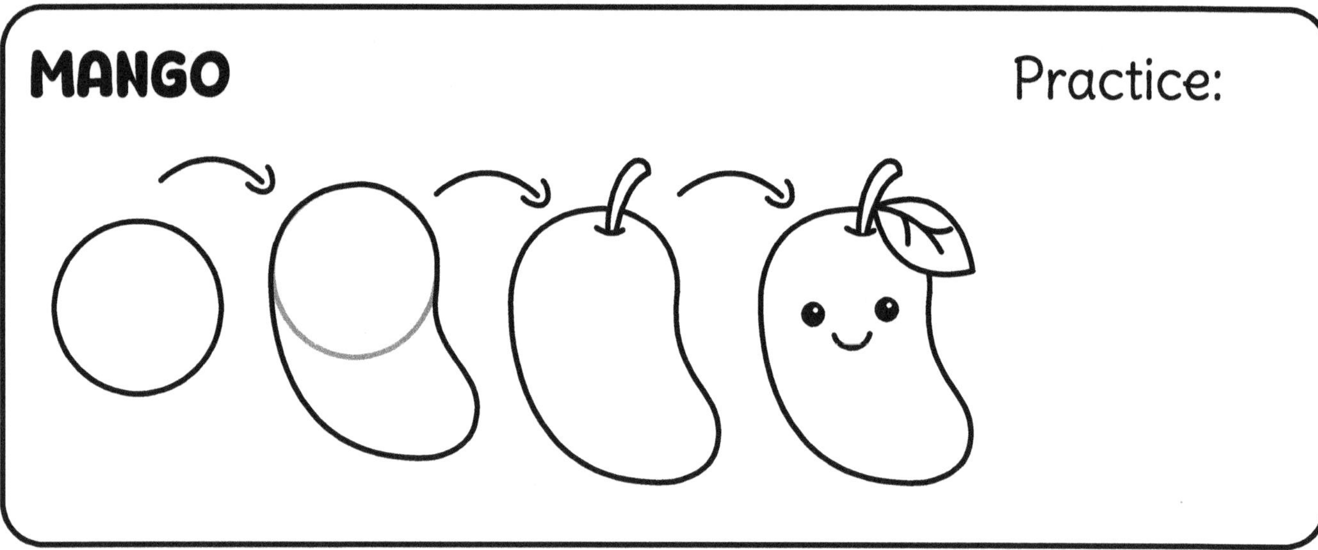

BLUEBERRY

Practice

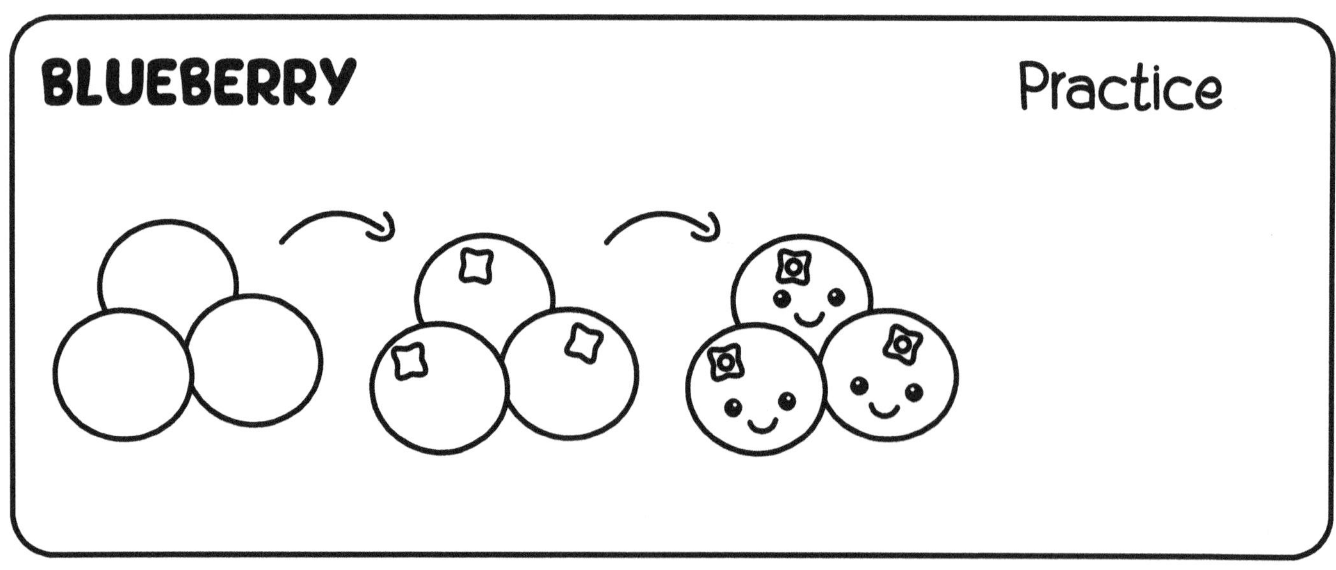

ORANGE

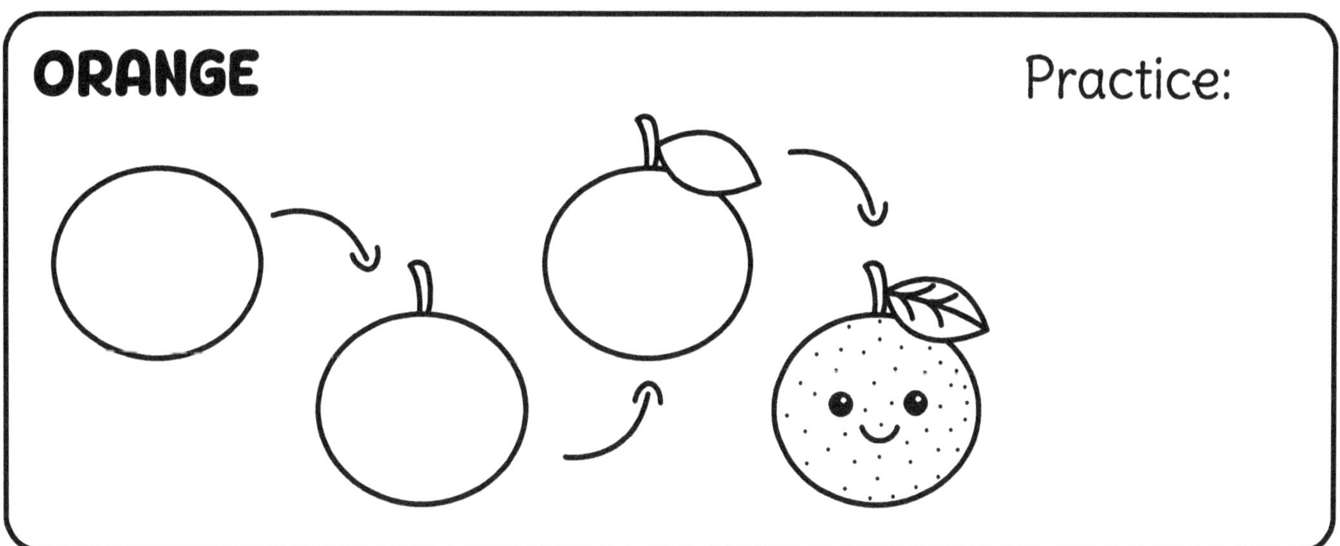

WATERMELON

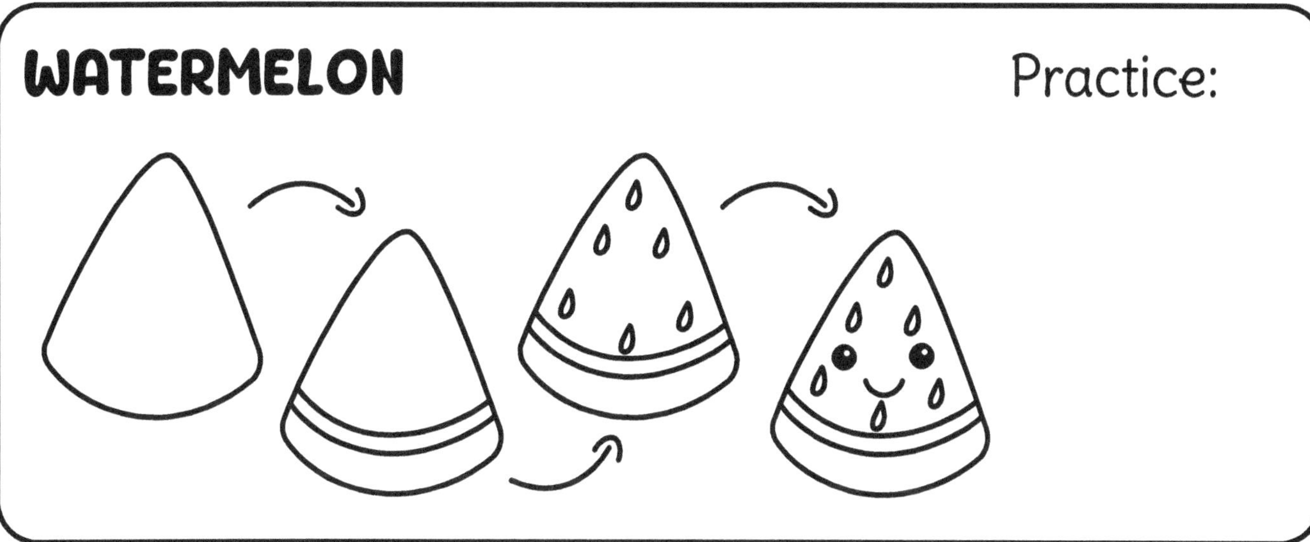

CHERRIES

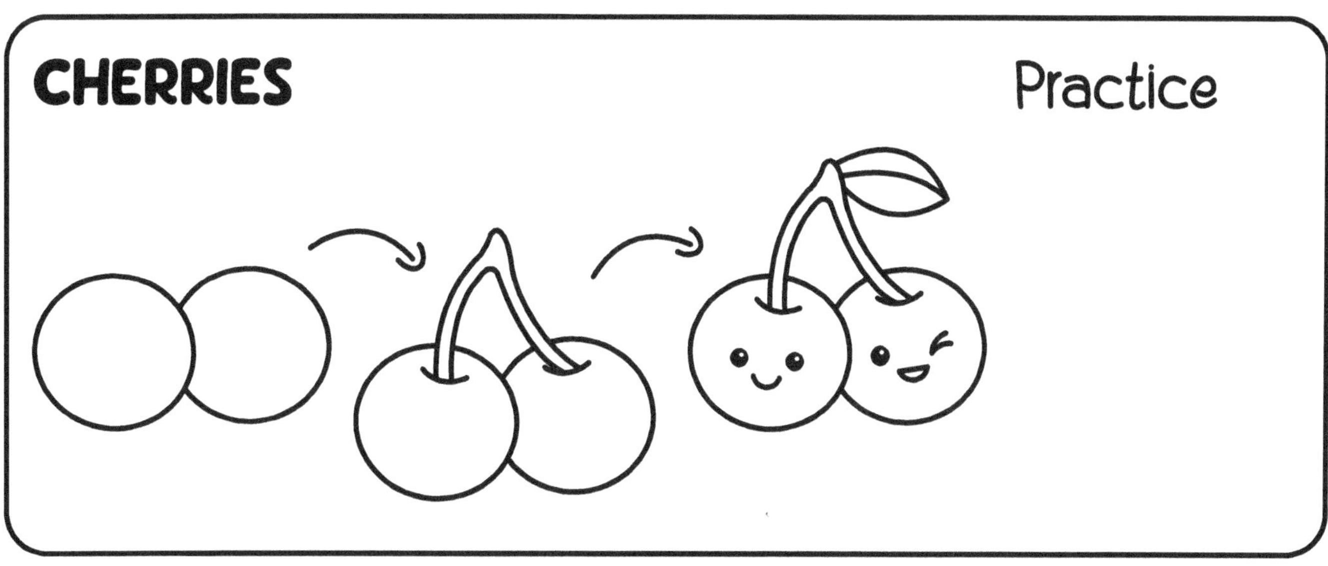

COCONUT

Practice:

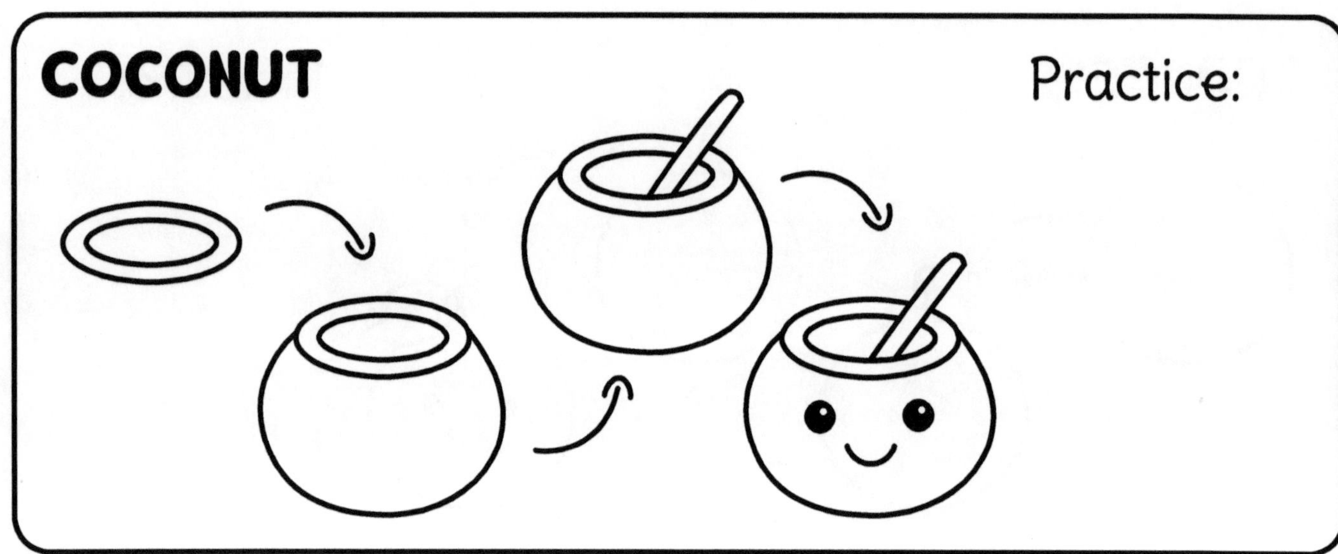

ONION

Practice:

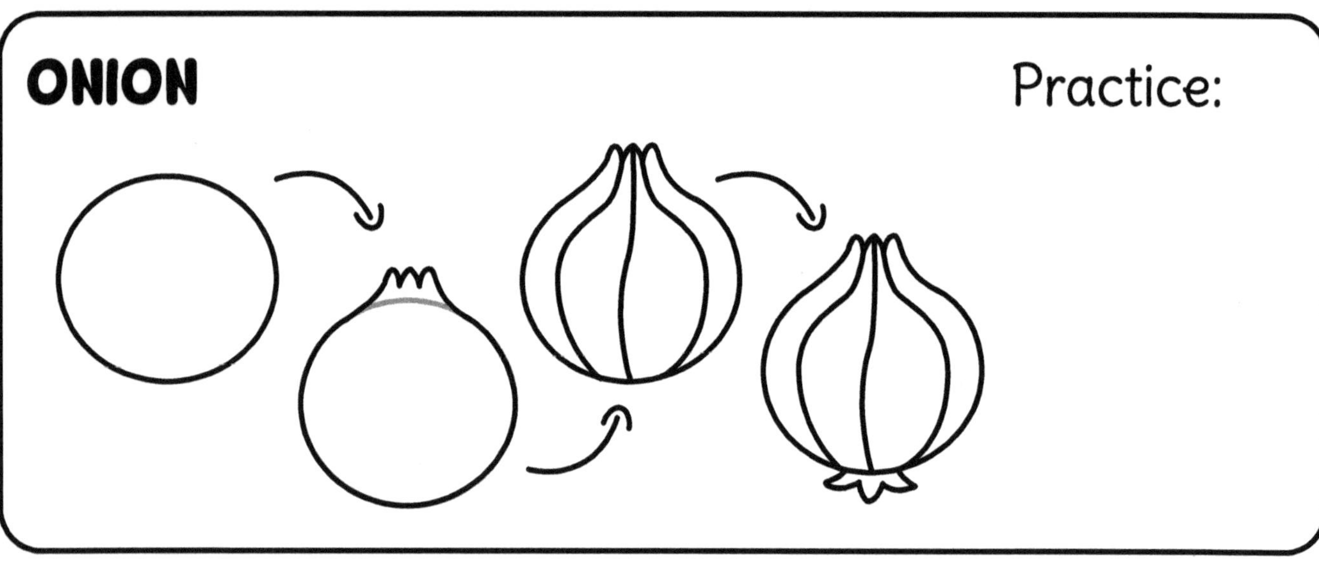

TOMATO

Practice

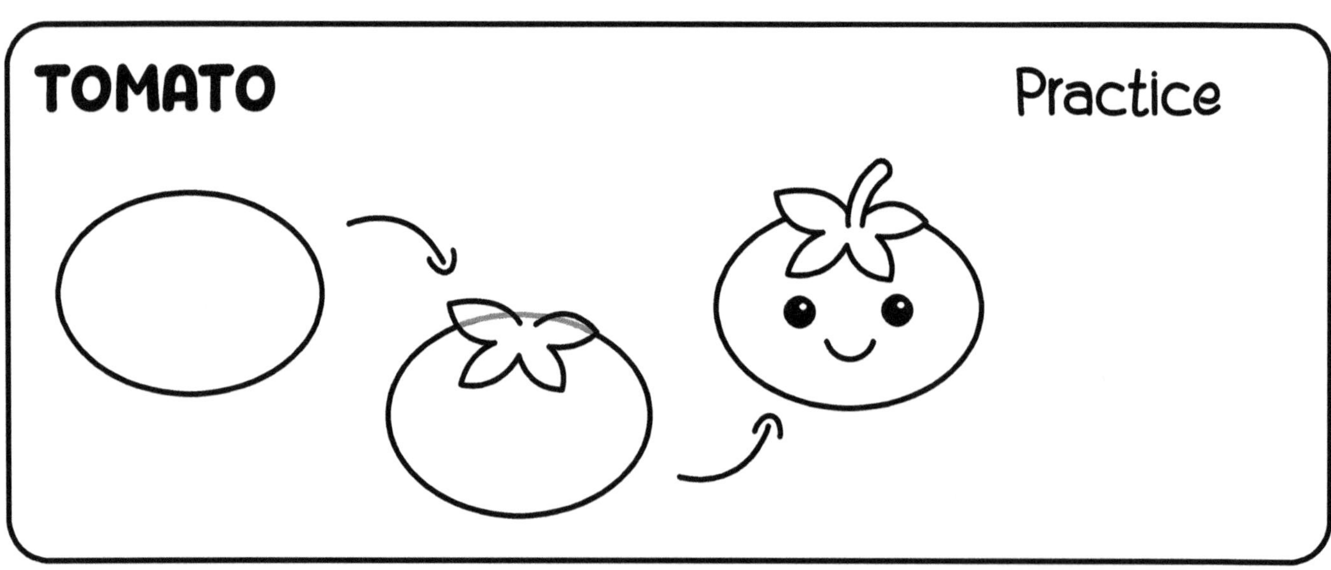

CABBAGE

Practice:

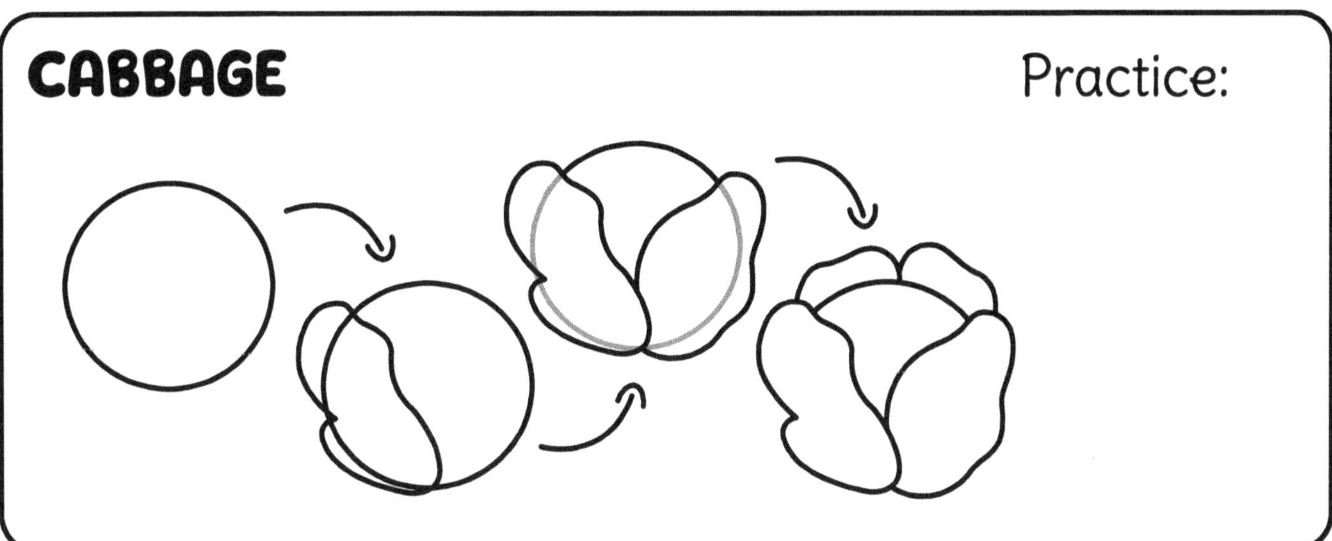

BROCCOLI

Practice:

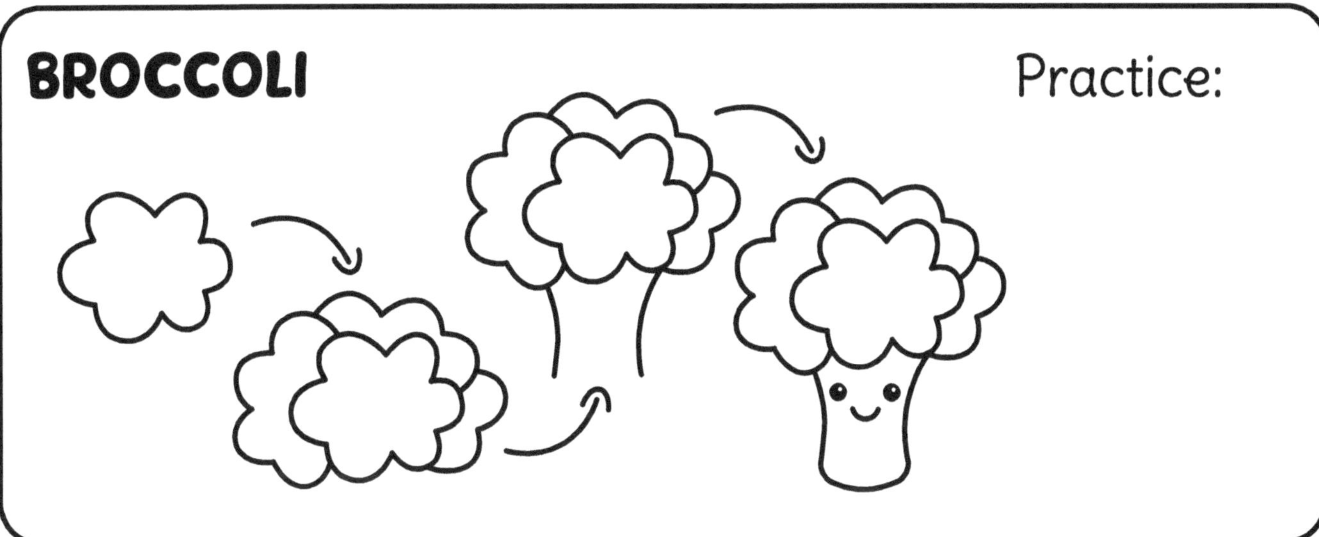

CARROT

Practice

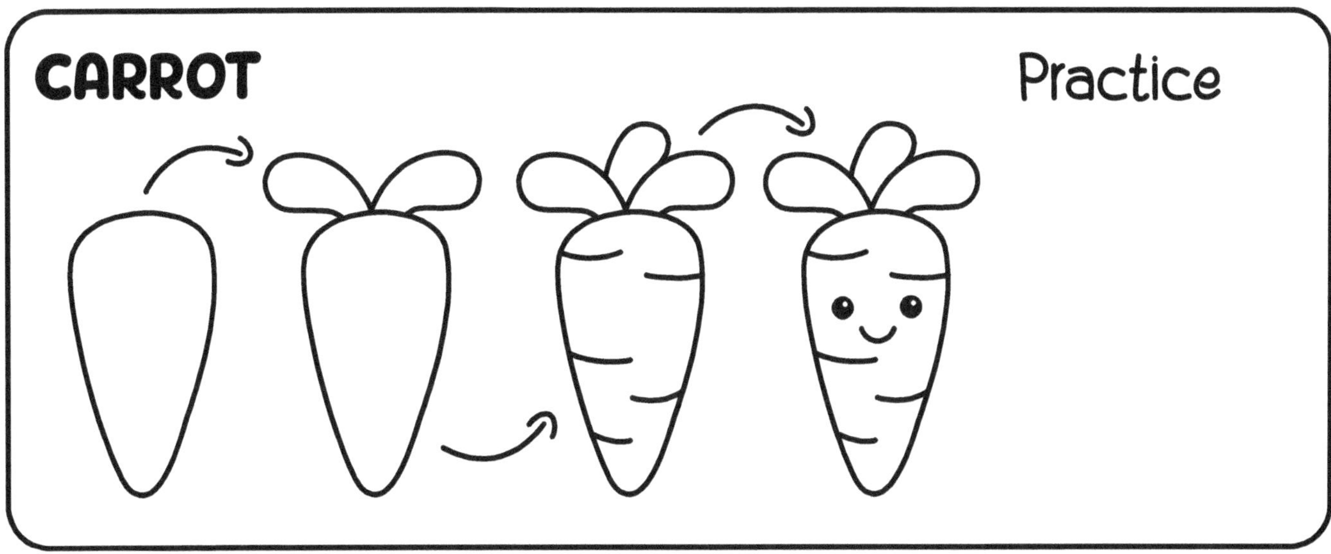

PEA

Practice:

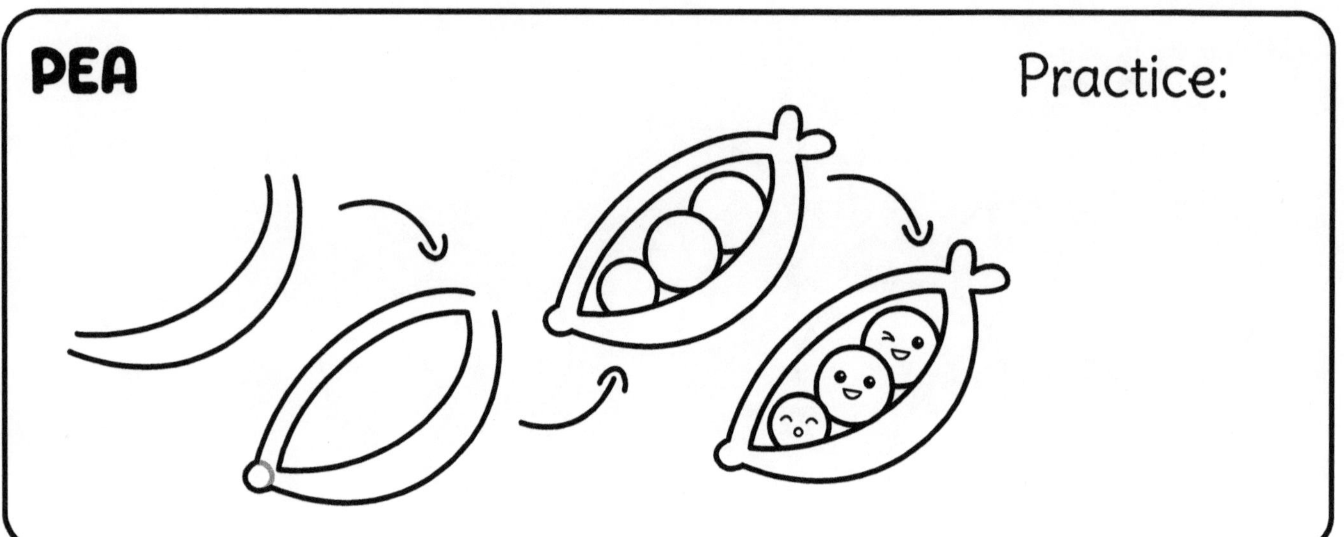

AVOCADO

Practice:

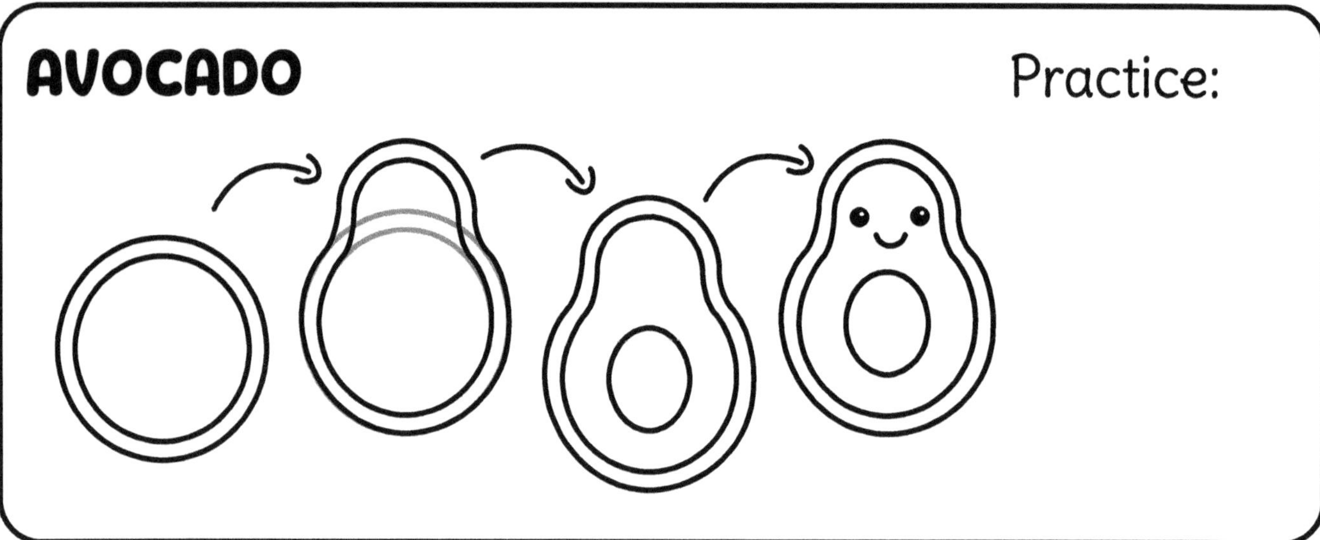

LEMON

Practice

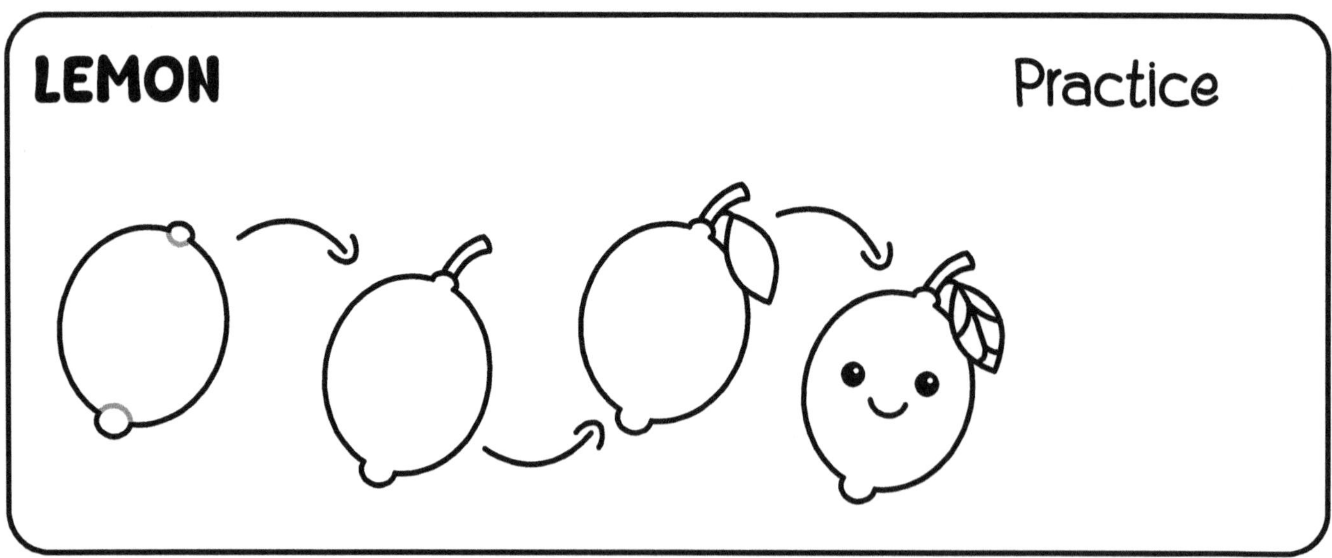

POTATO Practice:

BELL PEPPER Practice:

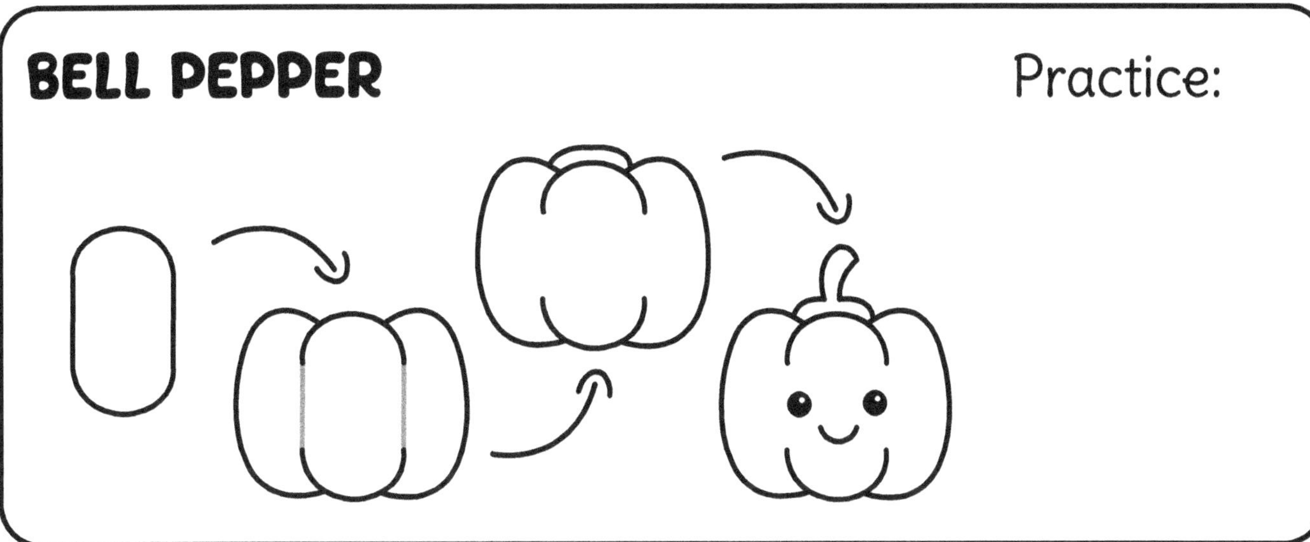

CHILLI Practice

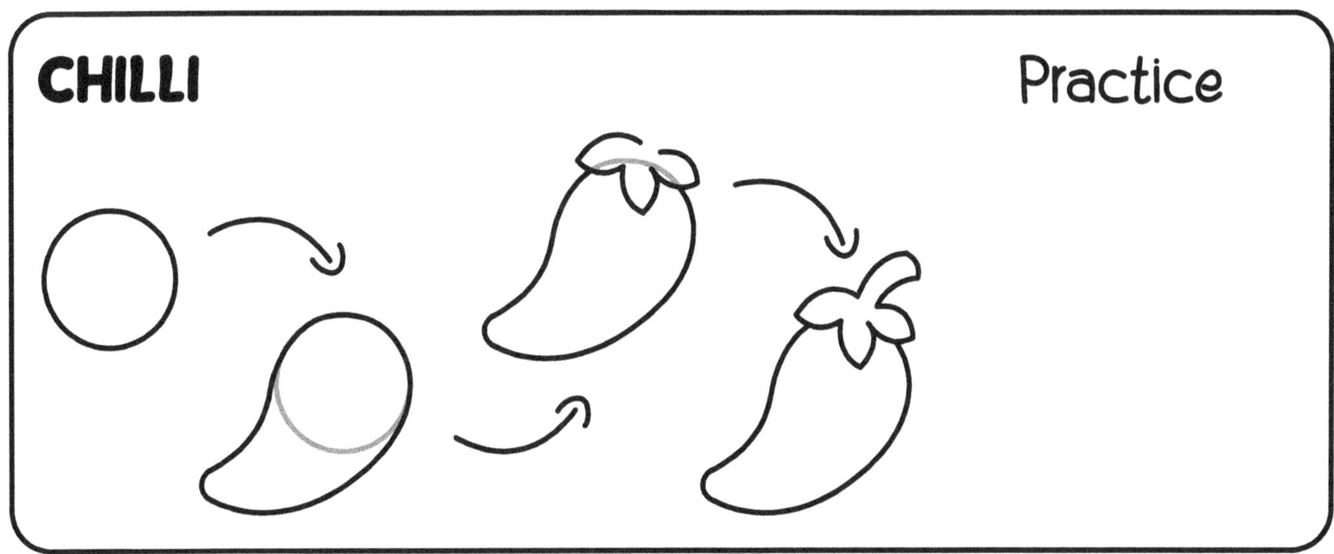

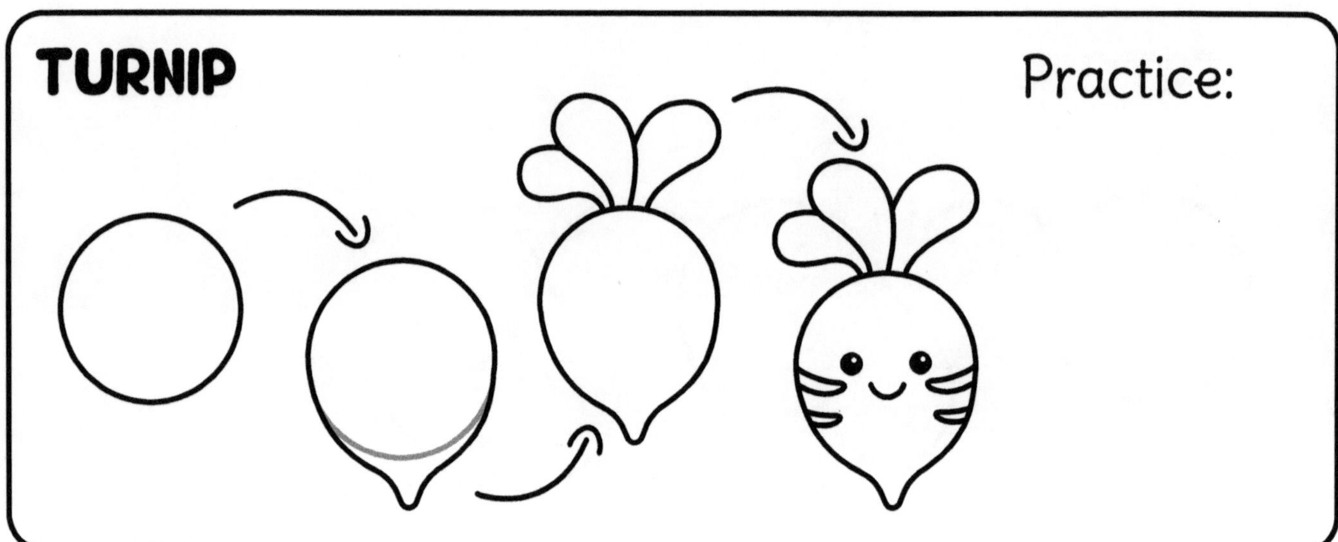

TURNIP
Practice:

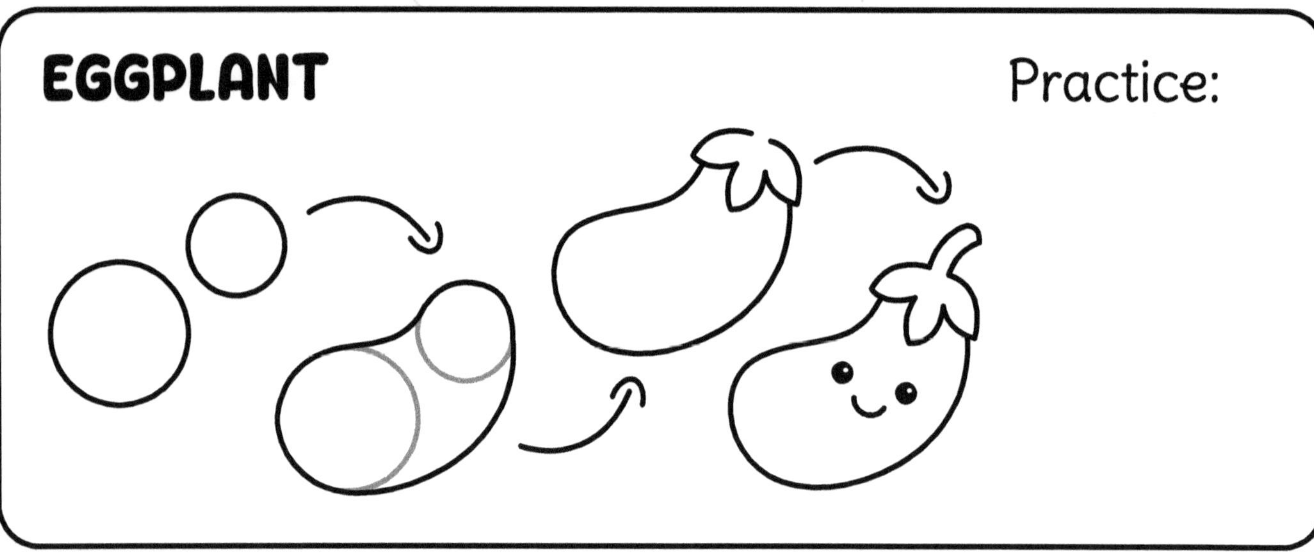

EGGPLANT
Practice:

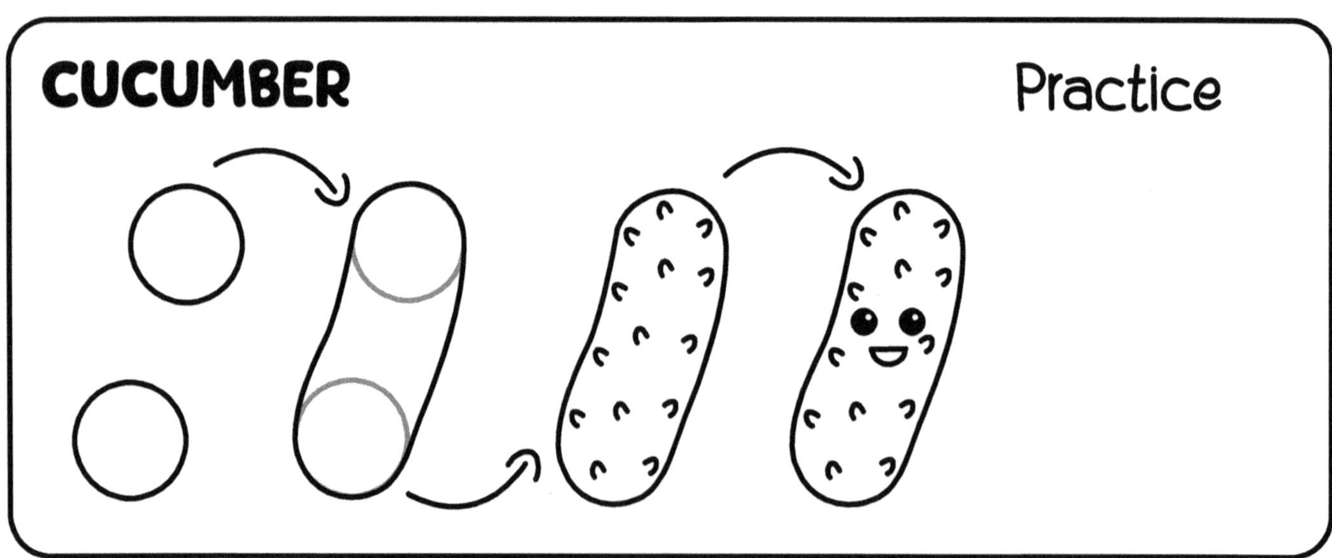

CUCUMBER
Practice

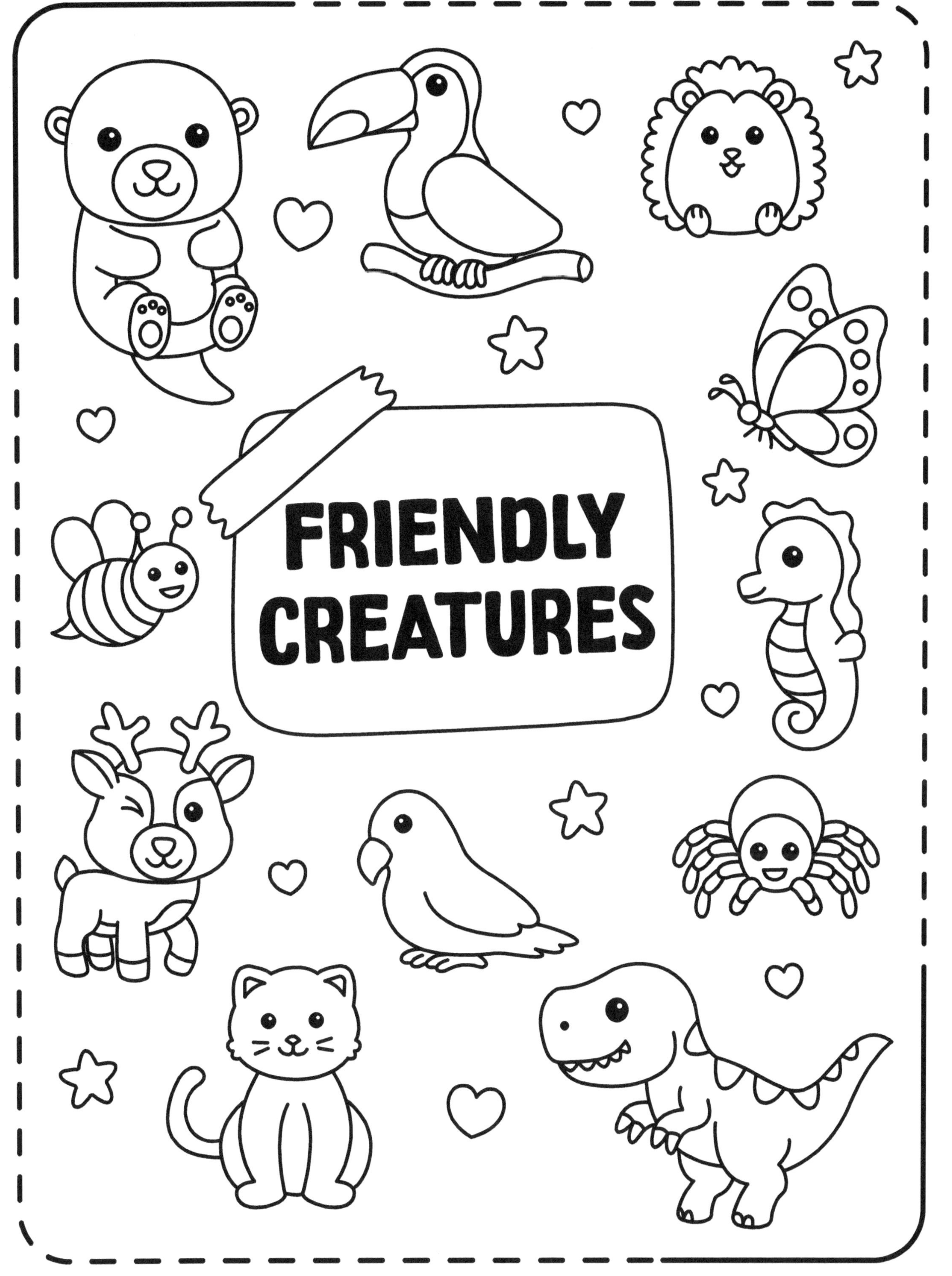
FRIENDLY CREATURES

CAT

Practice:

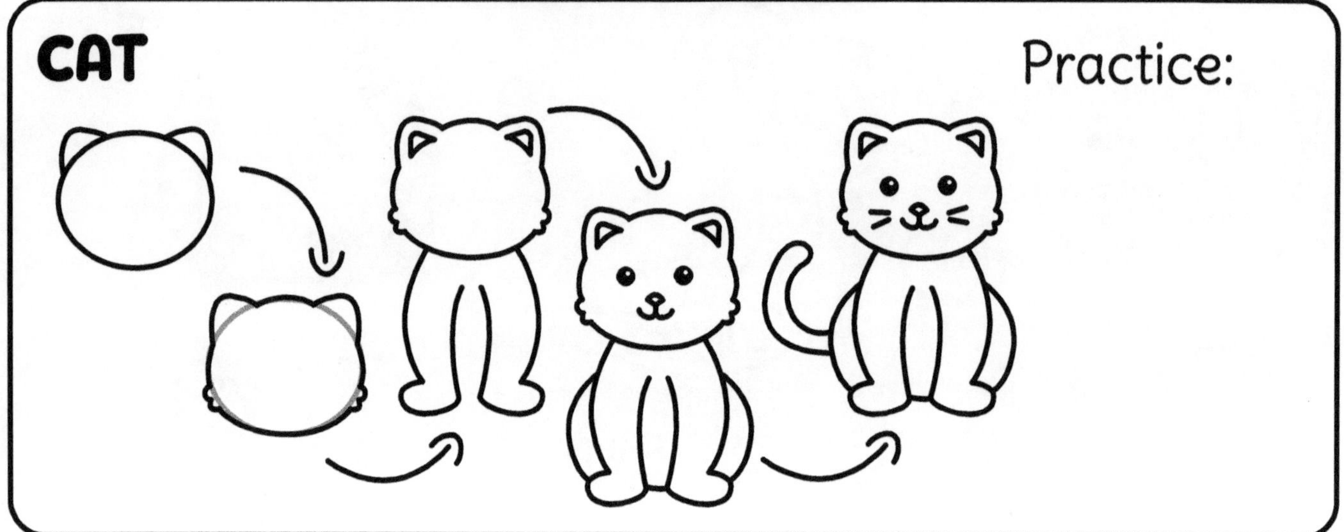

DOG

Practice:

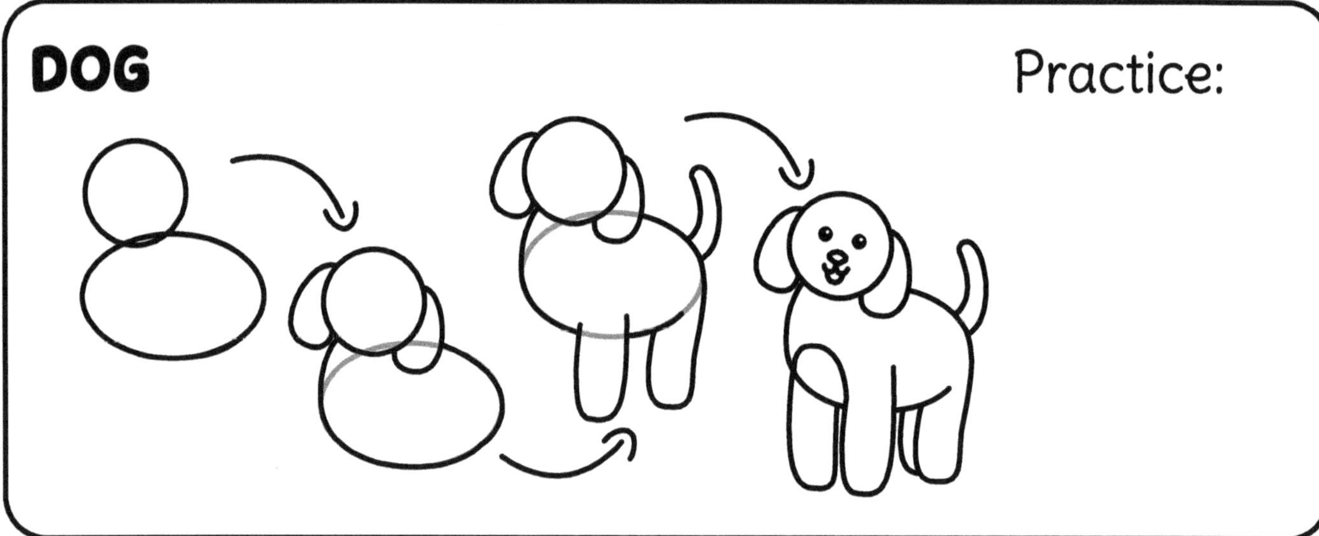

PIGGY

Practice

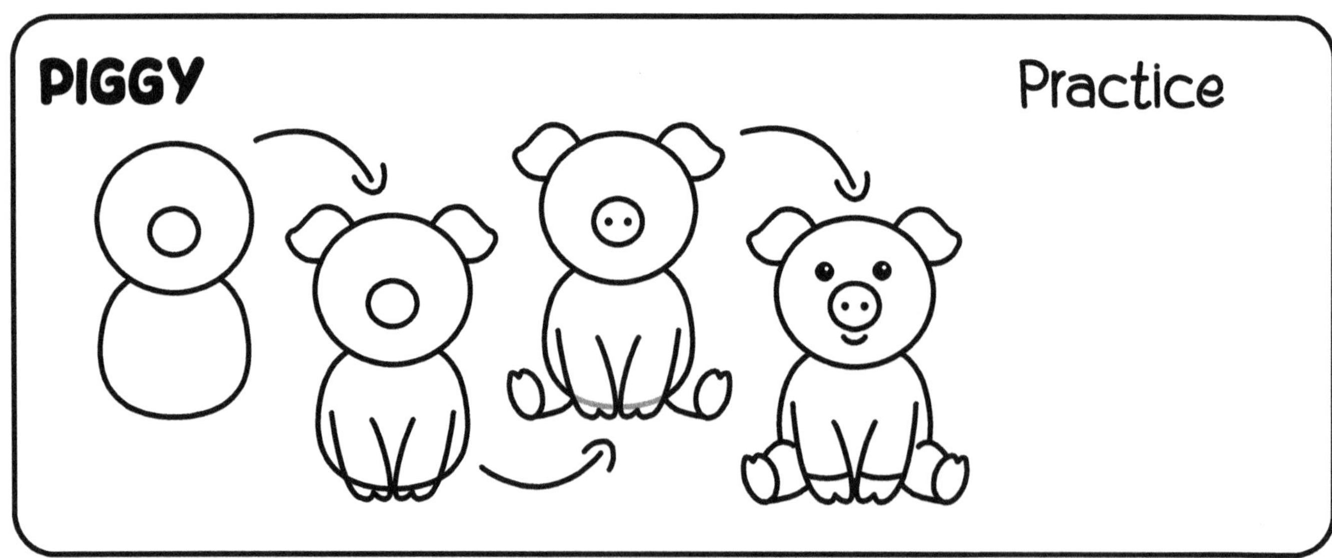

HAMSTER

Practice:

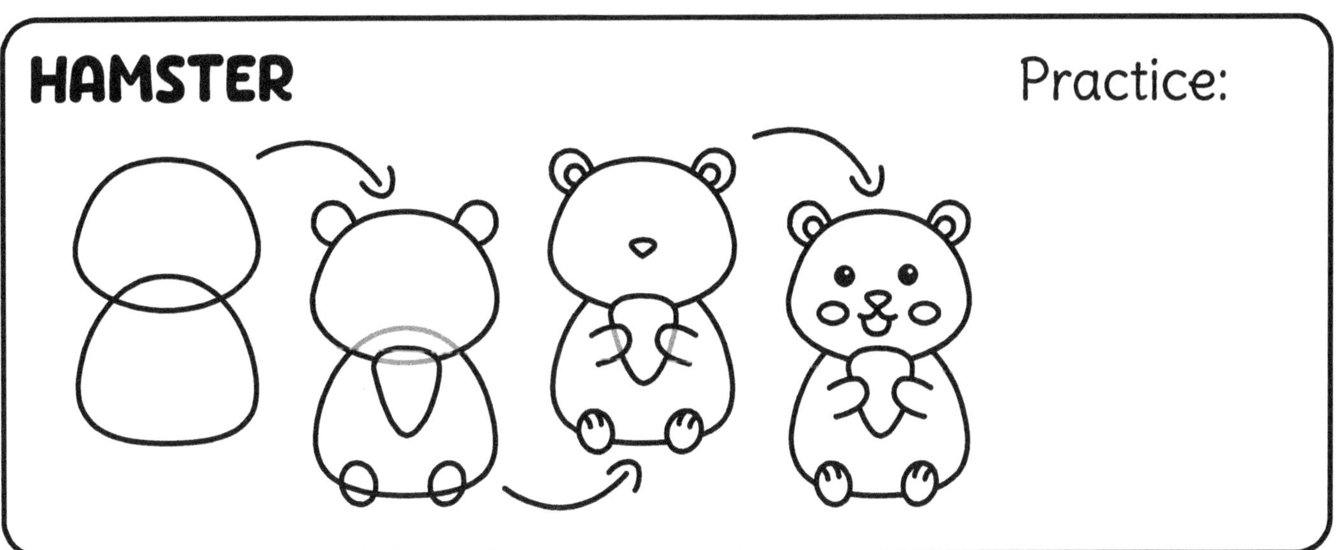

BUNNY

Practice:

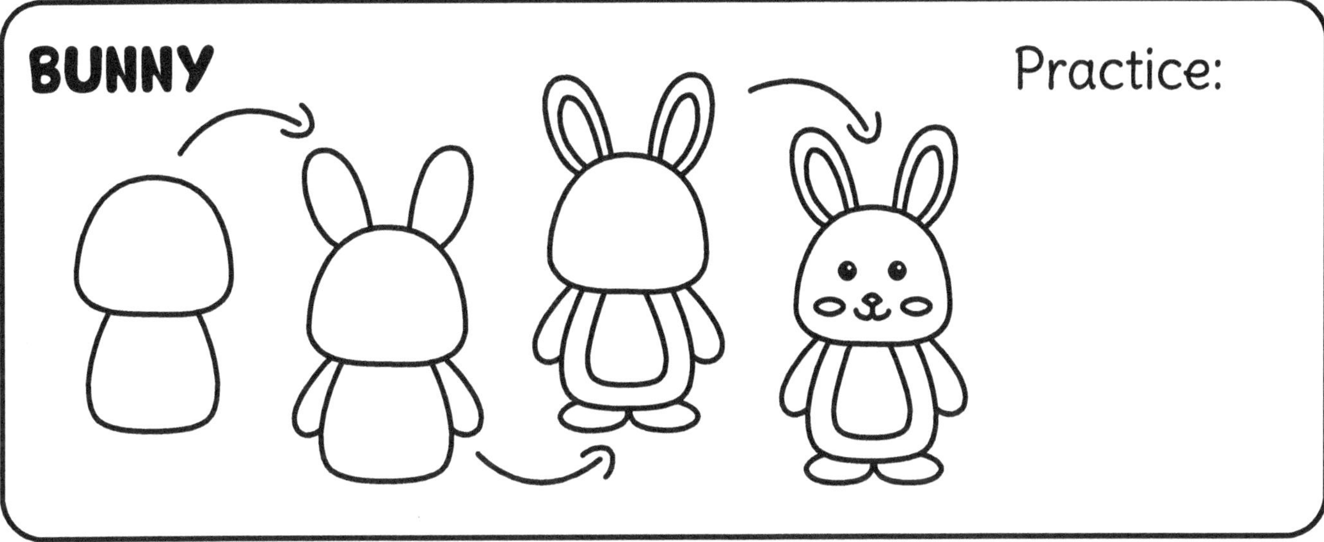

COW

Practice

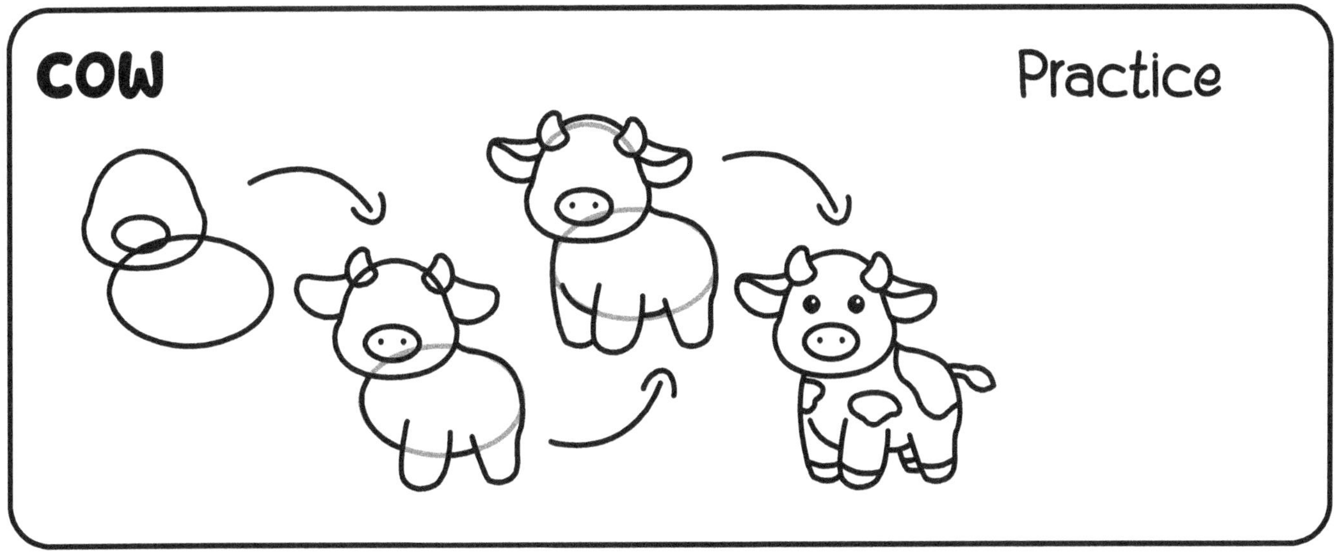

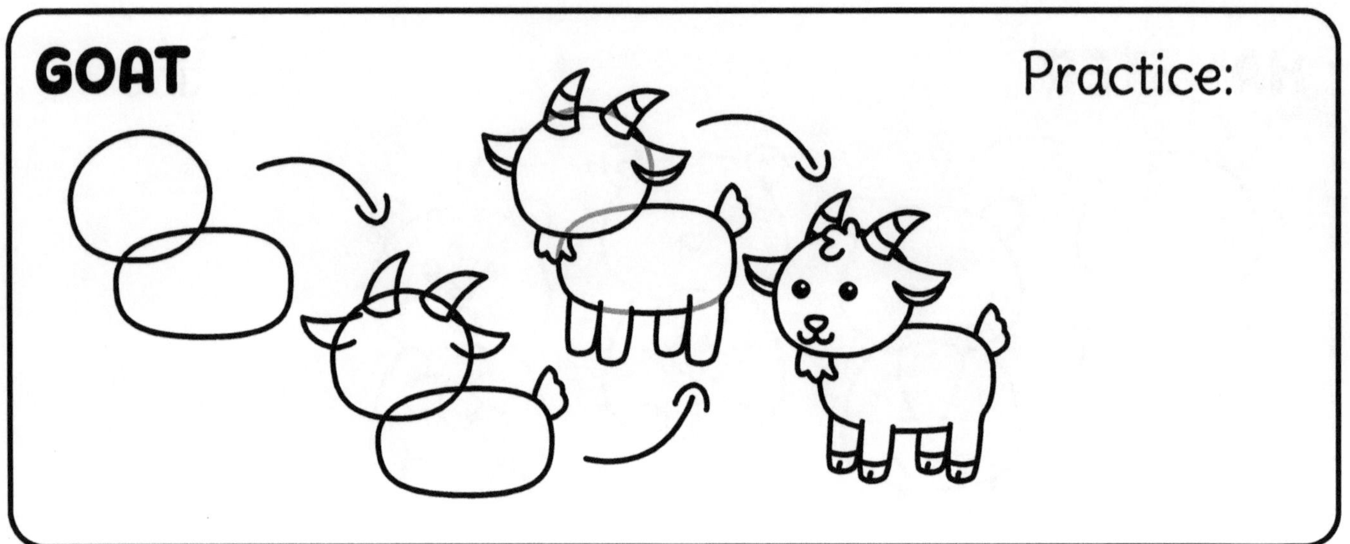

GOAT
Practice:

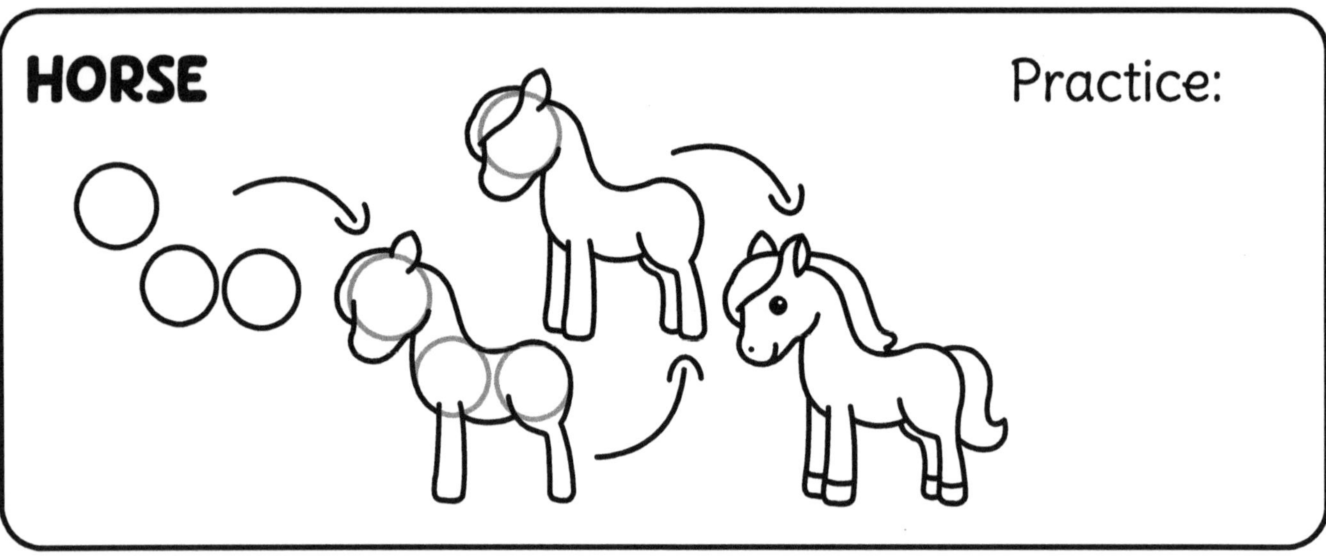

HORSE
Practice:

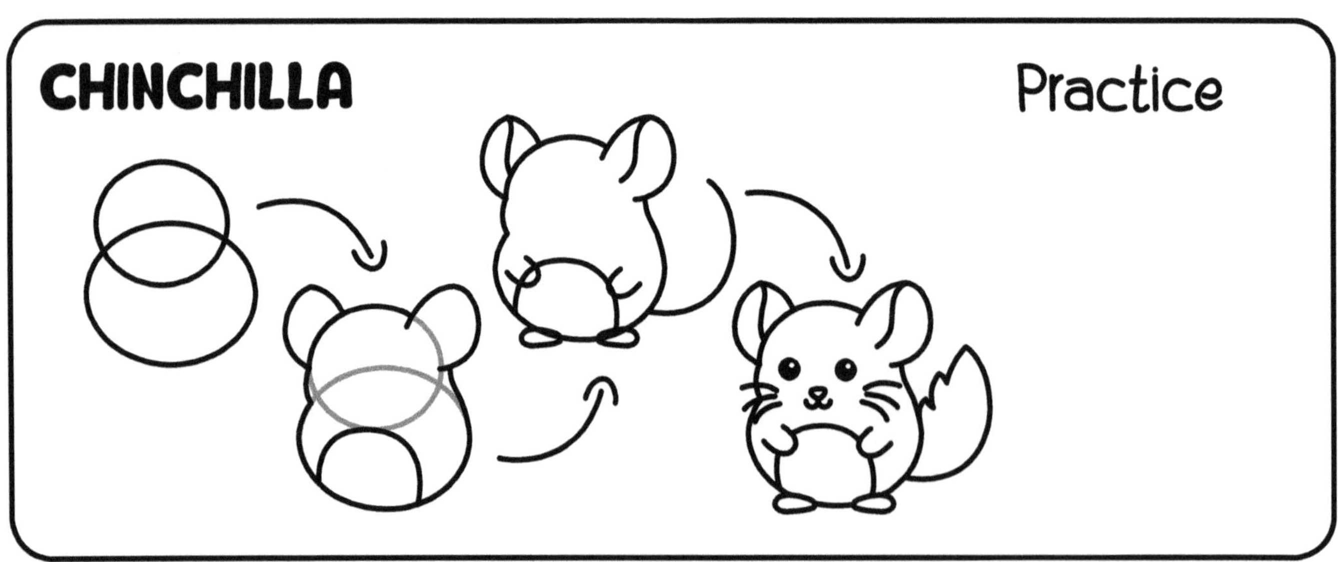

CHINCHILLA
Practice

AMAZING WILD ANIMALS

BEAR

Practice:

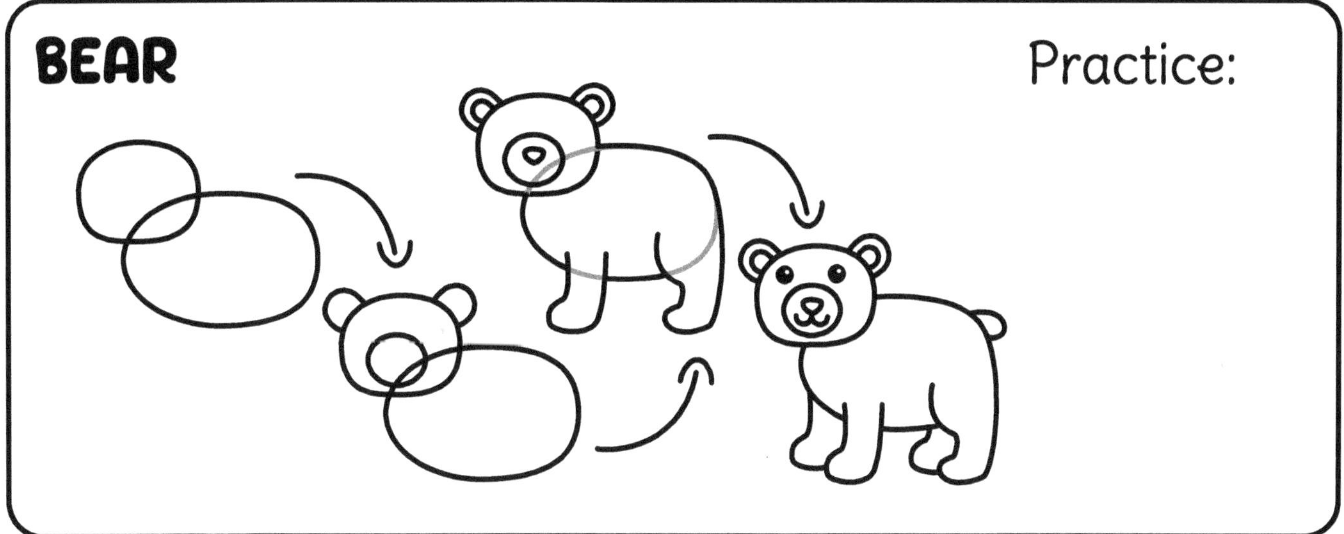

REINDEER

Practice:

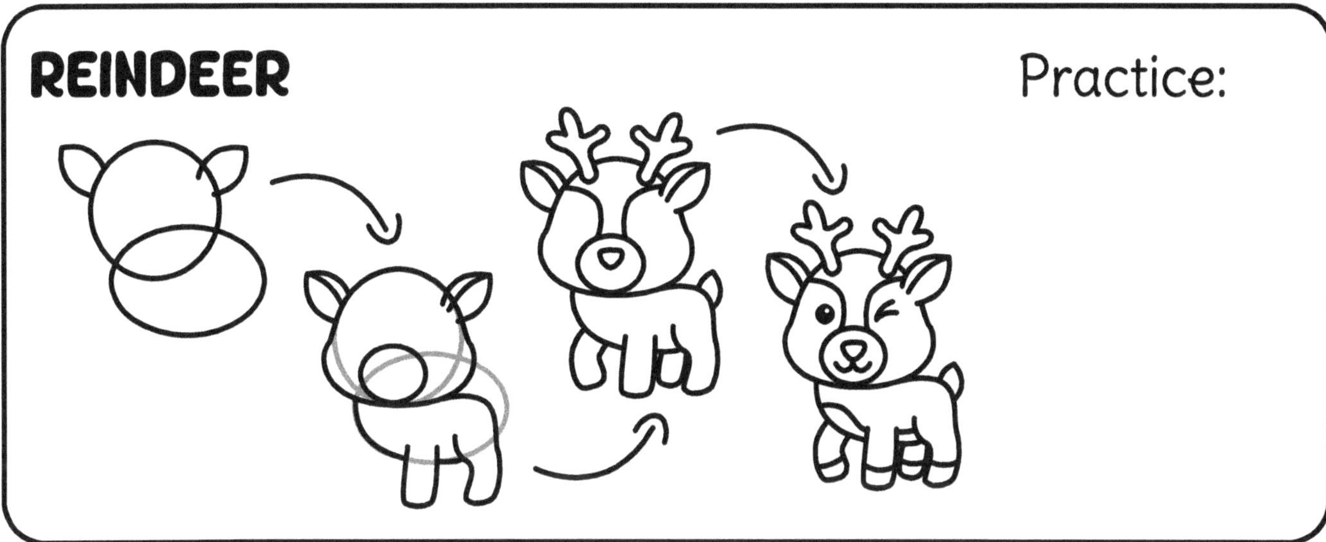

PANDA

Practice

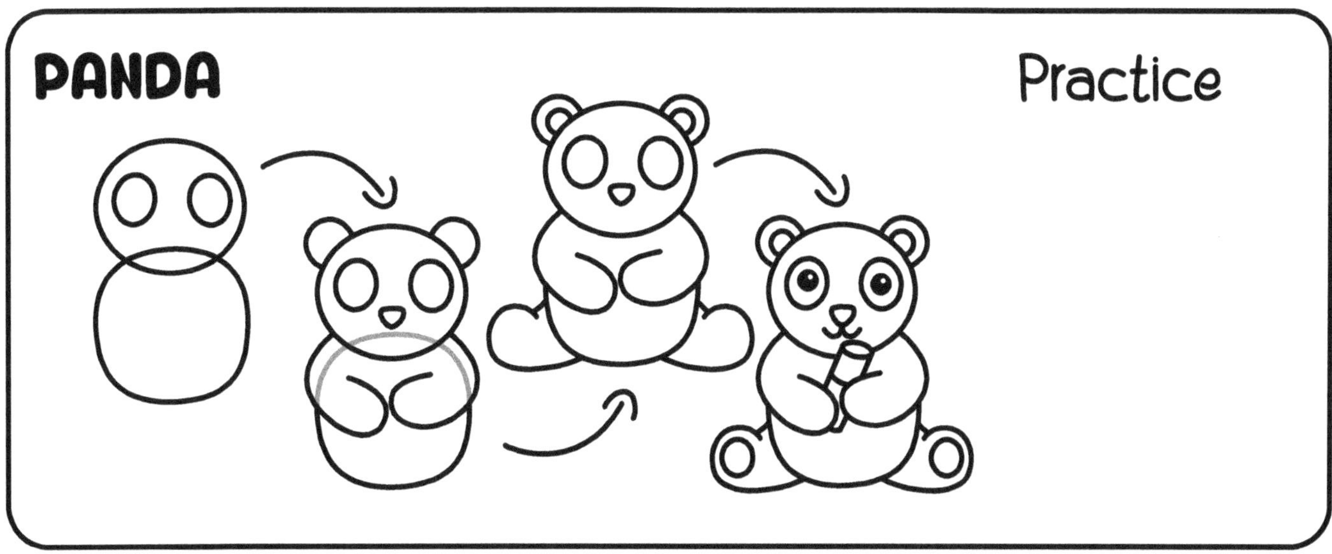

FOX

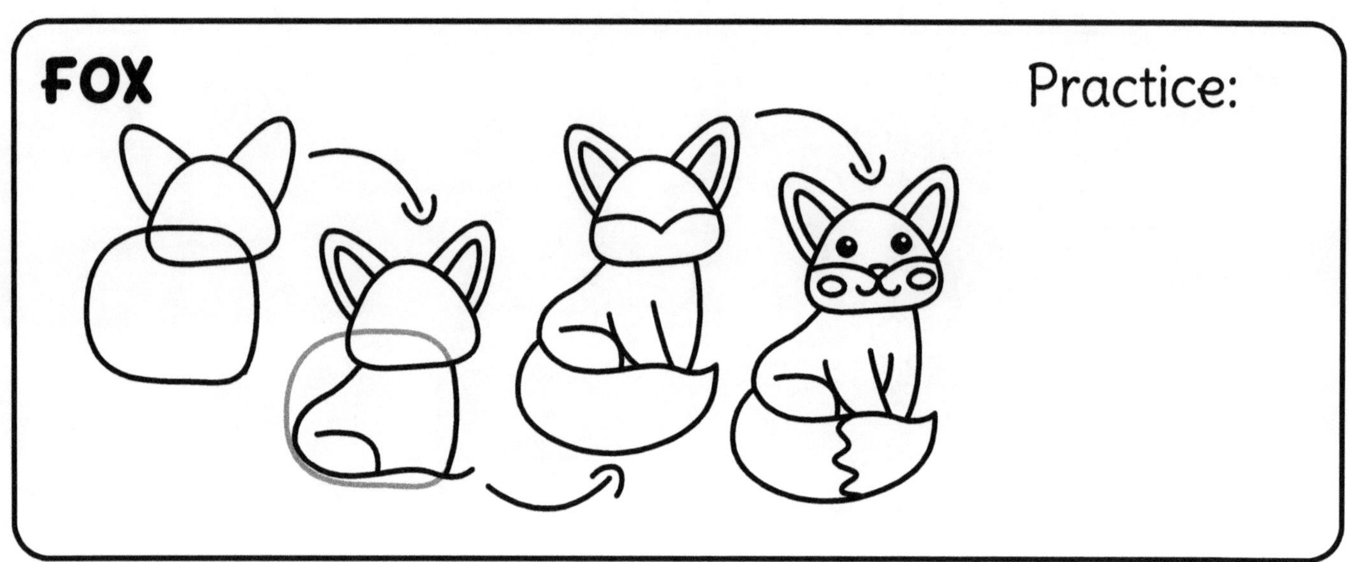

WOLF

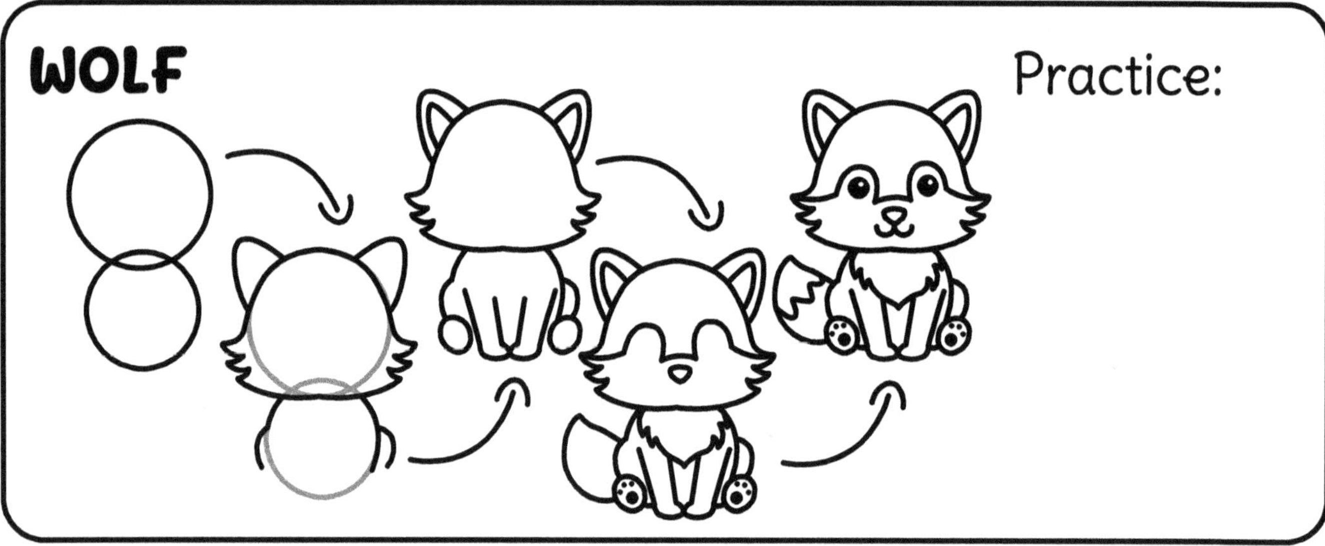

LAMA

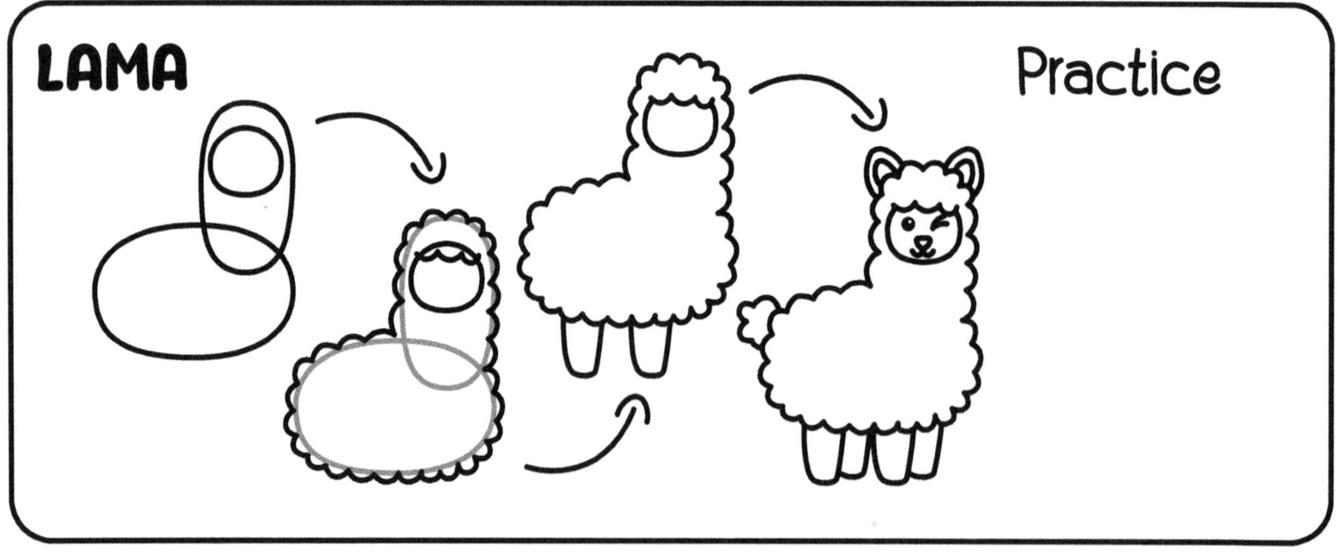

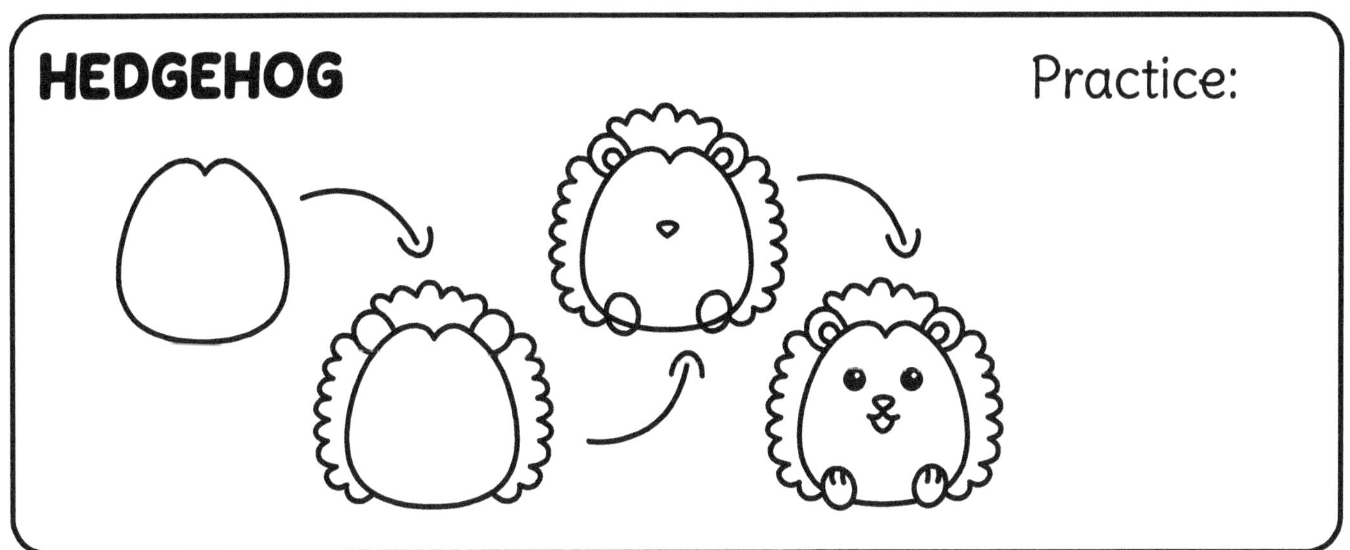

HEDGEHOG
Practice:

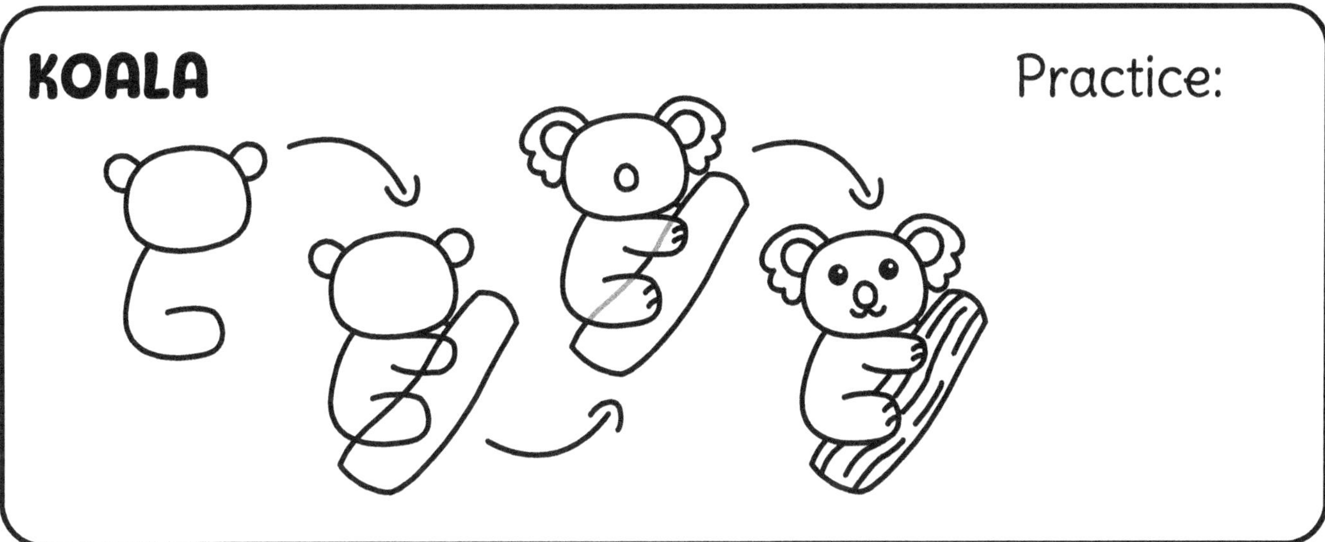

KOALA
Practice:

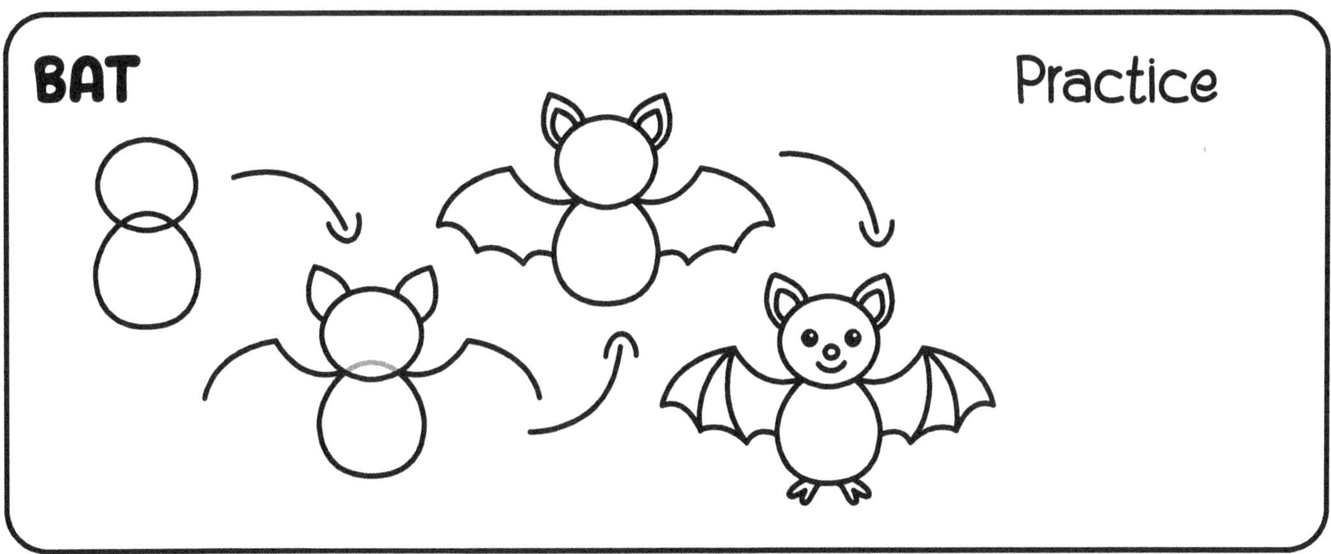

BAT
Practice

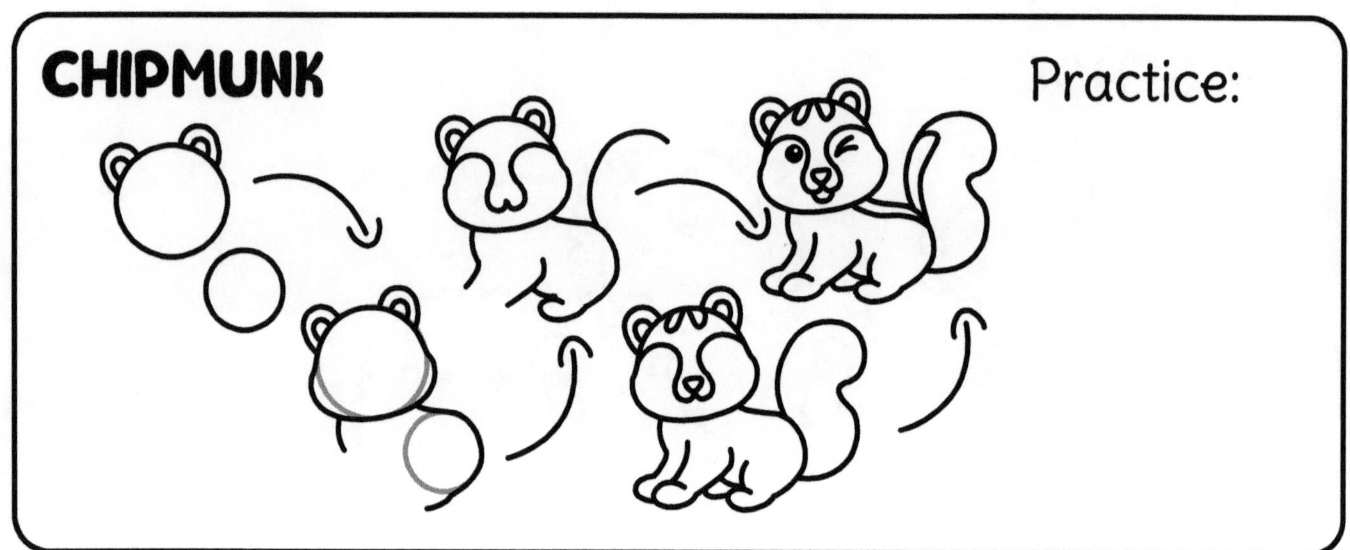

CHIPMUNK
Practice:

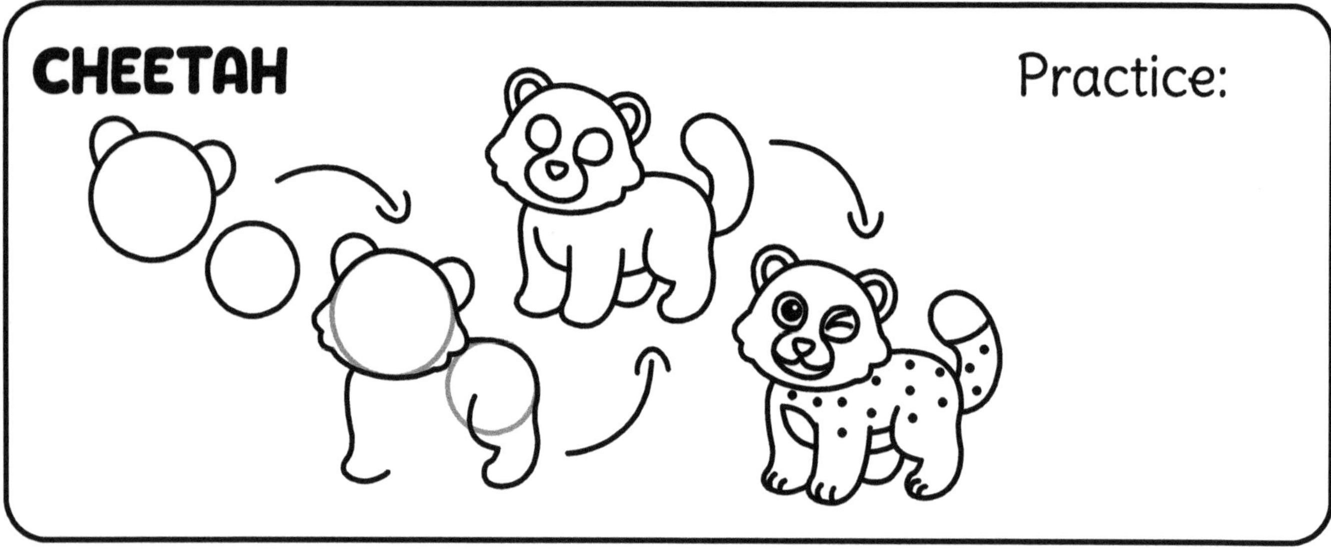

CHEETAH
Practice:

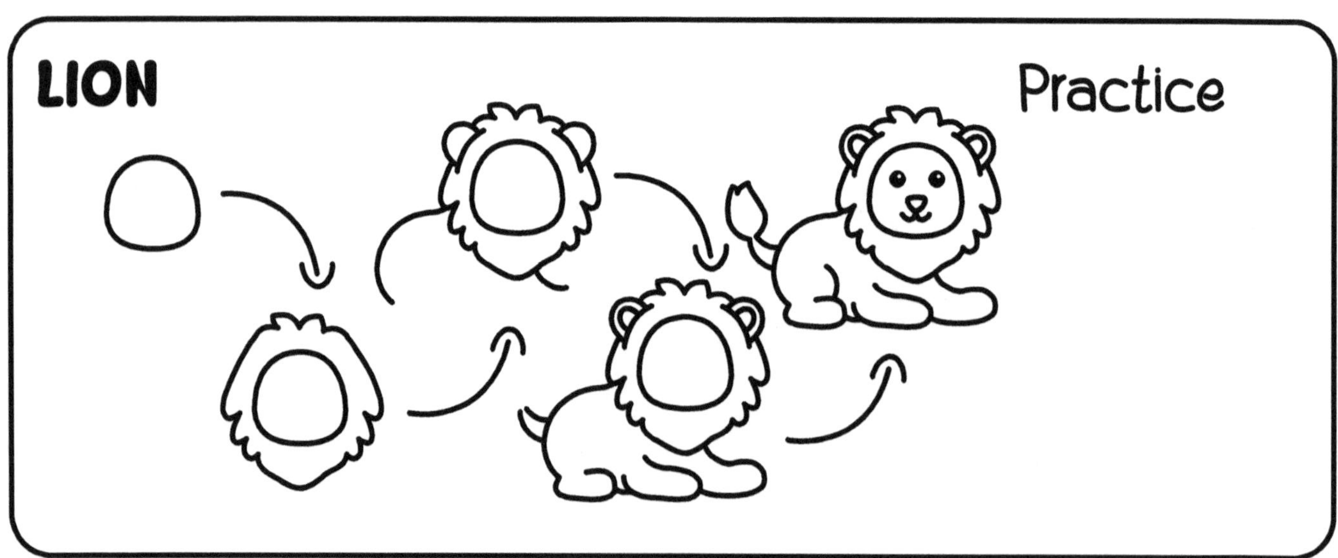

LION
Practice

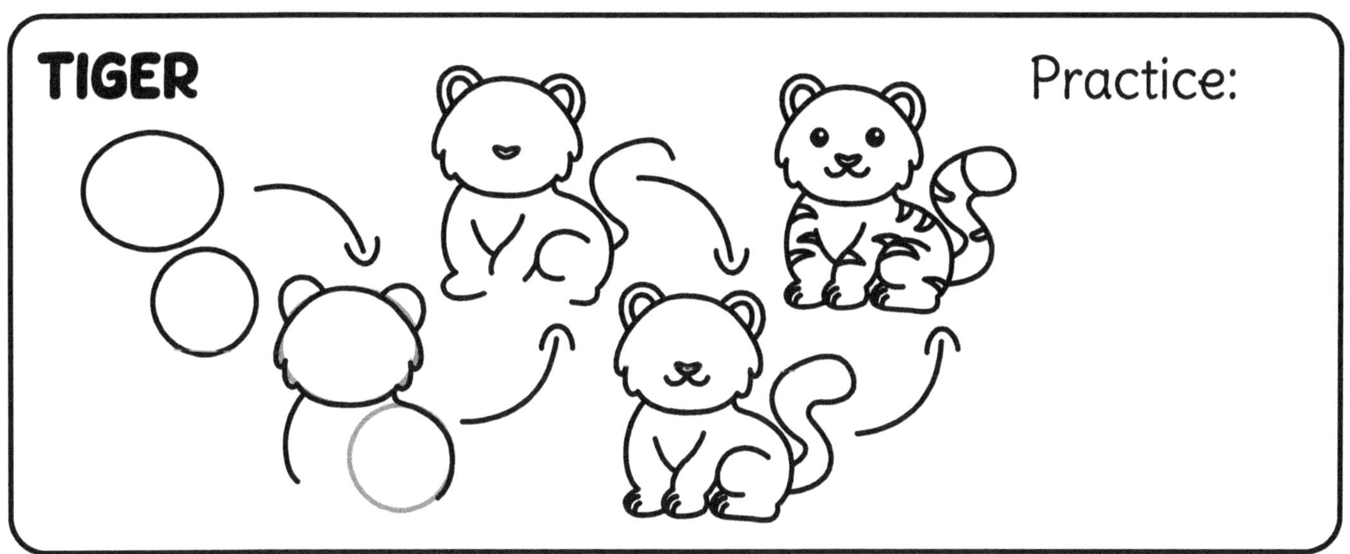

TIGER
Practice:

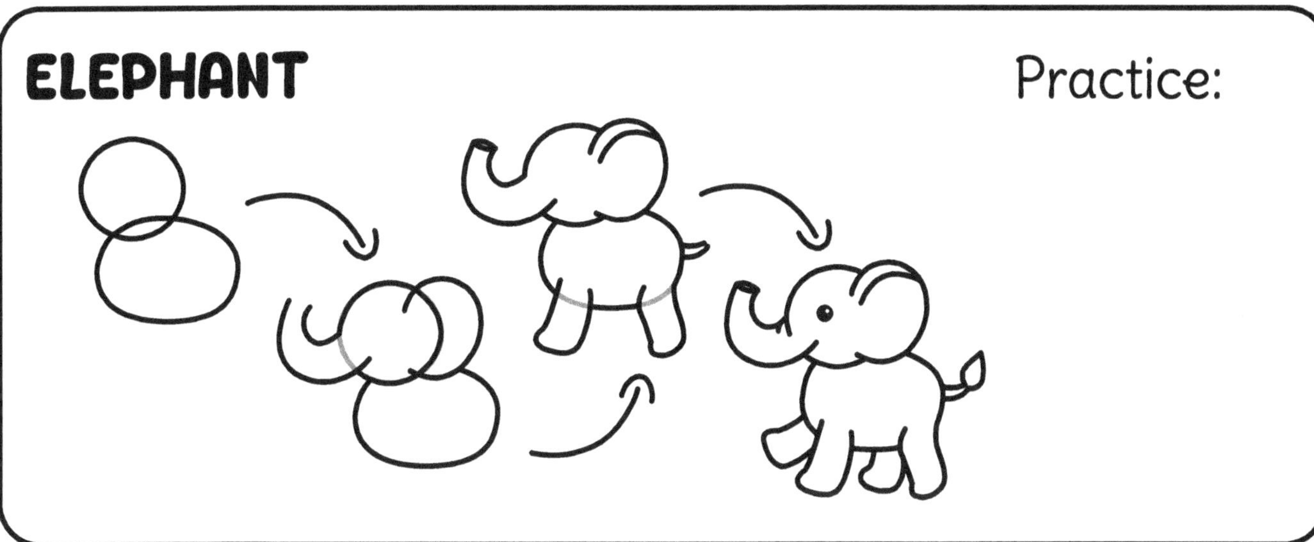

ELEPHANT
Practice:

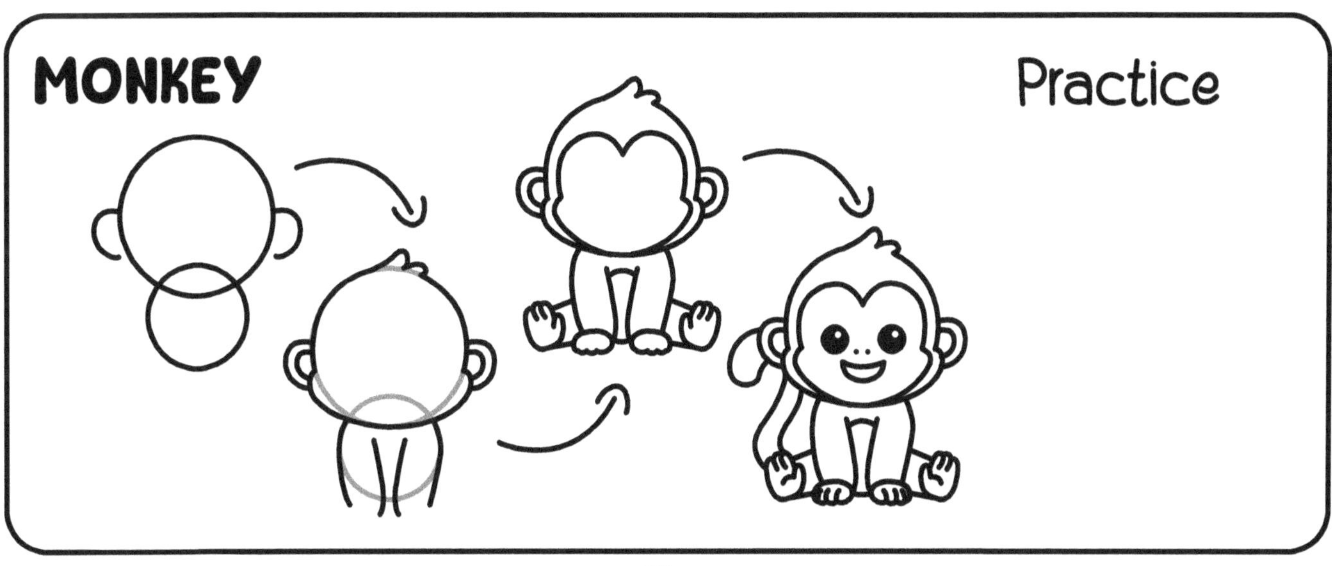

MONKEY
Practice

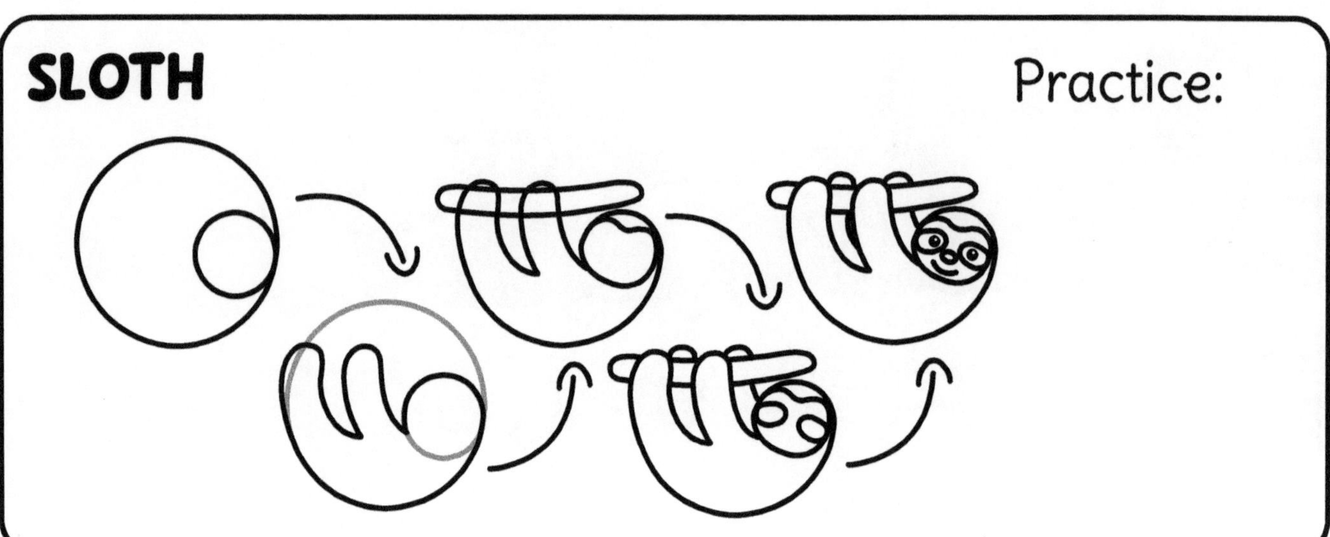
SLOTH
Practice:

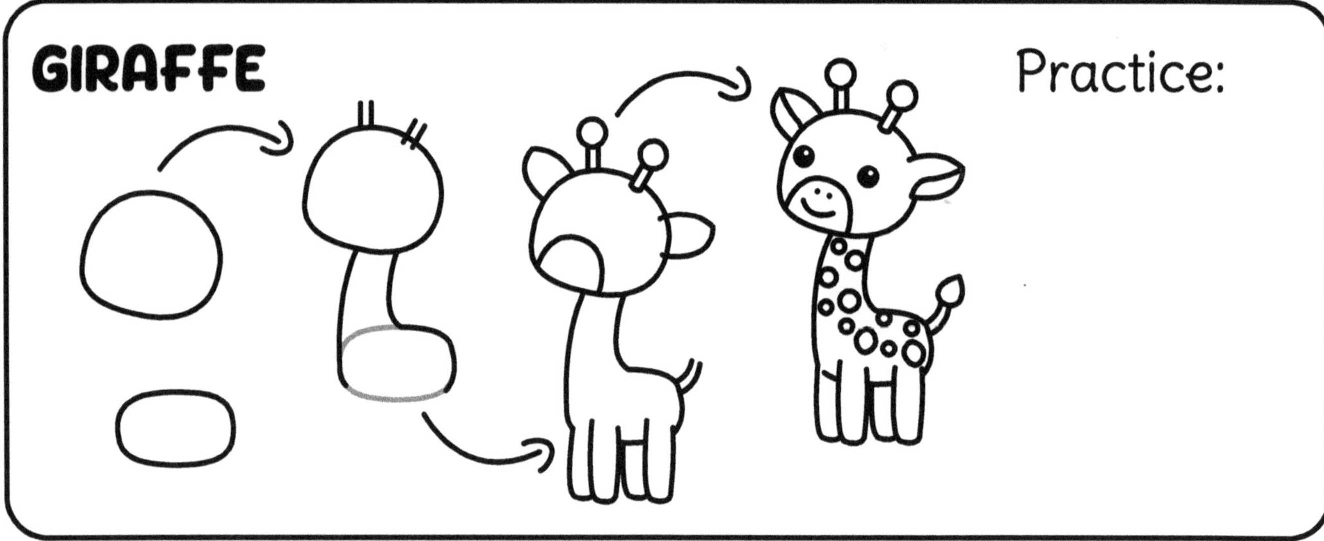
GIRAFFE
Practice:

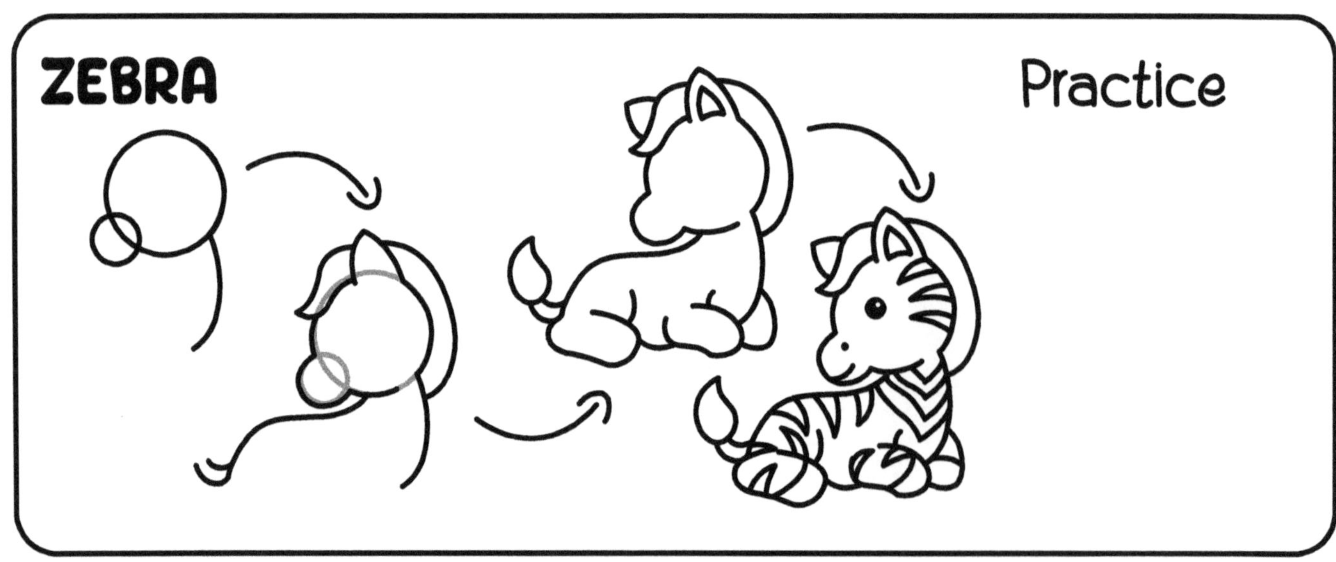
ZEBRA
Practice

CAMEL

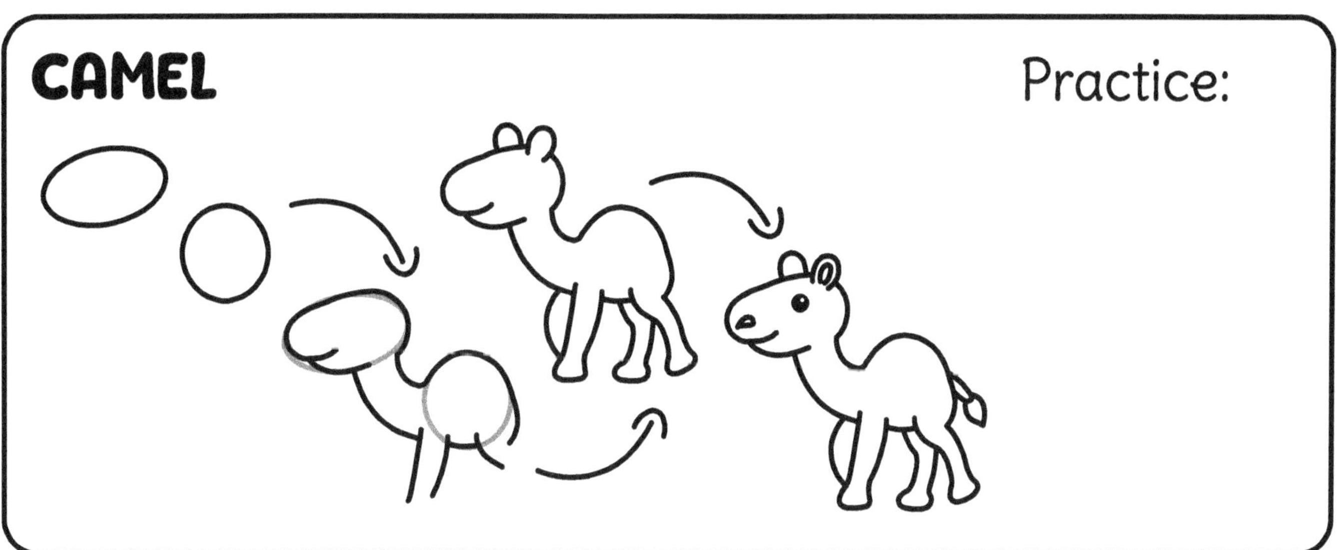

OTTER

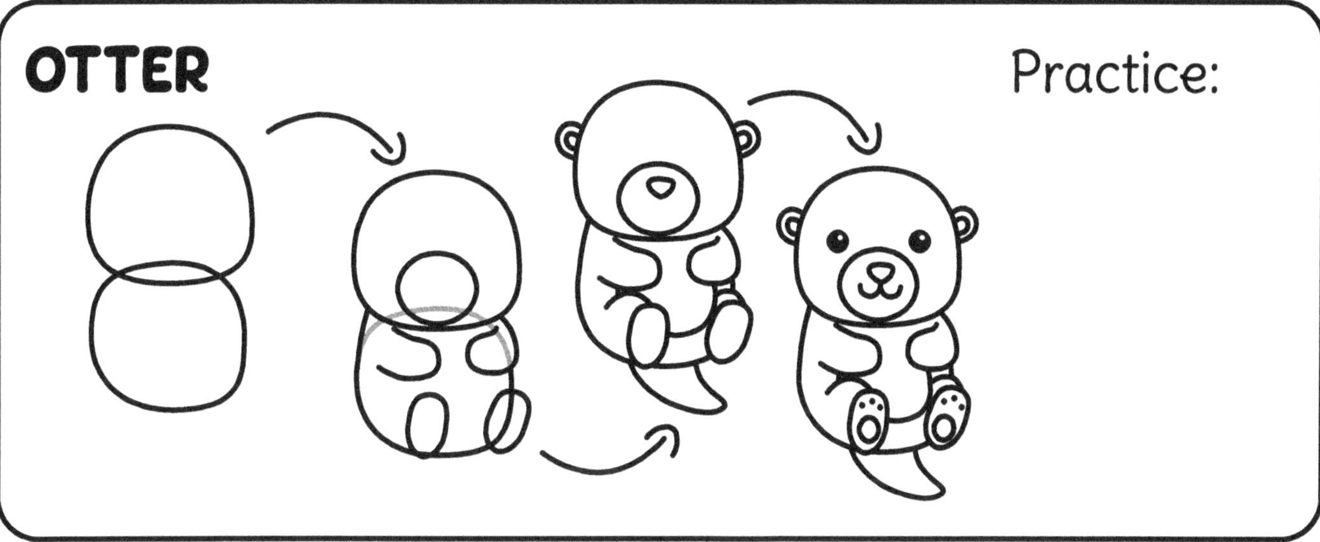

CROCODILE

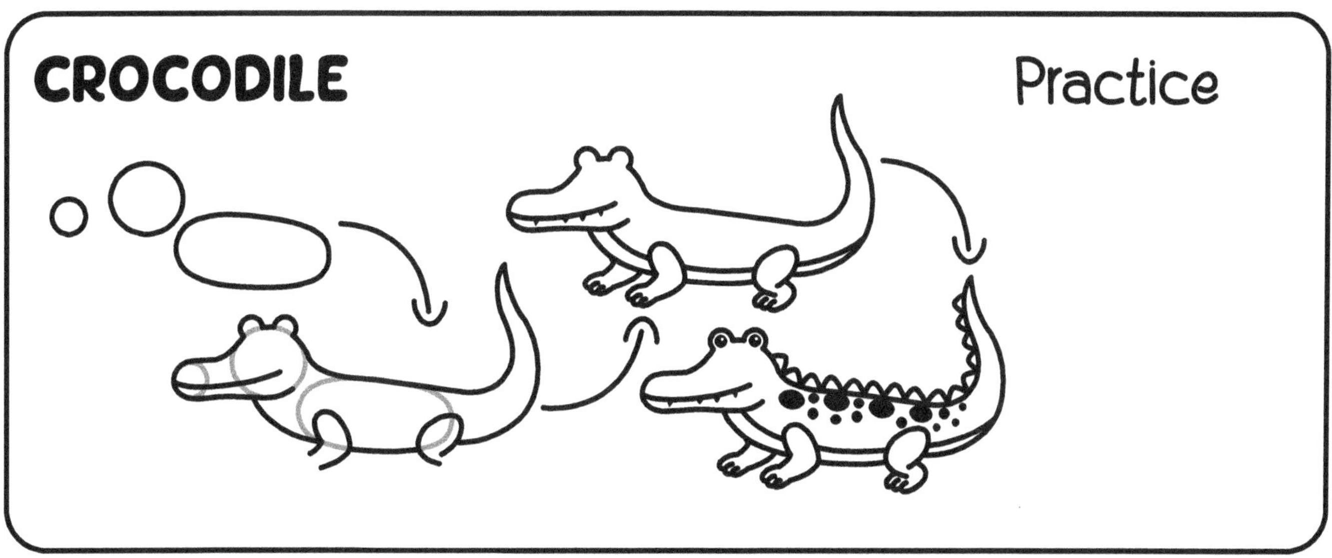

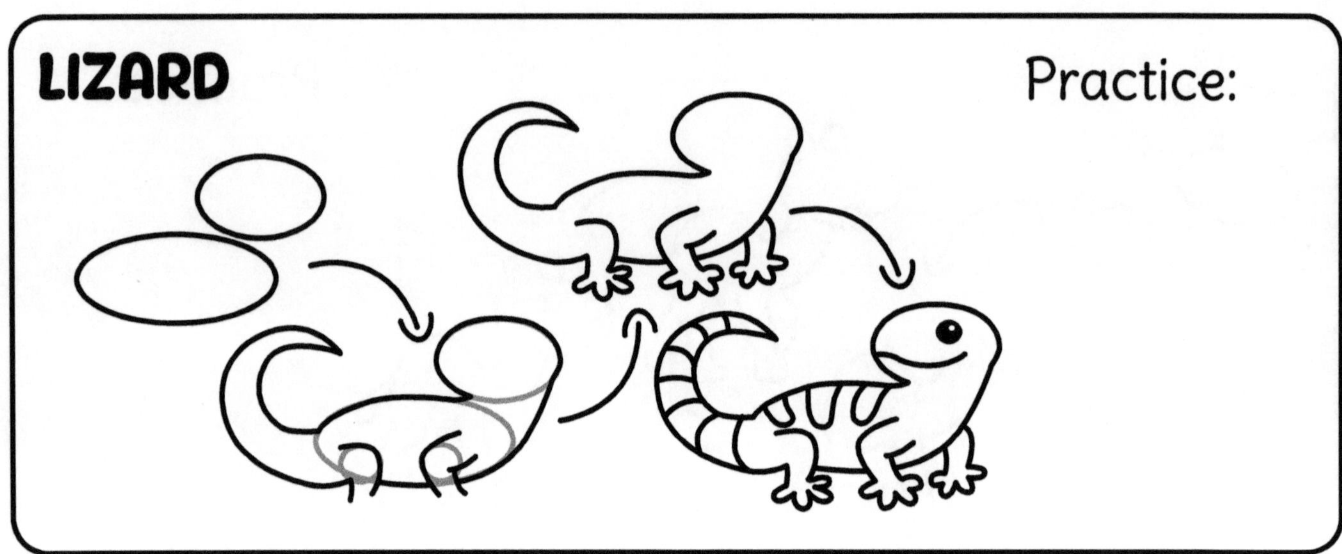

LIZARD
Practice:

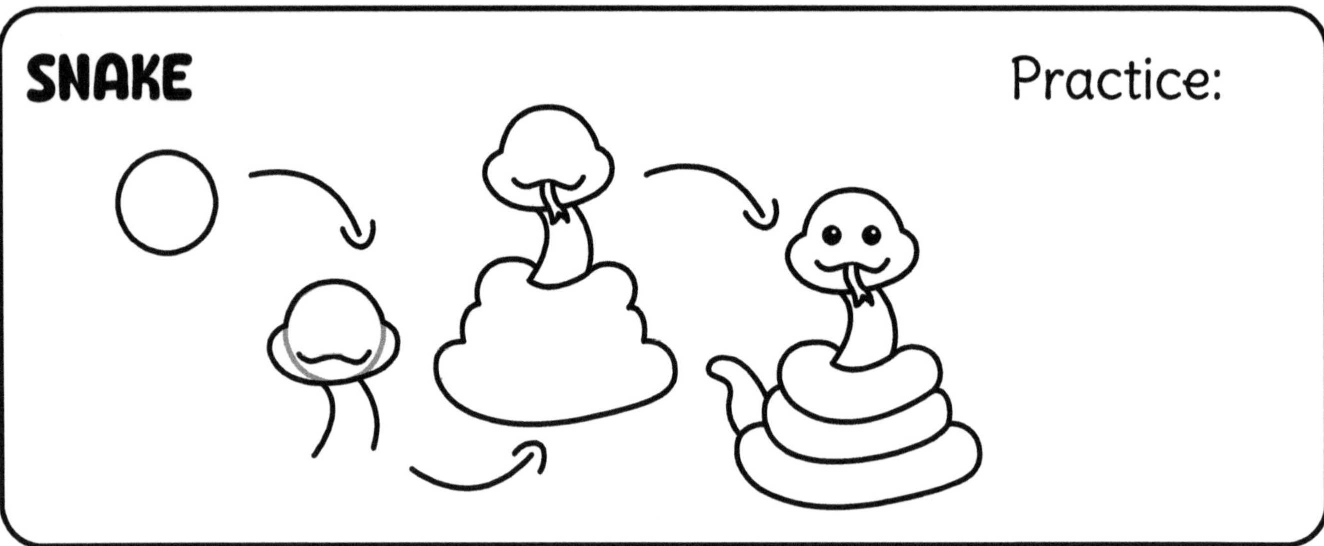

SNAKE
Practice:

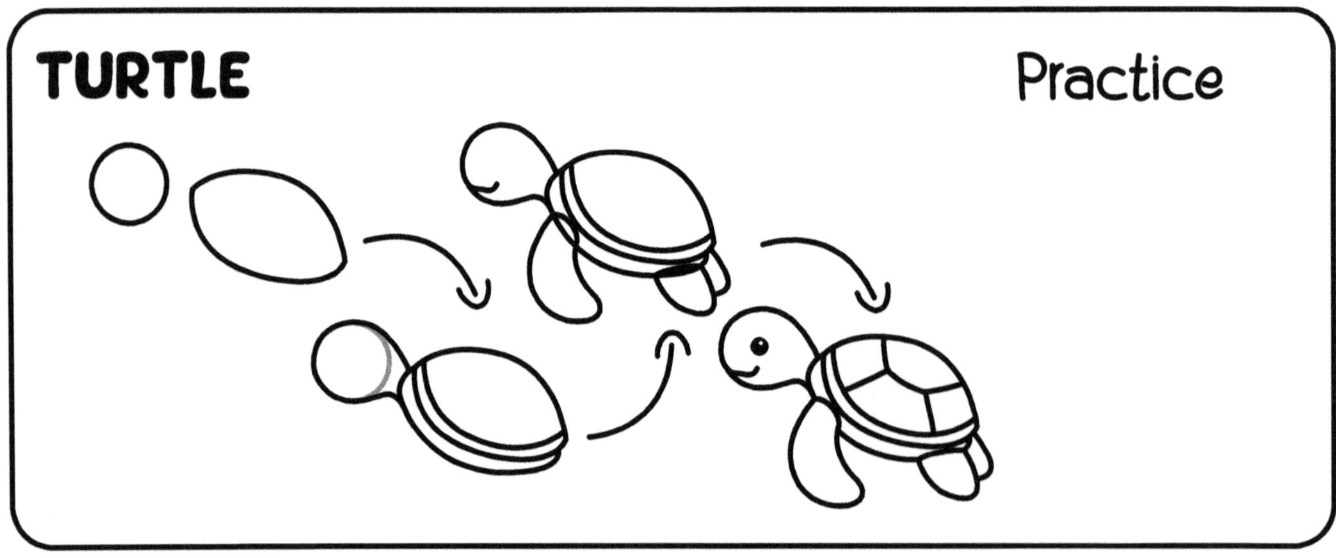

TURTLE
Practice

SEA ANIMALS

EEL

Practice:

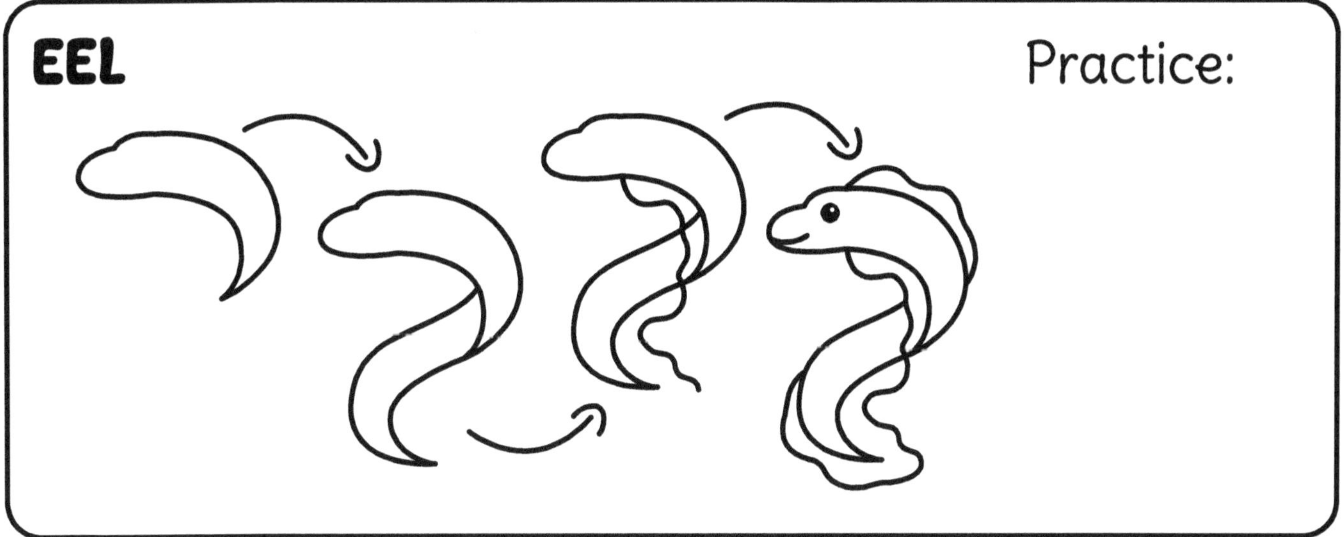

AXOLOTL

Practice:

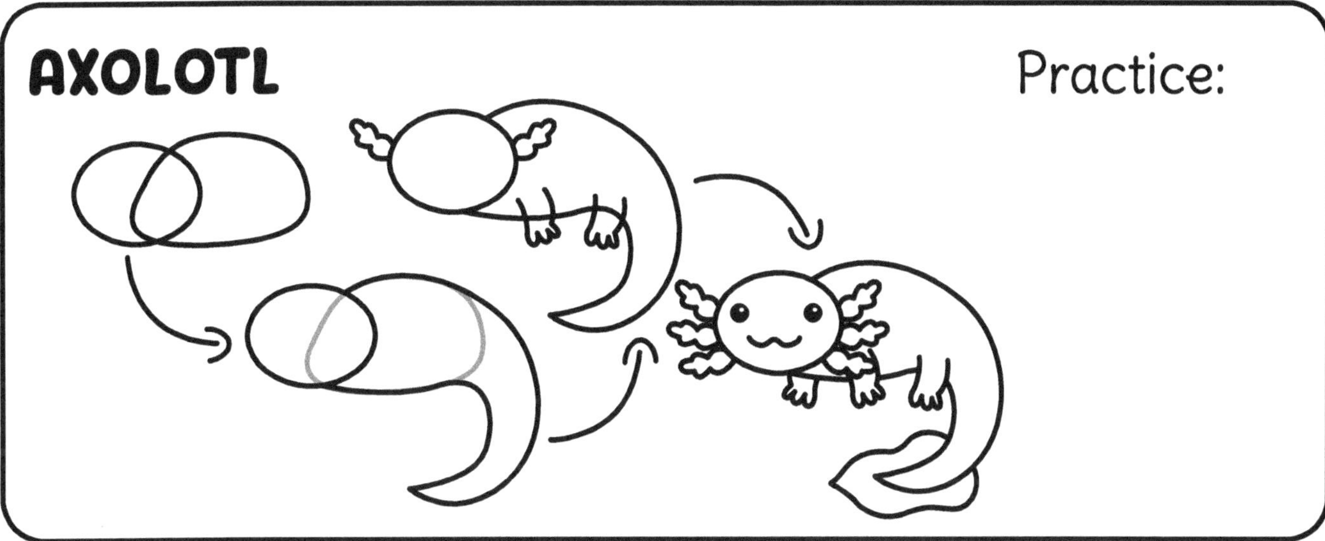

WHALE

Practice

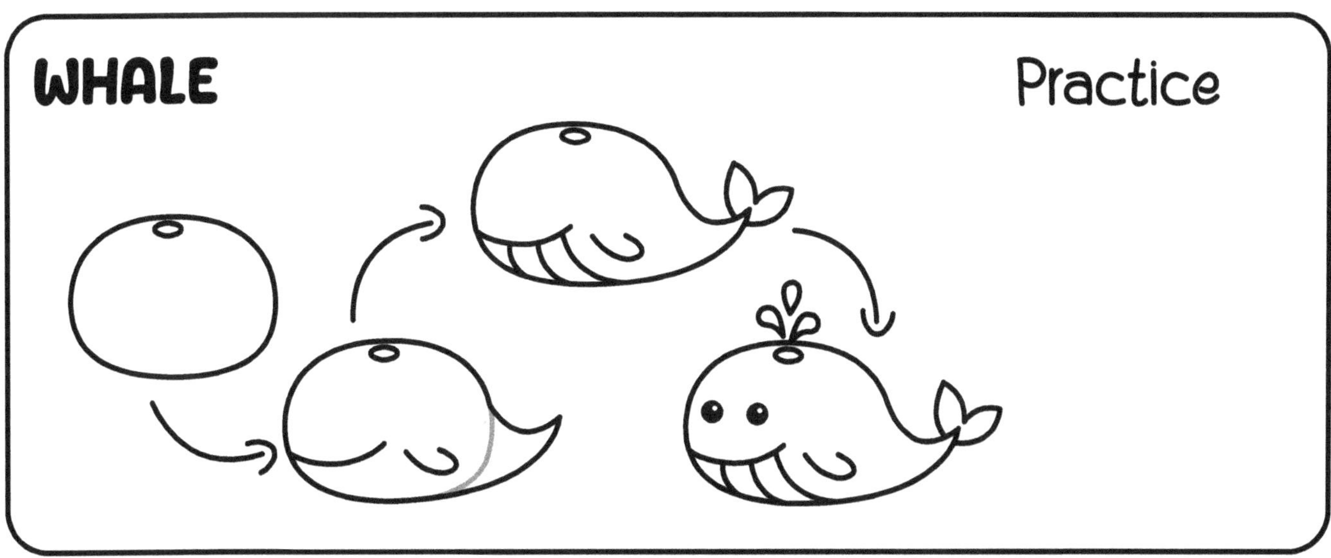

SHARK

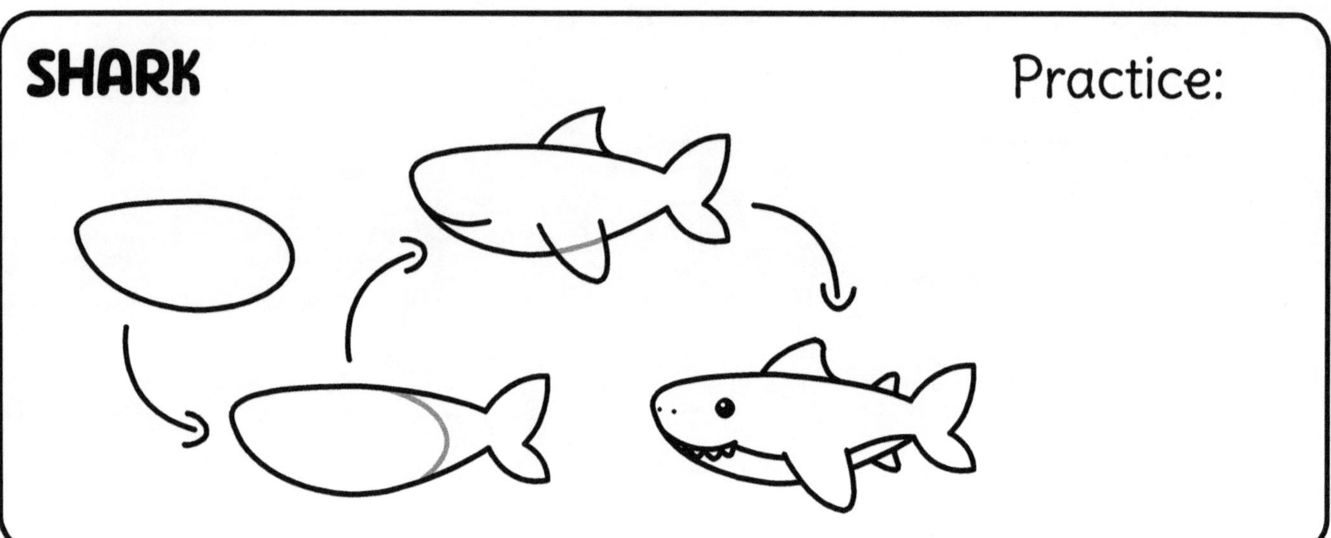

STARFISH

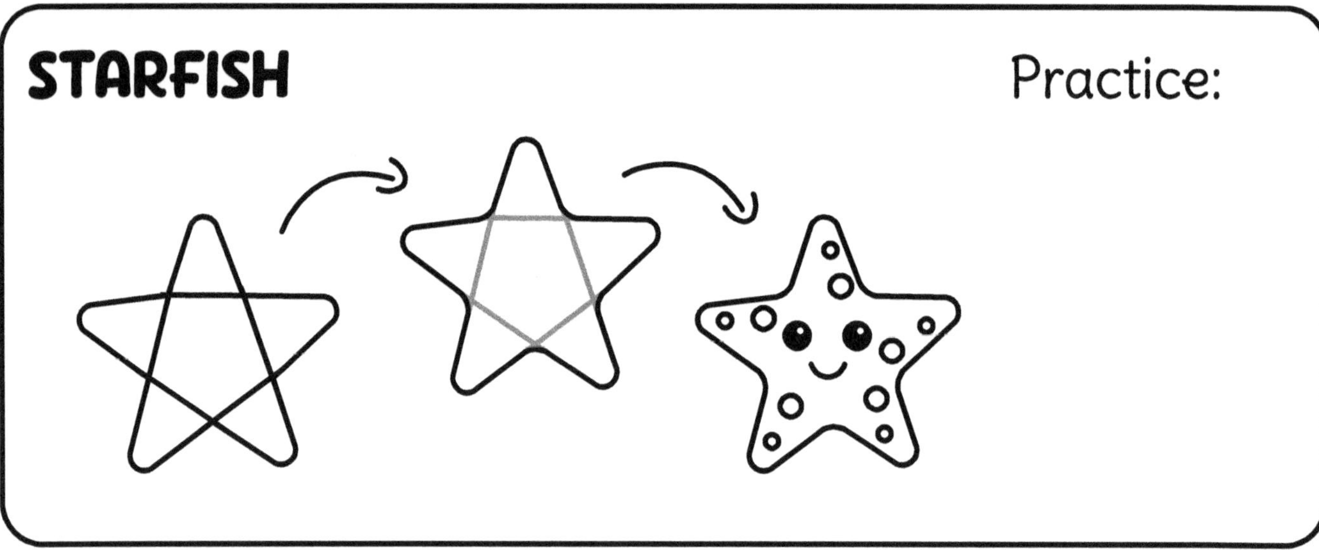

SEASHELL

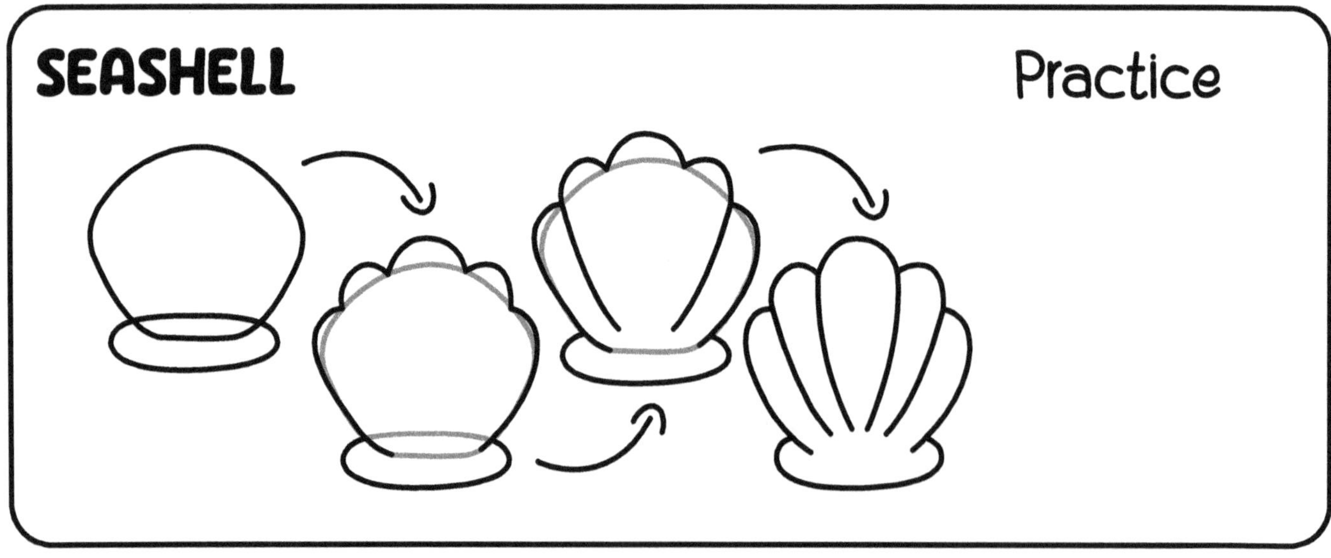

RAYS

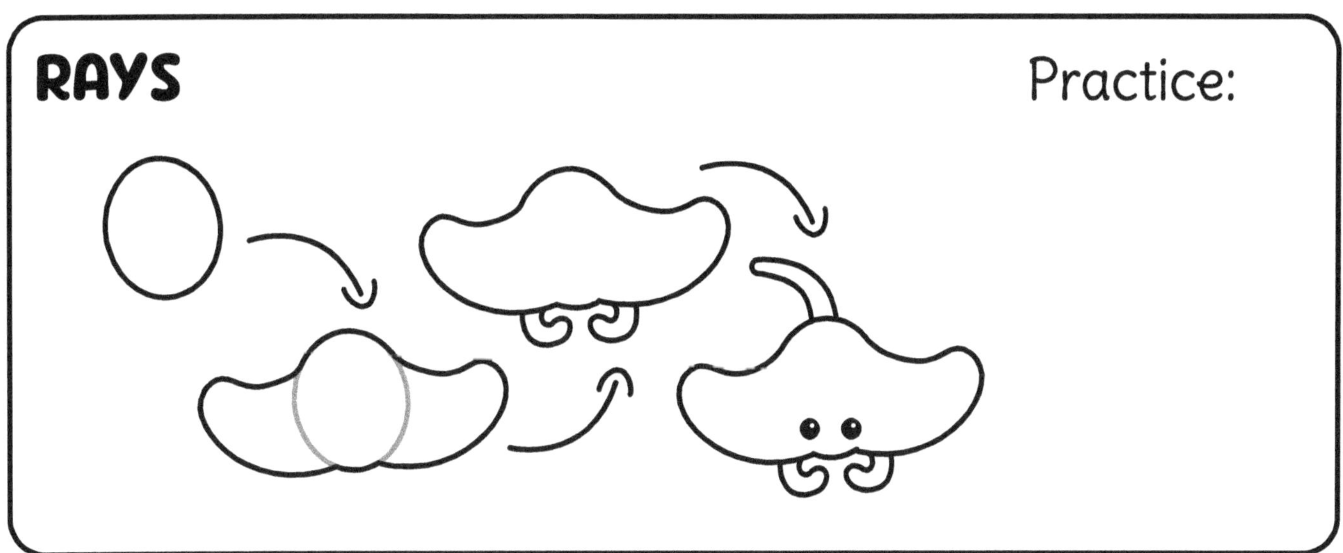

KOI FISH

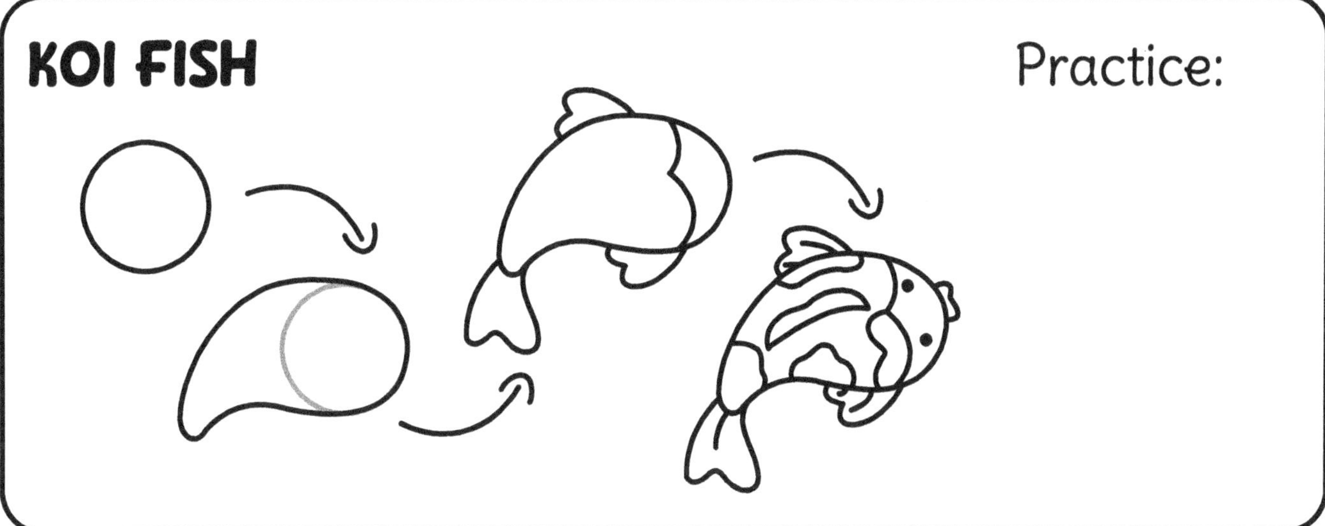

GOLDFISH

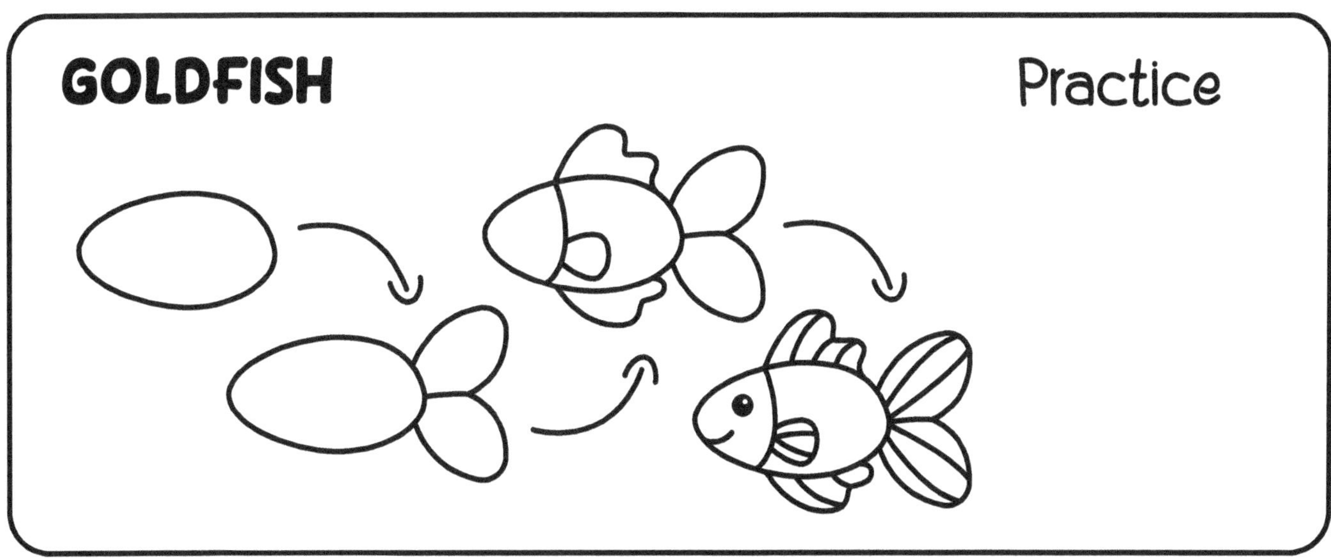

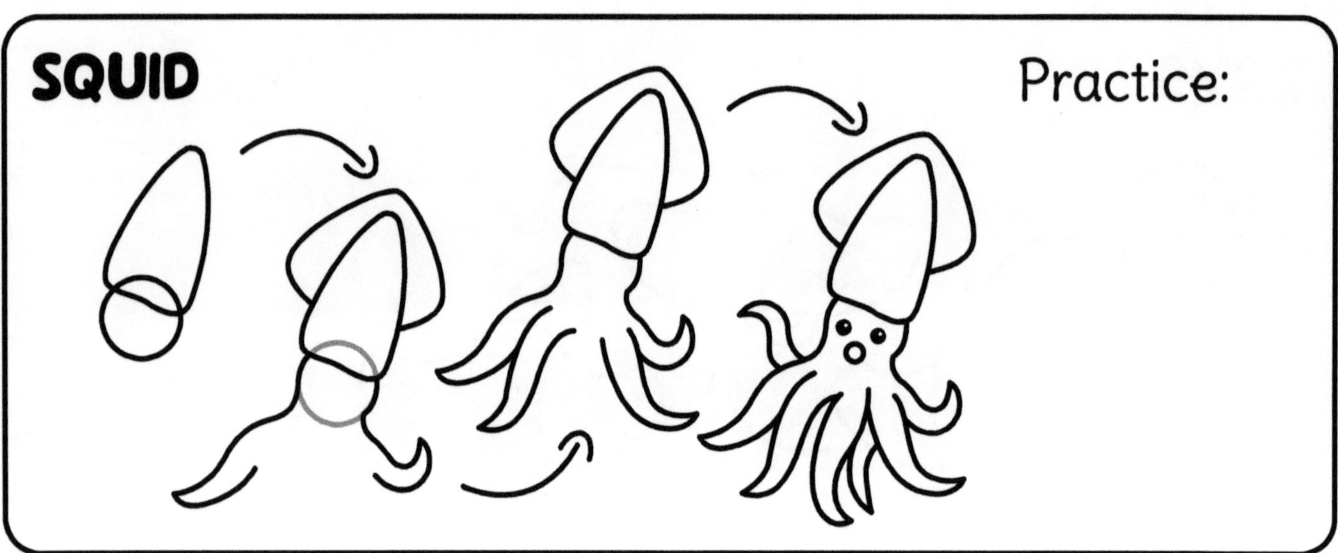

SQUID

Practice:

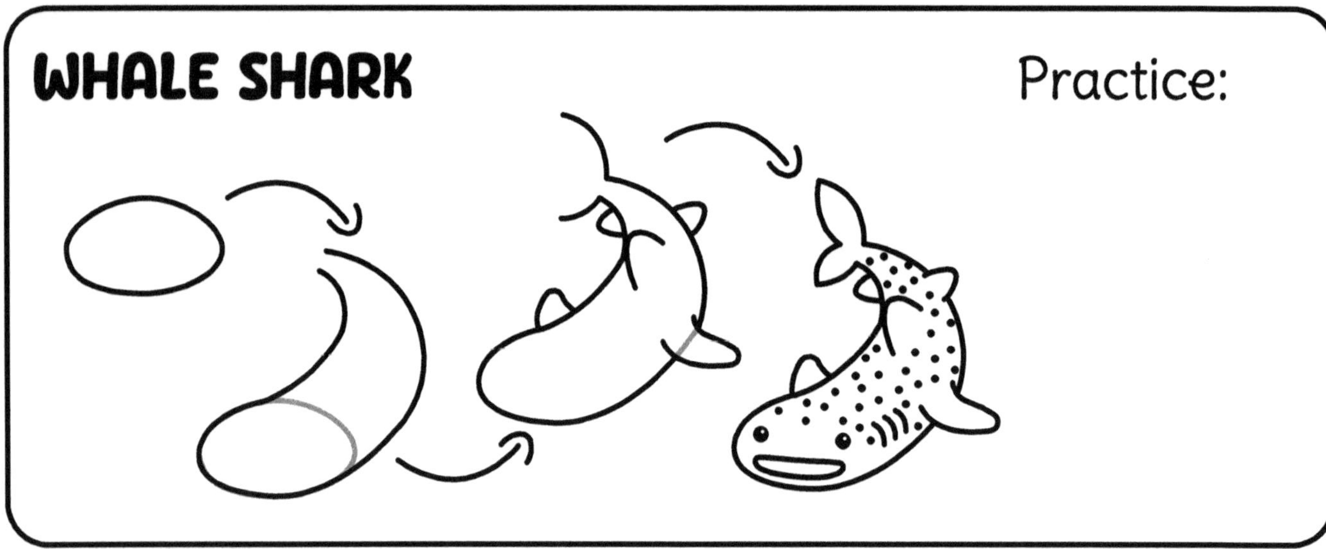

WHALE SHARK

Practice:

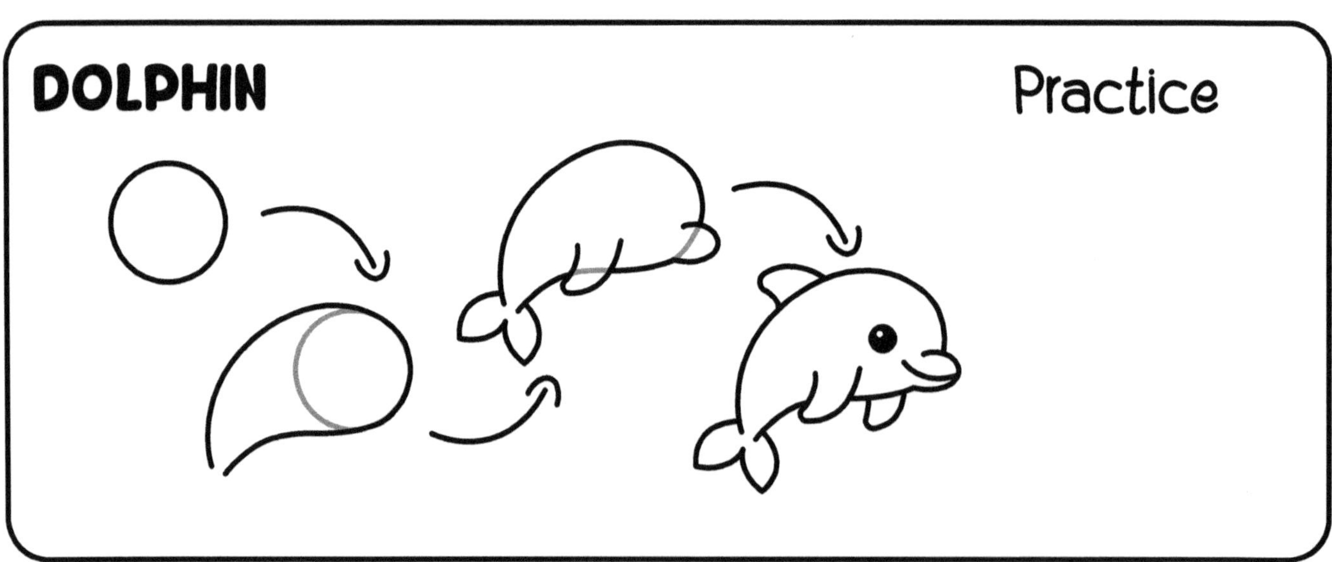

DOLPHIN

Practice

SEAL

Practice:

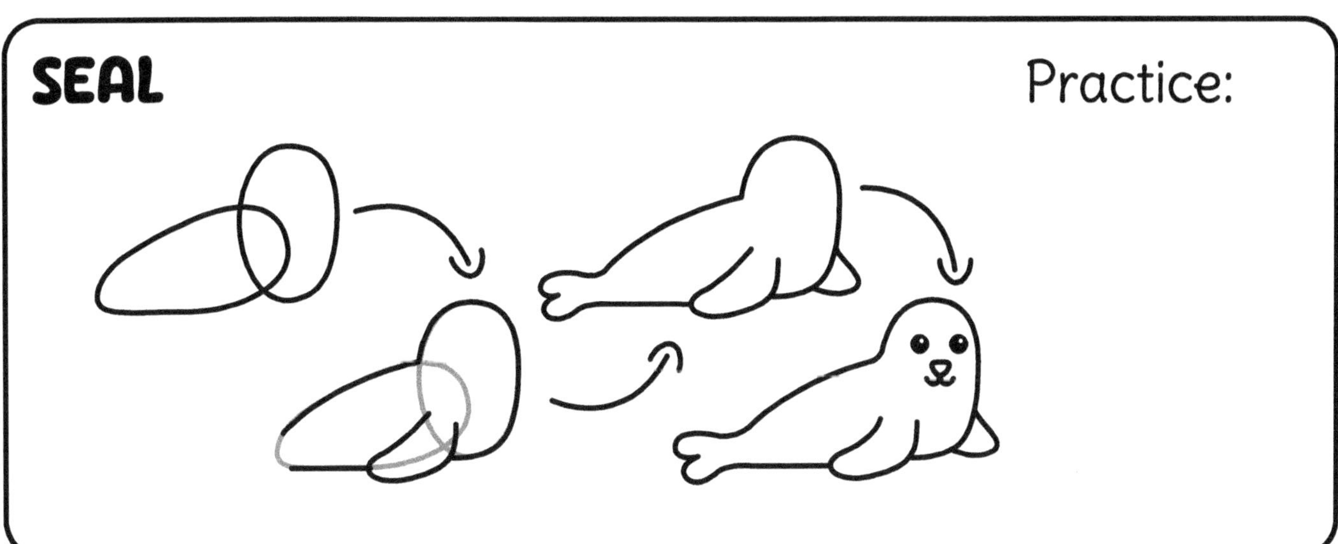

SEA HORSE

Practice:

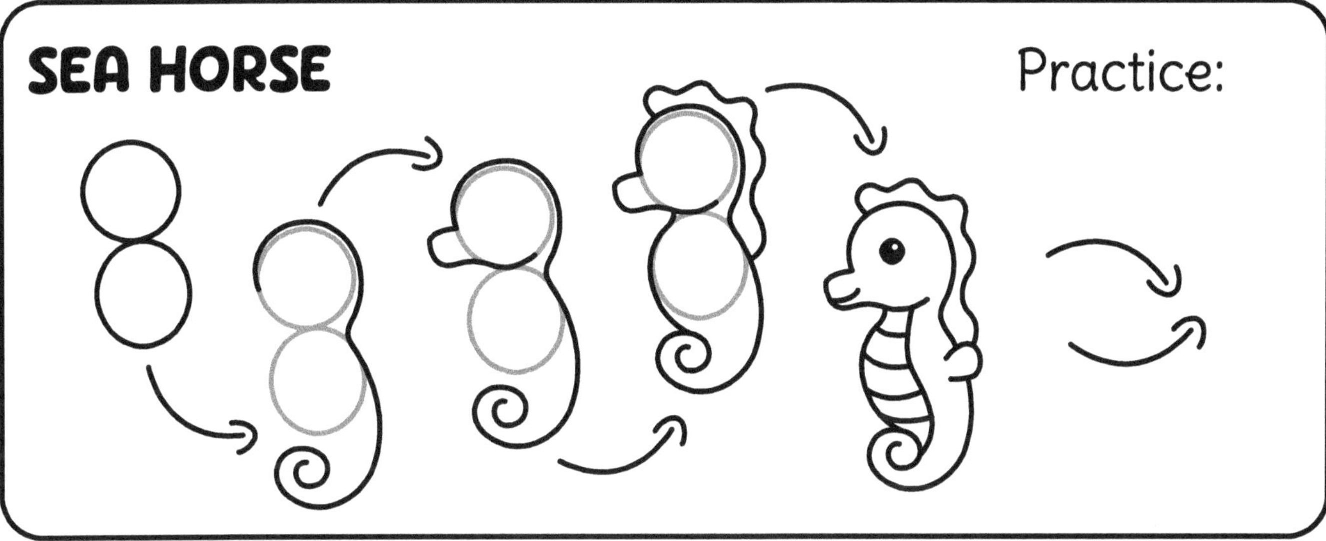

PUFFERFISH

Practice

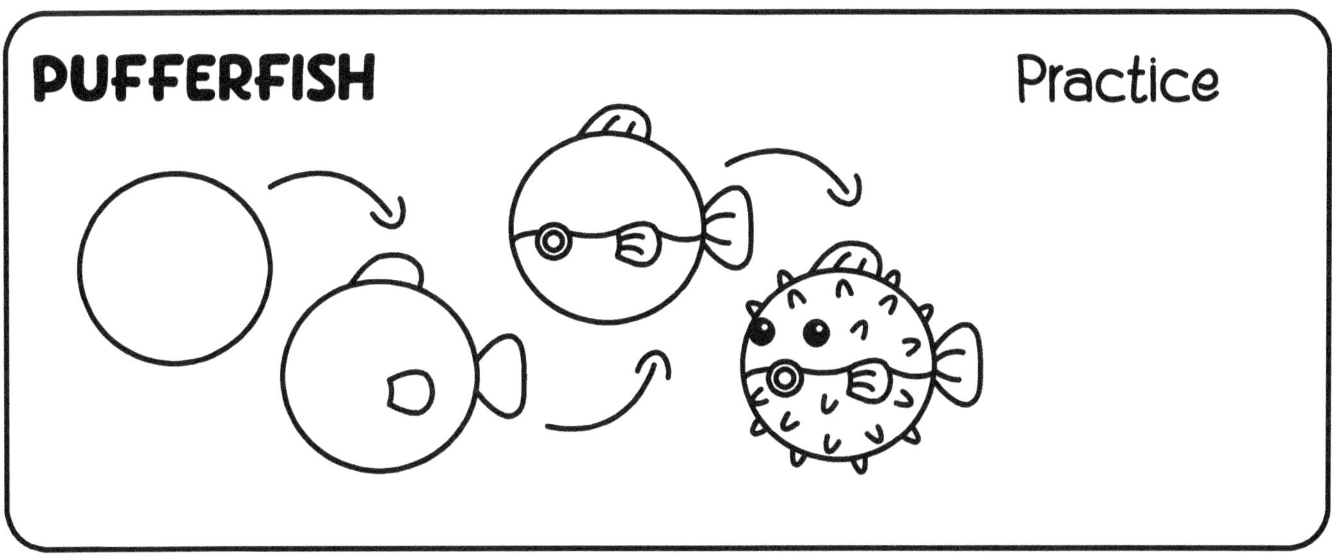

CRAB

Practice:

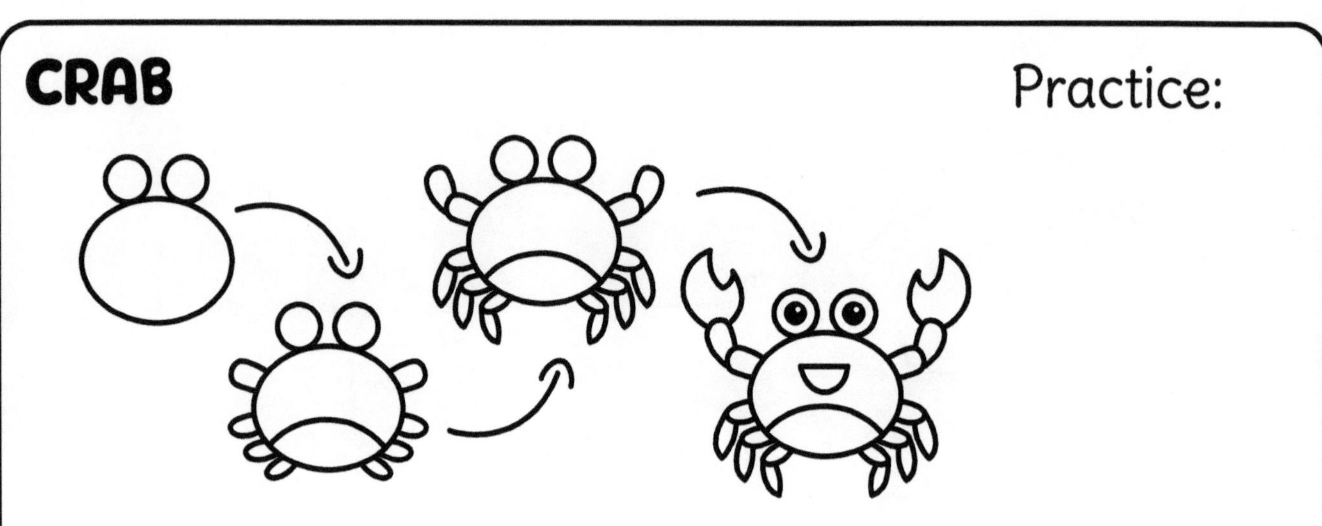

CUTTLE FISH

Practice:

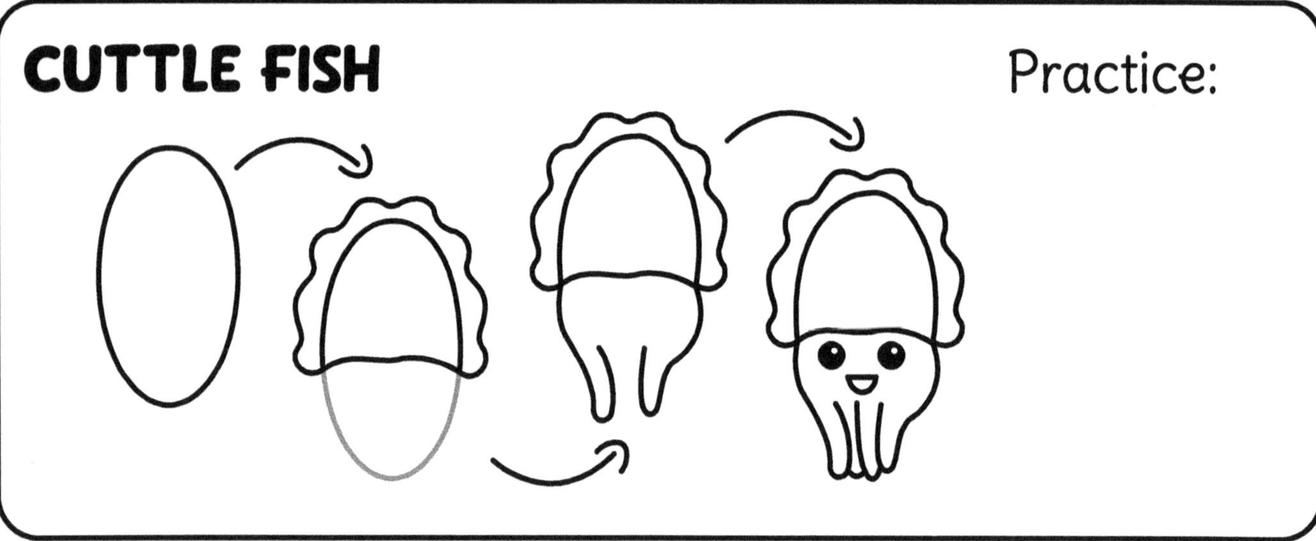

CLOWN FISH

Practice

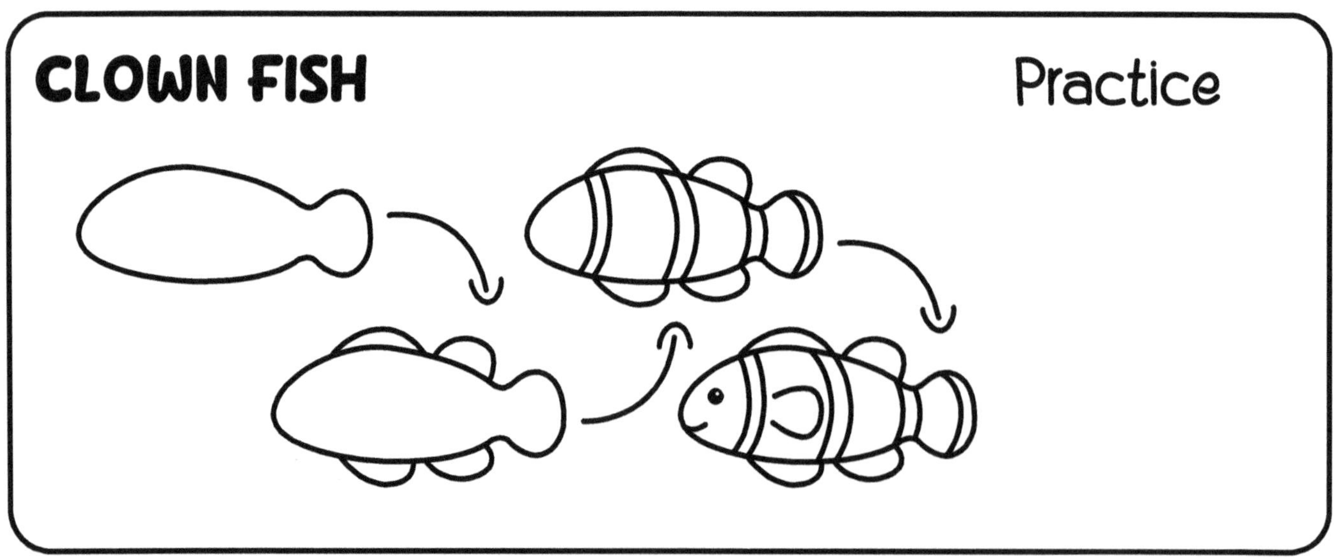

OCTOPUS

Practice:

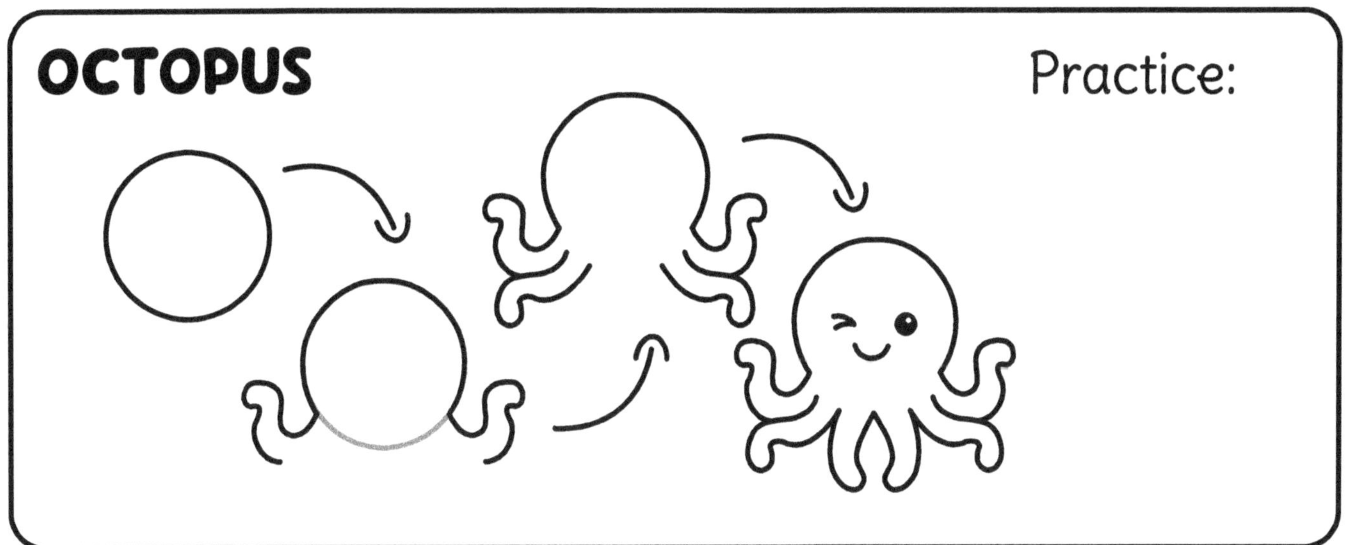

SEA ANEMONE

Practice:

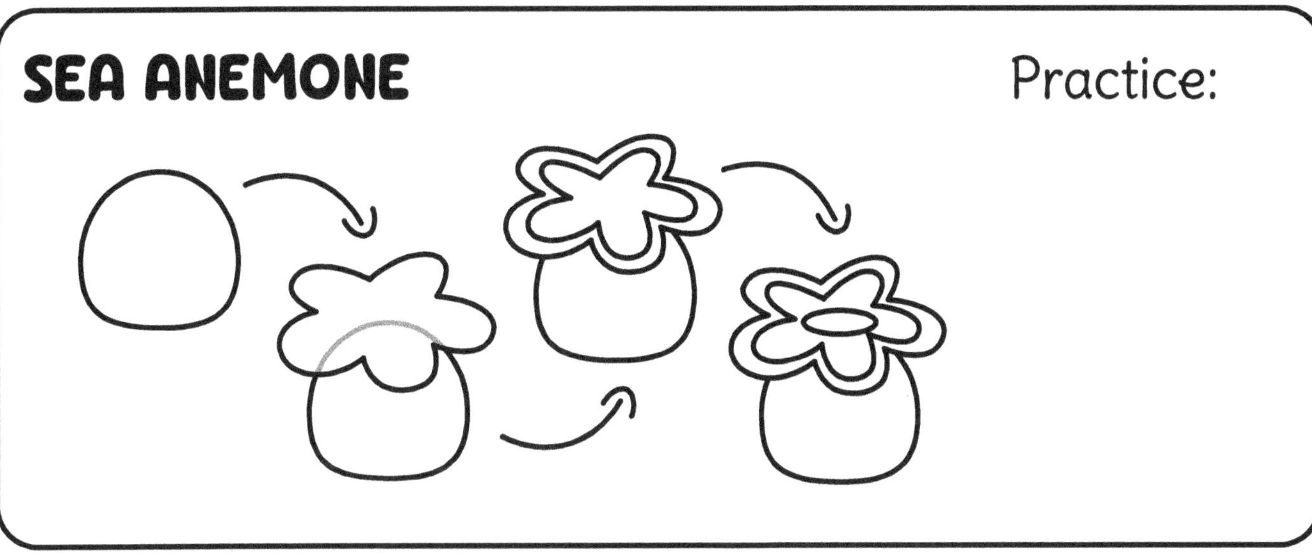

SUNFISH

Practice

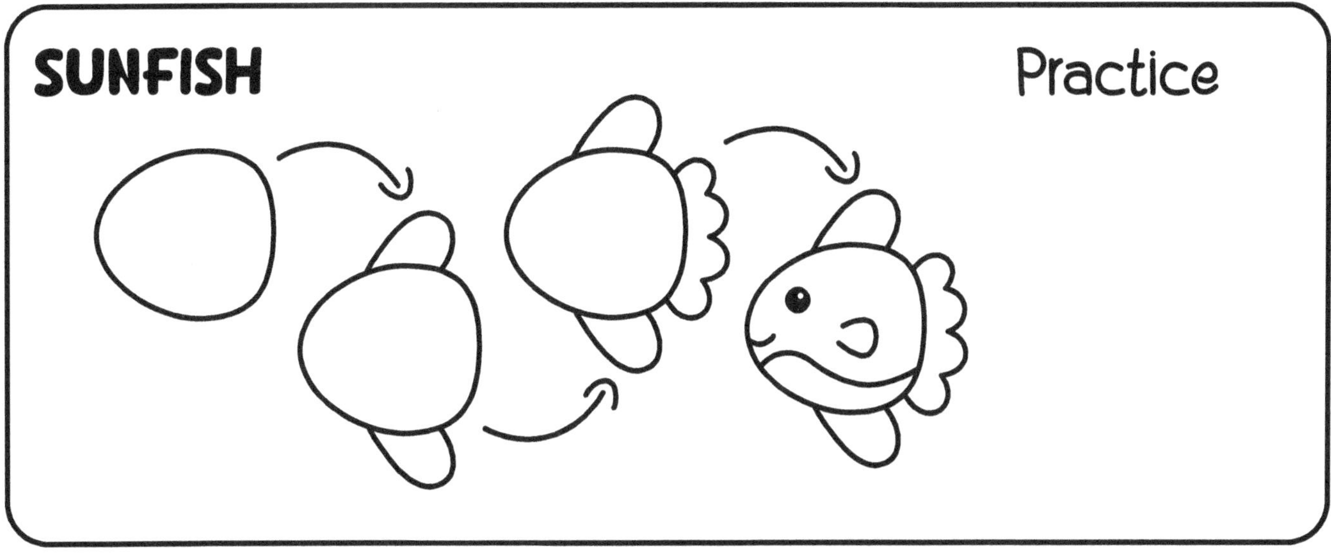

HONEYBEE

Practice:

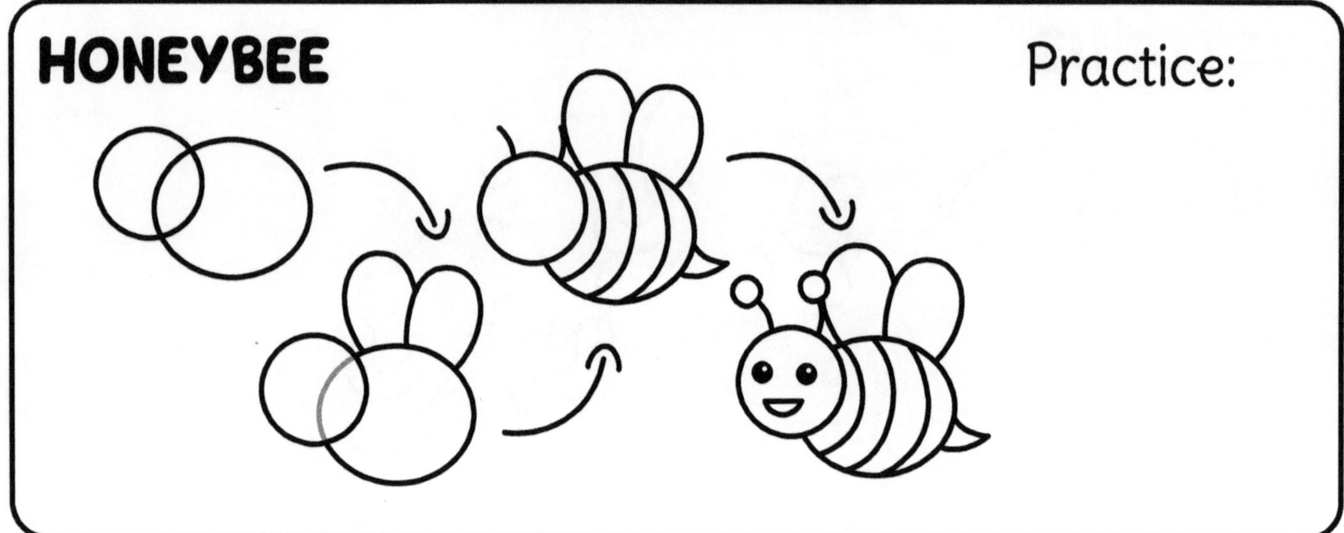

BUTTERFLY

Practice:

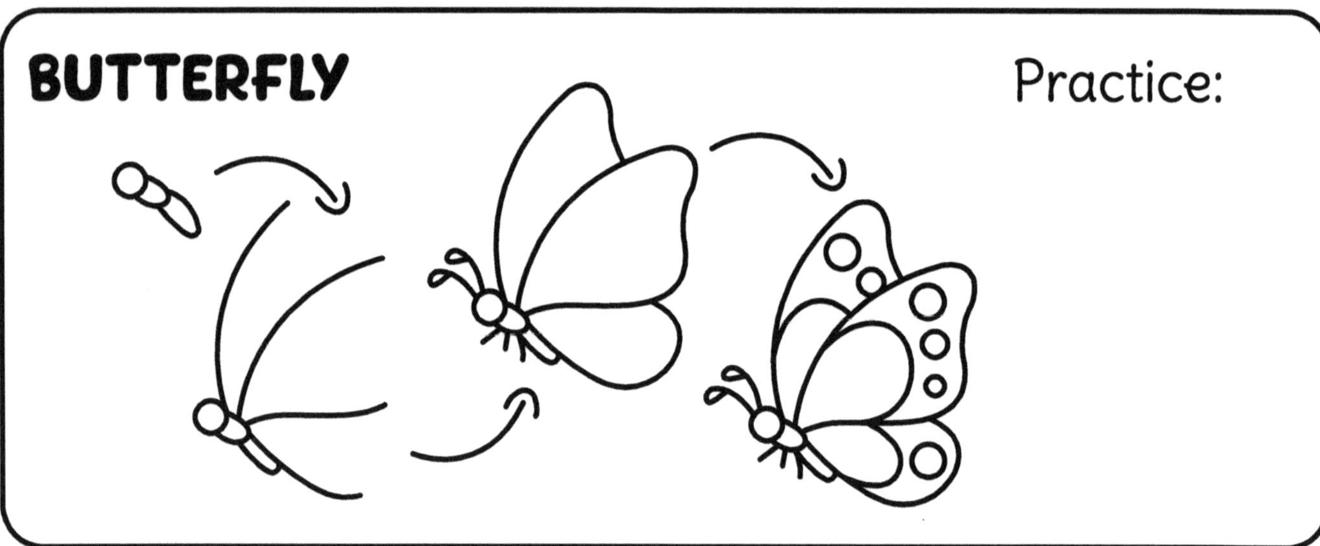

BEETLE

Practice

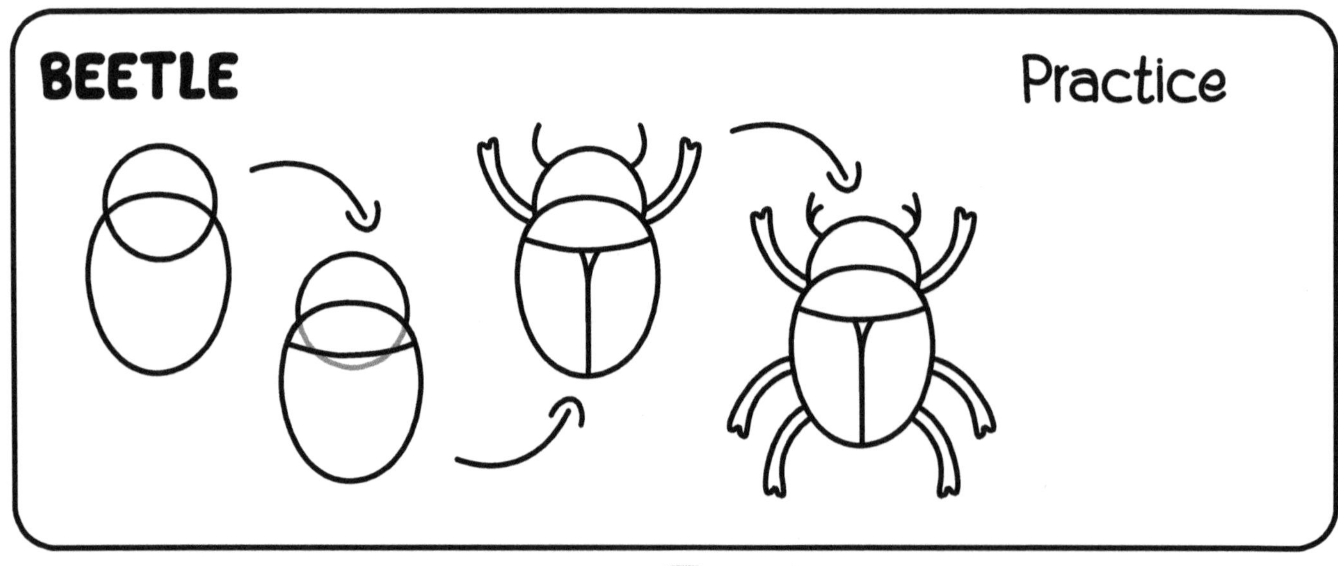

LADYBUG

Practice:

CATERPILLAR

Practice:

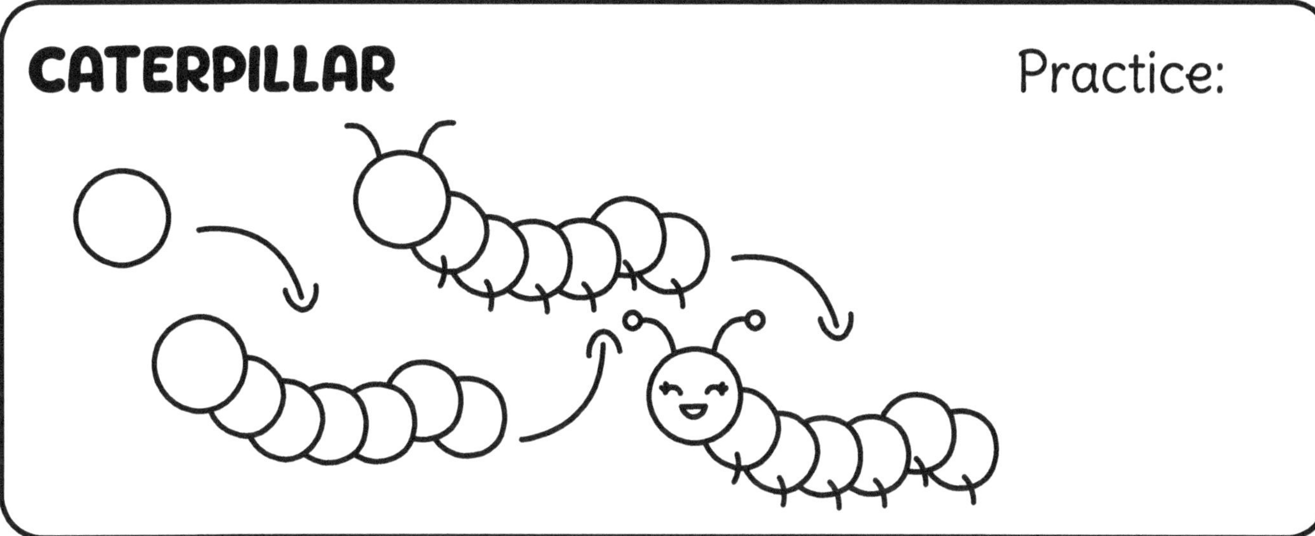

SPIDER

Practice

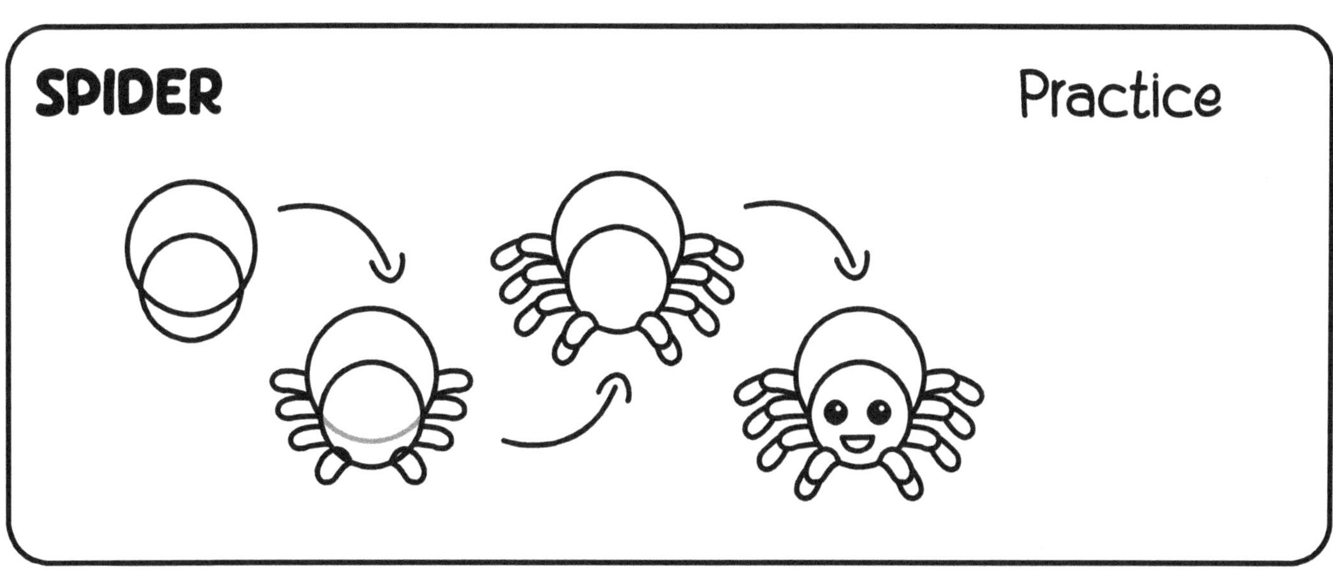

ANT

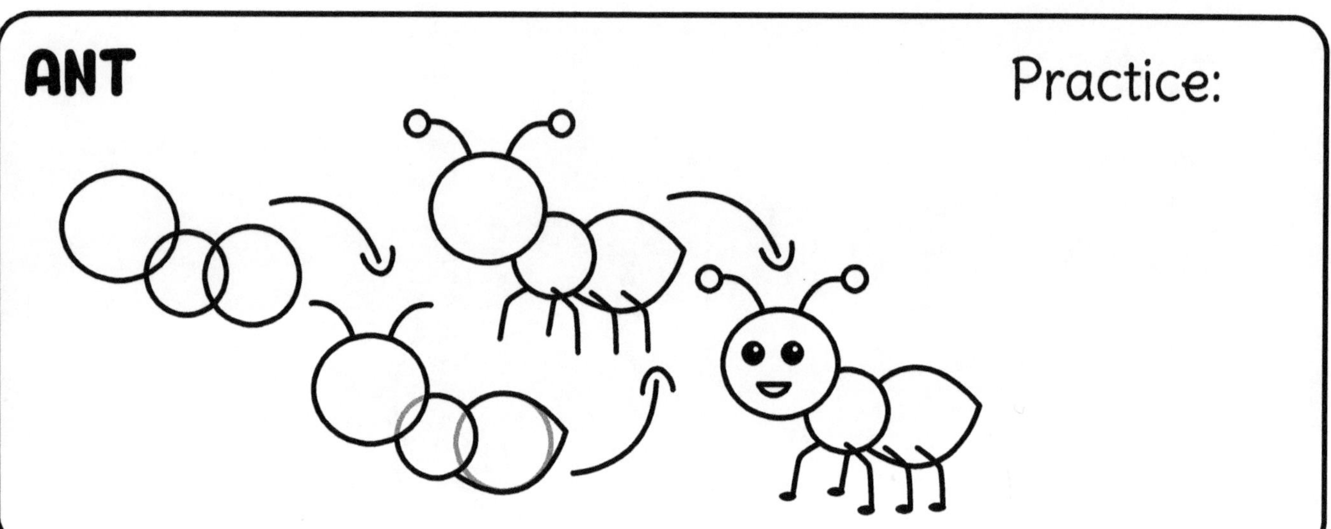

DRAGONFLY

Practice:

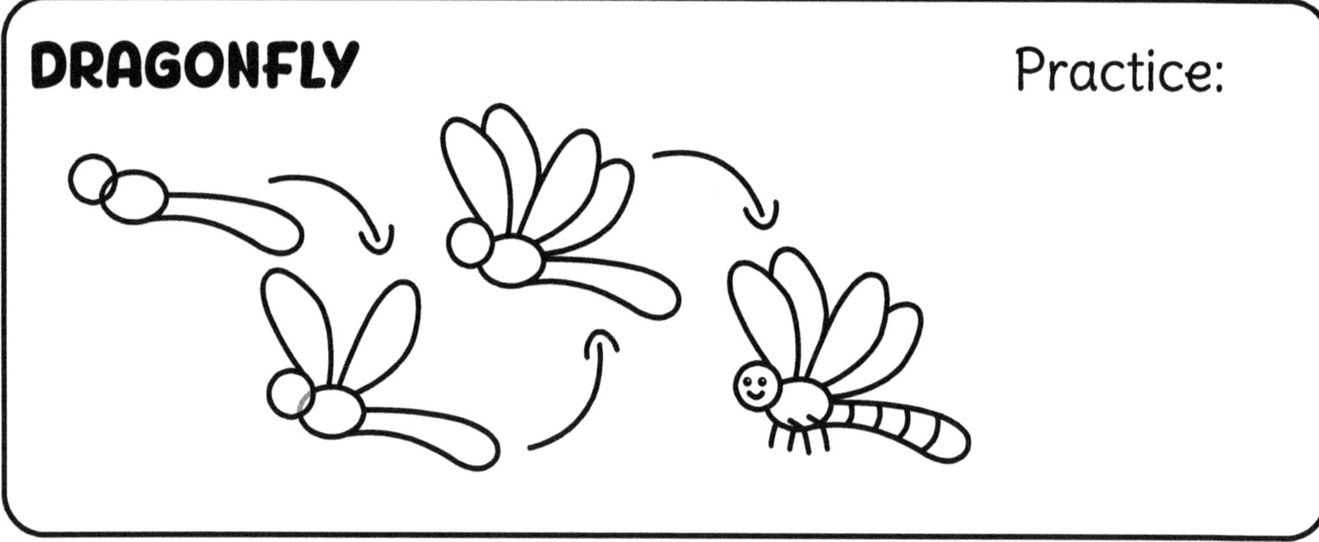

SNAIL

Practice

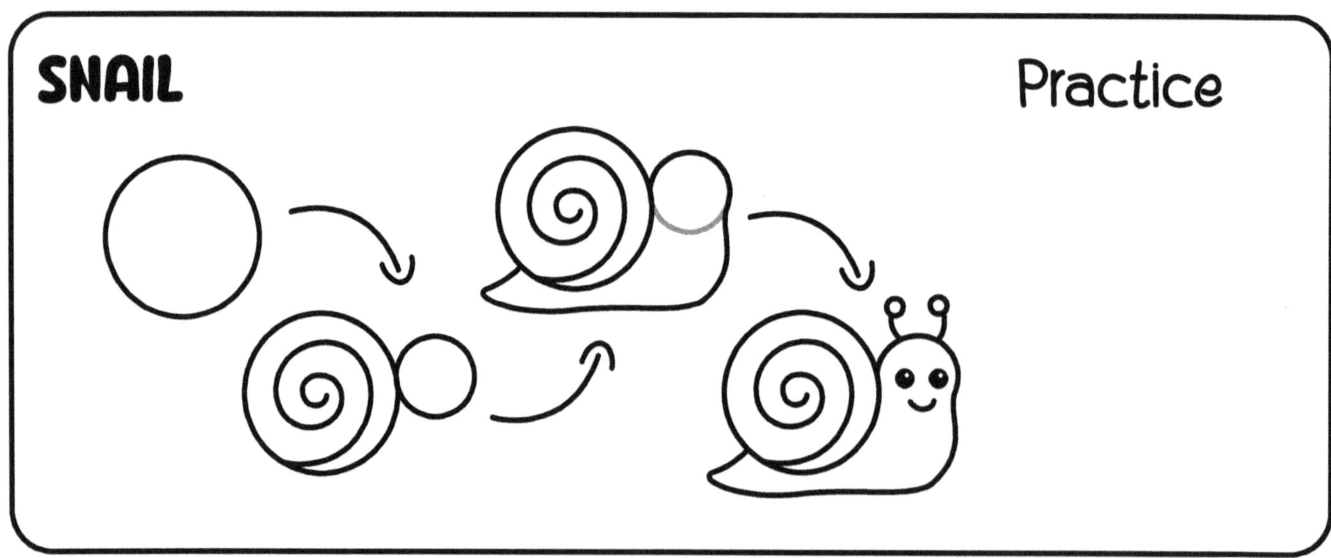

MAGICAL BEINGS

UNICORN

Practice:

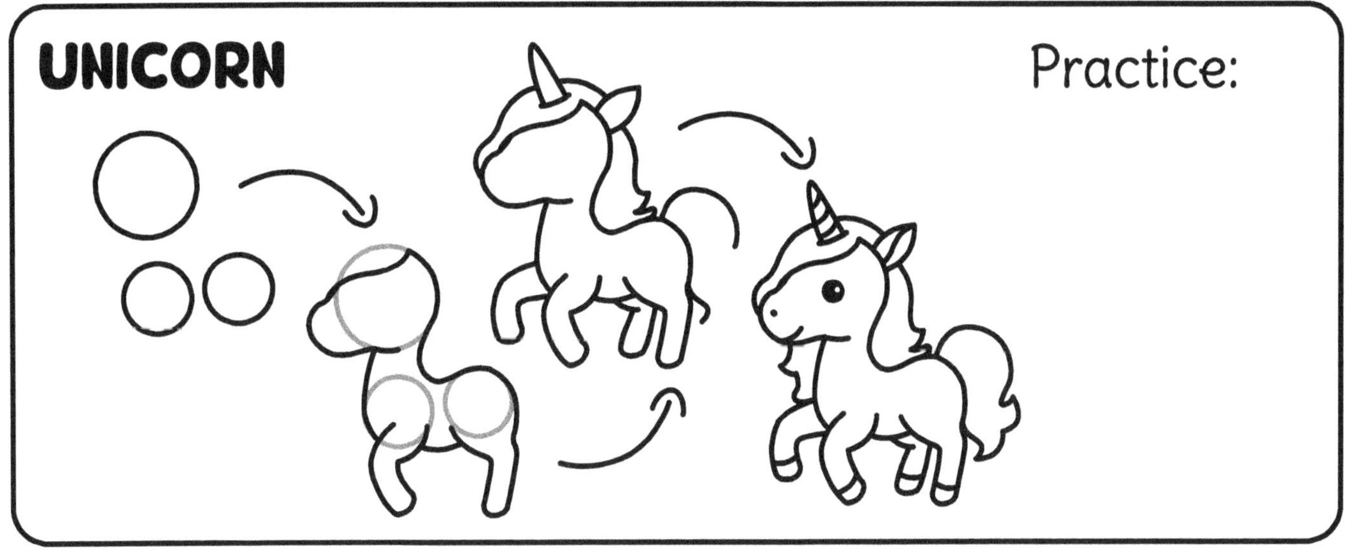

DRAGON

Practice:

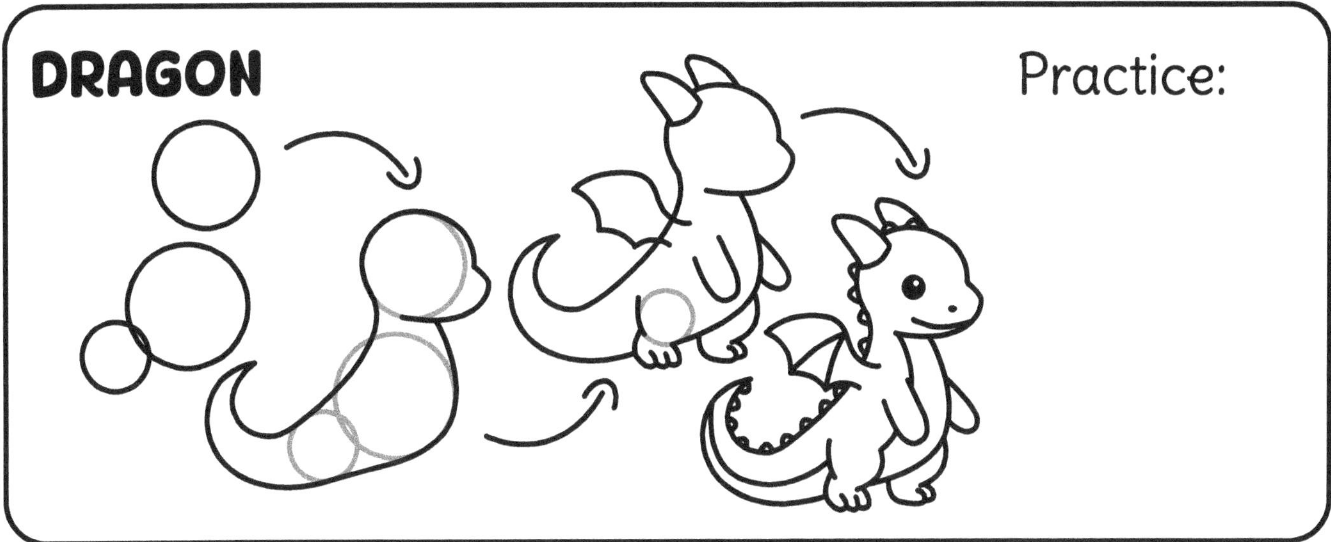

T-REX

Practice

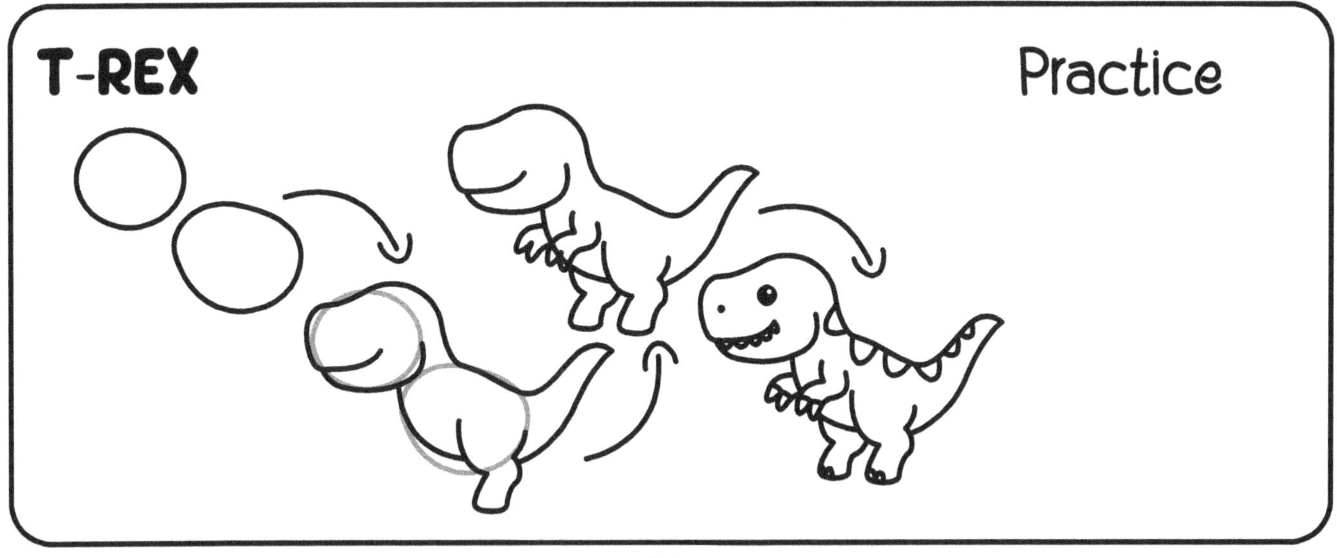

MERMAID

Practice:

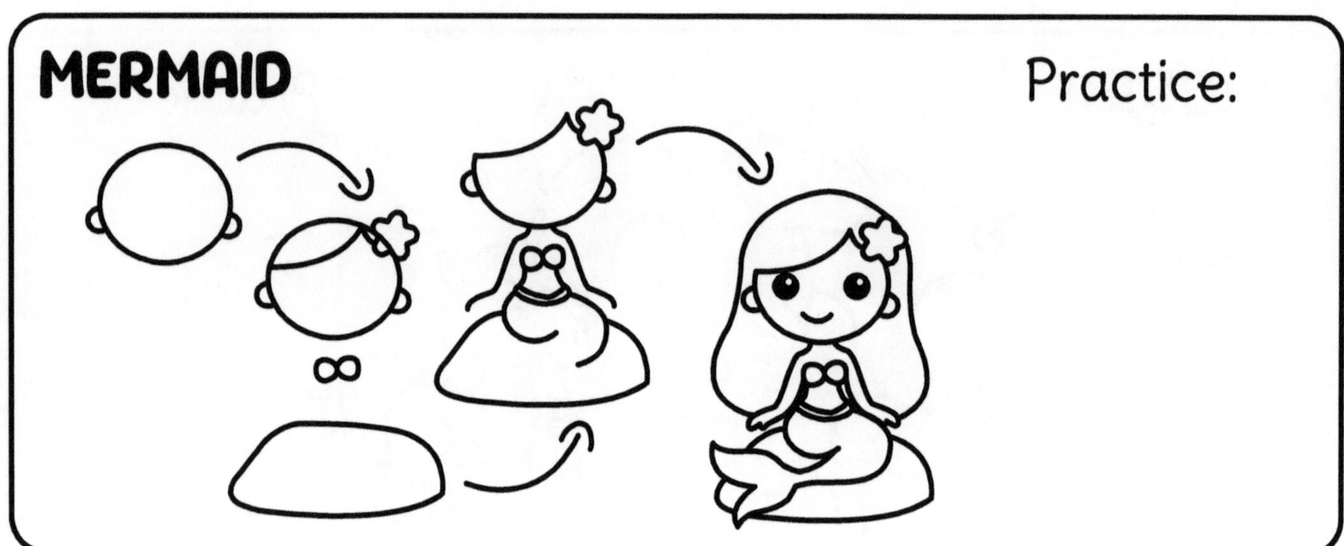

GRIFFIN

Practice:

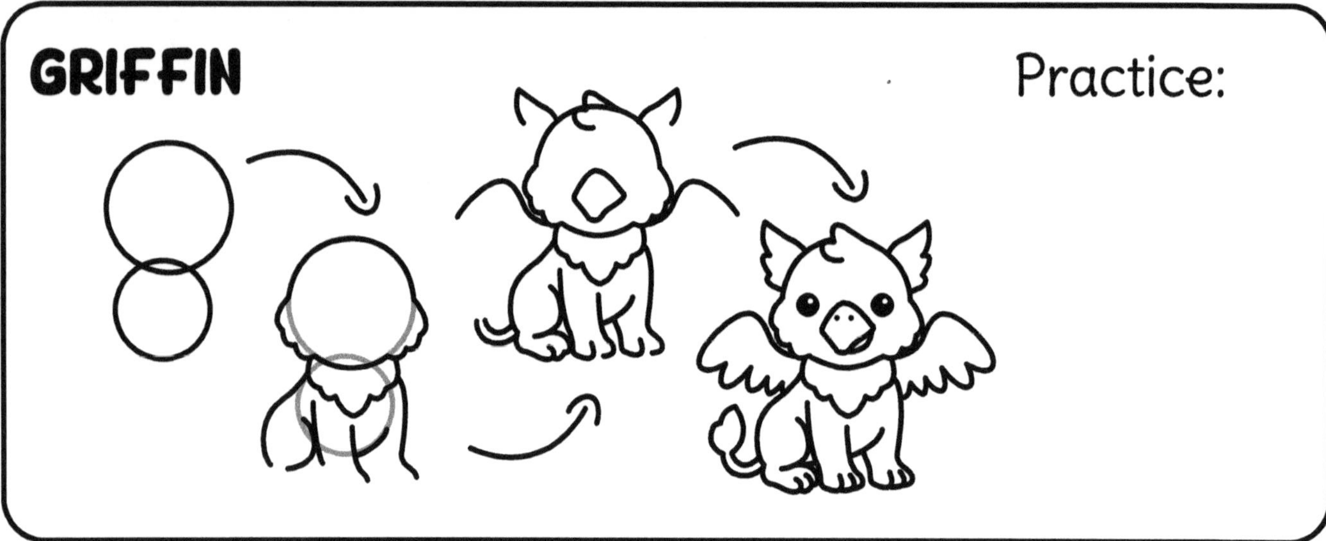

PHOENIX

Practice

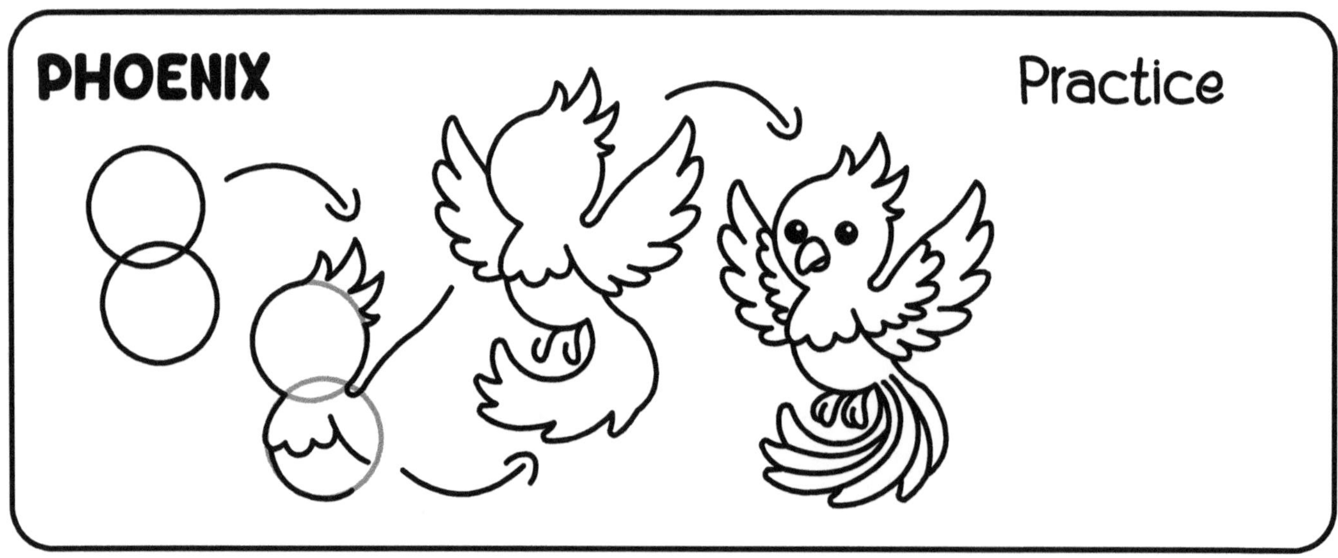

BIRDS

DUCK
Practice:

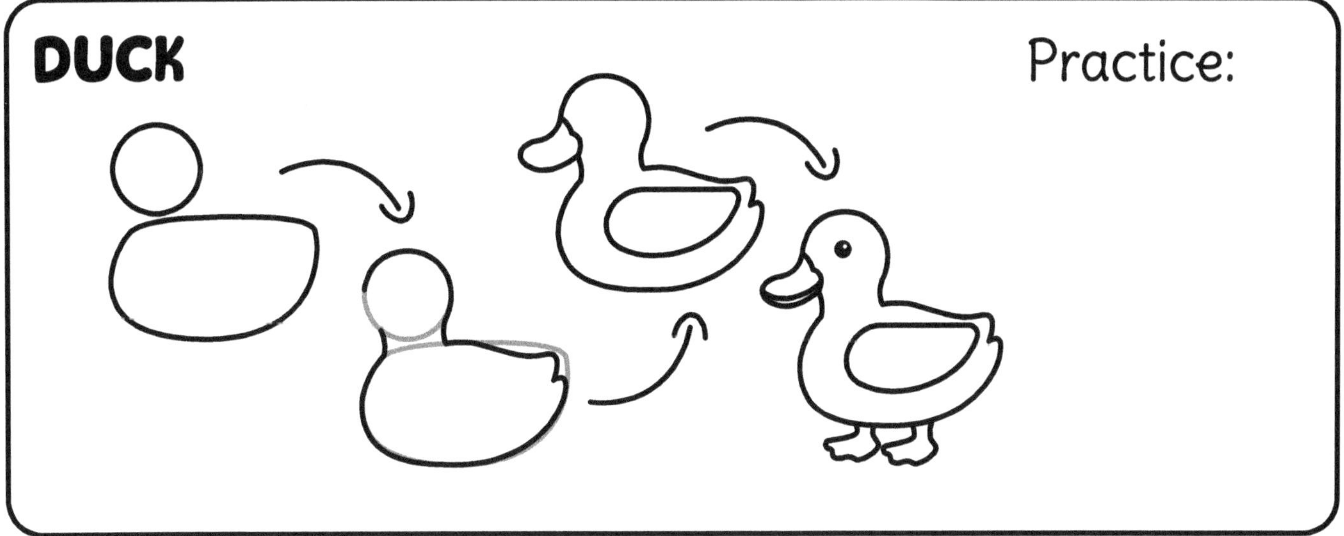

PARROT
Practice:

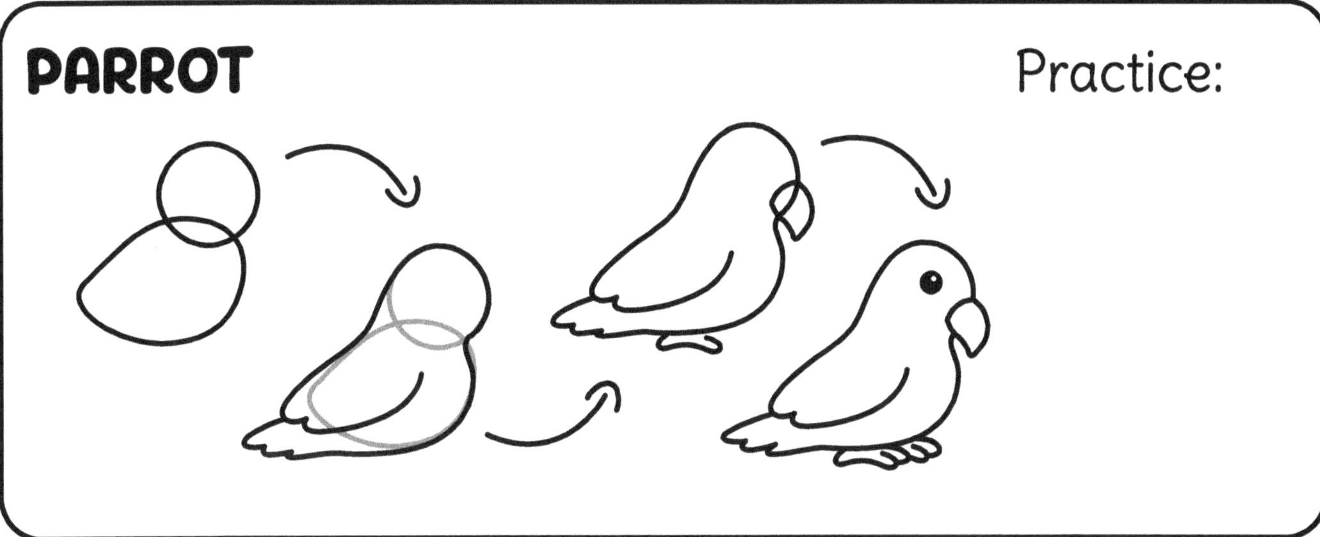

PENGUIN
Practice

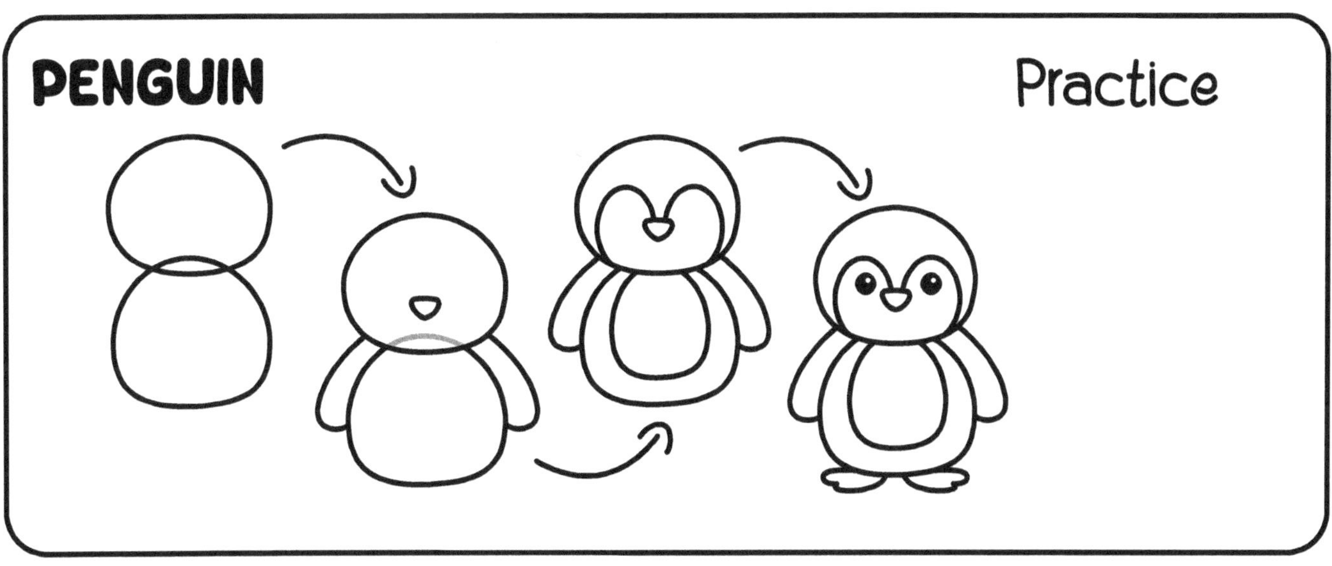

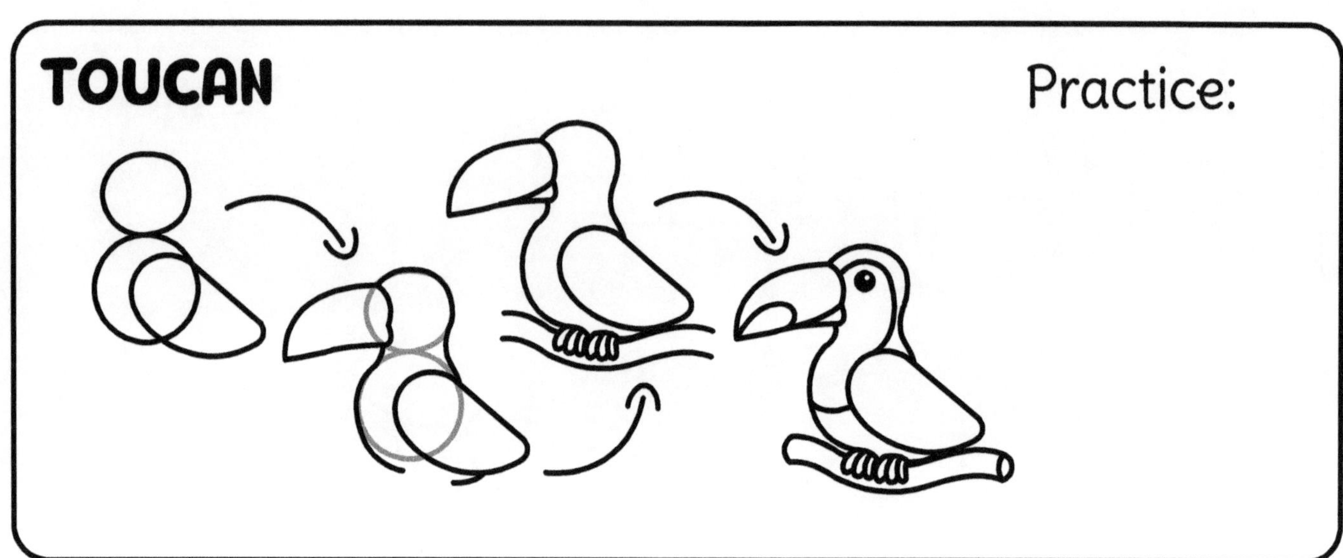

TOUCAN
Practice:

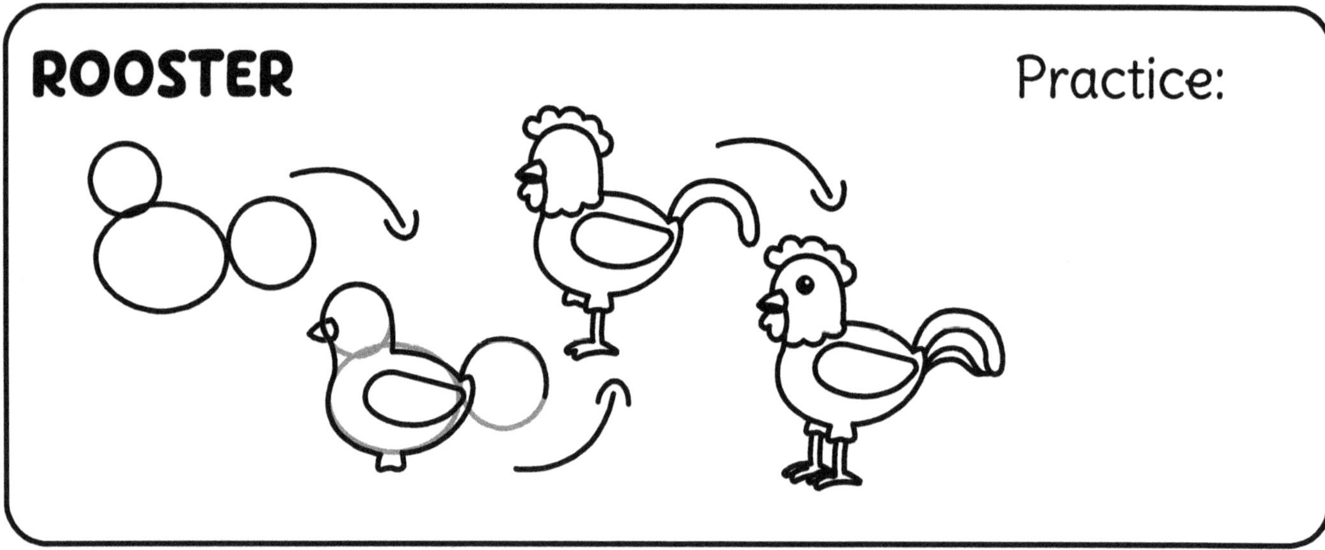

ROOSTER
Practice:

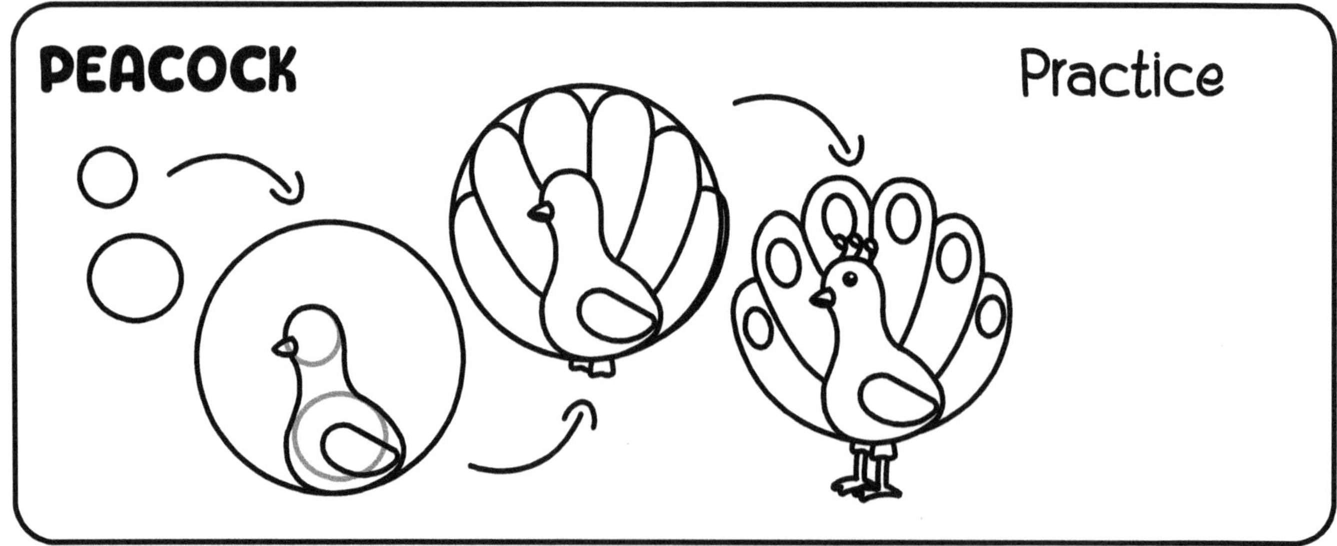

PEACOCK
Practice

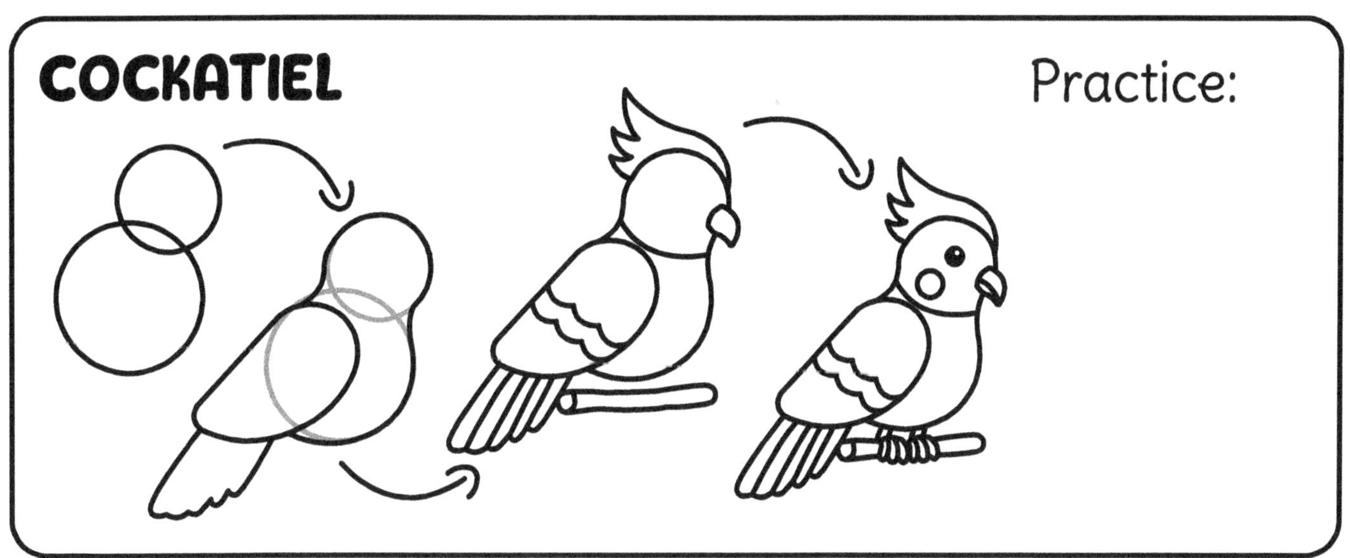

COCKATIEL
Practice:

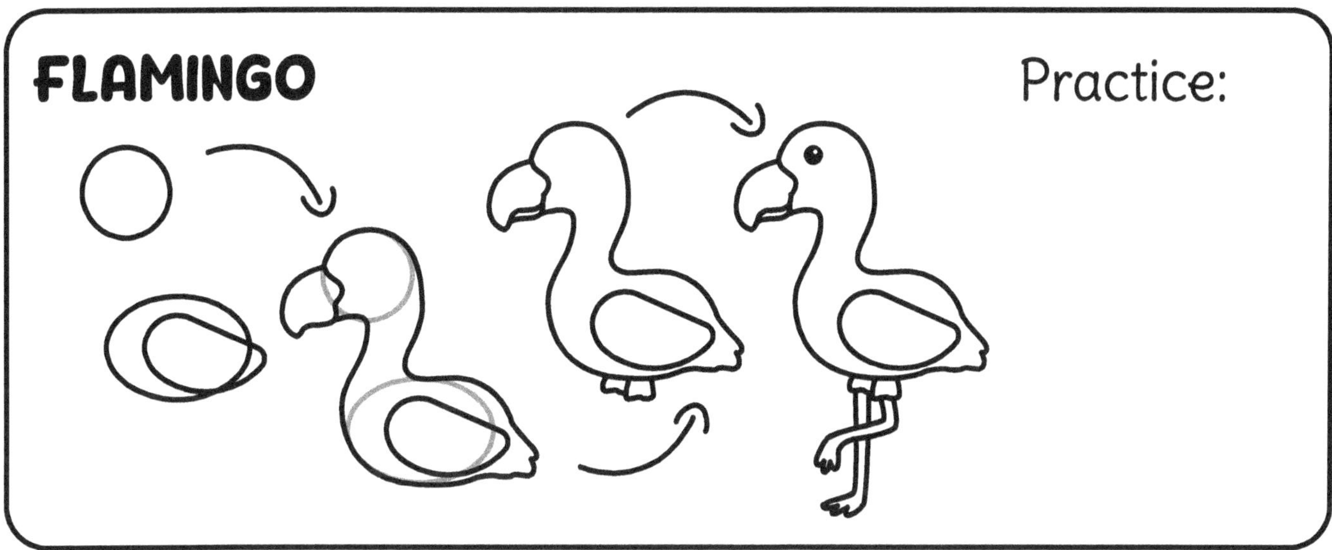

FLAMINGO
Practice:

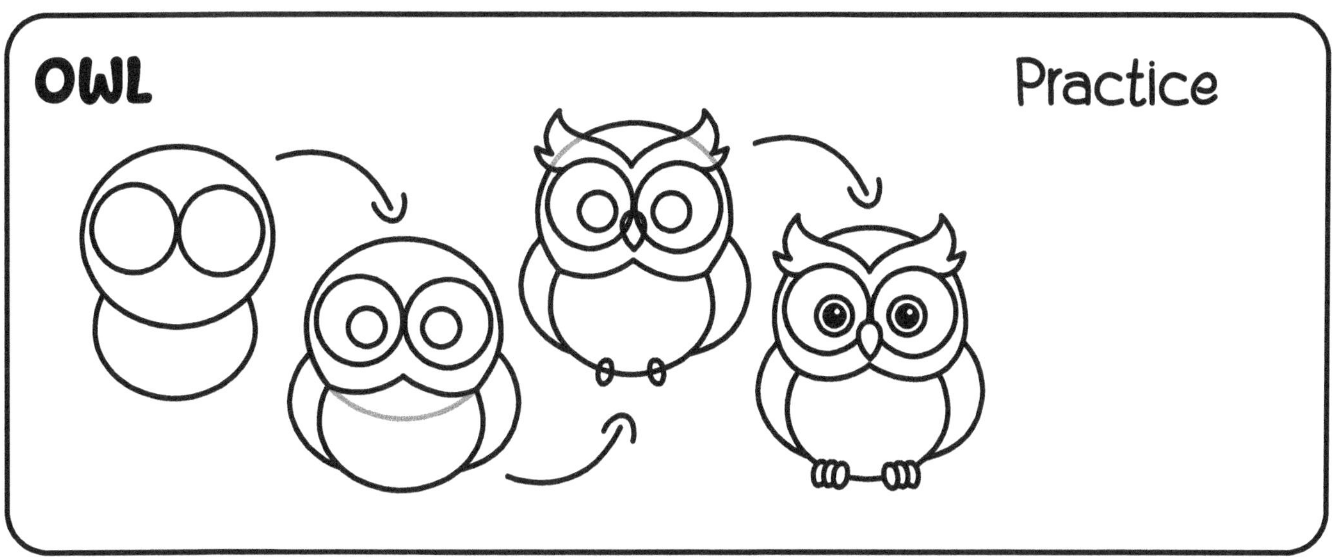

OWL
Practice

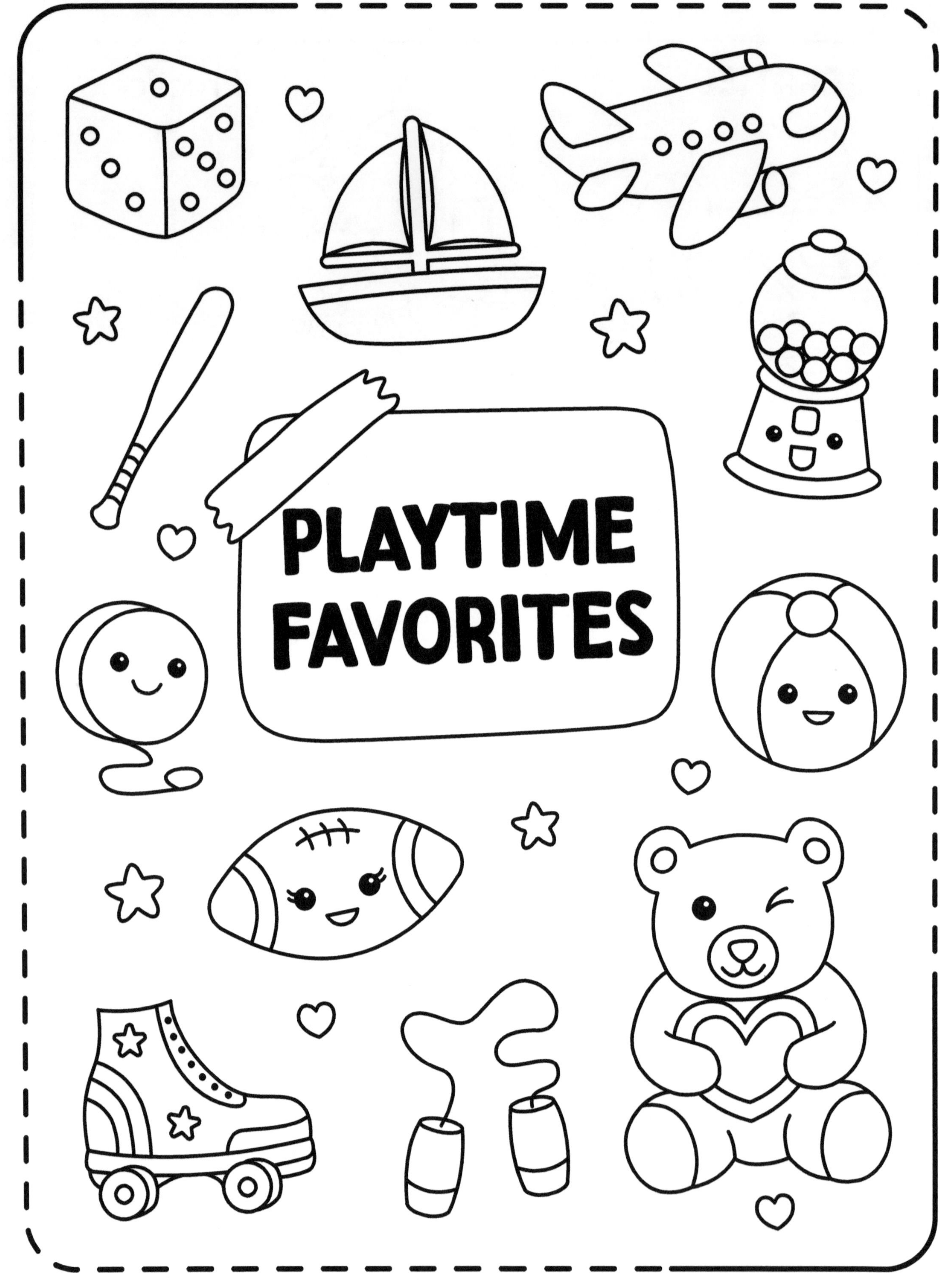
PLAYTIME FAVORITES

VEHICLES

CAR

Practice:

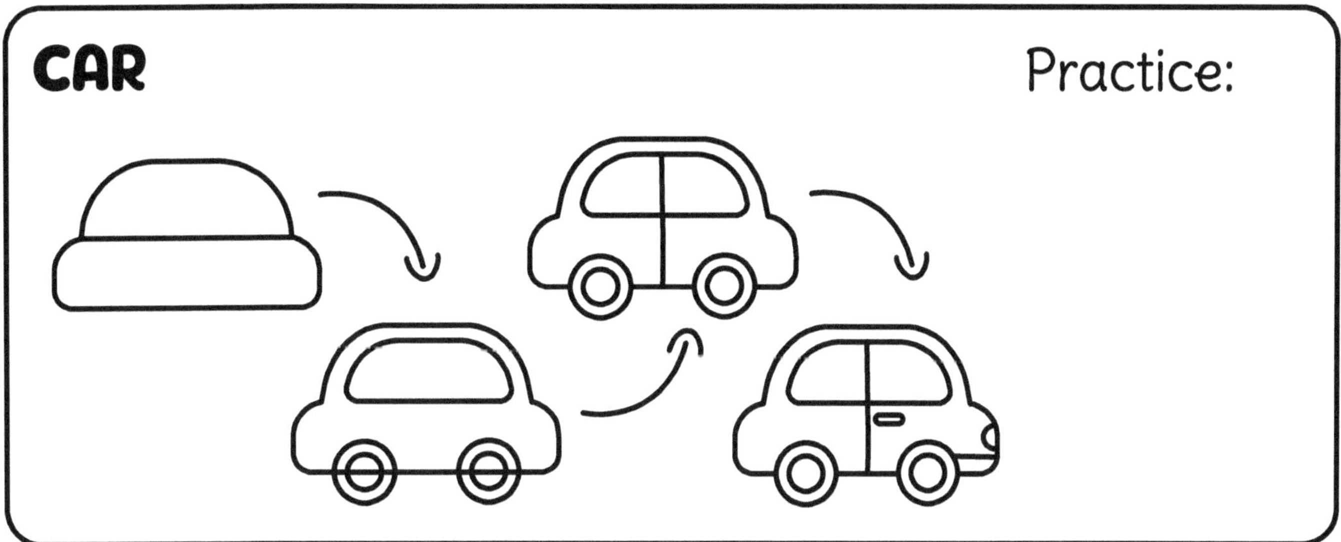

ICE CREAM TRUCK

Practice:

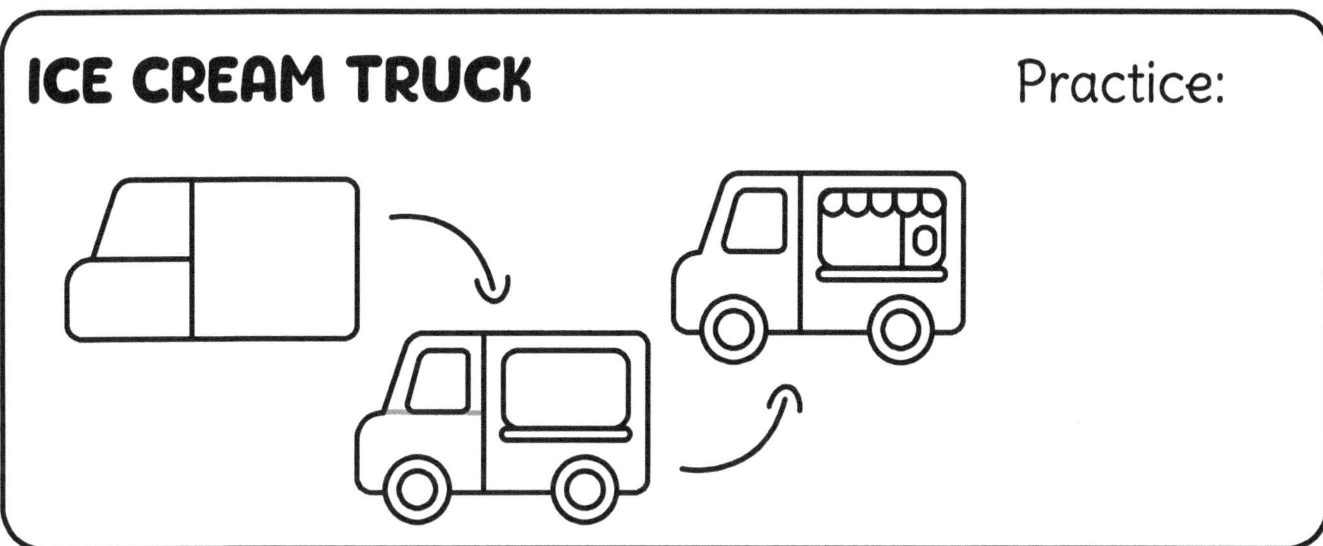

TIPPER TRUCK

Practice

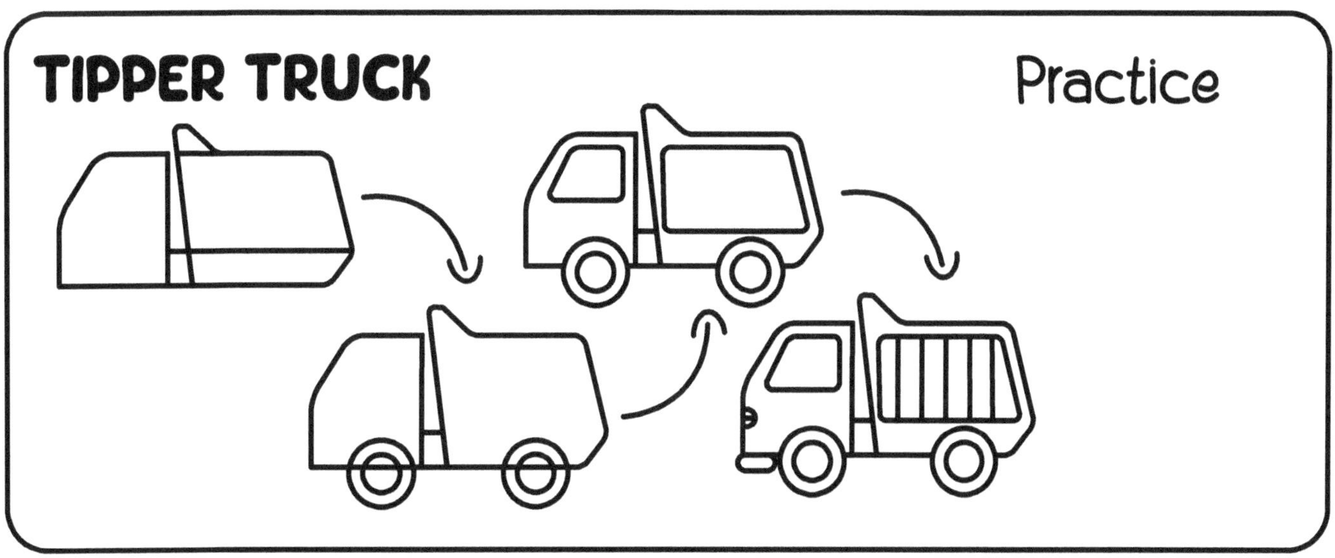

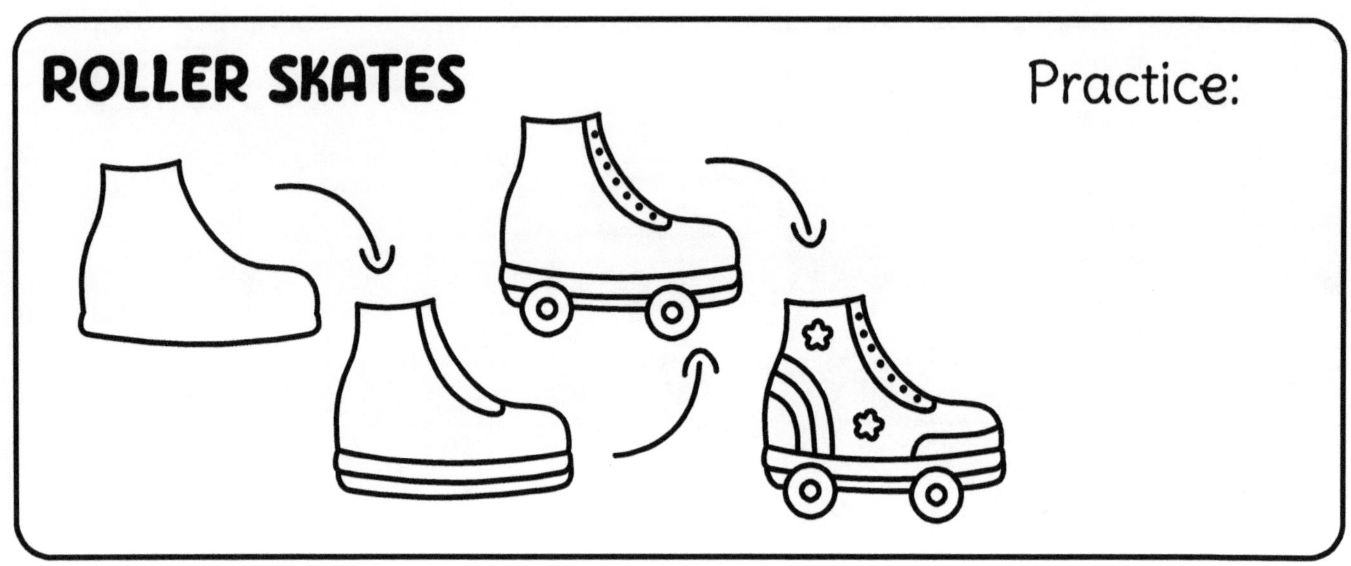

ROLLER SKATES
Practice:

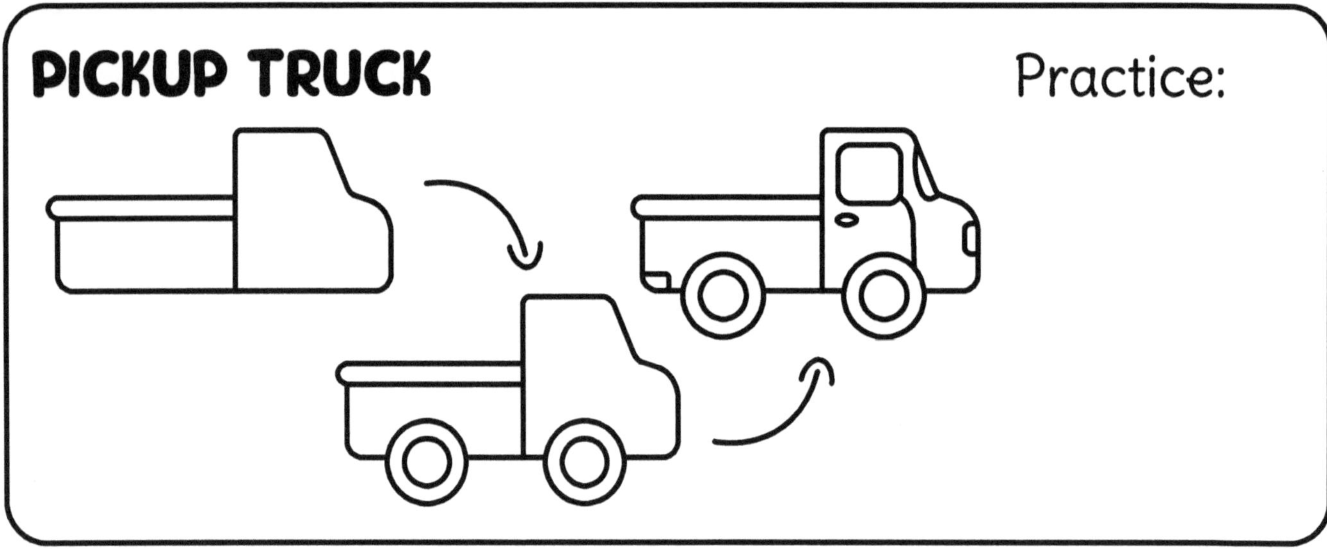

PICKUP TRUCK
Practice:

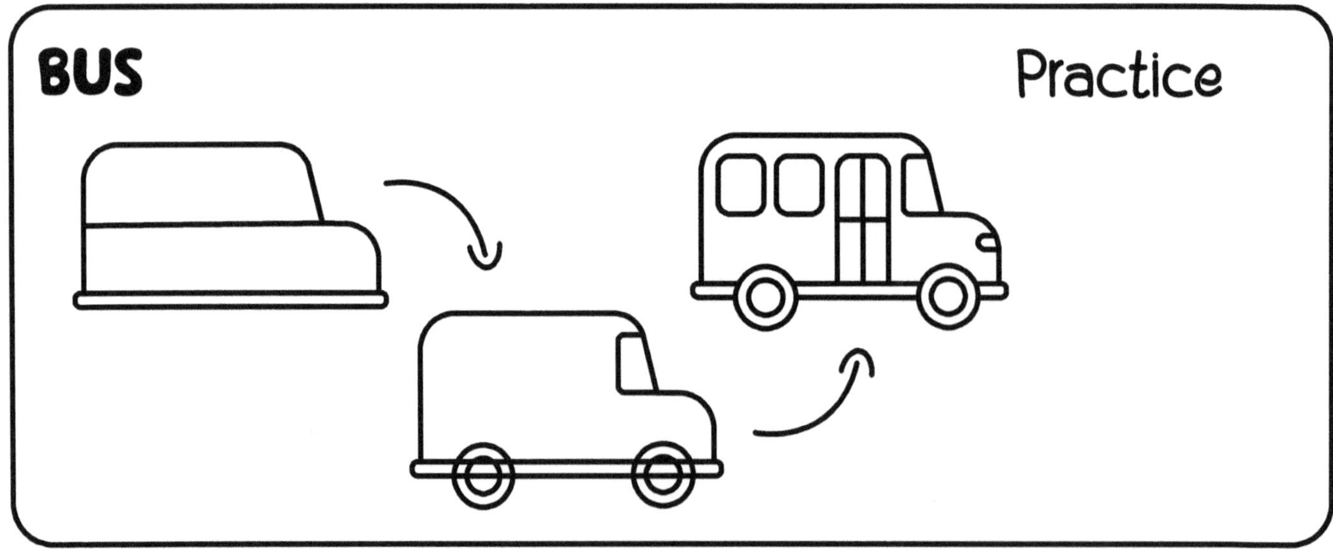

BUS
Practice

BOAT

Practice:

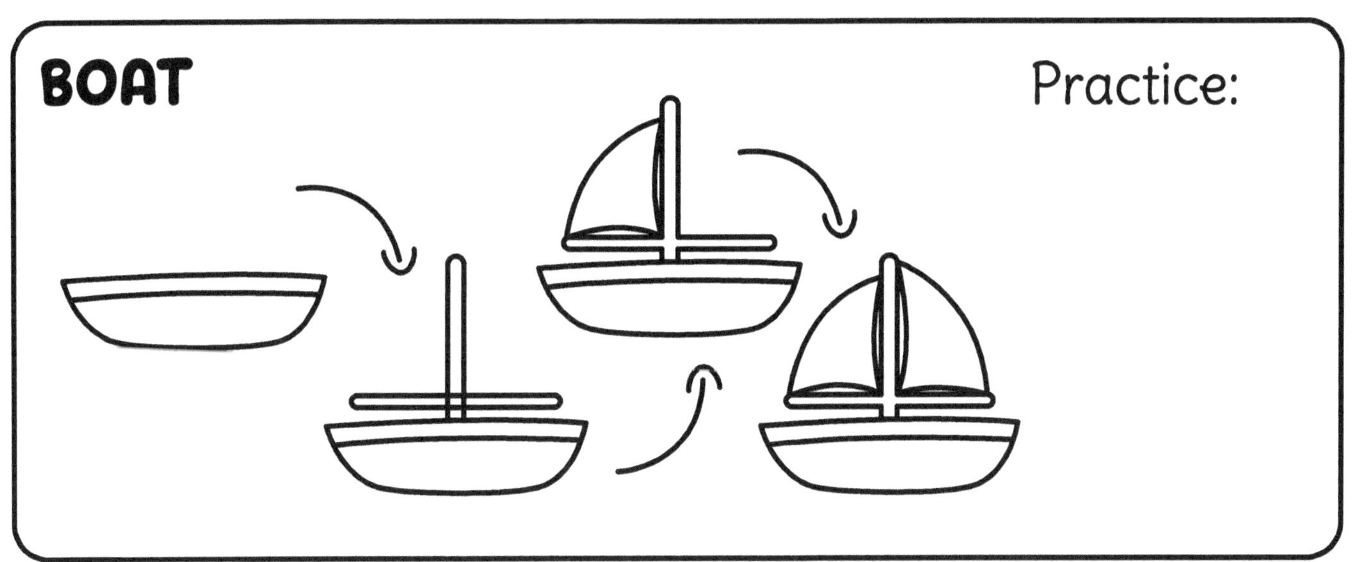

TRAIN

Practice:

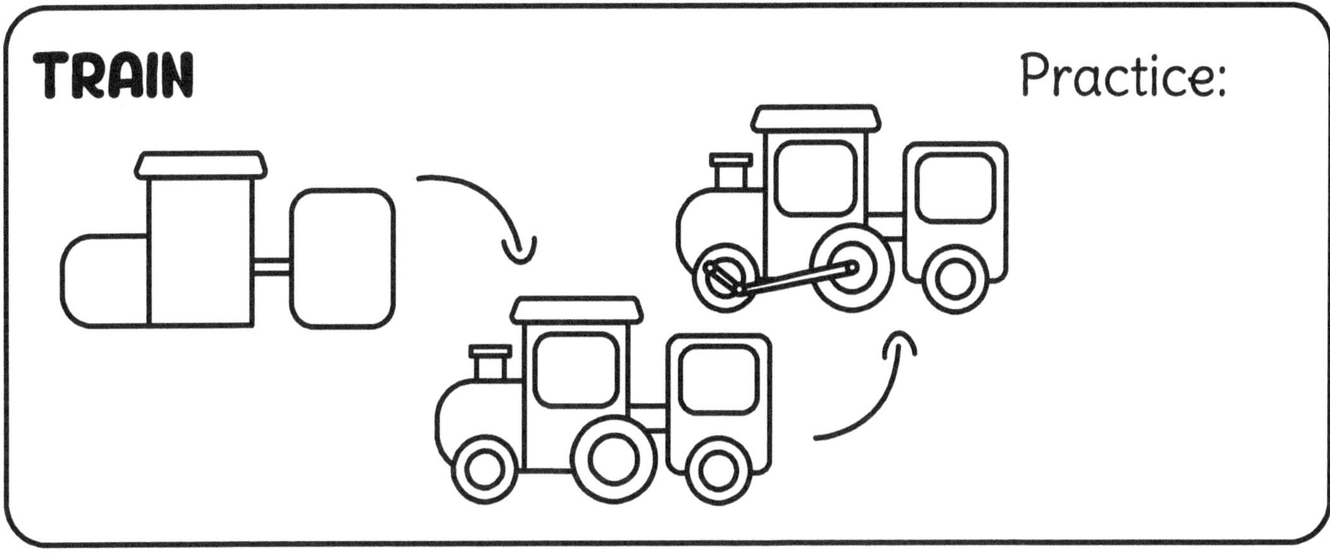

AIRPLANE

Practice

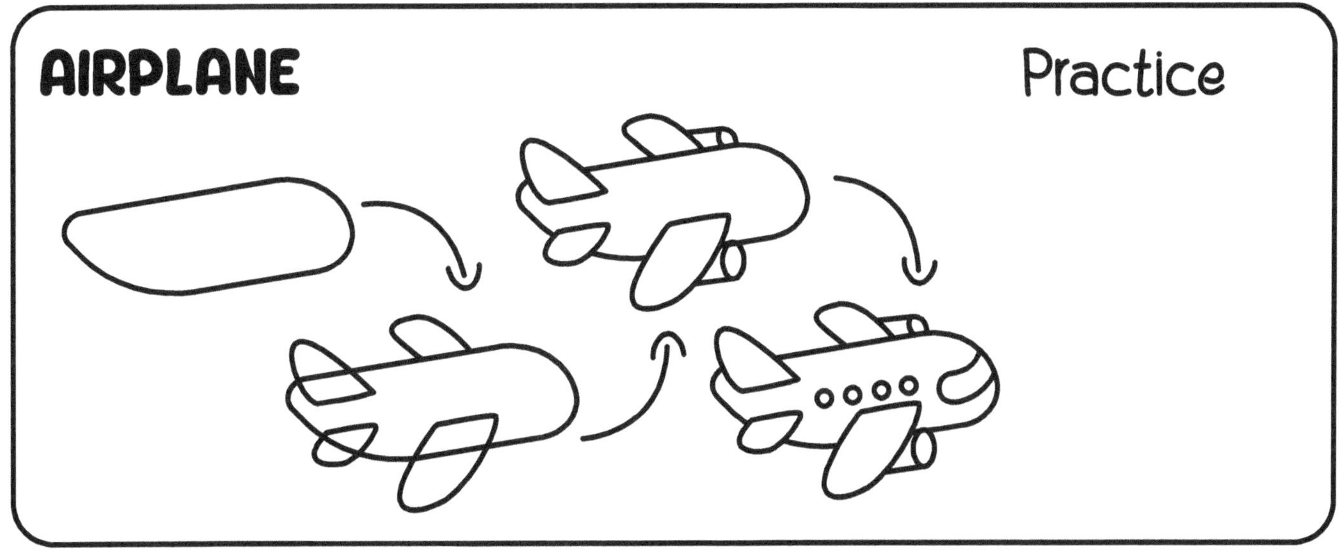

HAND SCOOTER

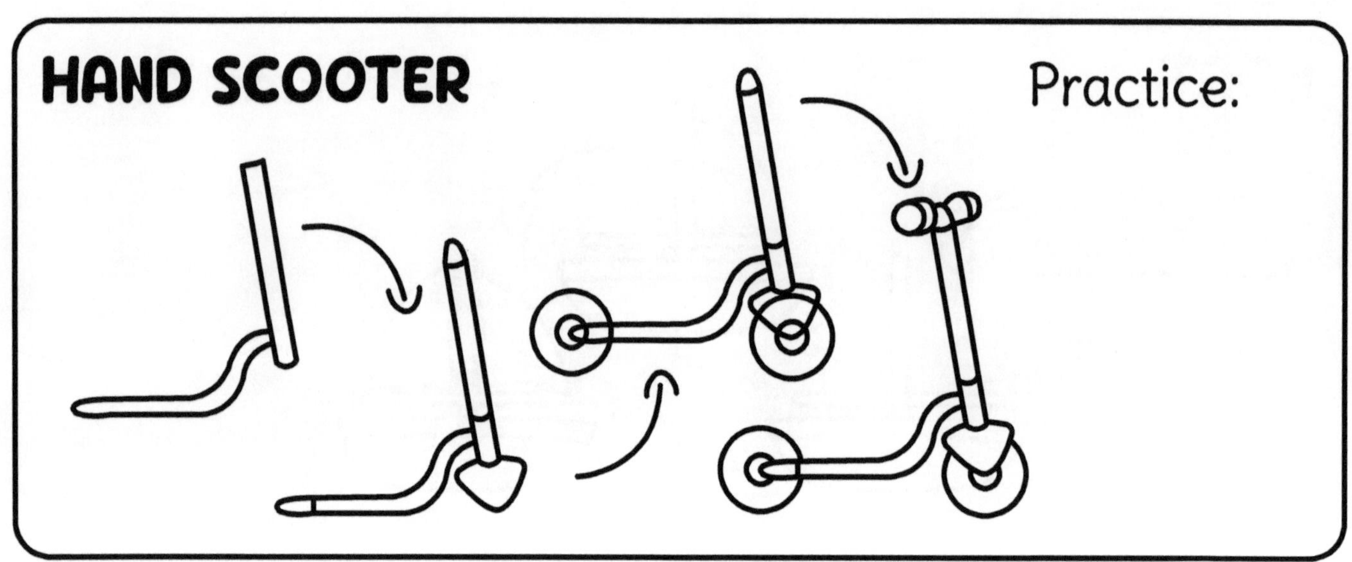

SKATEBOARD

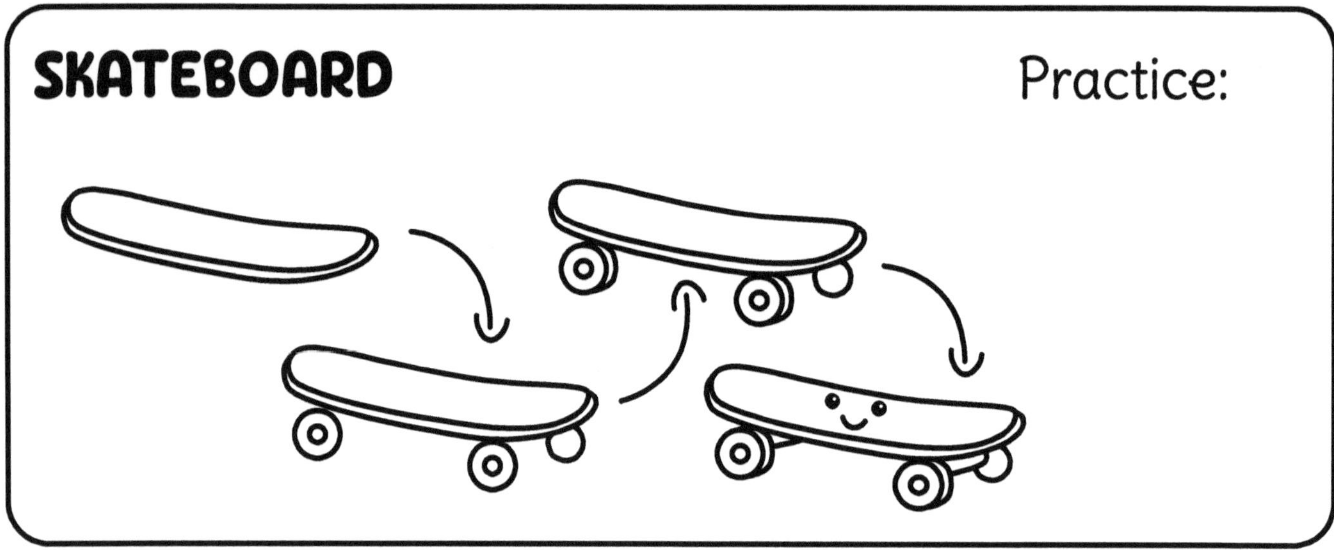

BICYCLE

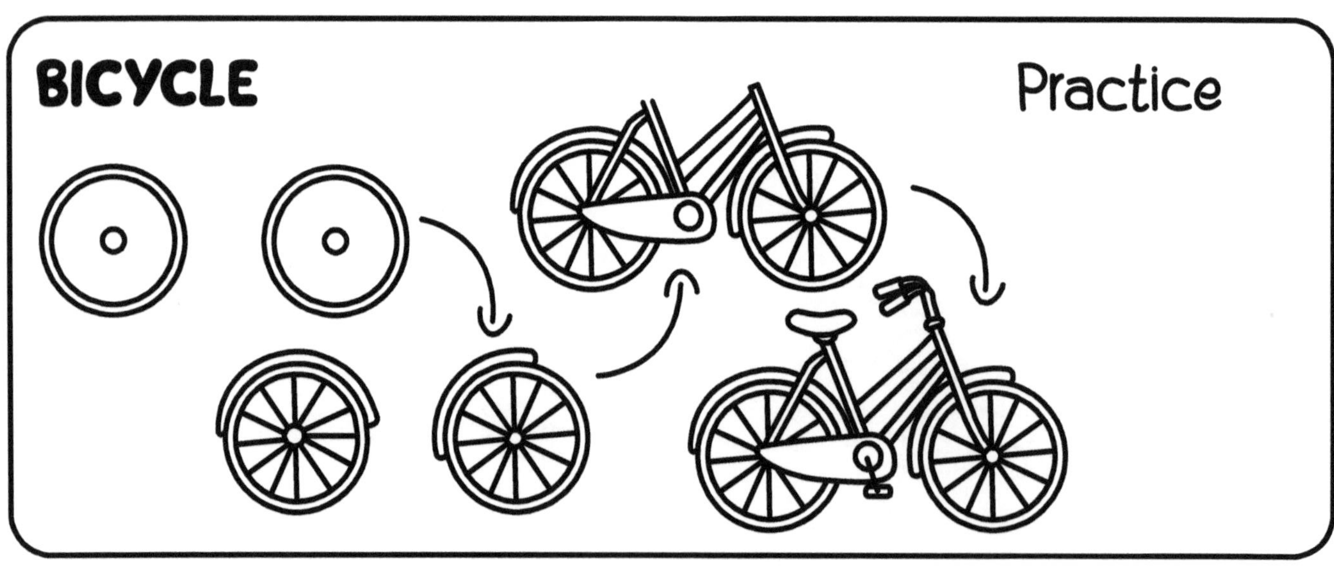

FRISBEES

Practice:

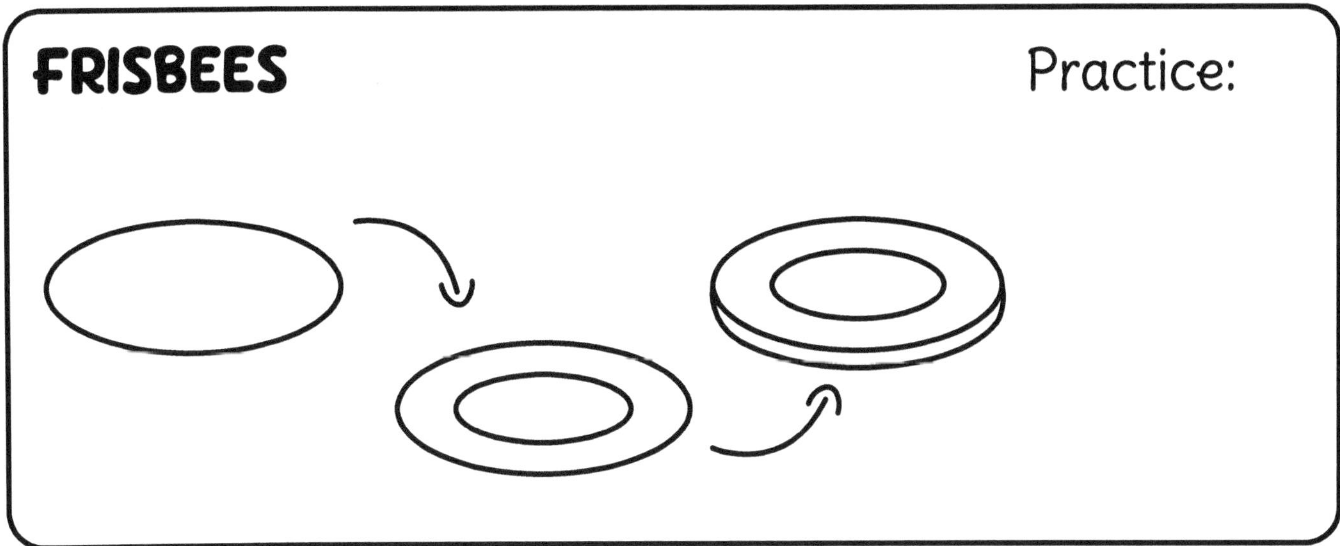

JUMP ROPES

Practice:

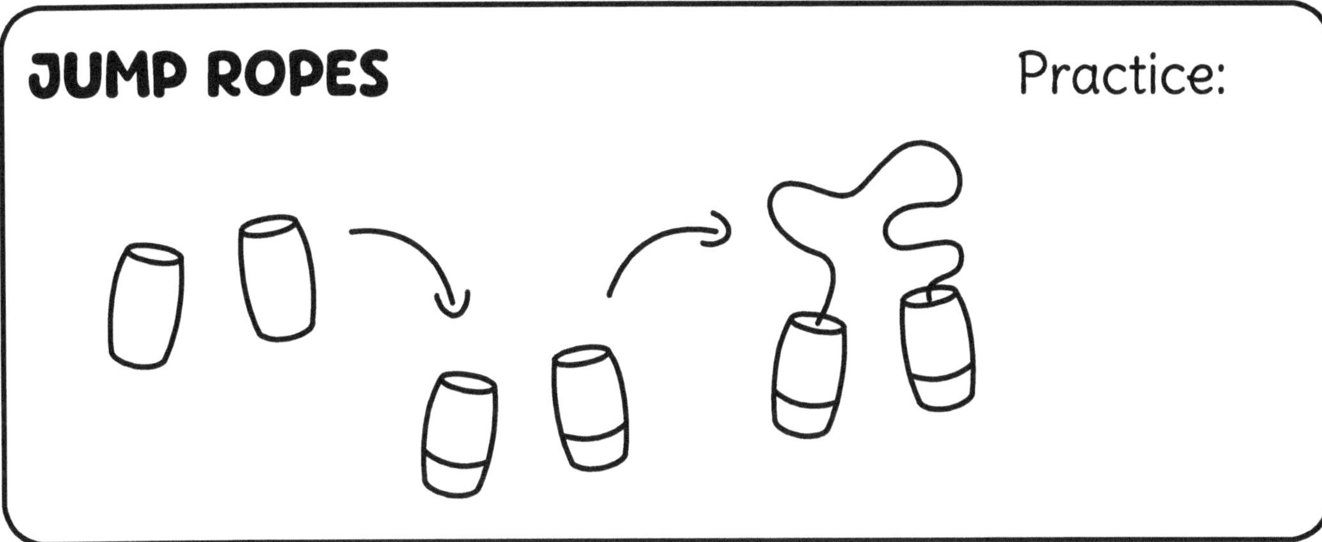

BASKETBALL

Practice

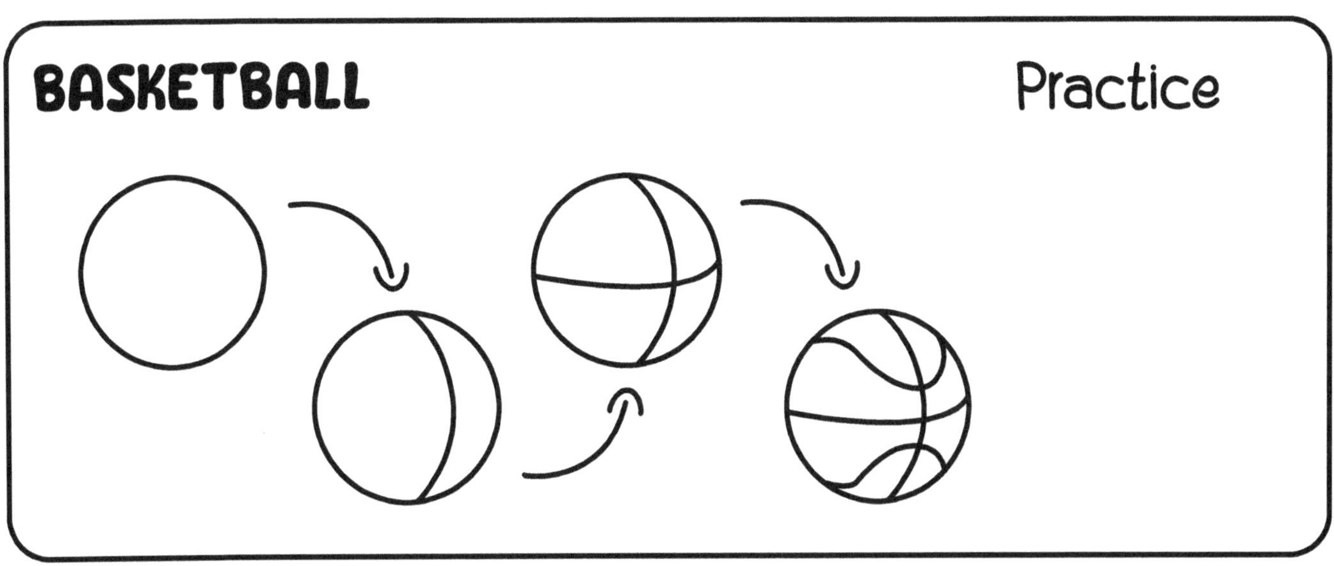

FOOTBALL

Practice:

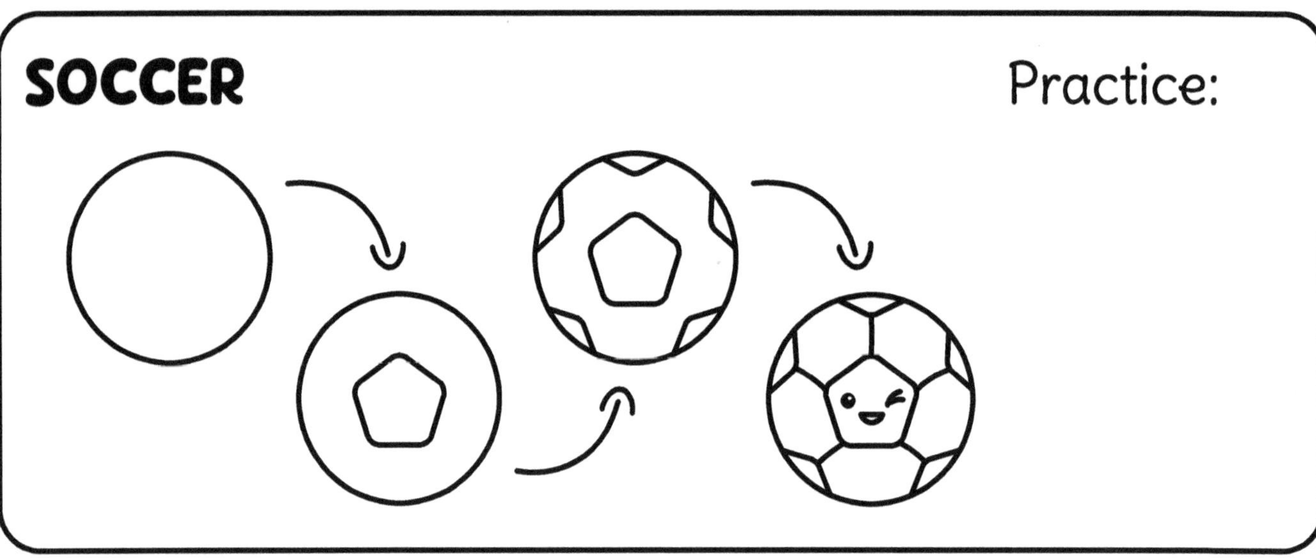

SOCCER

Practice:

BASEBALL BAT

Practice

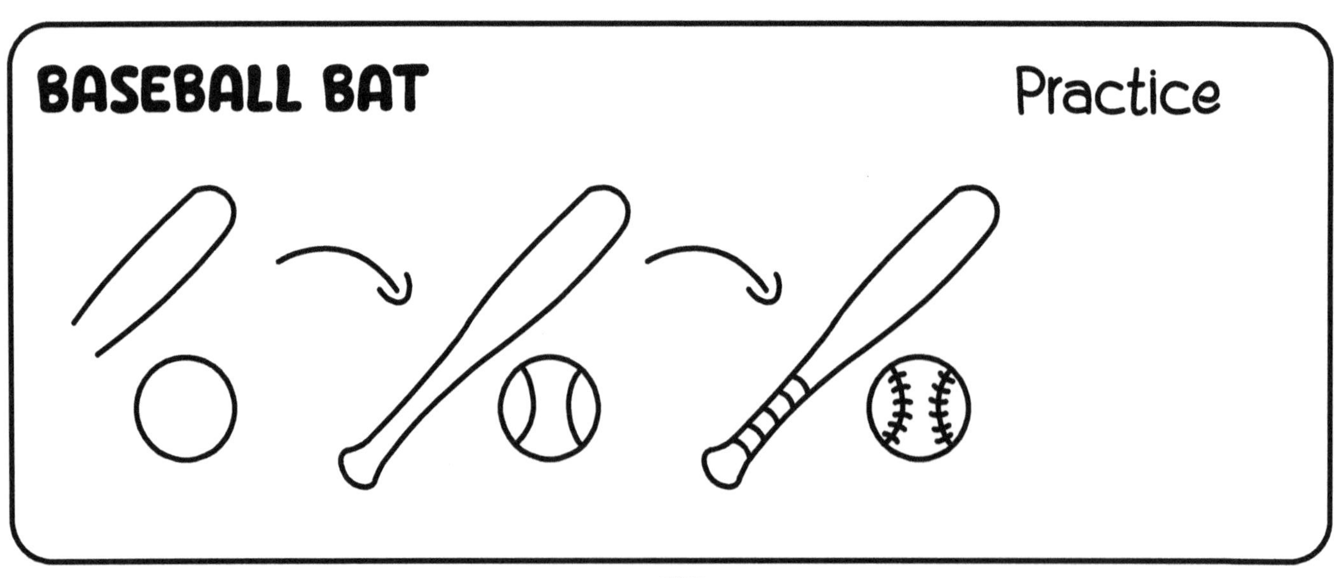

BASEBALL GLOVE

Practice:

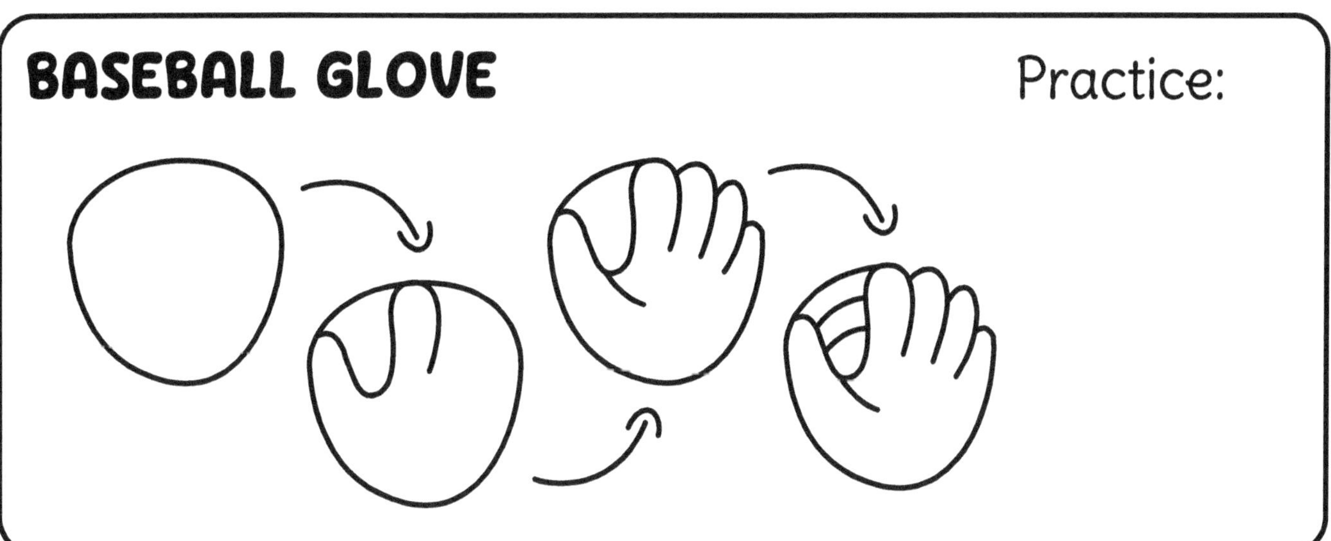

BOXING GLOVES

Practice:

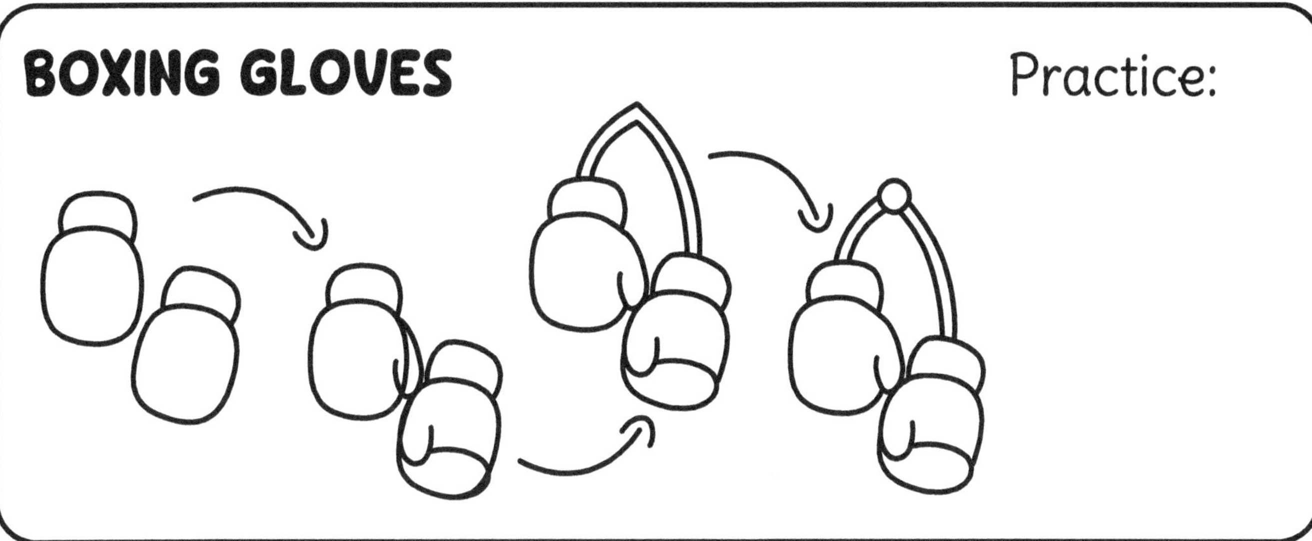

HOCKEY STICK

Practice

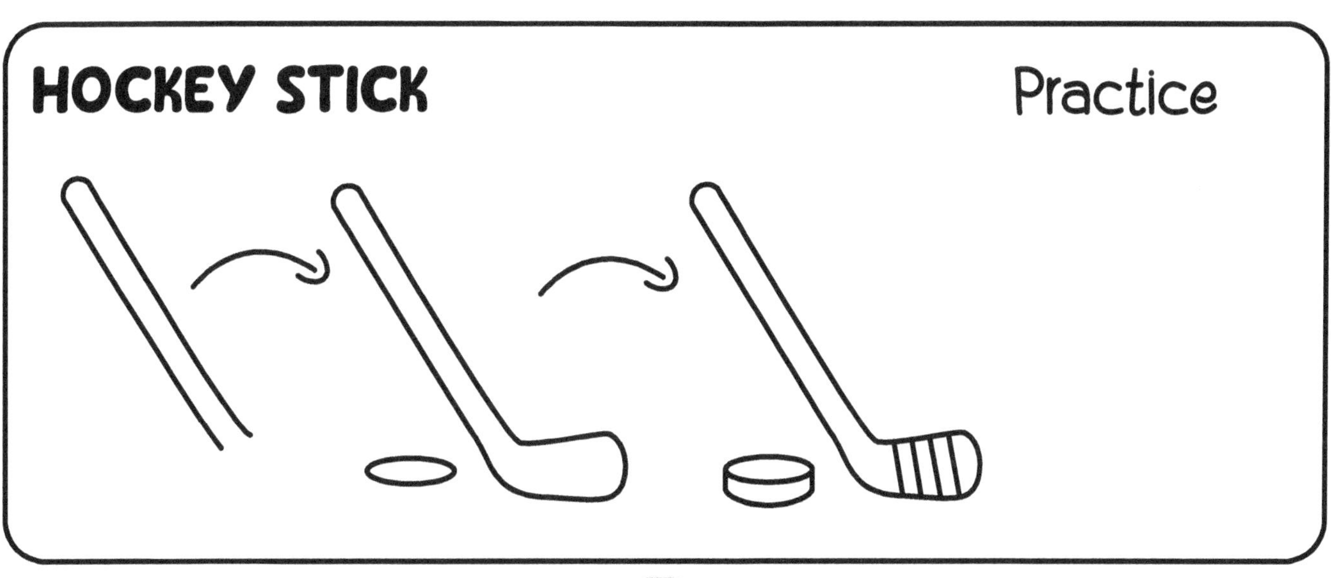

Practice:

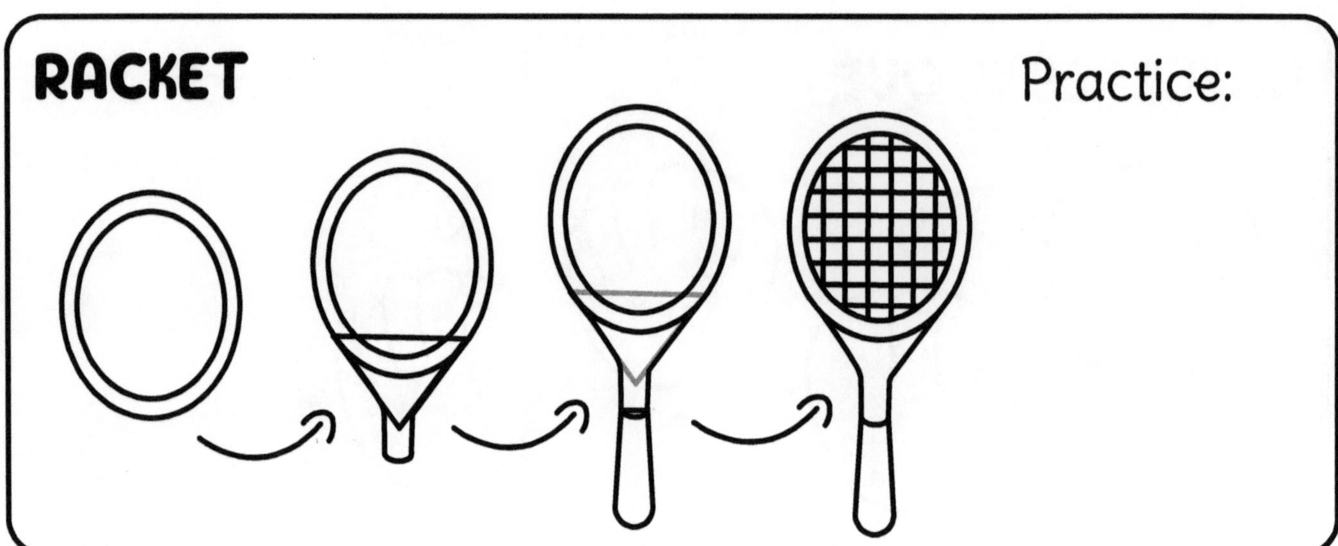

Practice:

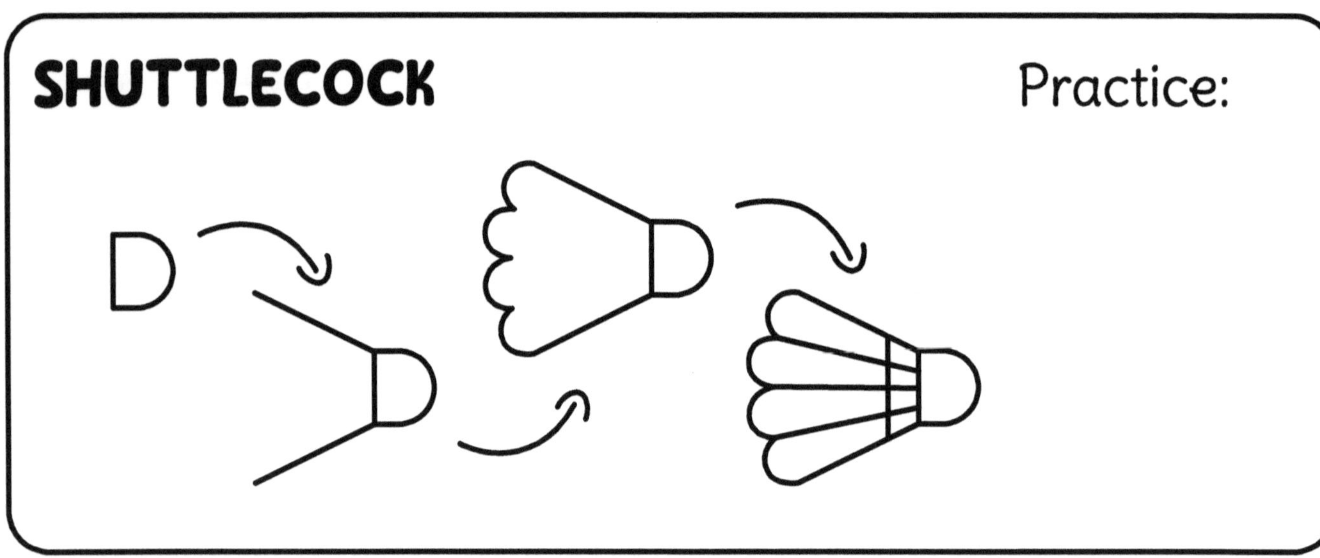

Practice

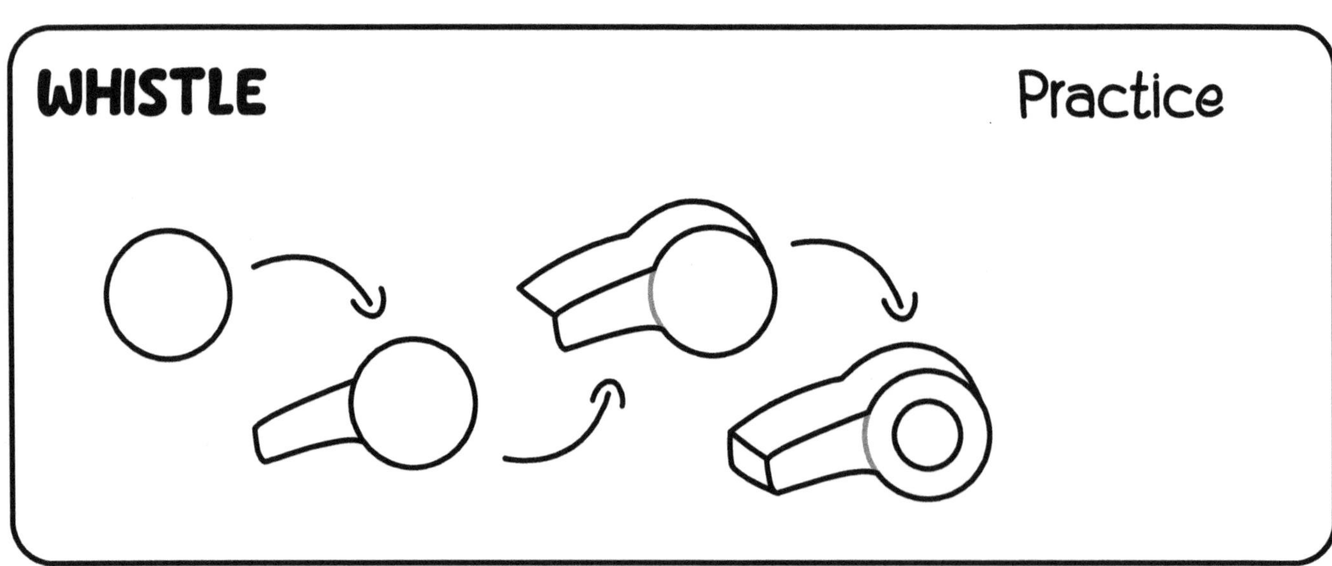

TOYS

TEDDY BEAR

Practice:

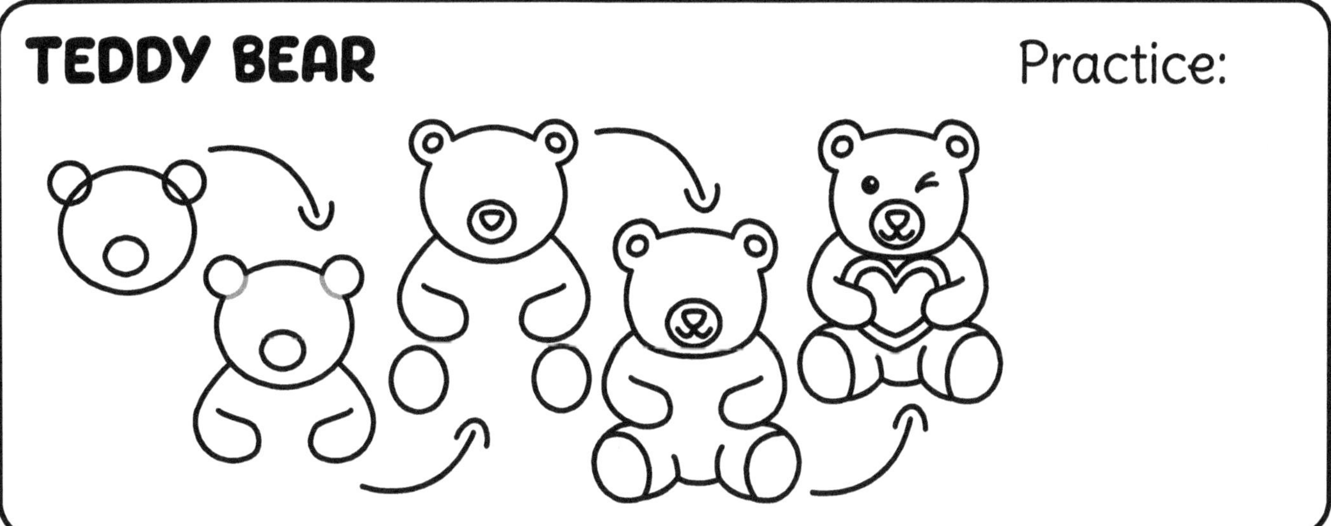

YOYO

Practice:

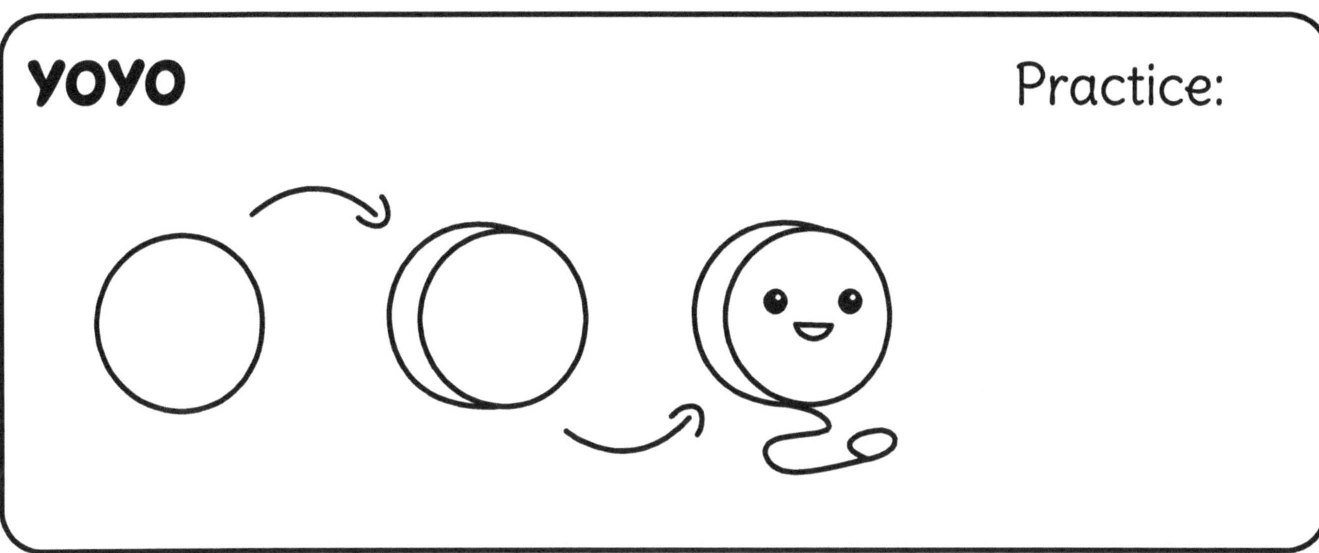

SPINNER

Practice

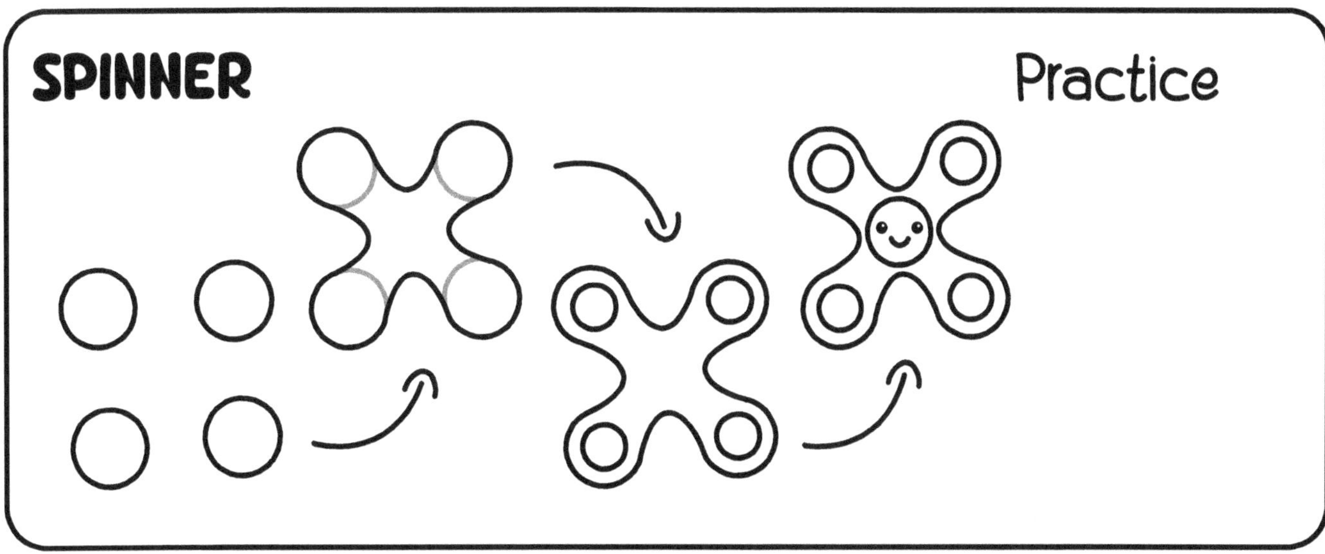

GUM BALL
Practice:

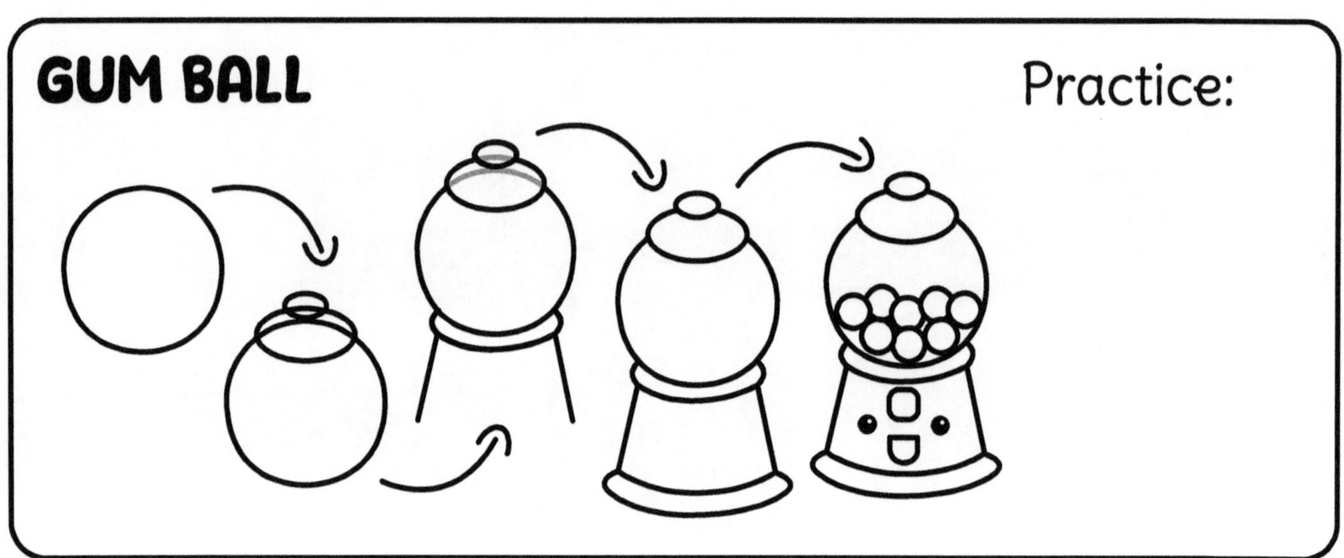

TOY CAMERA
Practice:

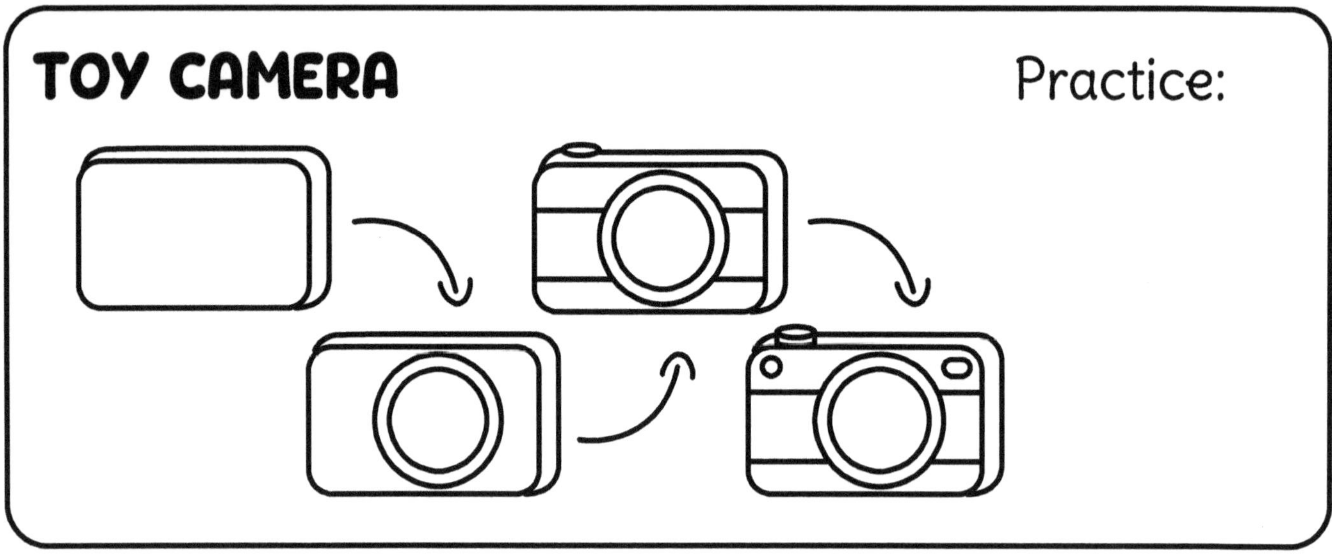

DOLL
Practice

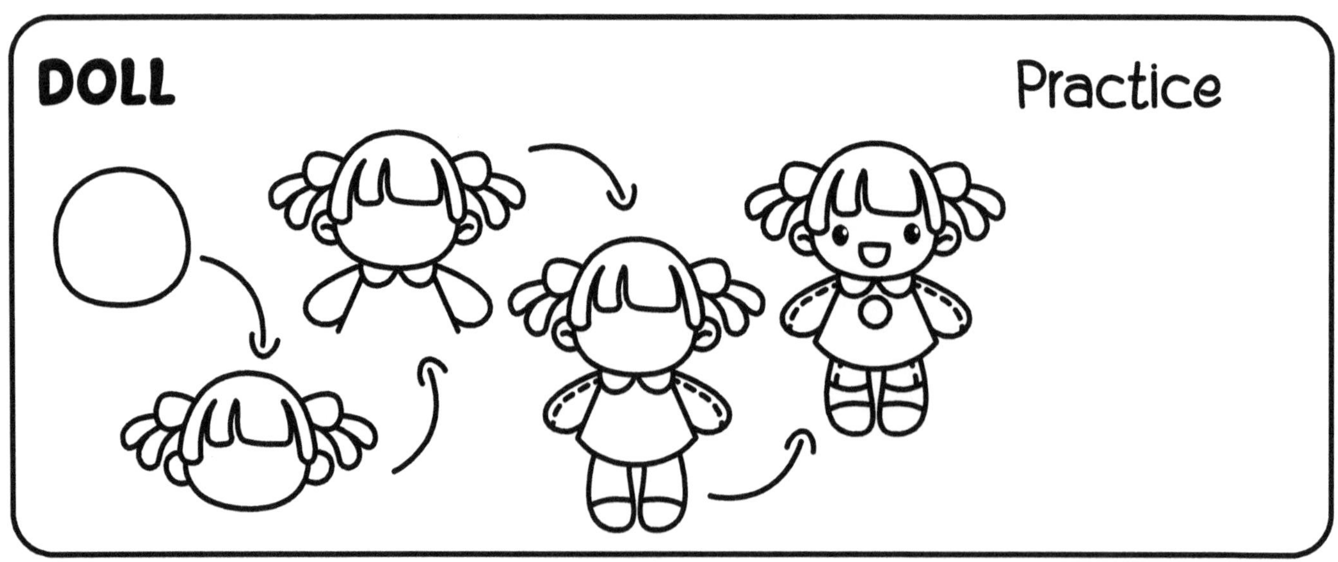

WALKIE-TALKIE

Practice:

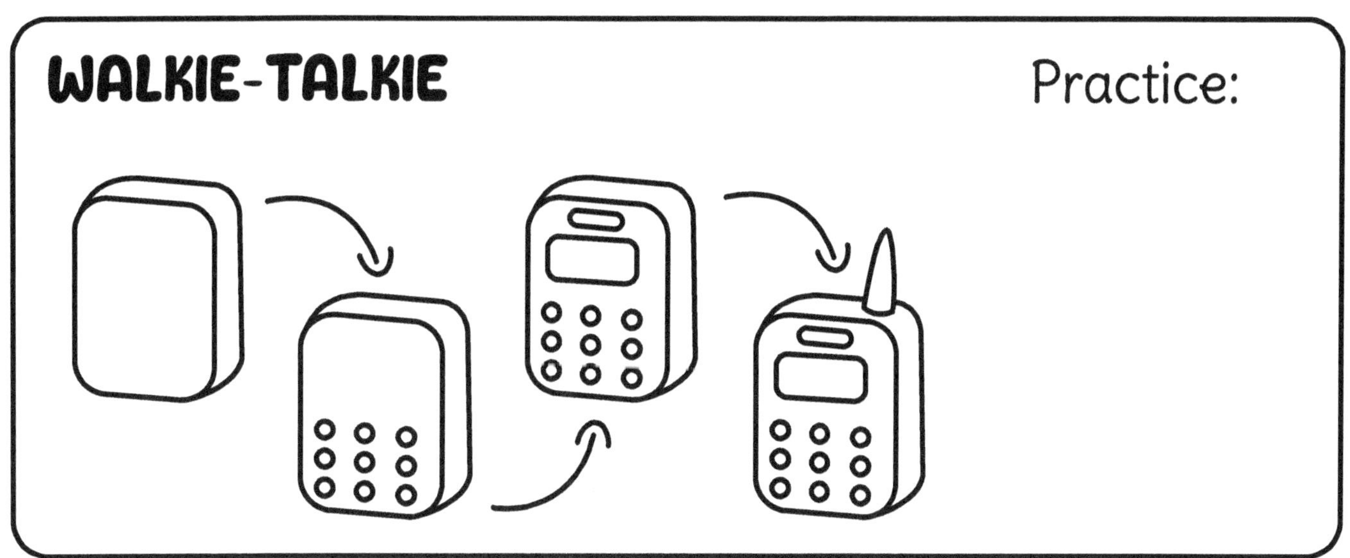

BALLOON

Practice:

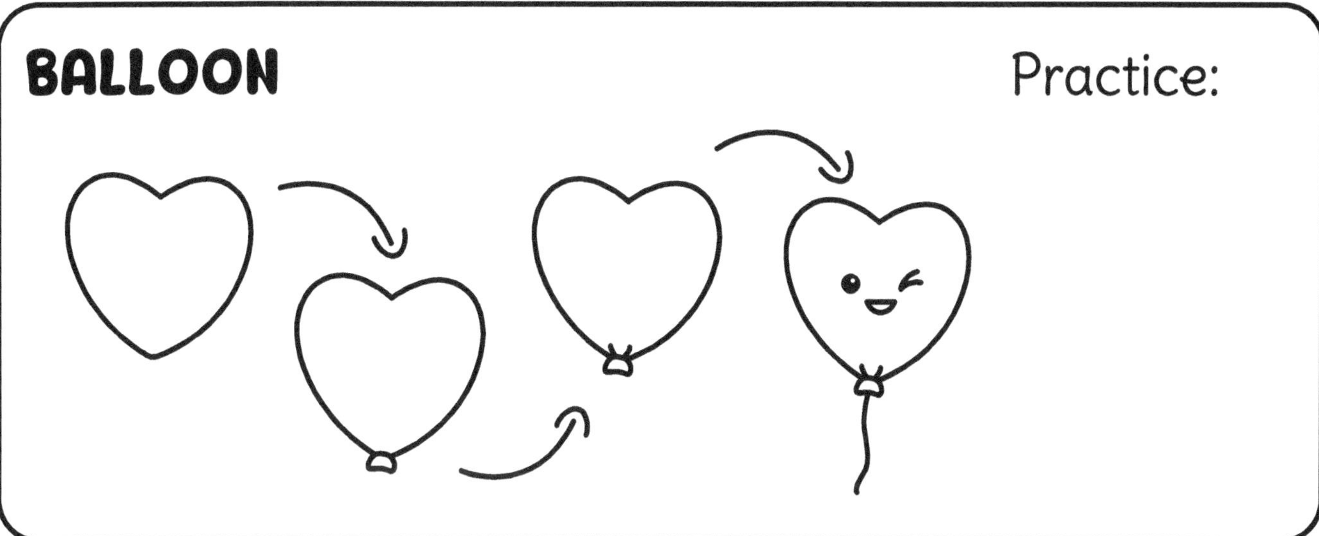

PLAYDOH

Practice

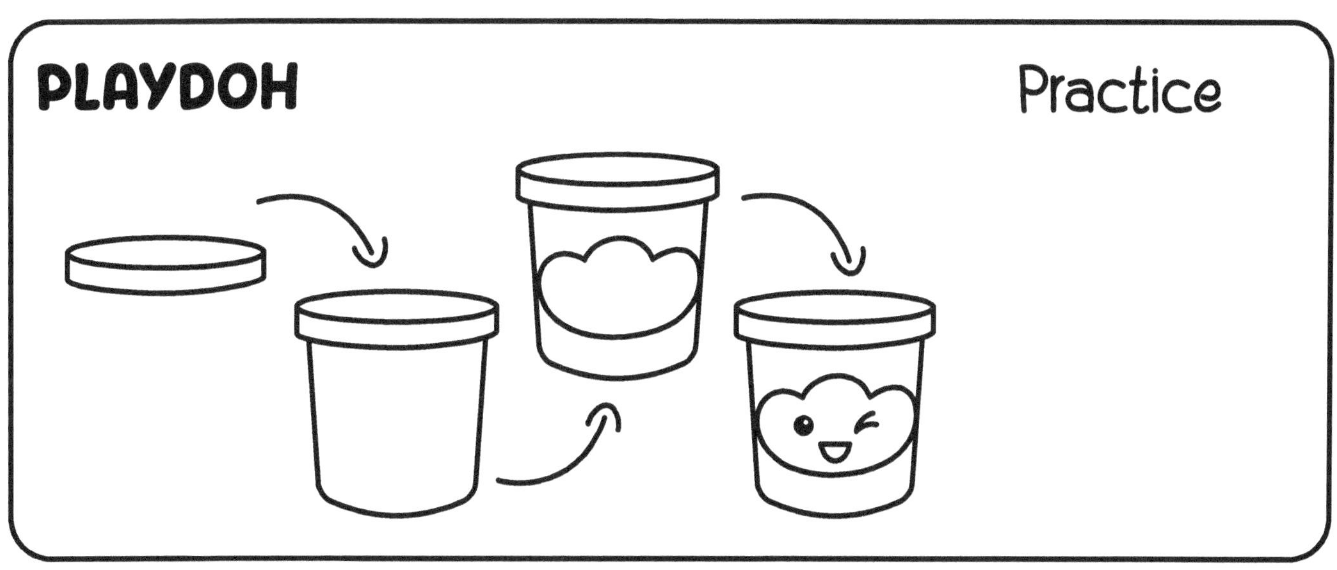

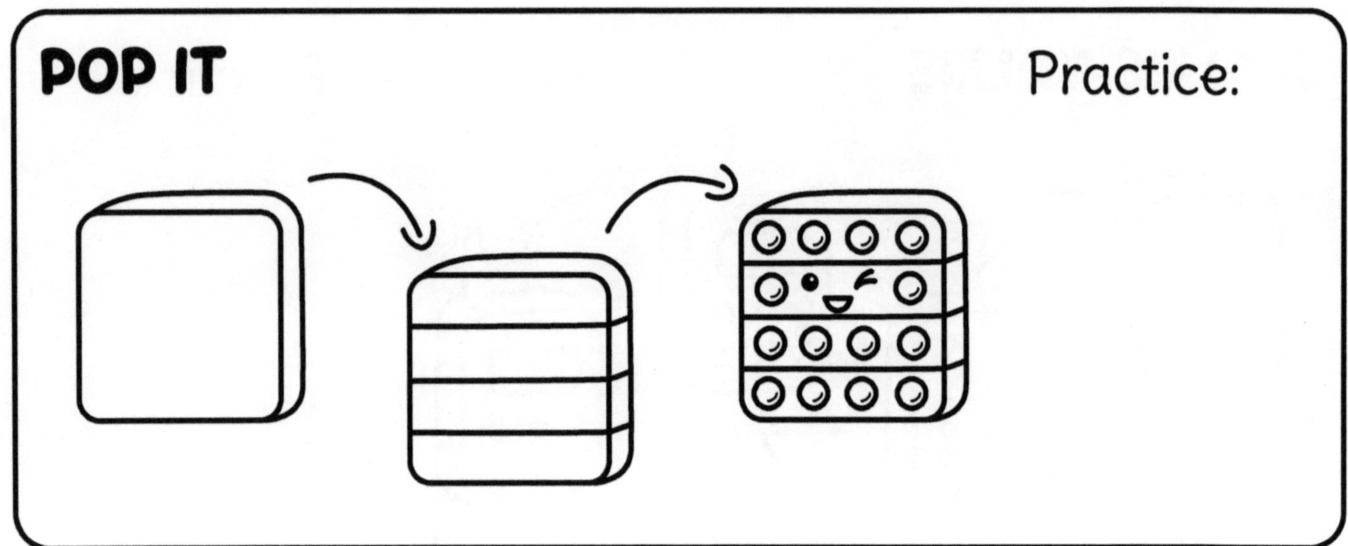
POP IT
Practice:

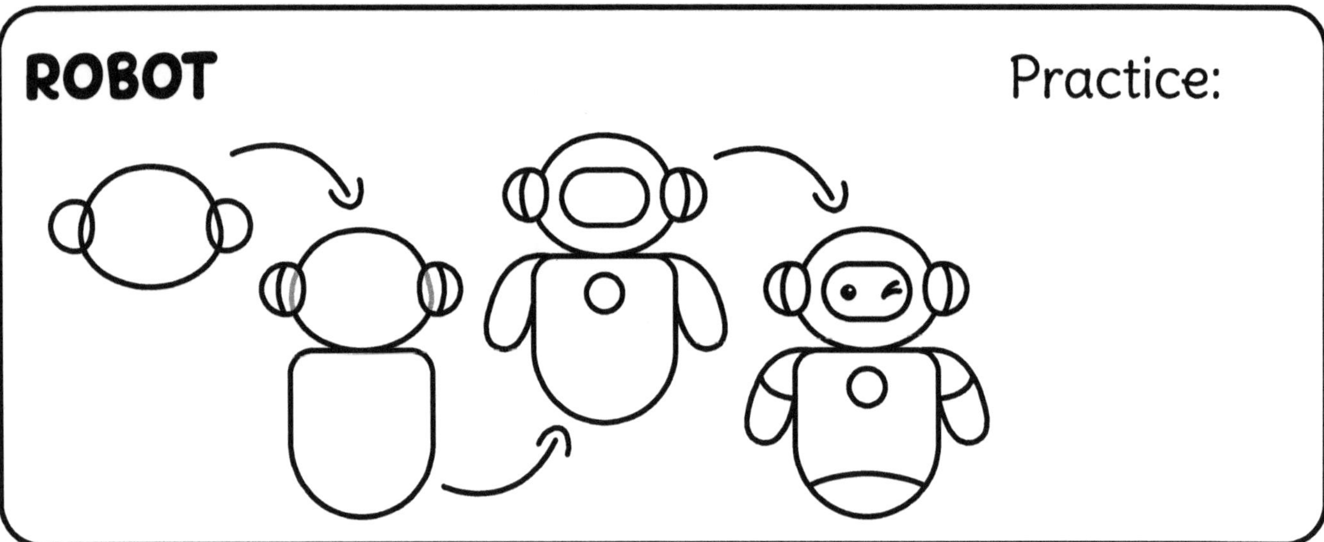
ROBOT
Practice:

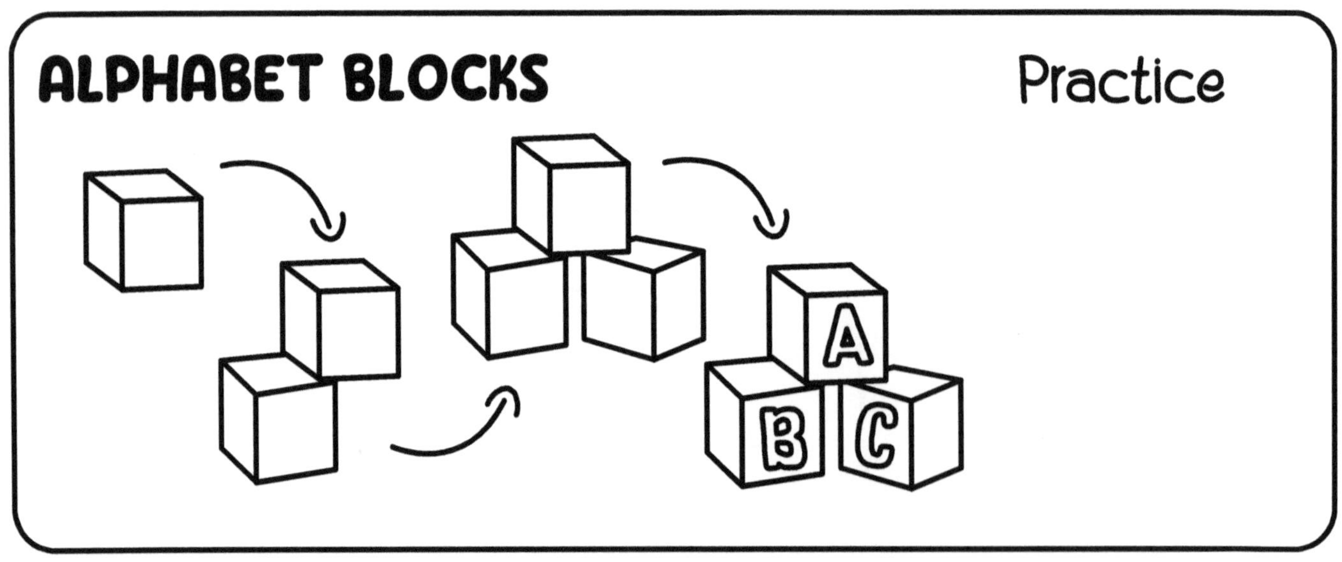
ALPHABET BLOCKS
Practice
A
B
C

INTERLOCKING BRICKS Practice:

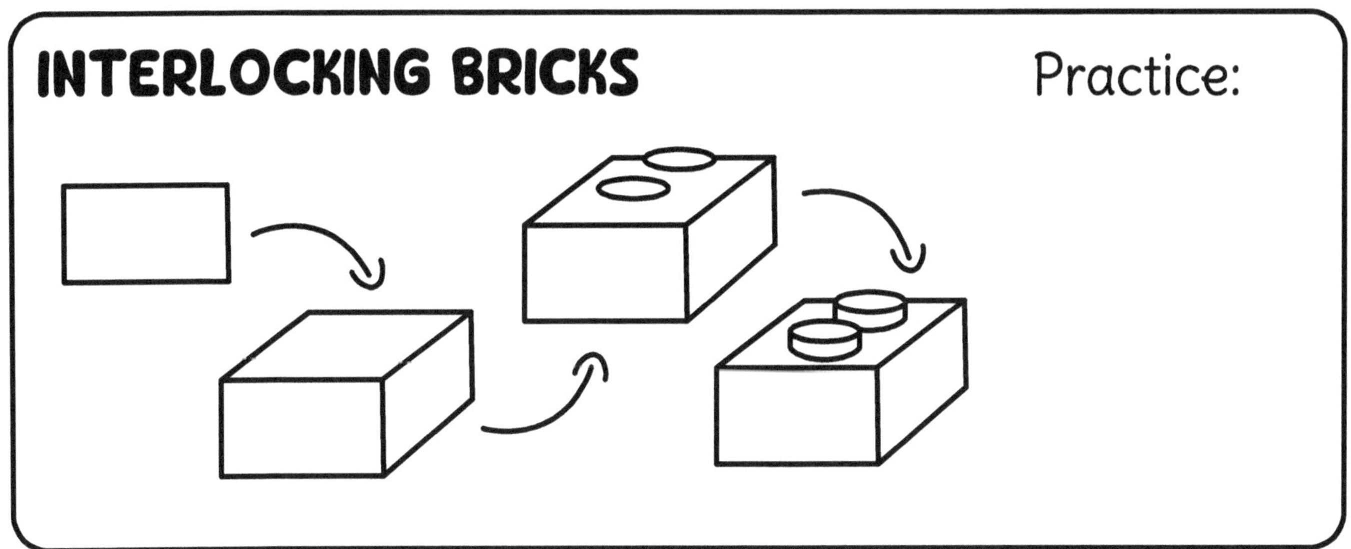

DICE Practice:

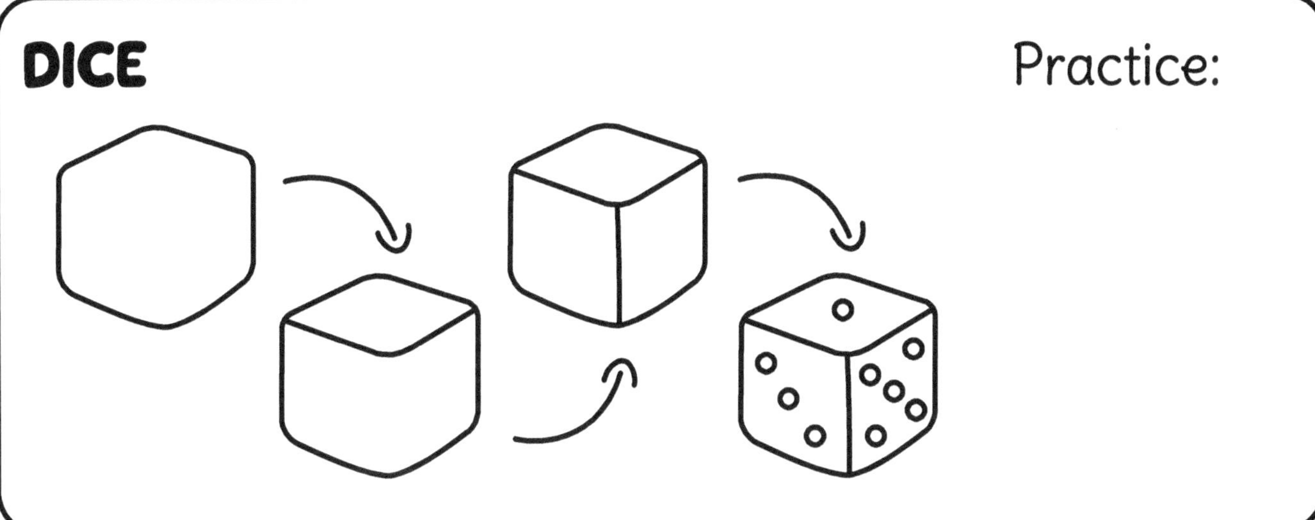

DOMINOES Practice

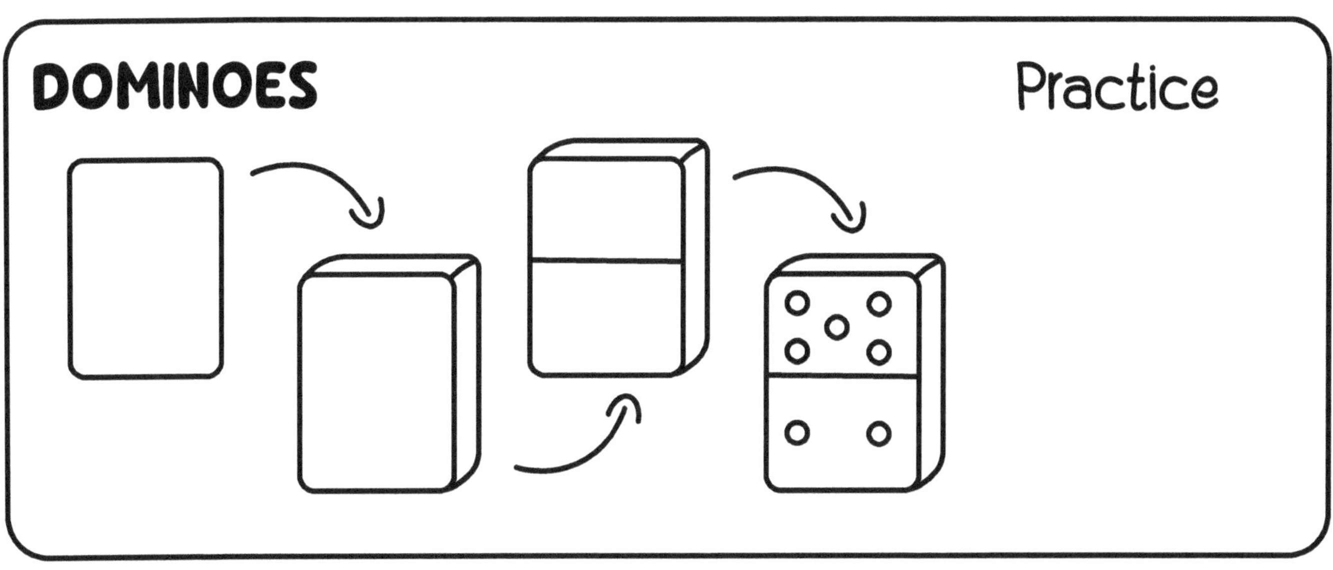

SLIME JAR

Practice:

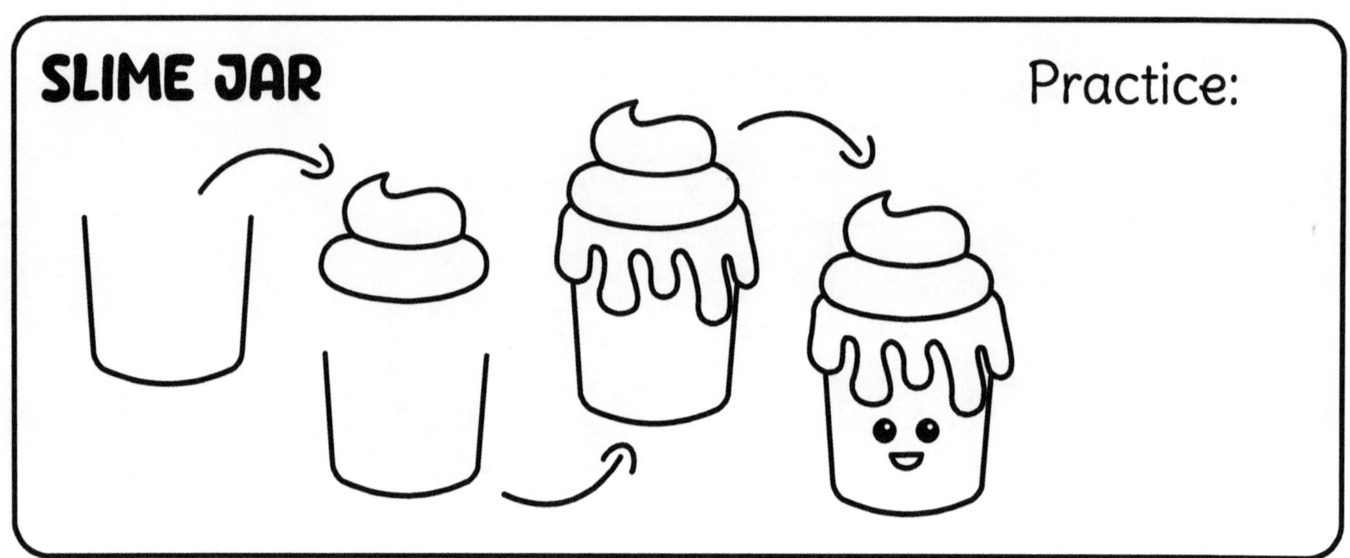

TOY PHONE

Practice:

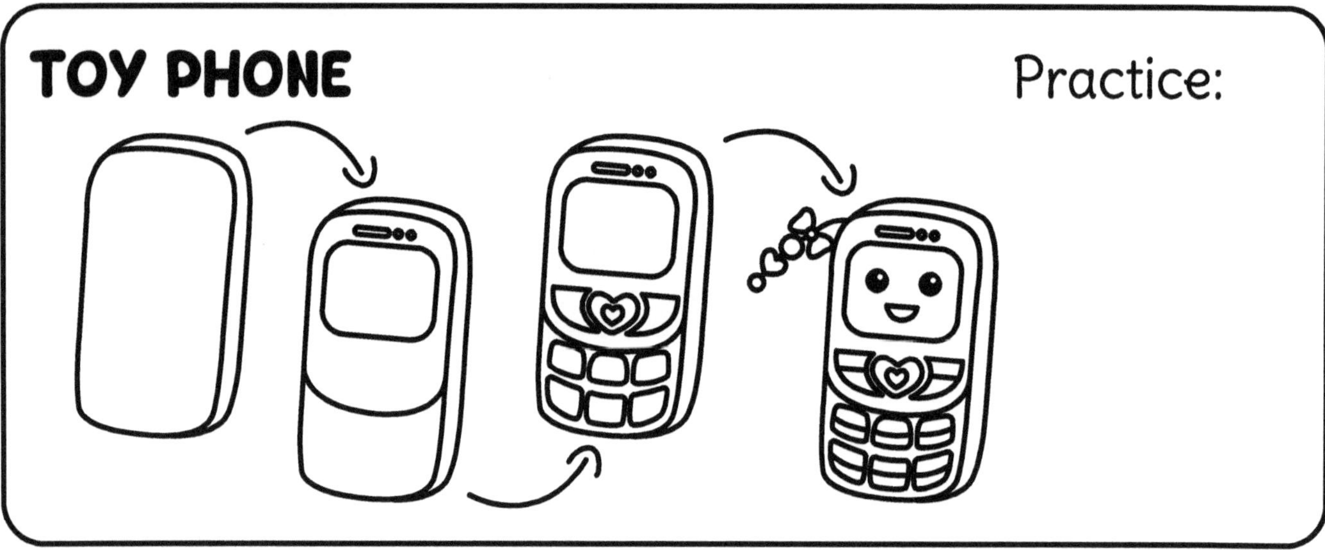

DRUM

Practice

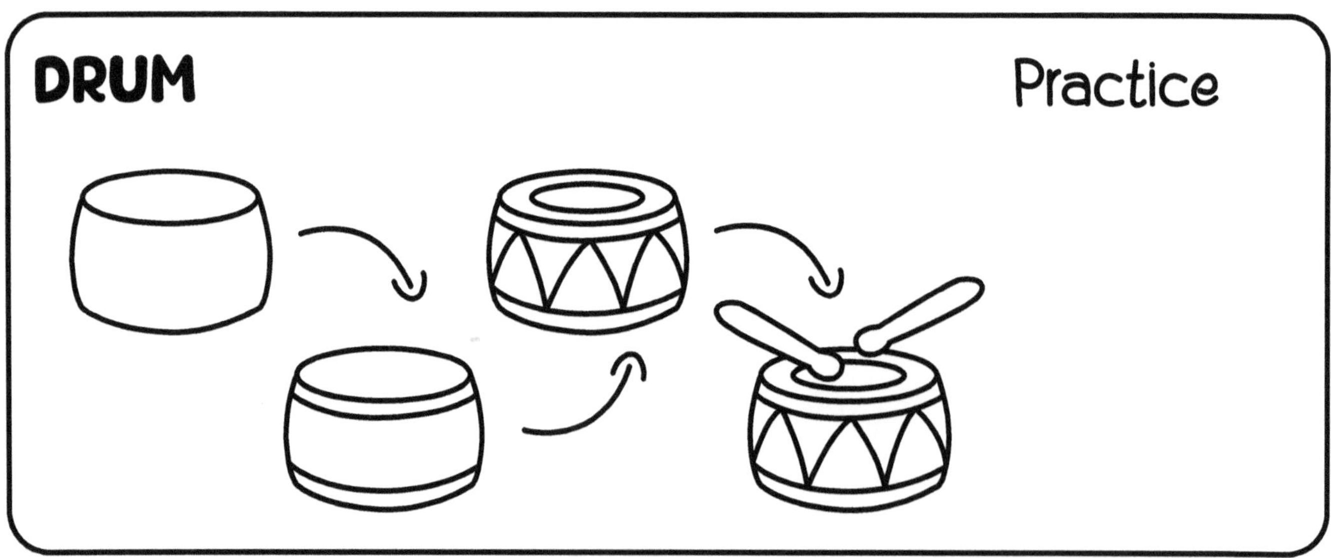

BELL Practice:

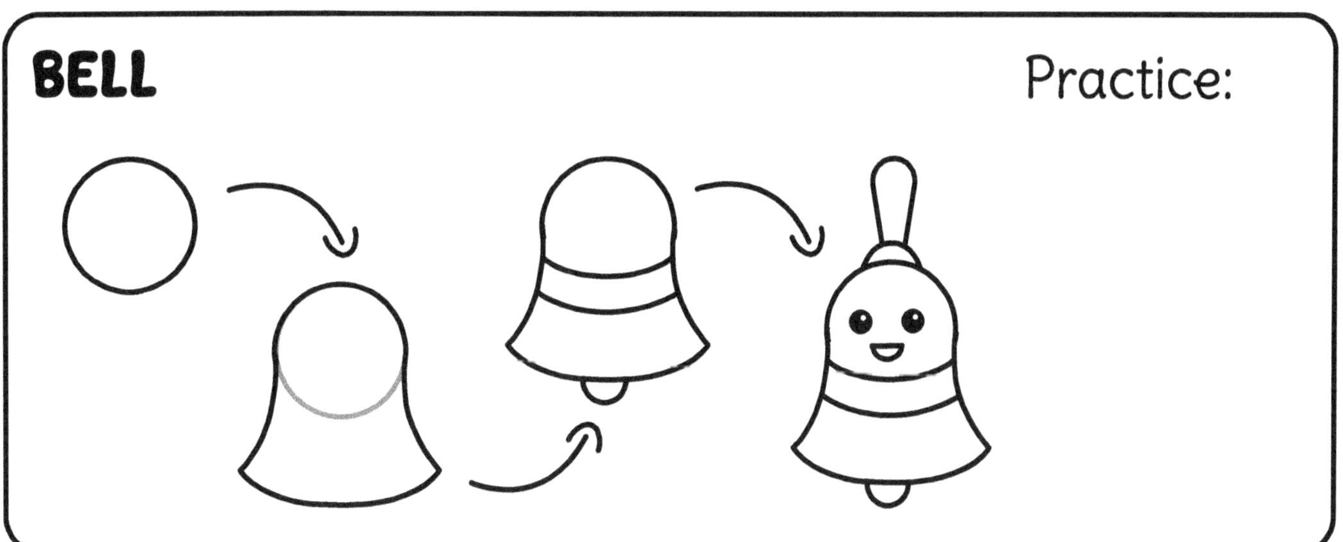

CRAYONS Practice:

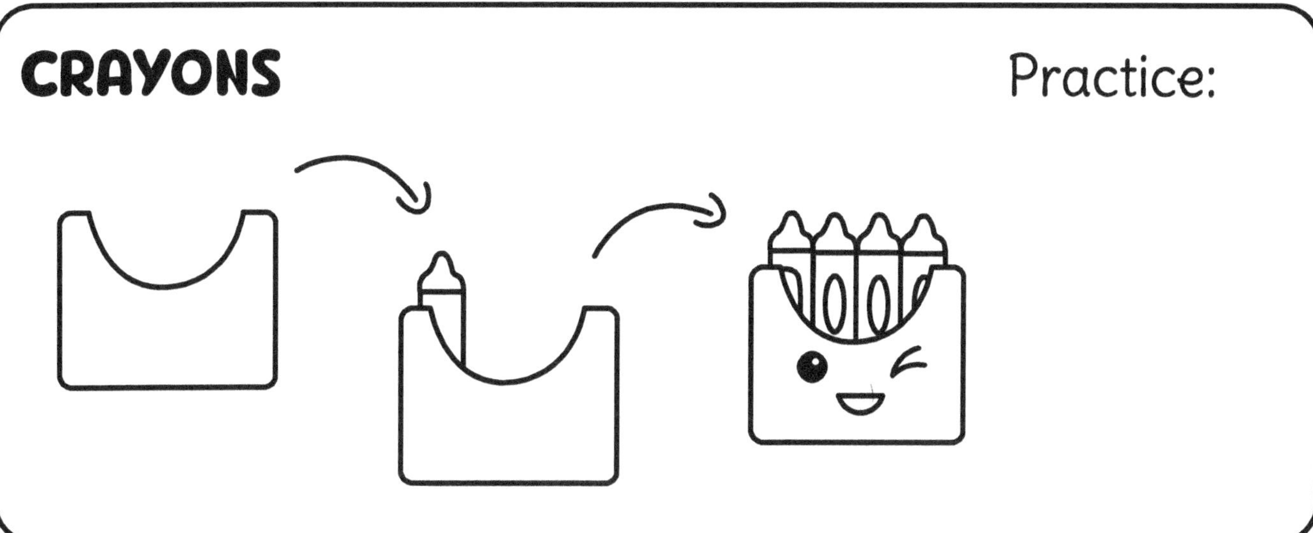

PYRAMID Practice

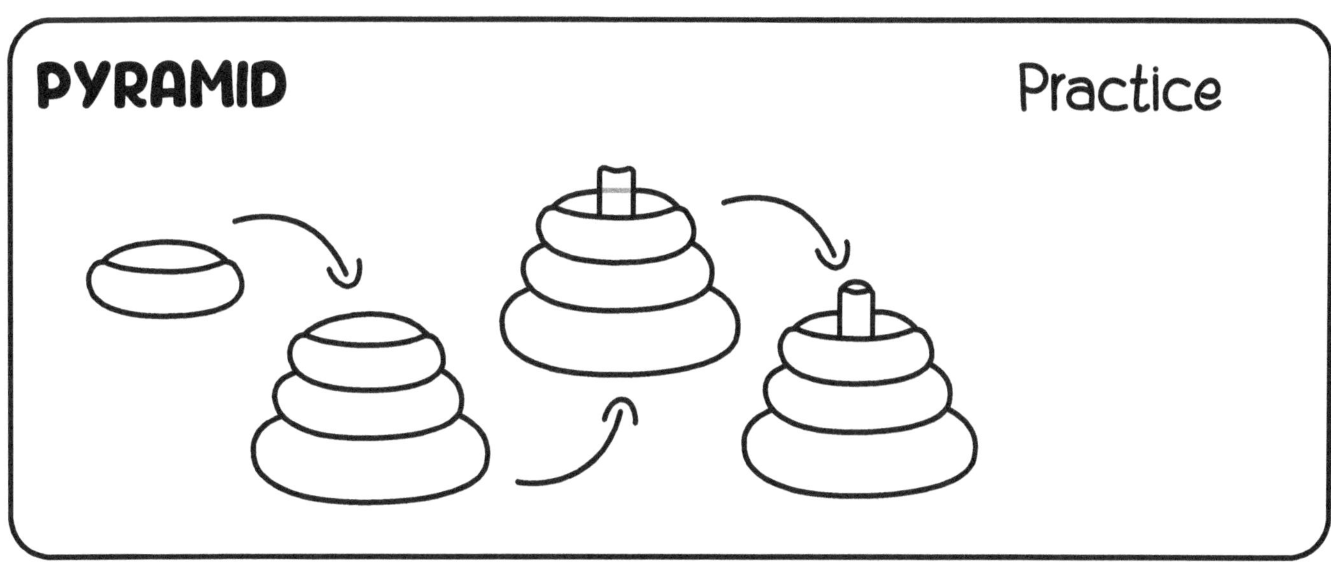

ROCKET

Practice:

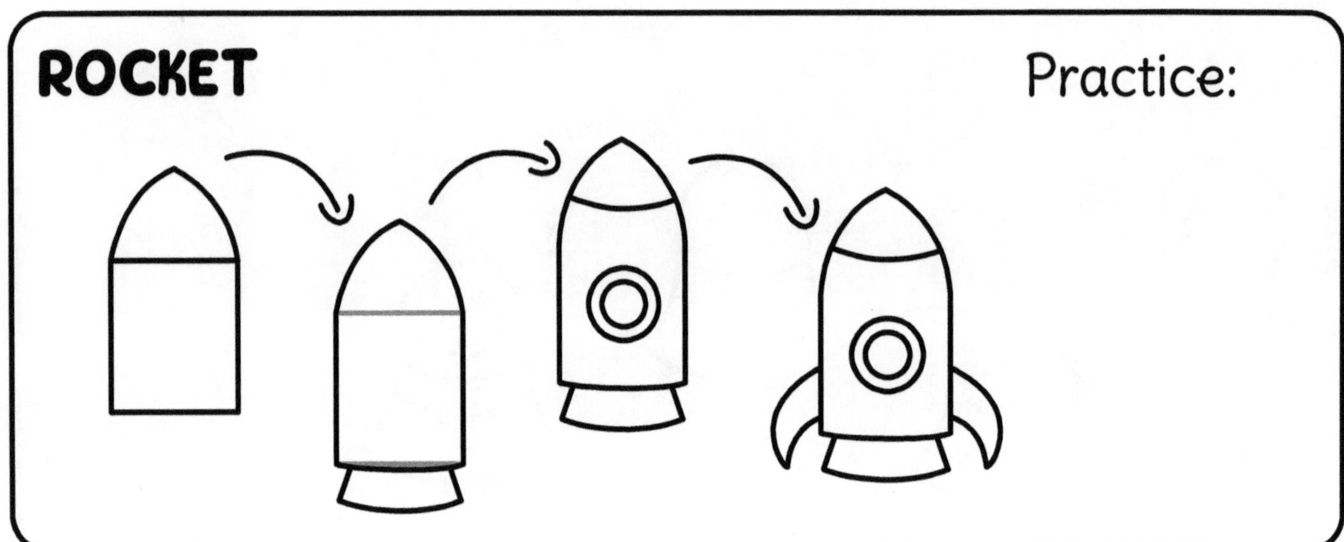

BINOCULARS

Practice:

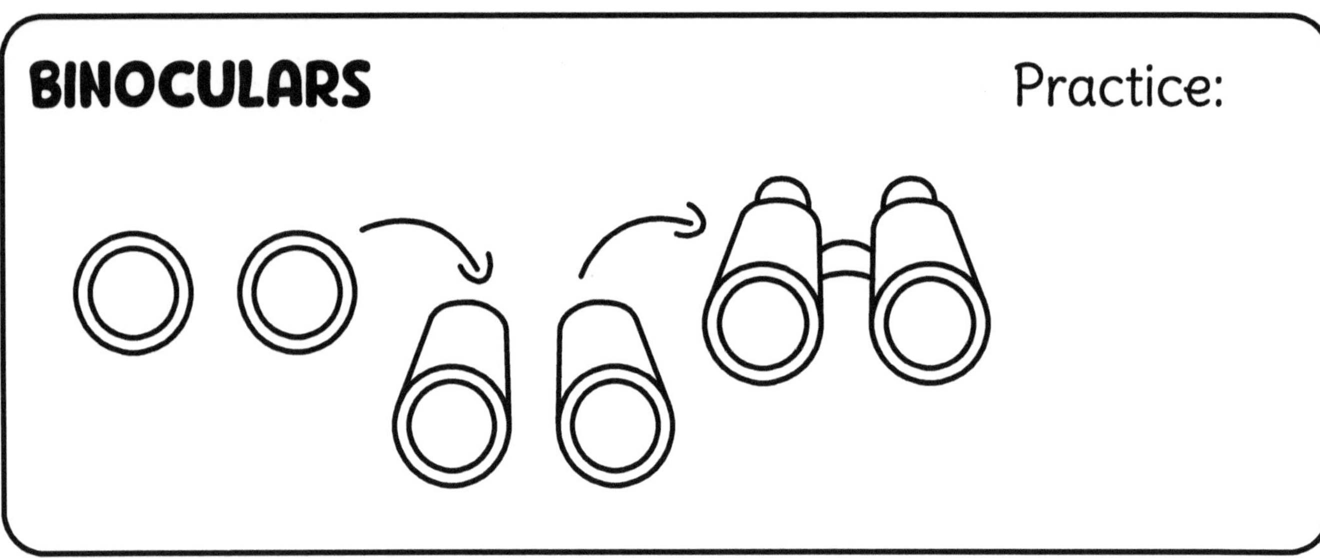

XYLOPHONE

Practice

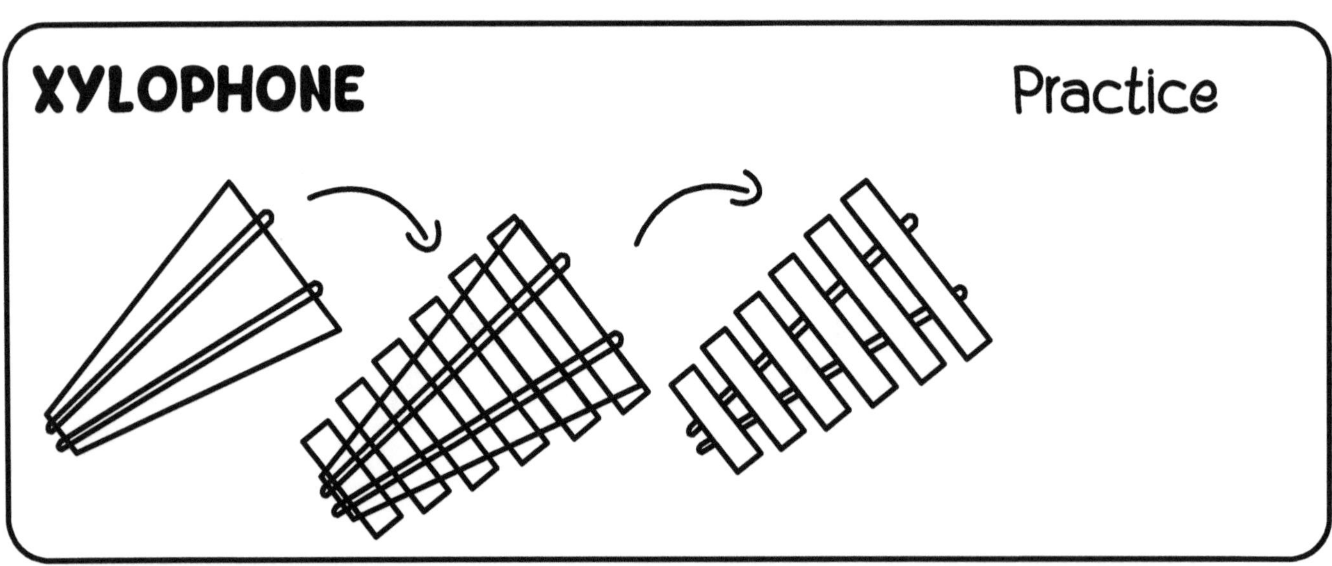

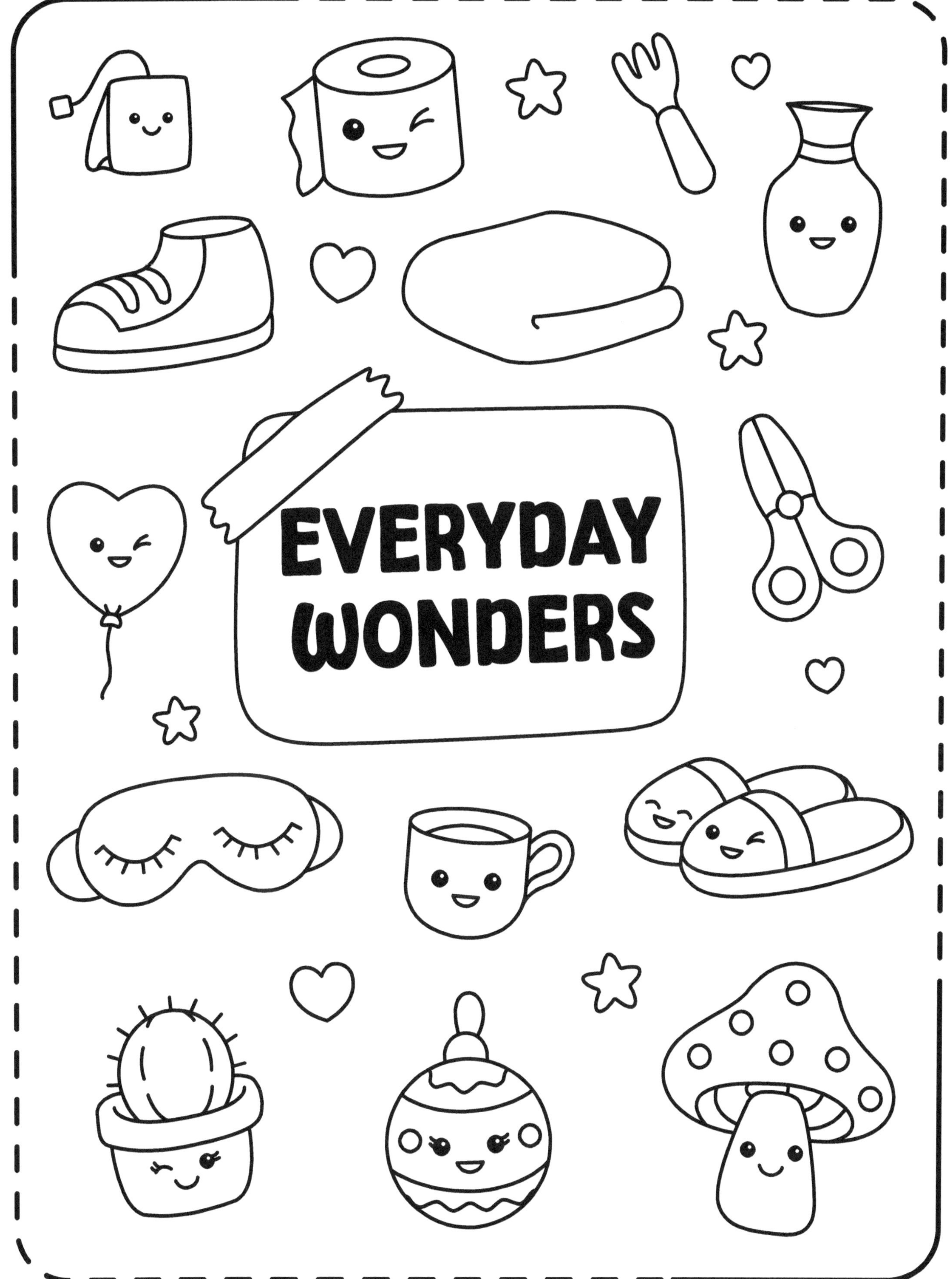
EVERYDAY
WONDERS

SUN

Practice:

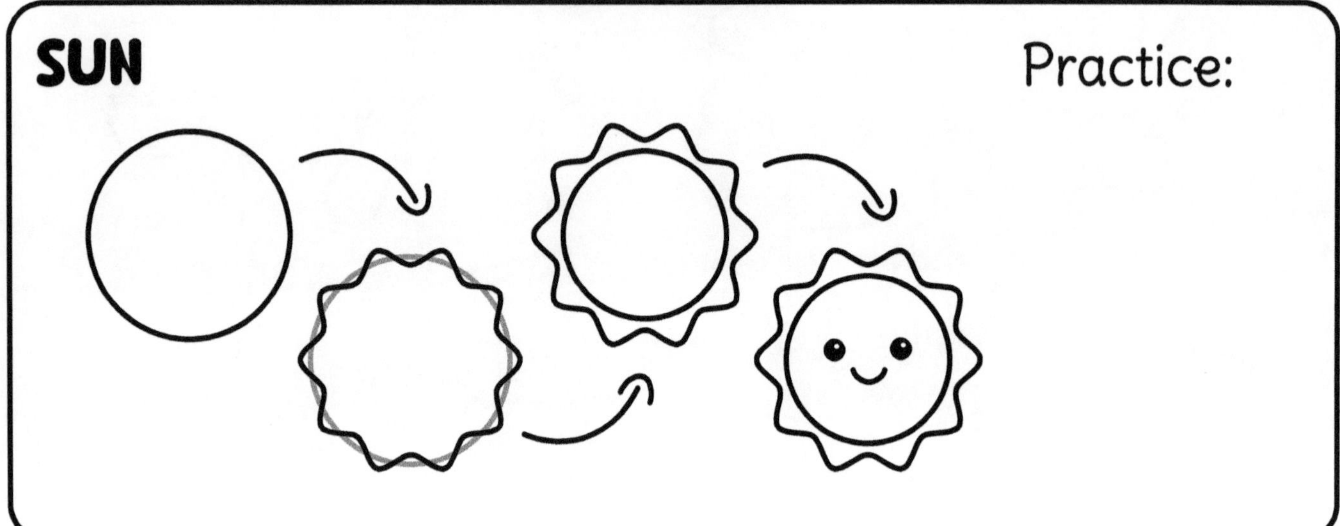

MOON

Practice:

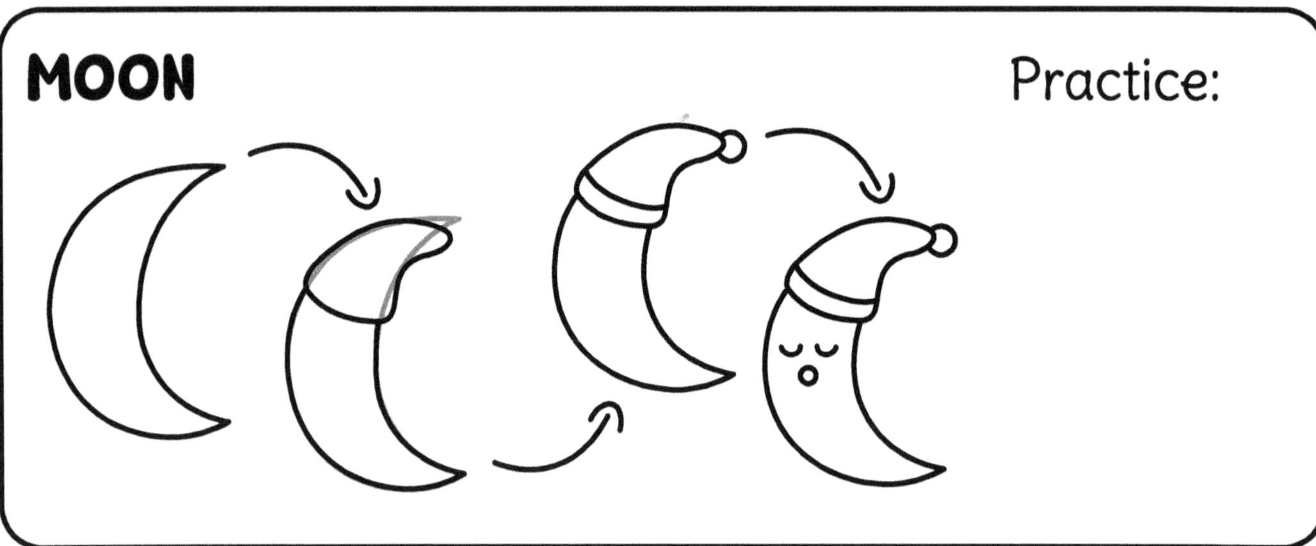

STARS

Practice

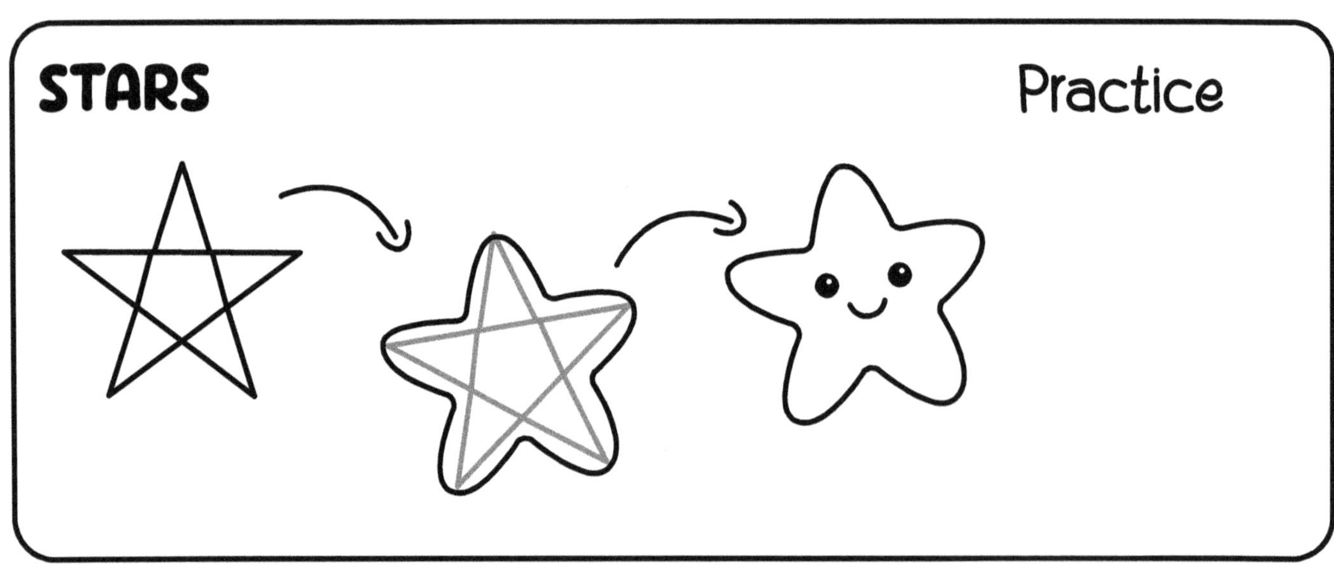

RAINBOW Practice:

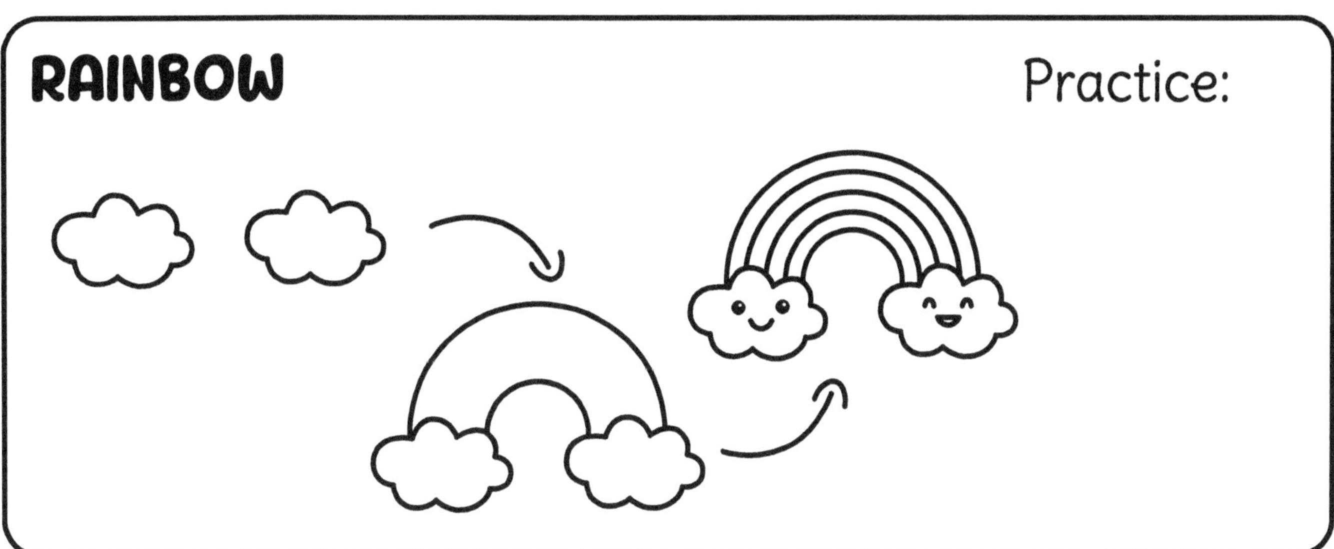

CLOUDS Practice:

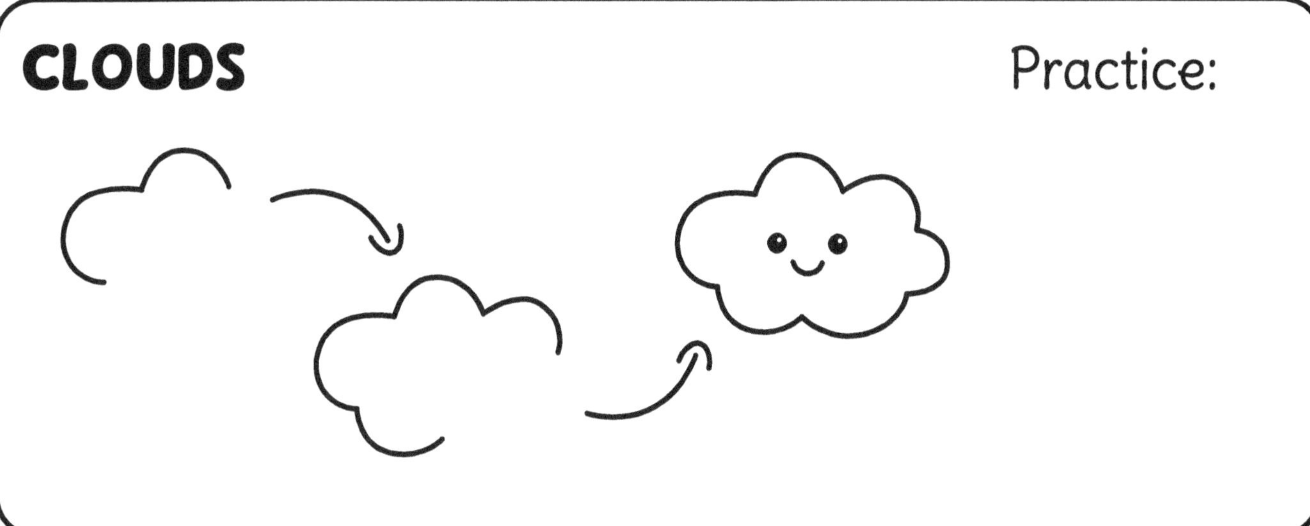

RAIN Practice

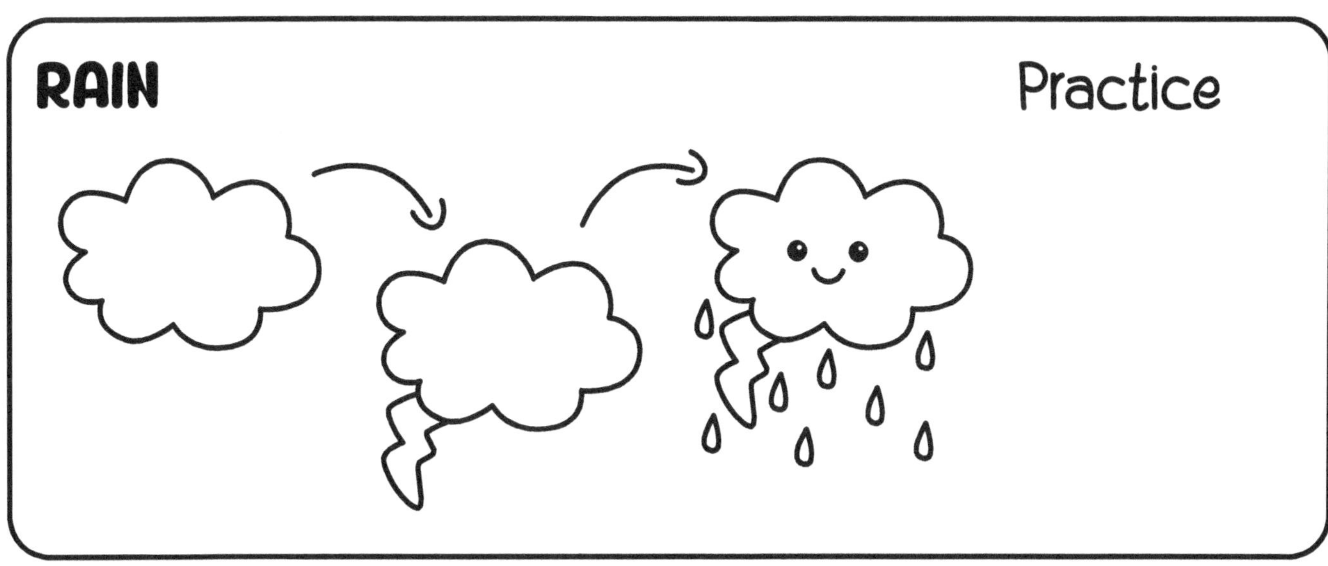

WATER DROP

SNOWFLAKE
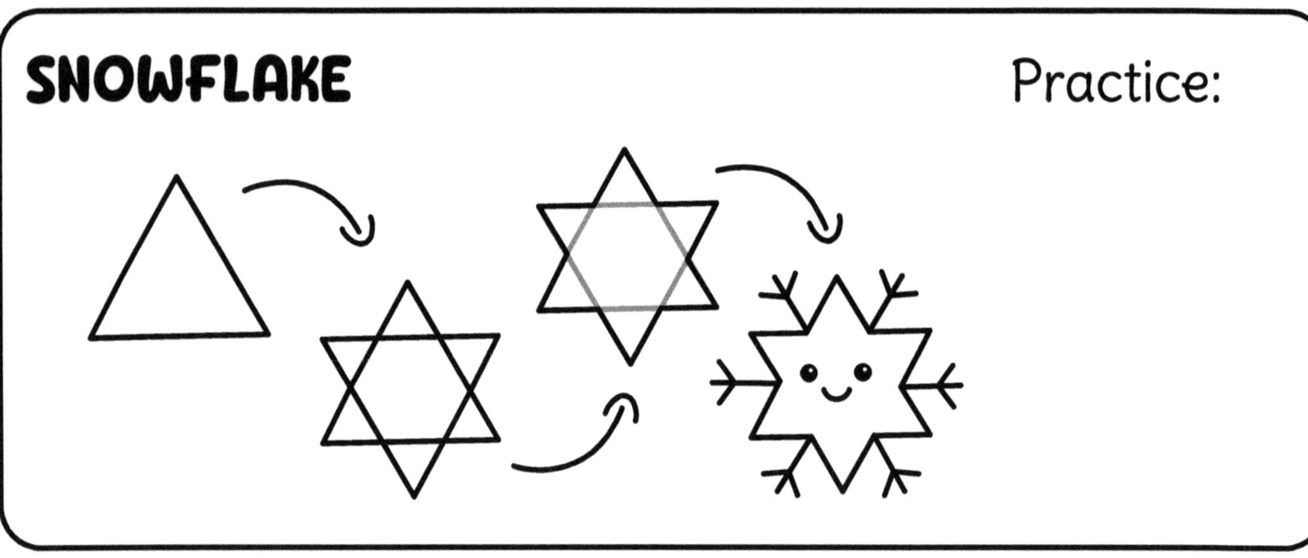

MOUNTAIN
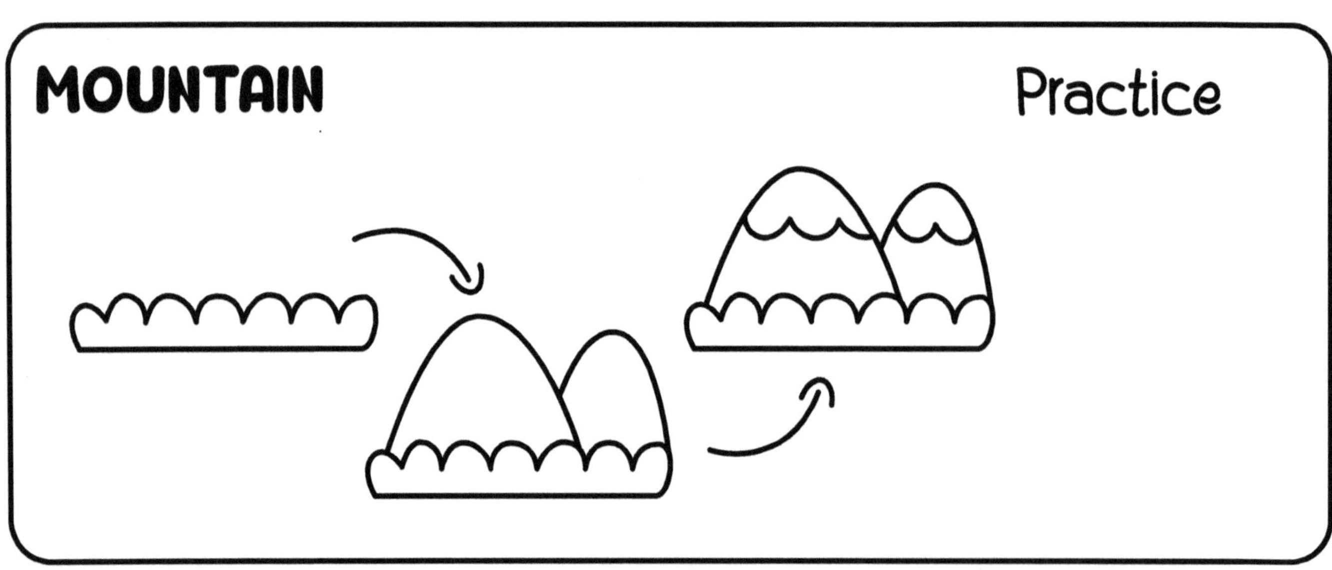

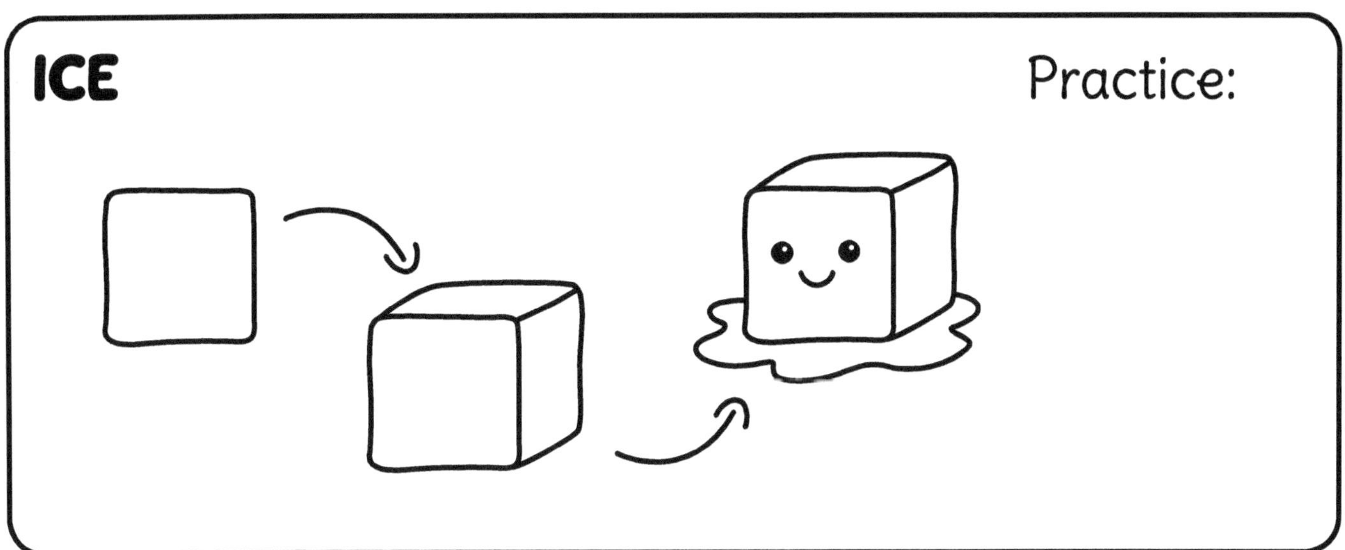

ICE
Practice:

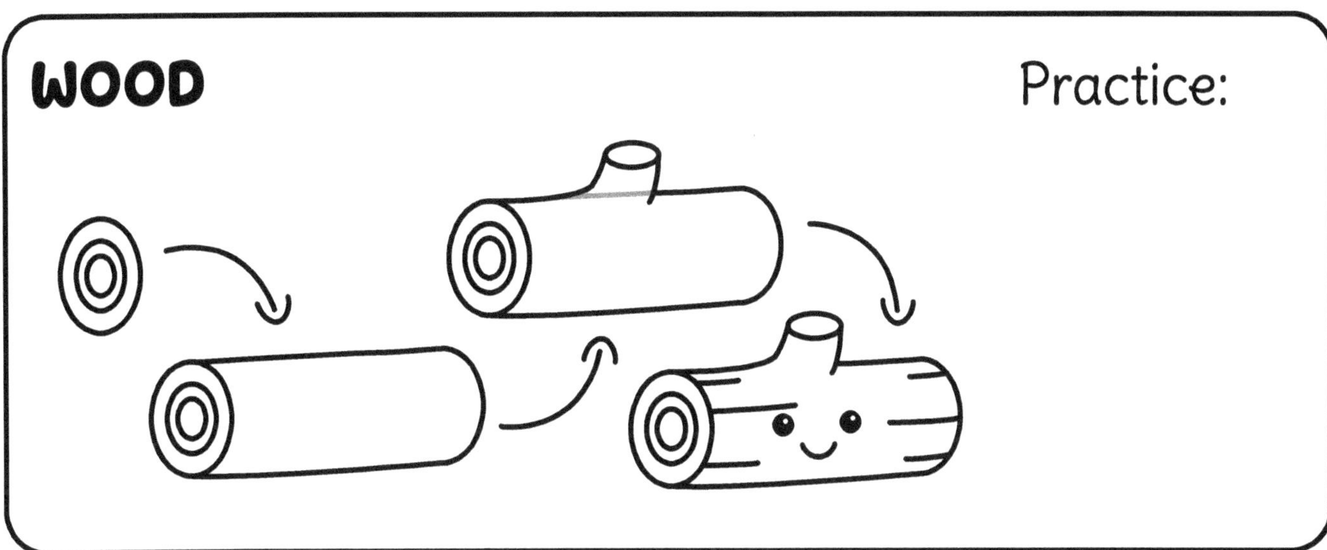

WOOD
Practice:

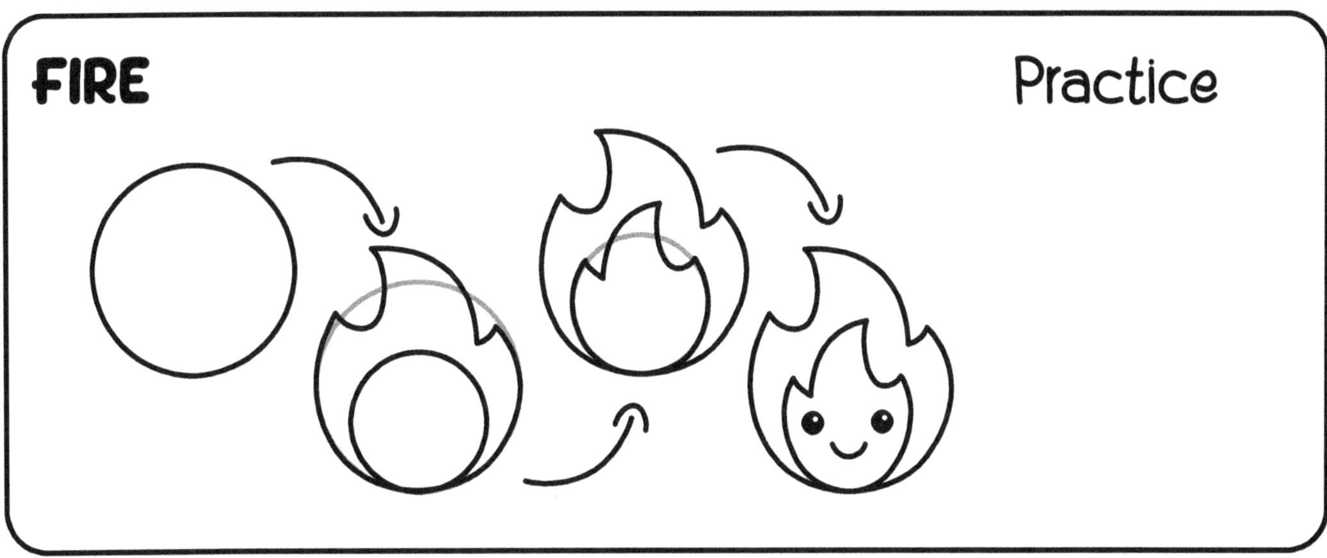

FIRE
Practice

EARTH
Practice:

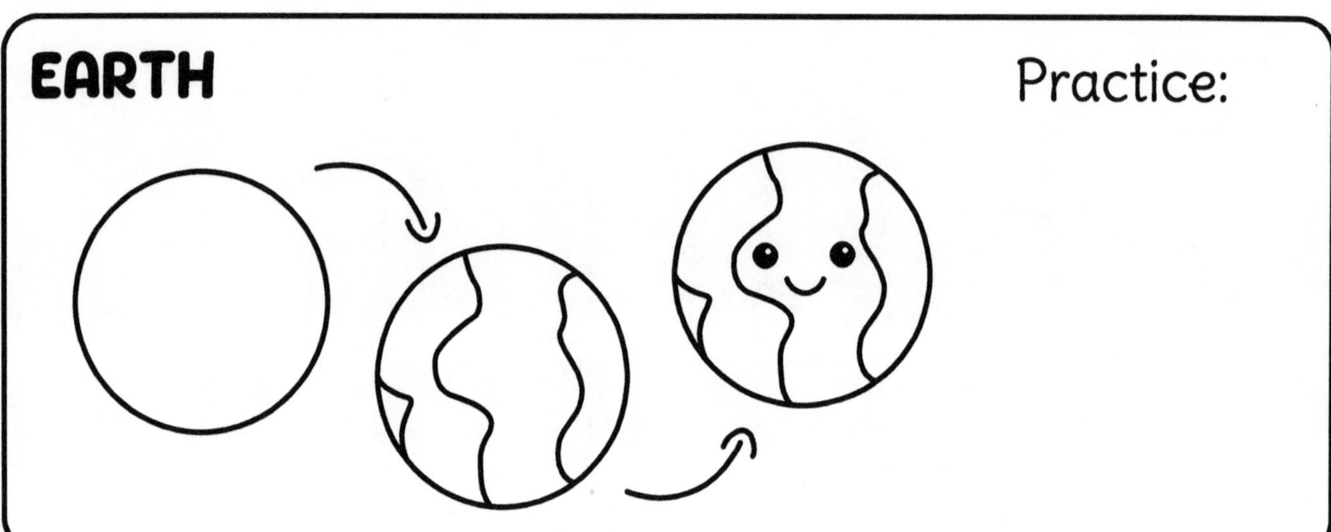

SATURN
Practice:

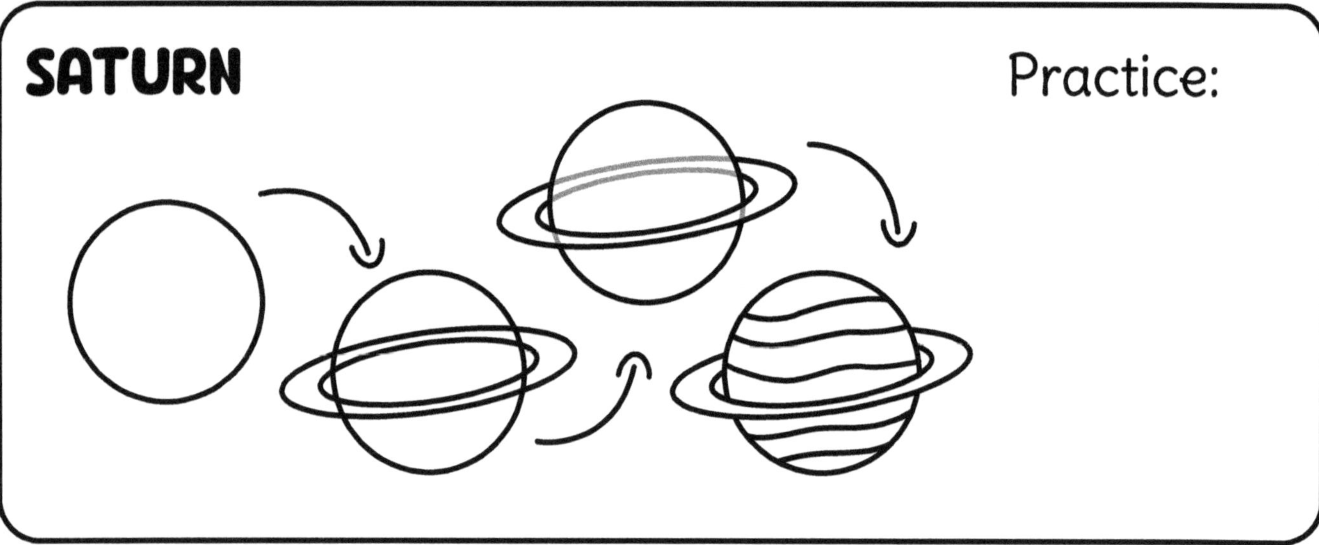

TORNADO
Practice

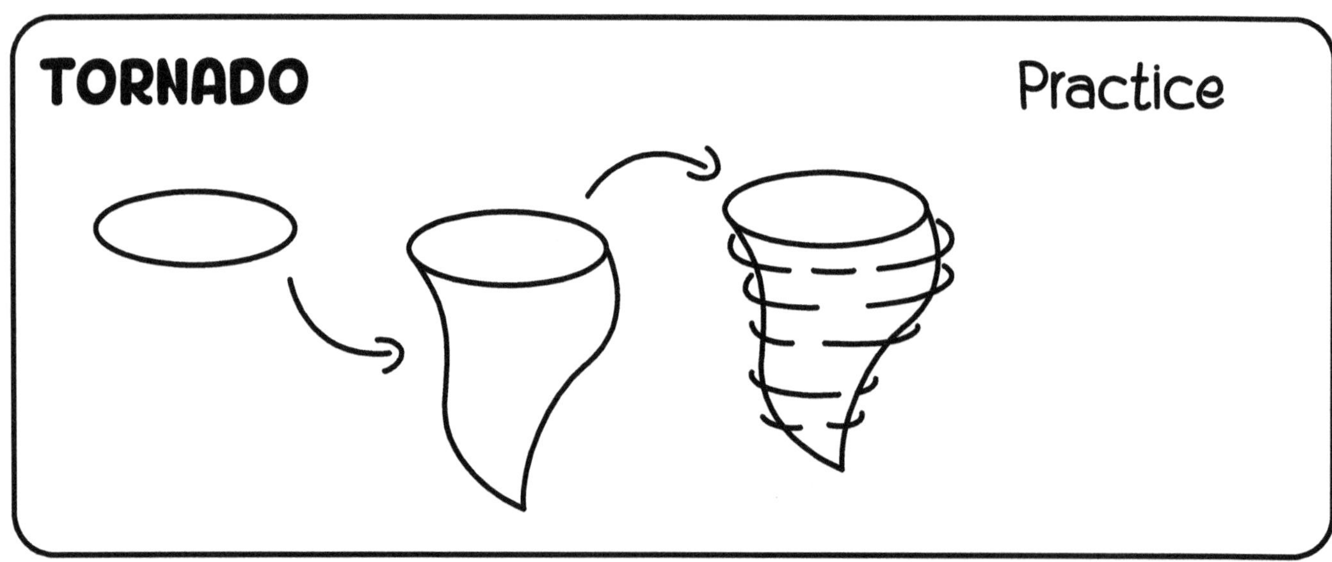

PLANTS

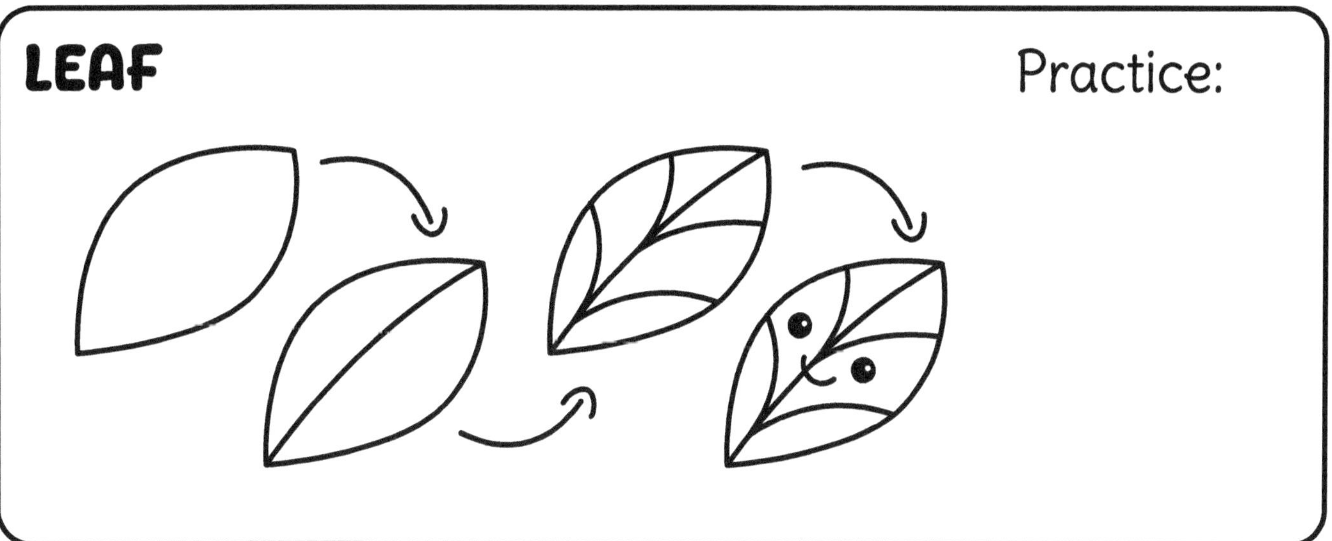

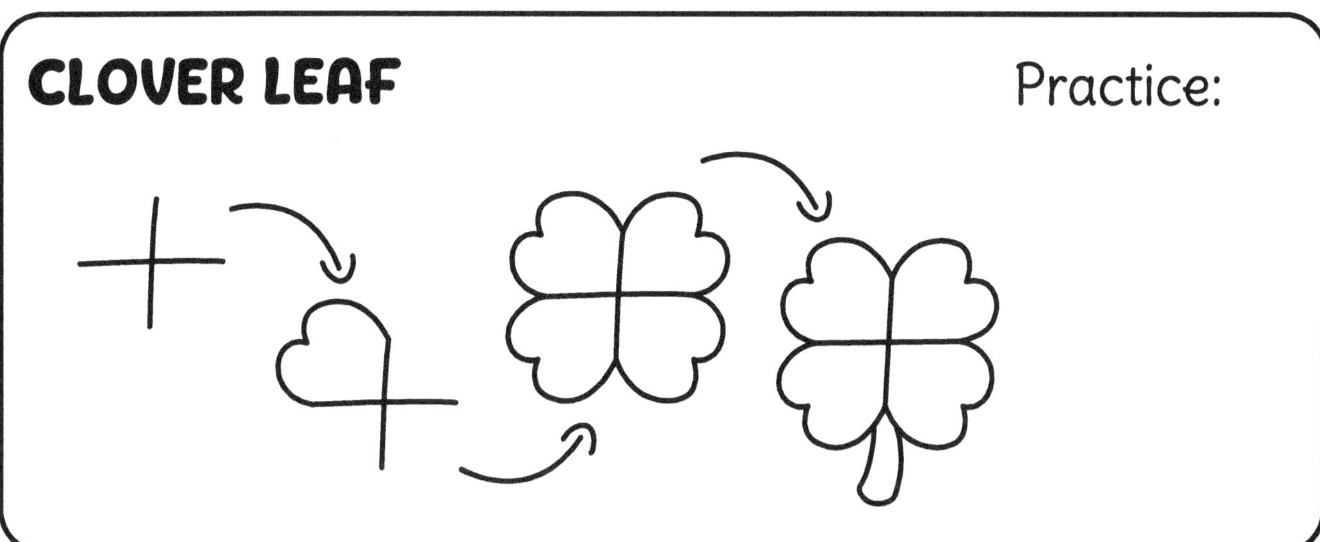

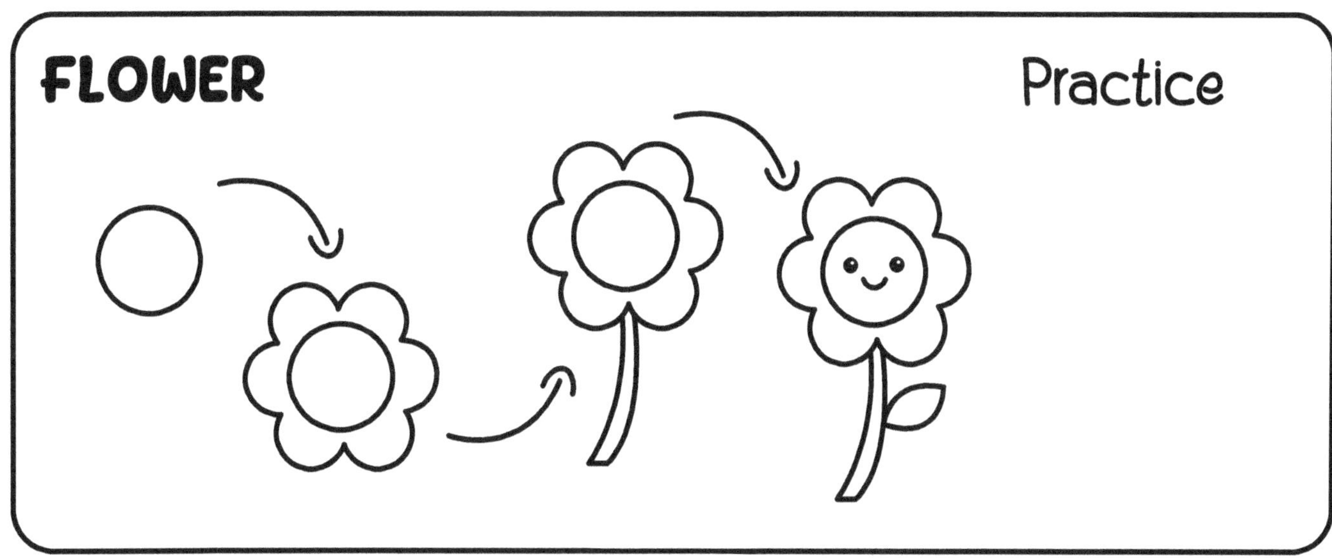

MUSHROOM

Practice:

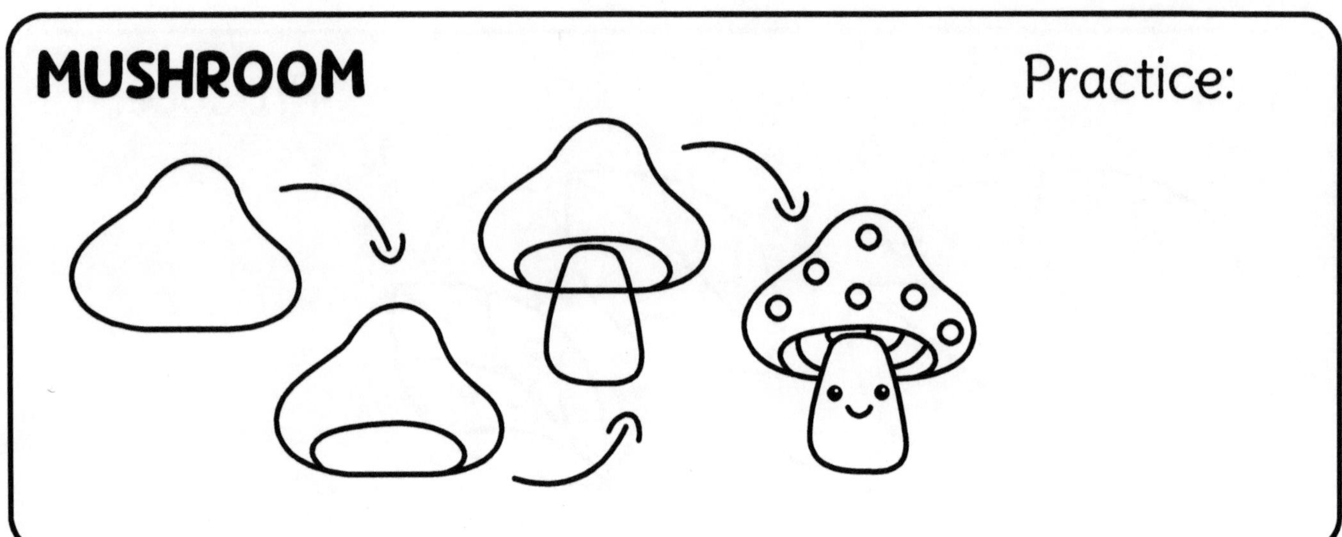

CACTUS

Practice:

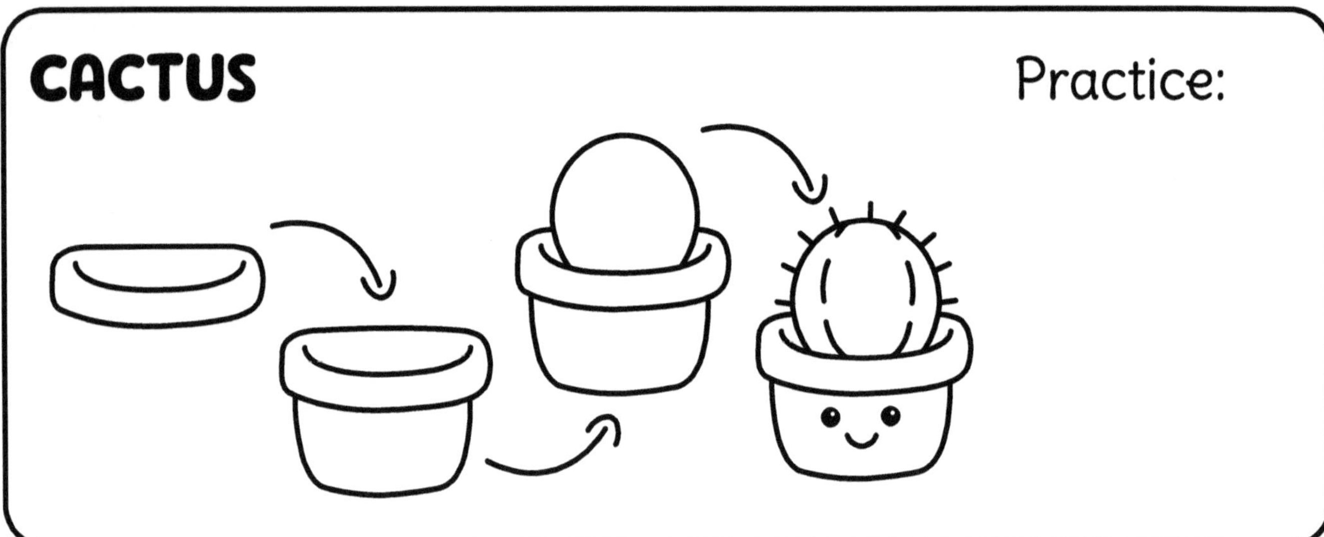

BONSAI

Practice

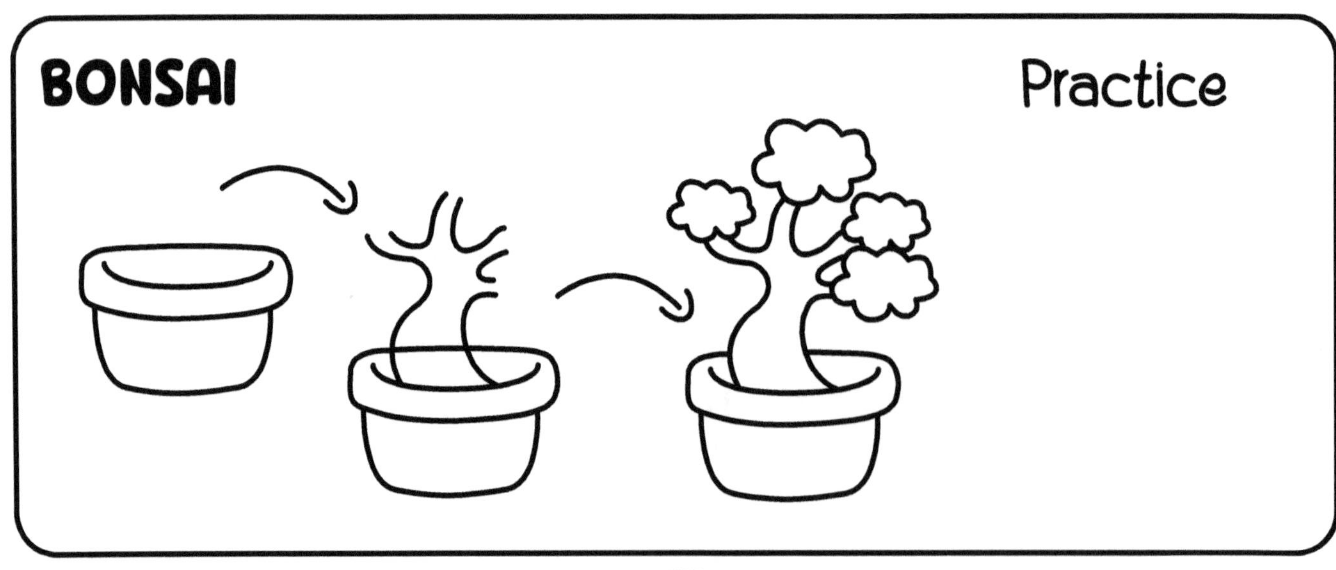

SNOWMAN

Practice:

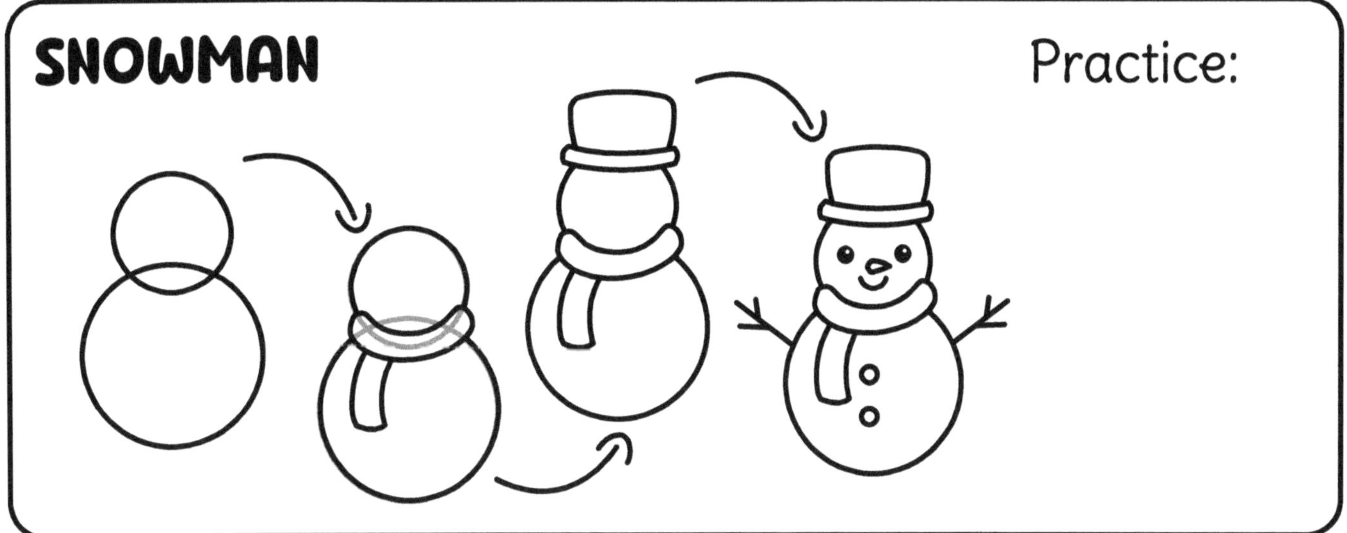

CHRISTMAS TREE

Practice:

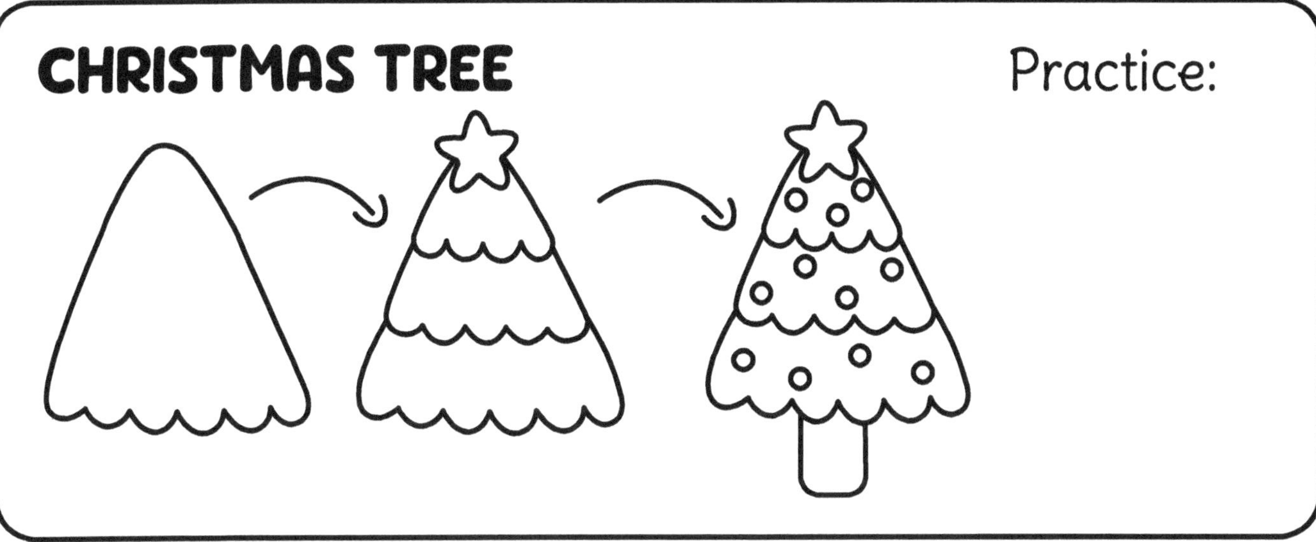

CHRISTMAS HAT

Practice

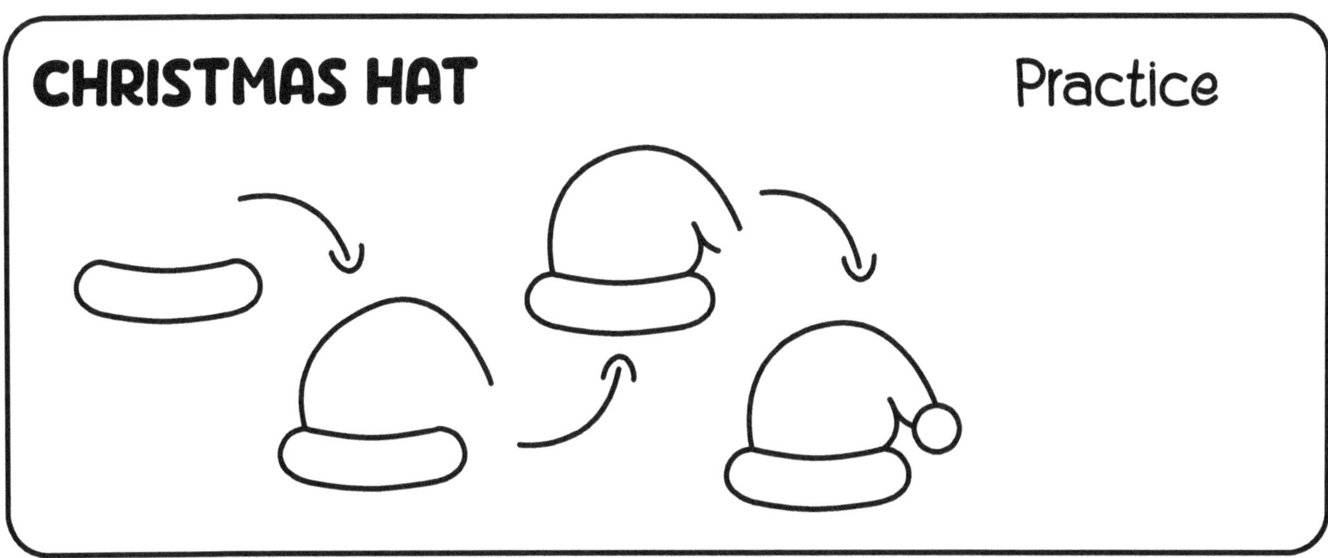

CHRISTMAS BALL

Practice:

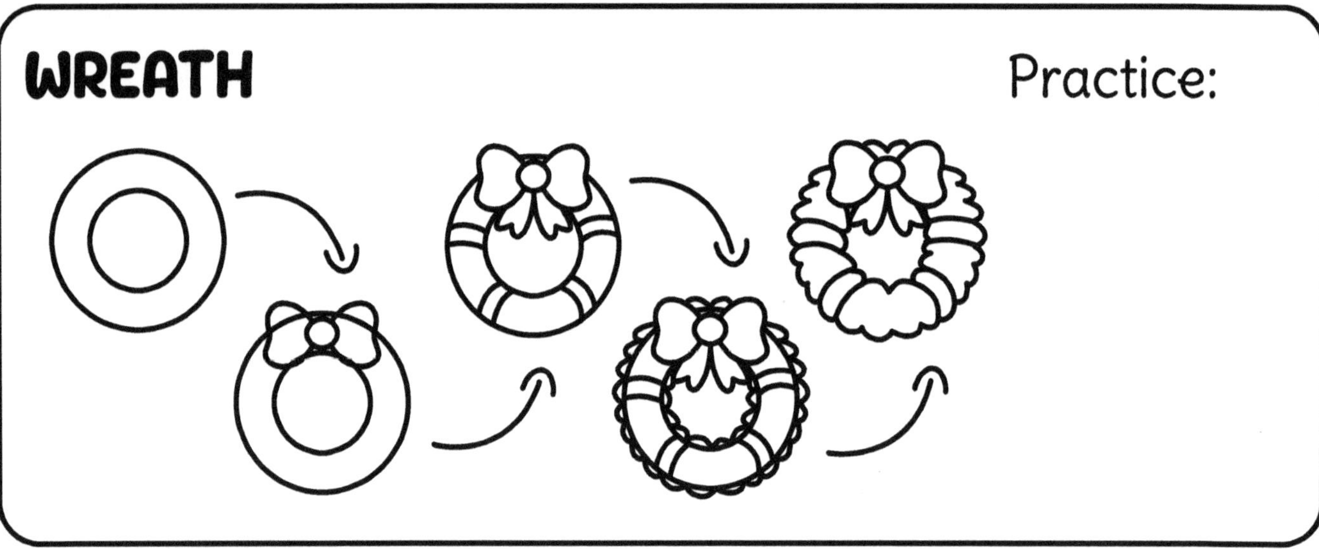

WREATH

Practice:

PUMPKIN BASKET

Practice

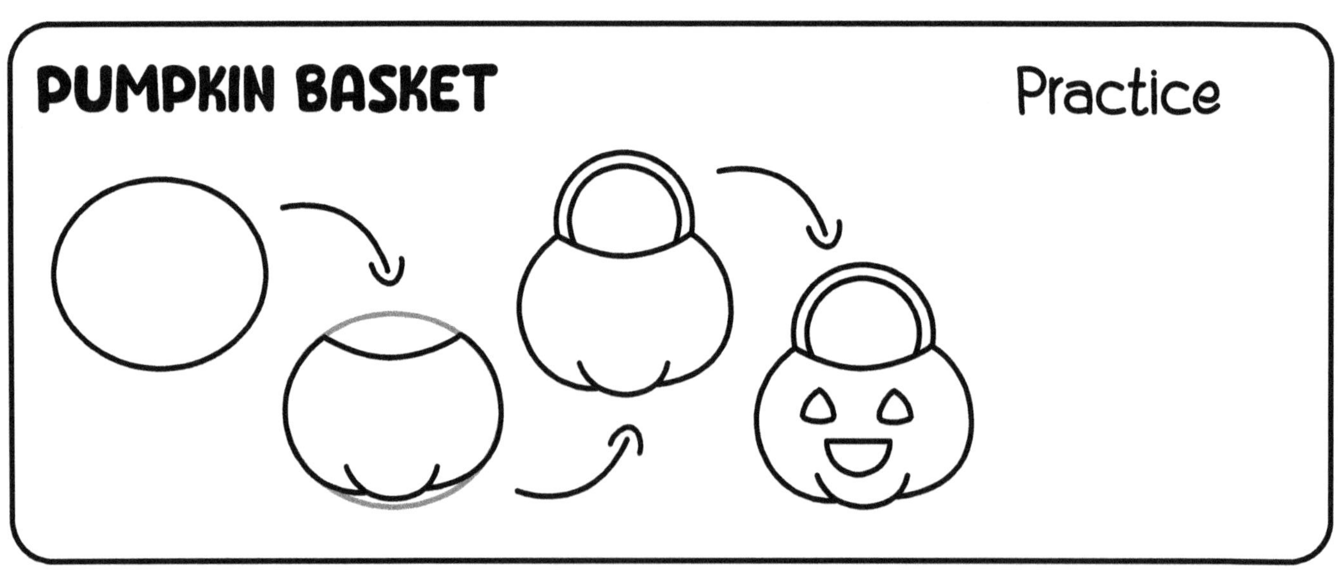

WITCH HAT

Practice:

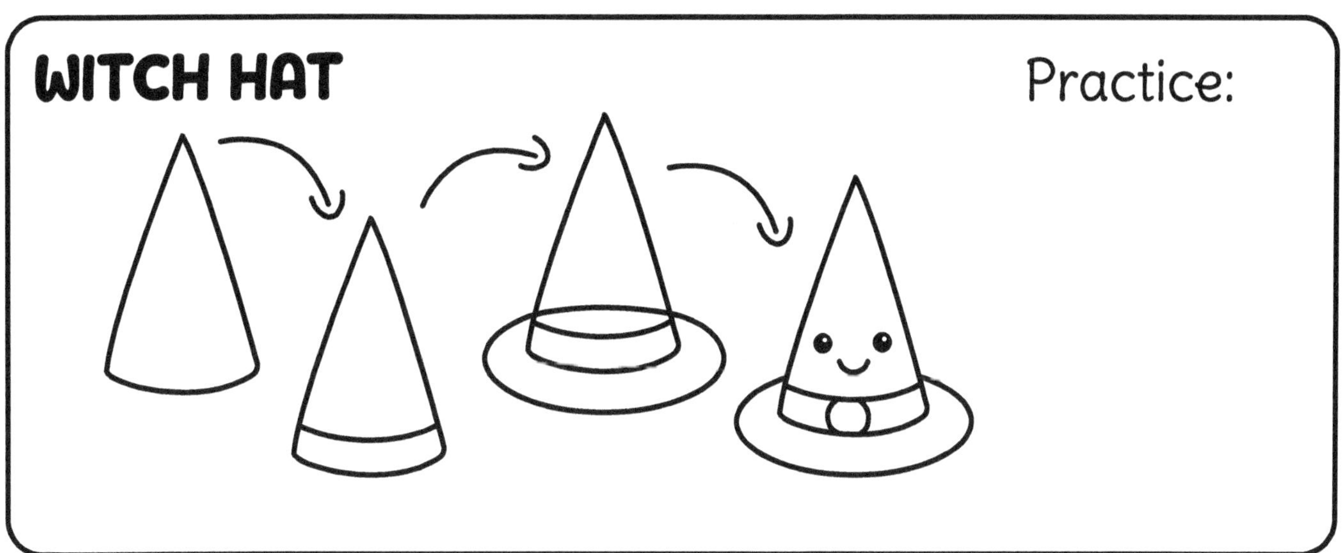

BROOM

Practice:

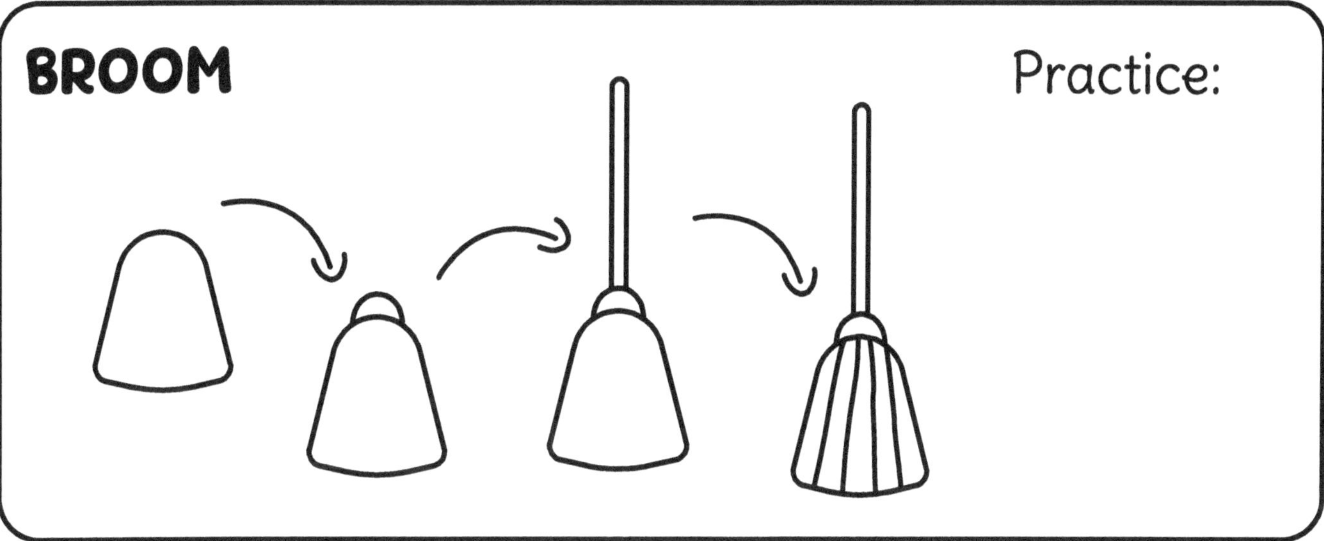

GHOST

Practice

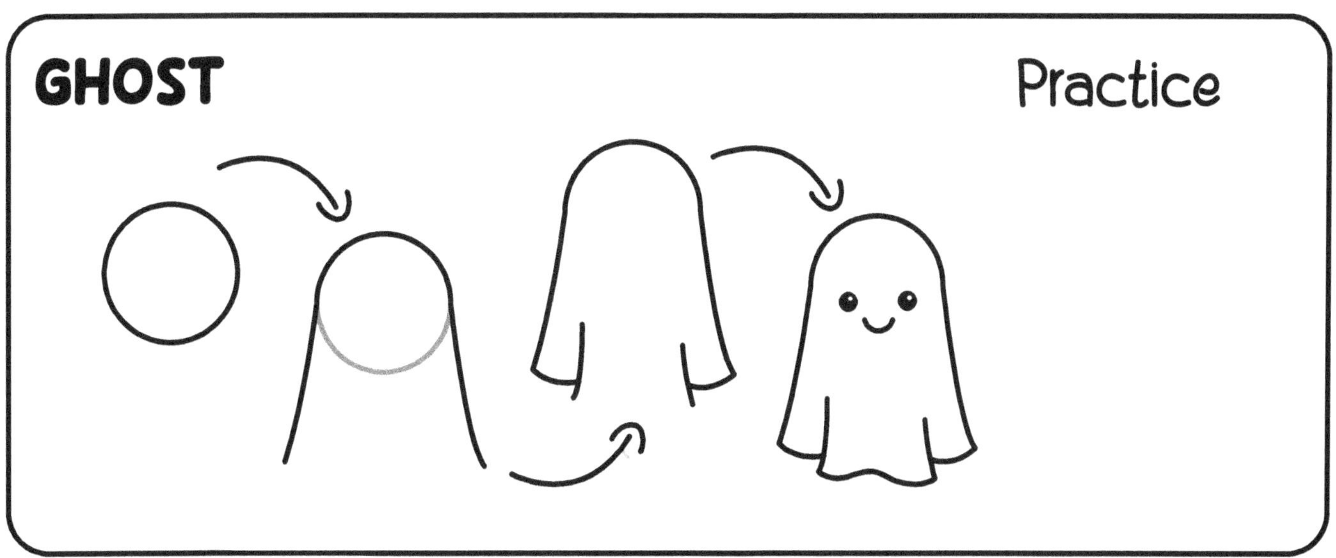

SKULL

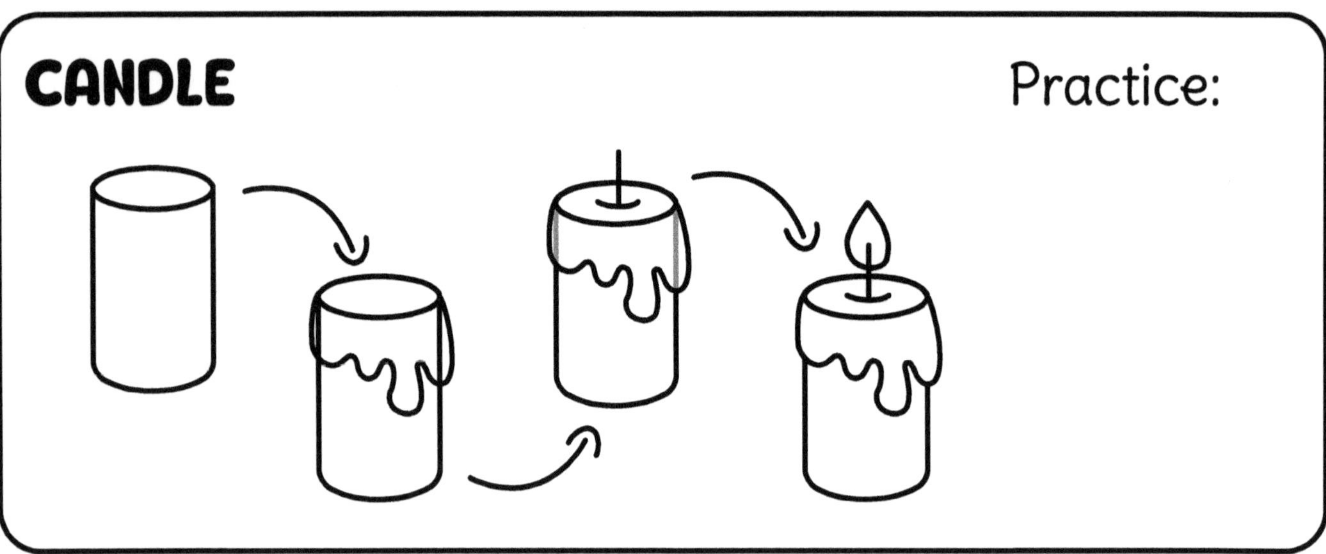

CANDLE

EYEBALL CANDY

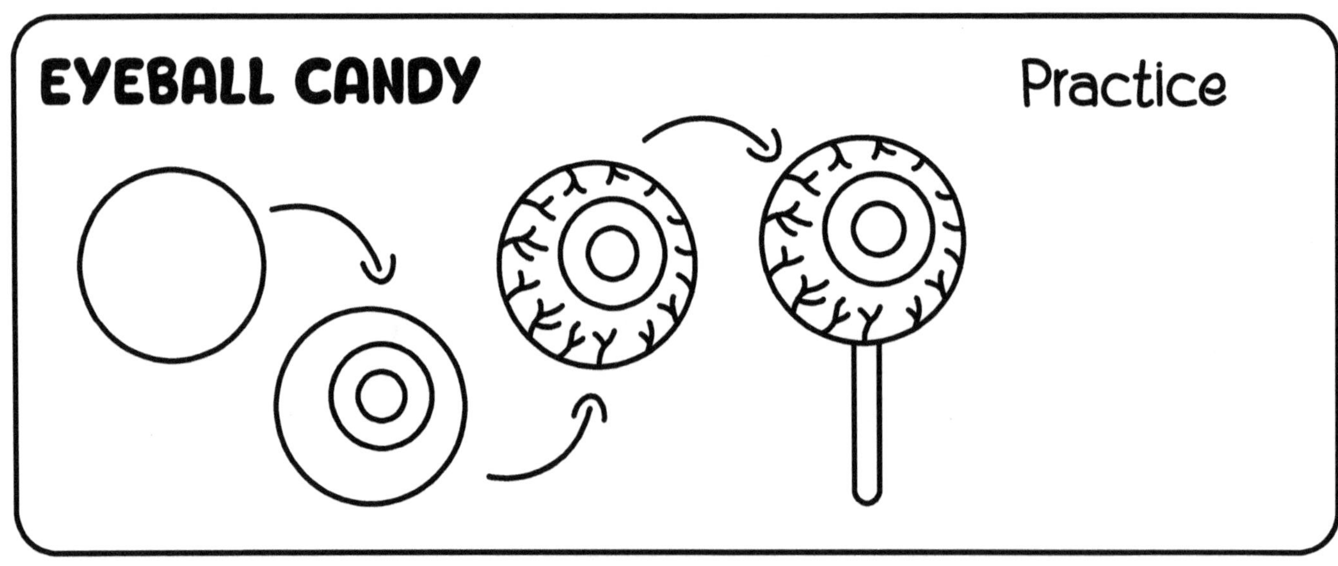

CLOTHES

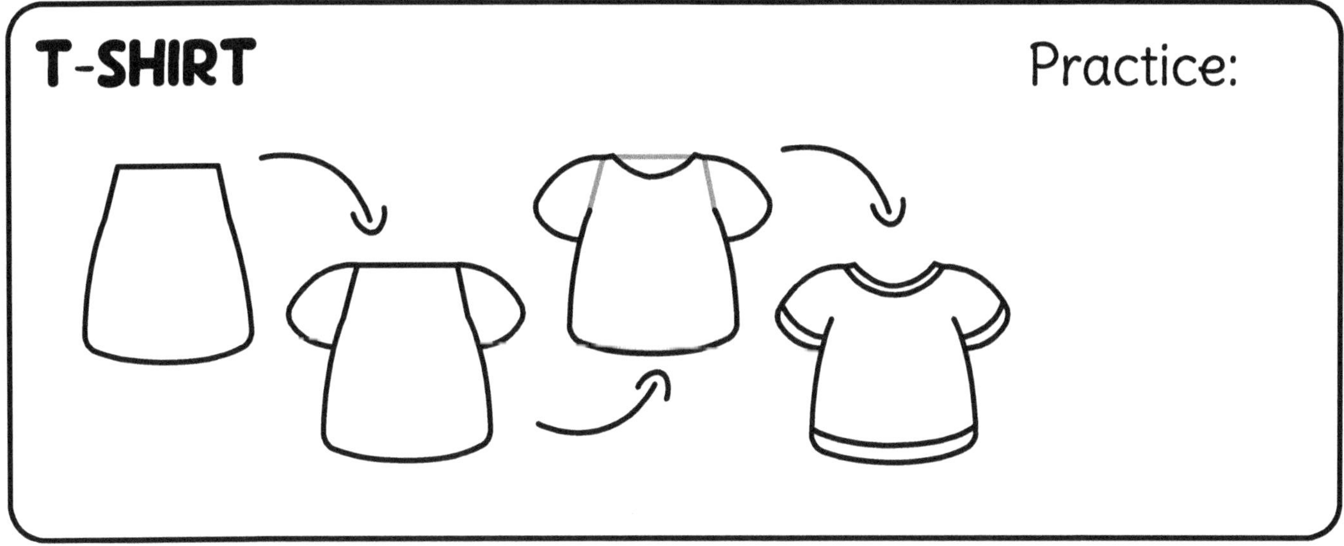

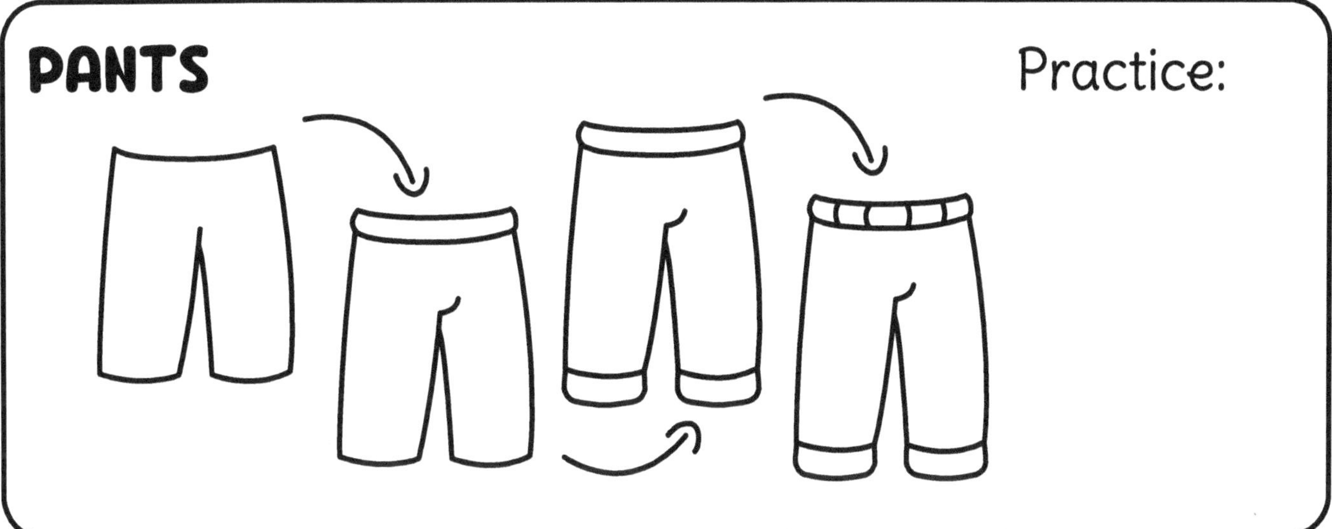

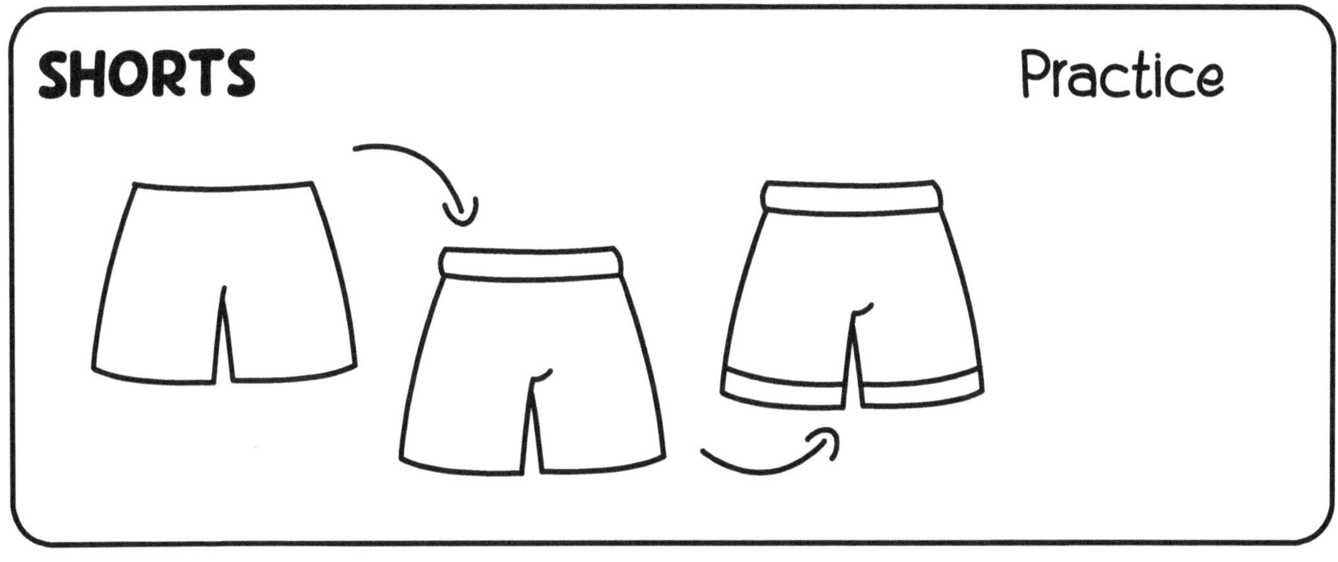

DRESS

Practice:

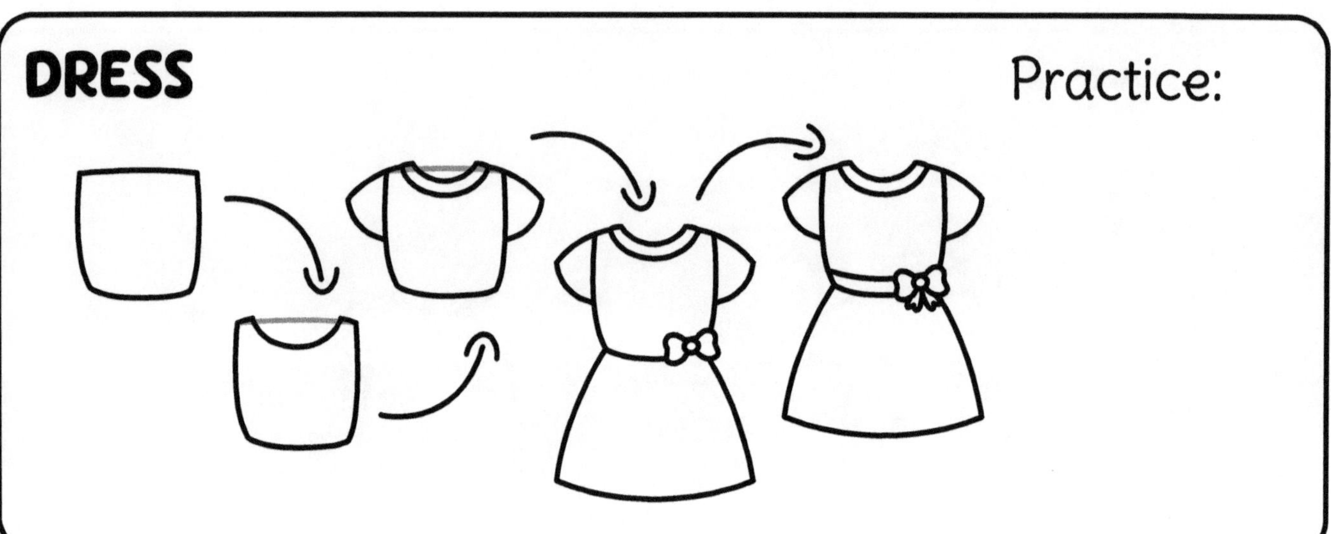

SKIRT

Practice:

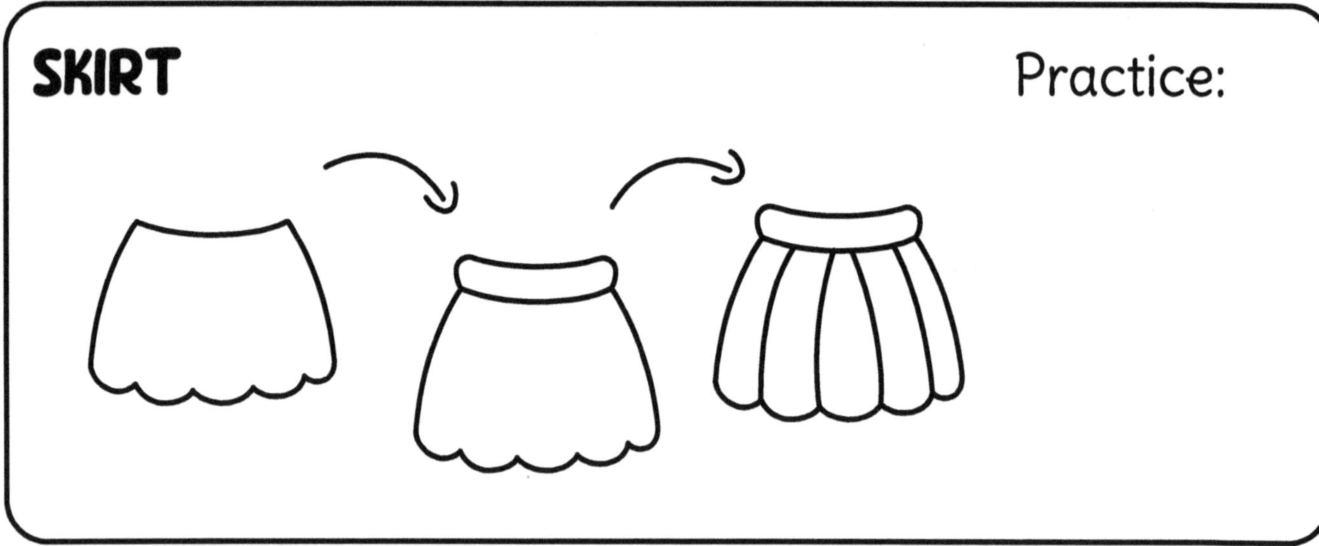

UNDERWEAR

Practice

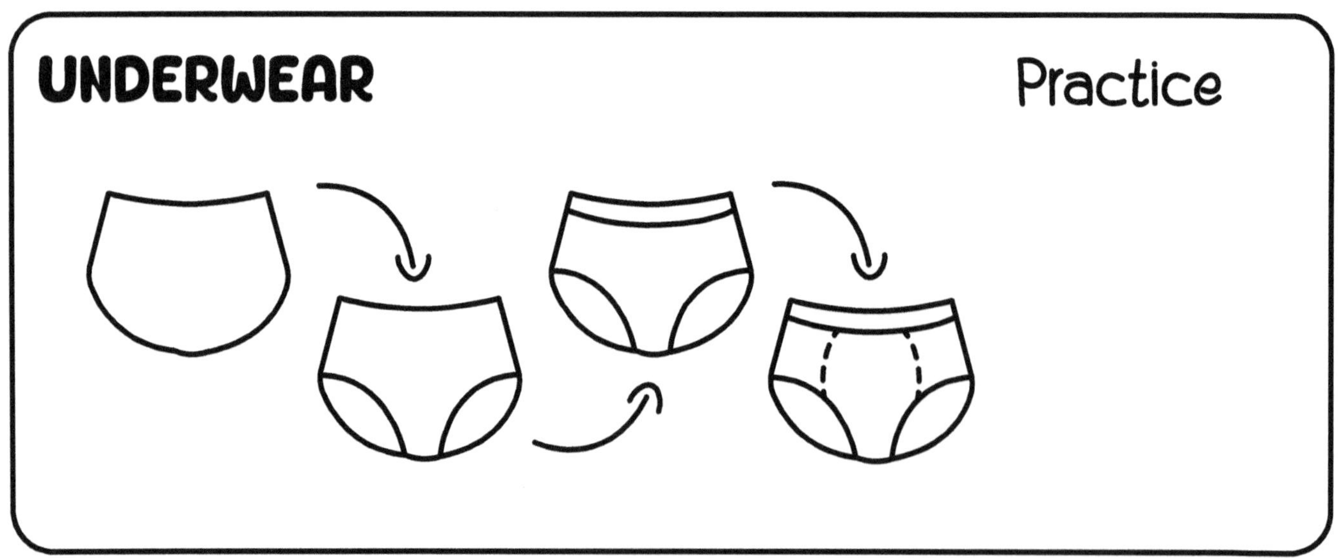

SWEATER

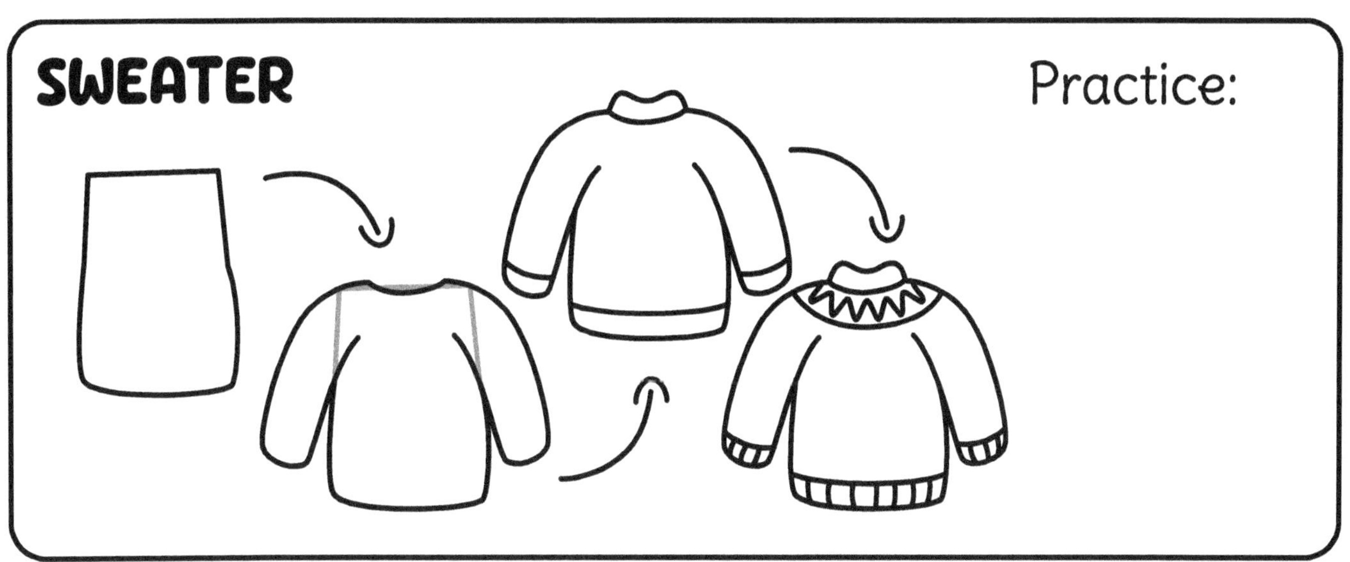

Practice:

JACKET

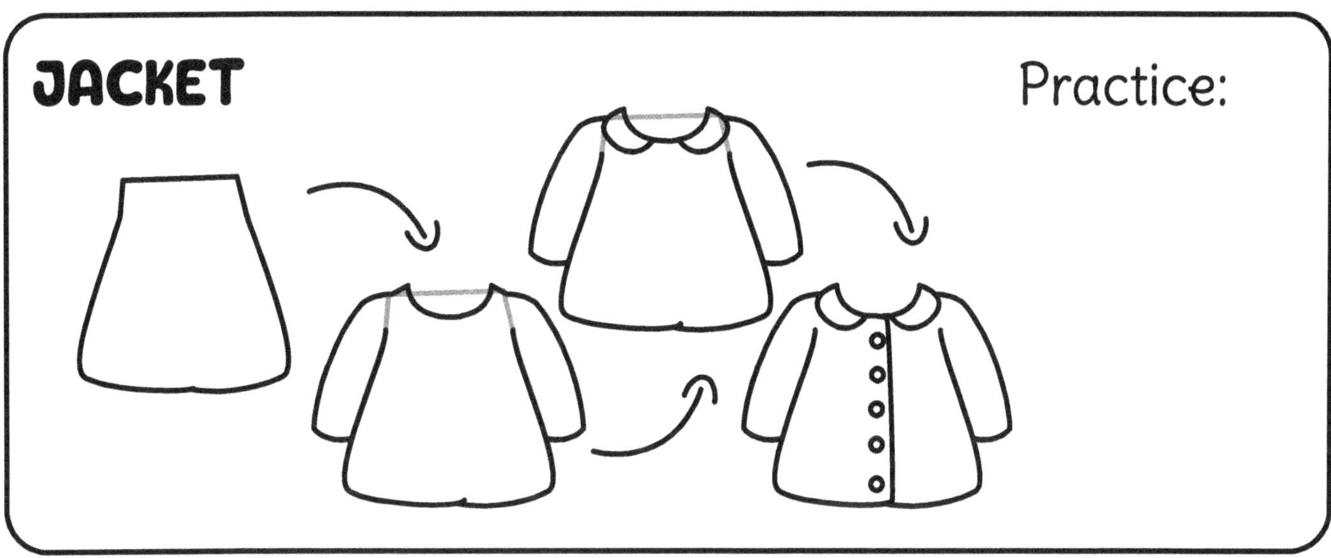

Practice:

SWIM WEAR

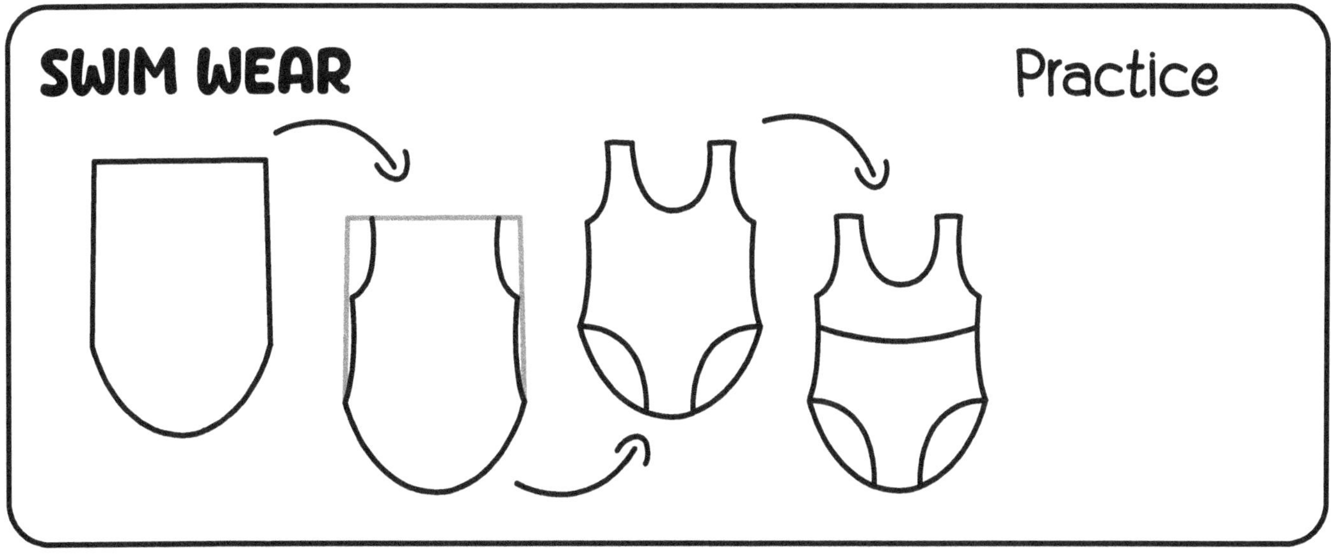

Practice

SNEAKERS

Practice:

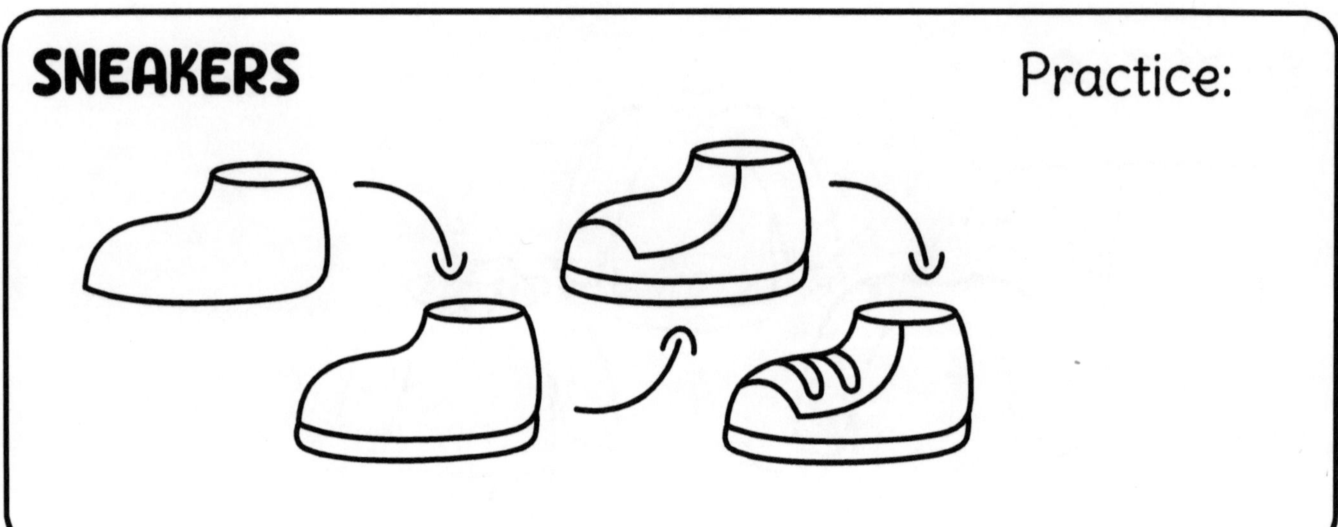

BOOTS

Practice:

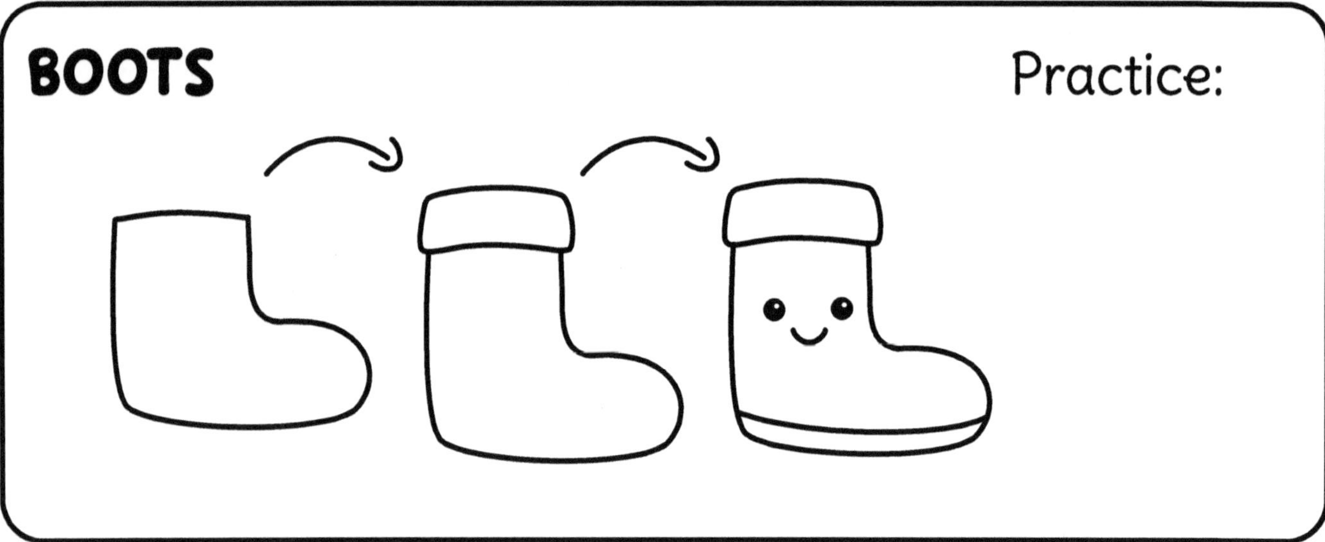

SLIPPERS

Practice

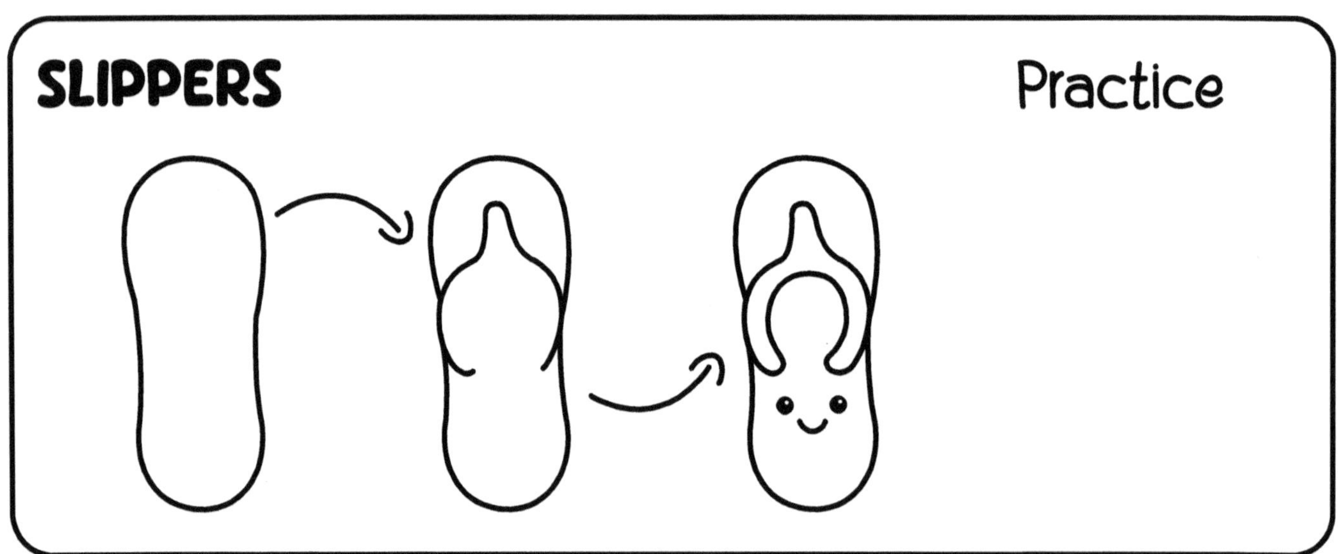

HOUSE SHOES

Practice:

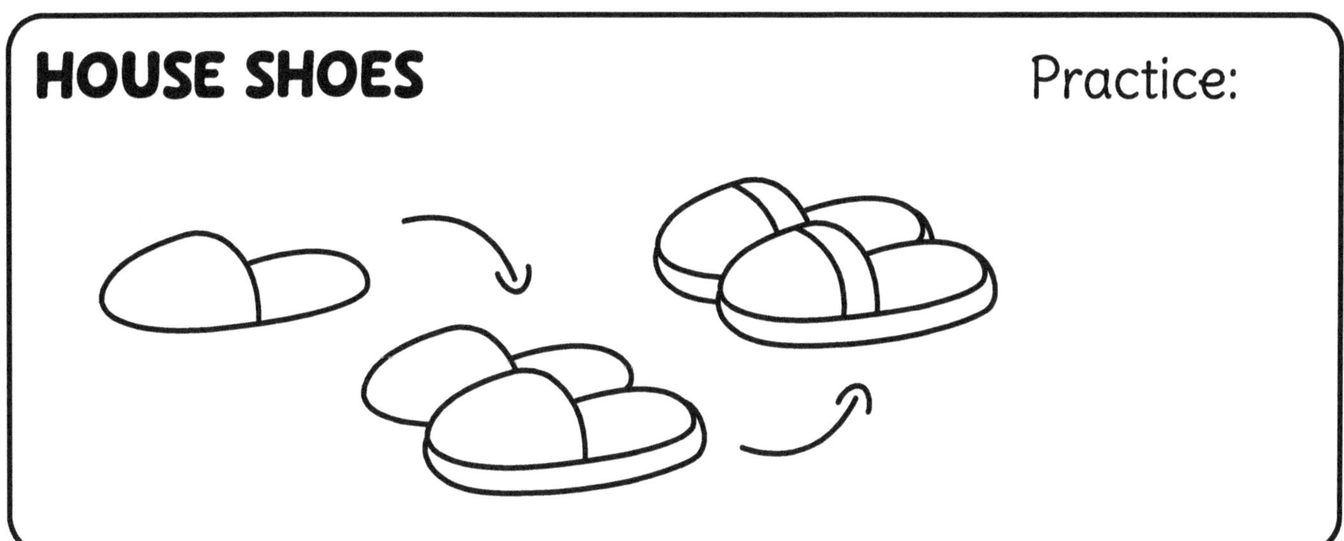

SOCKS

Practice:

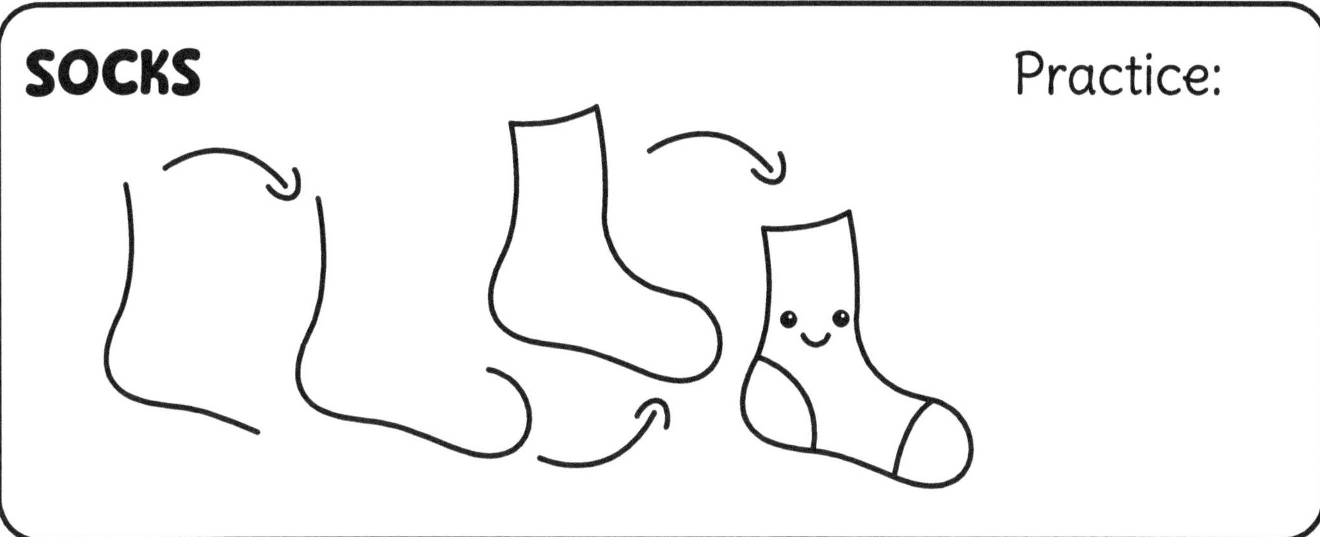

OVERALLS

Practice

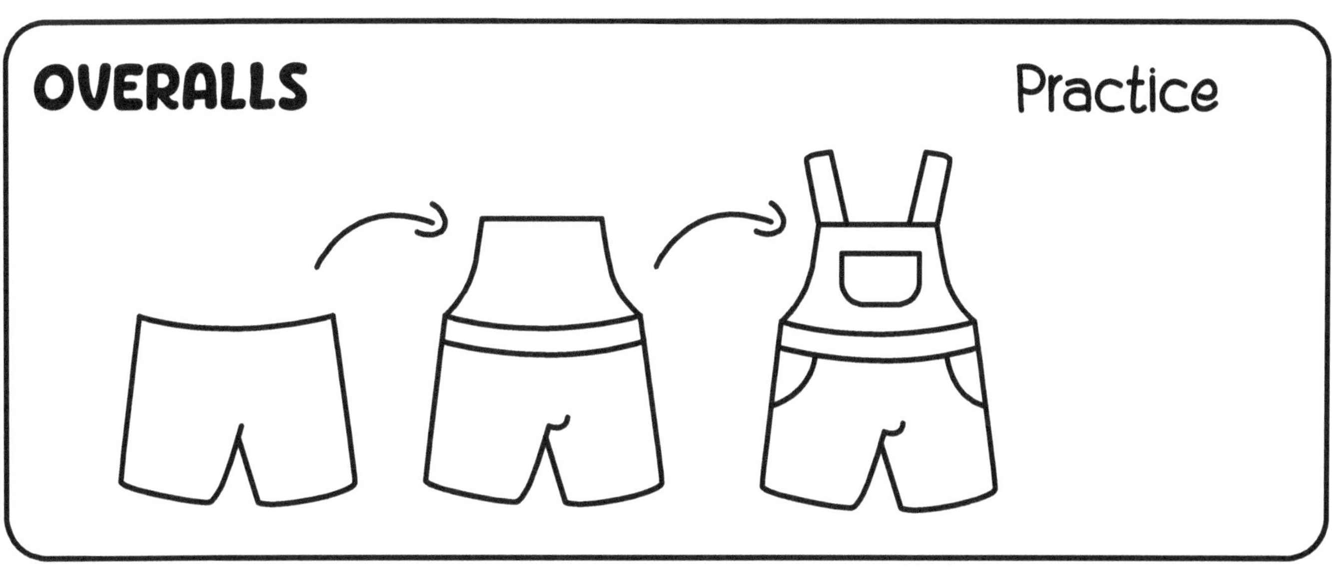

ACCESSORIES

CAP

Practice:

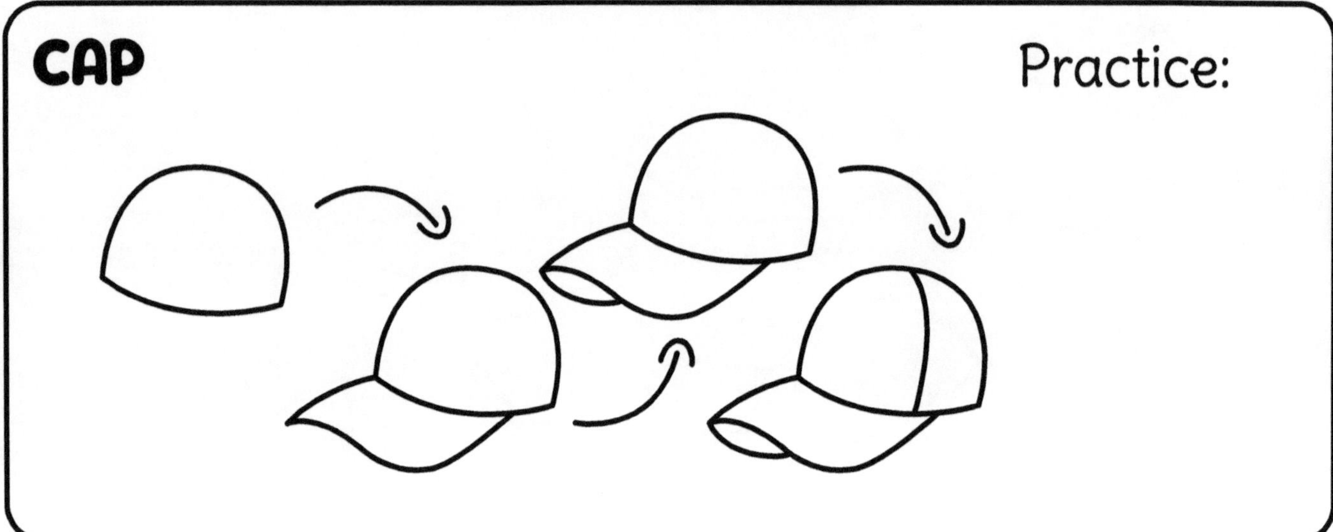

BUCKET HAT

Practice:

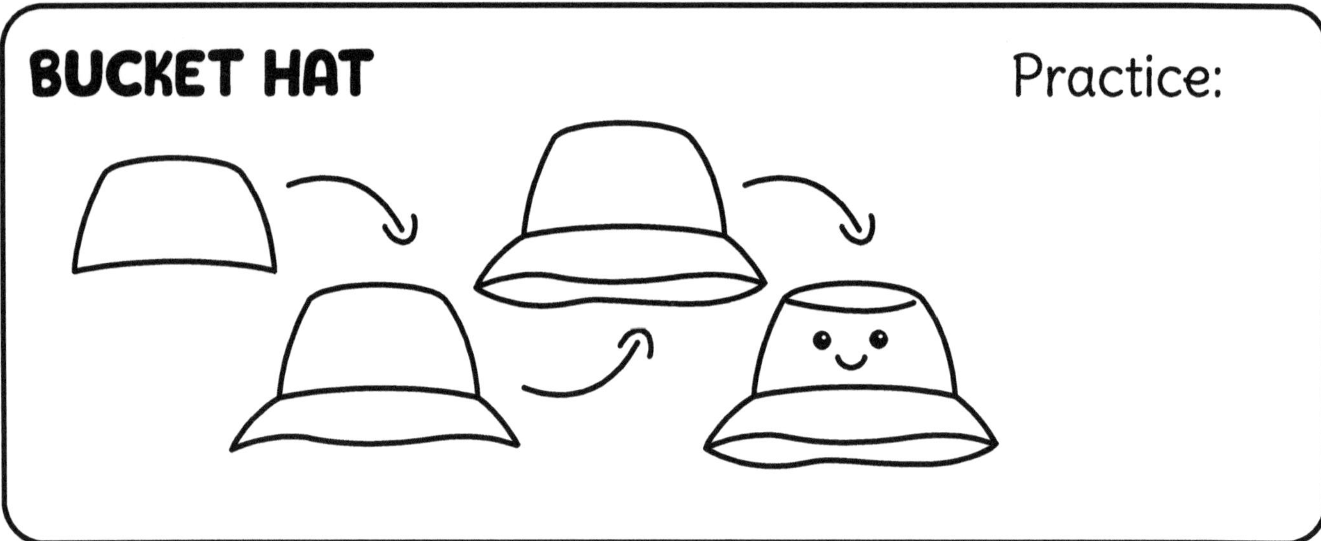

GLOVES

Practice

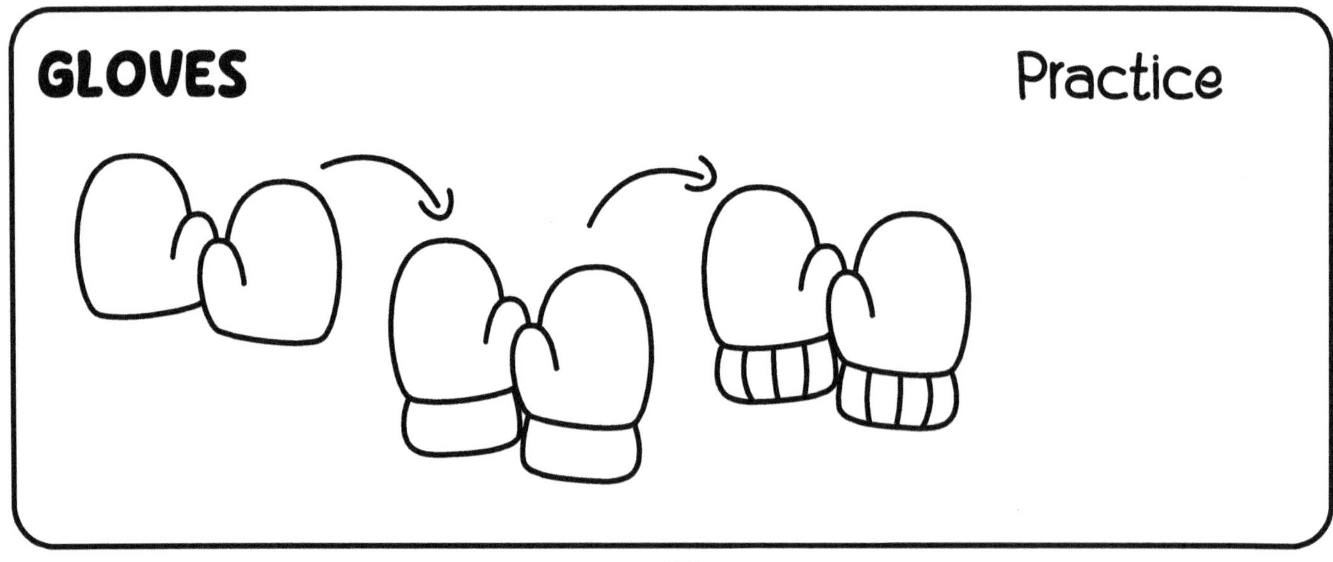

MUFFS

Practice:

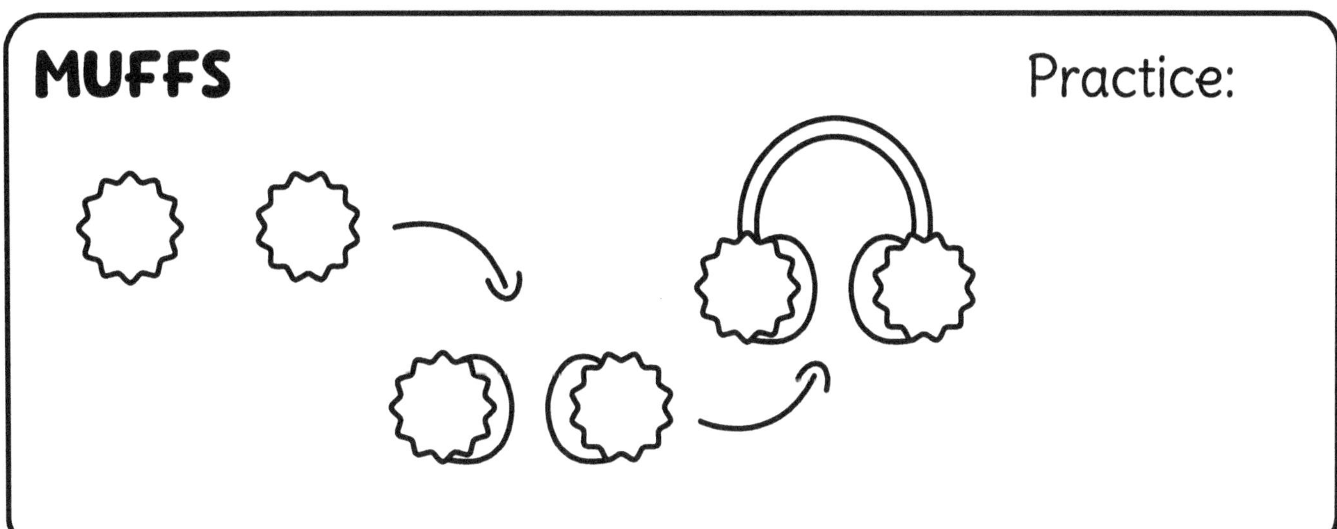

PURSE

Practice:

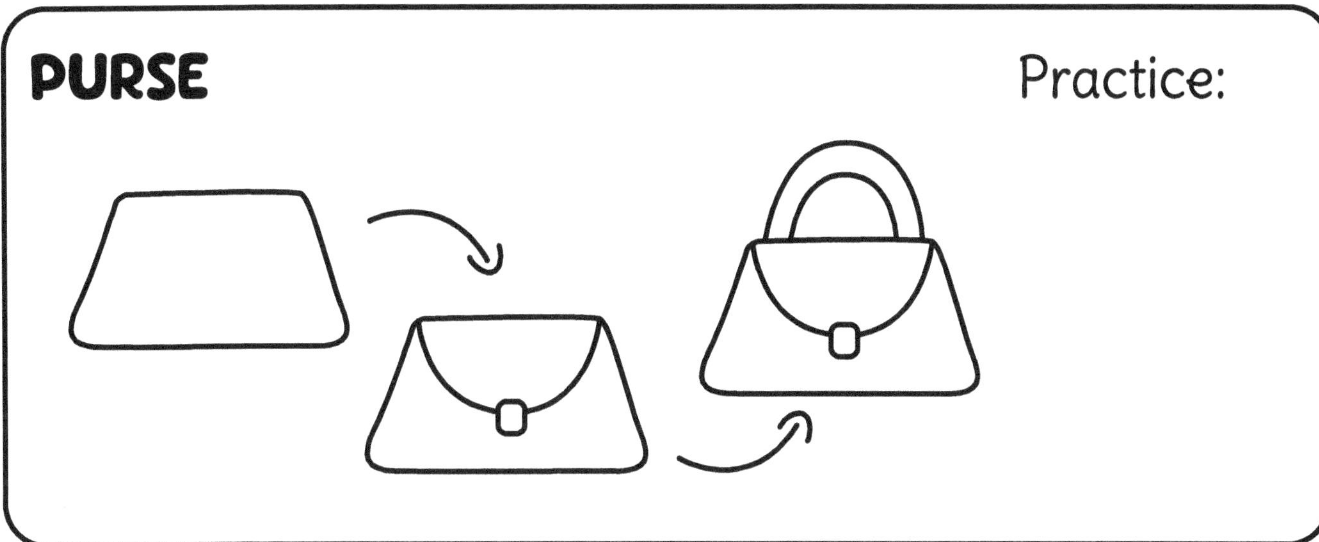

HAIRCLIP

Practice

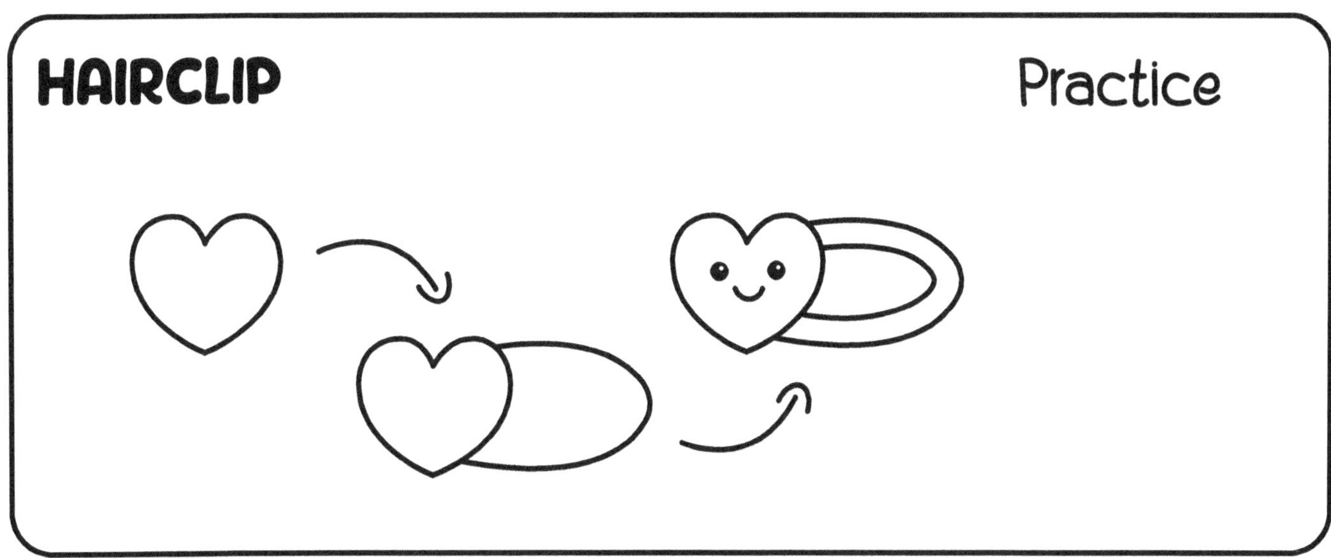

EARRINGS

Practice:

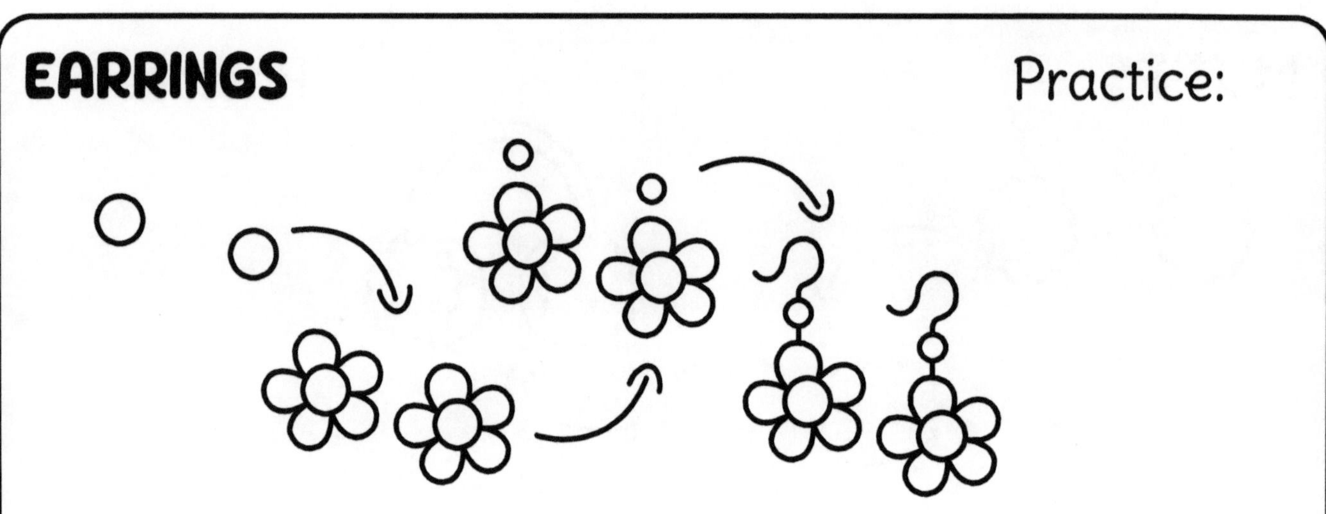

RINGS

Practice:

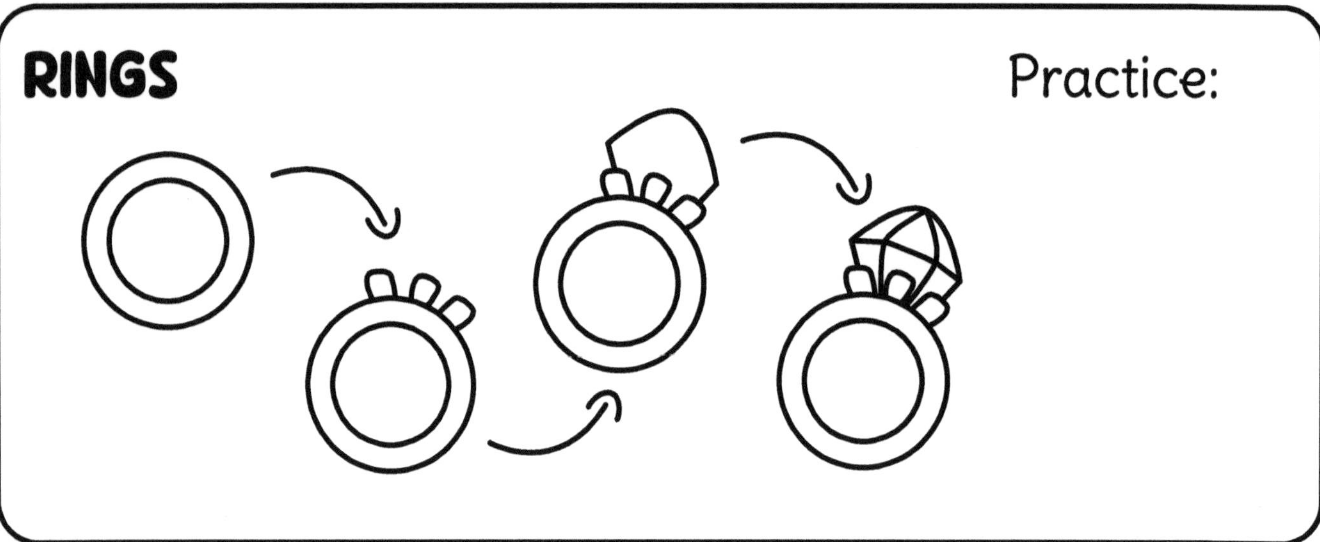

CLAW CLIP

Practice

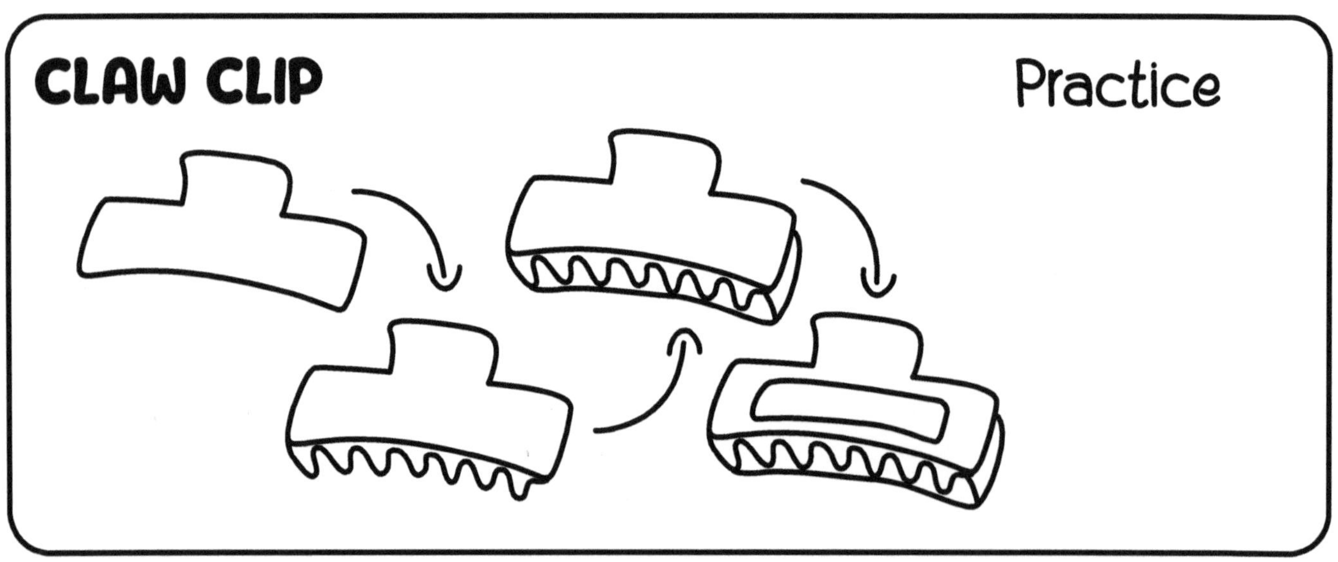

EYE MASK

Practice:

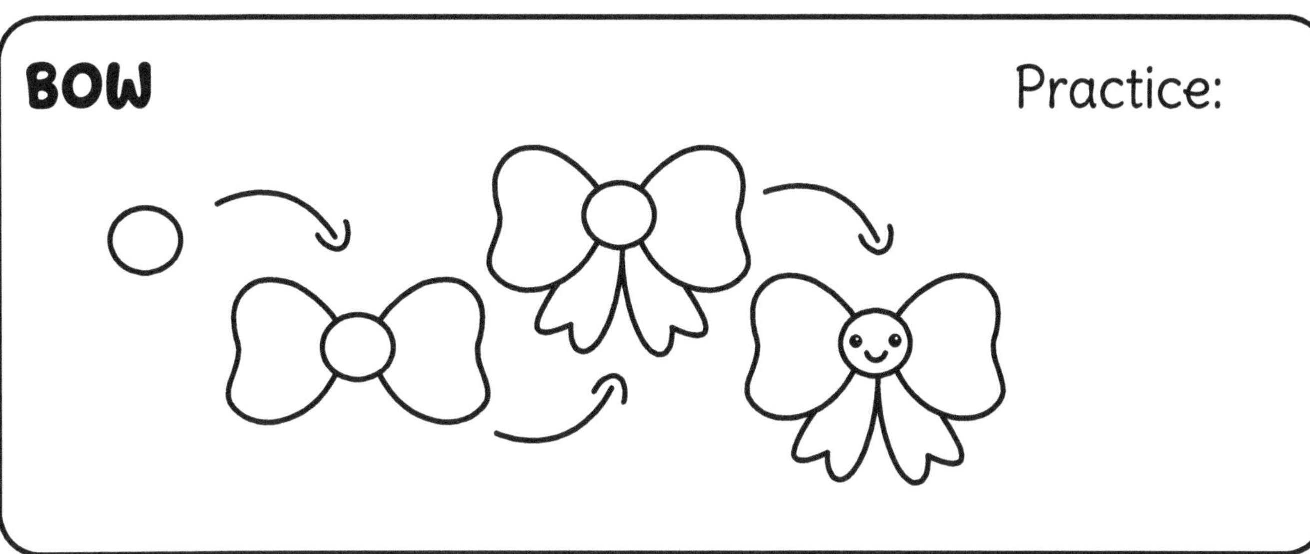

BOW

Practice:

SUNGLASSES

Practice

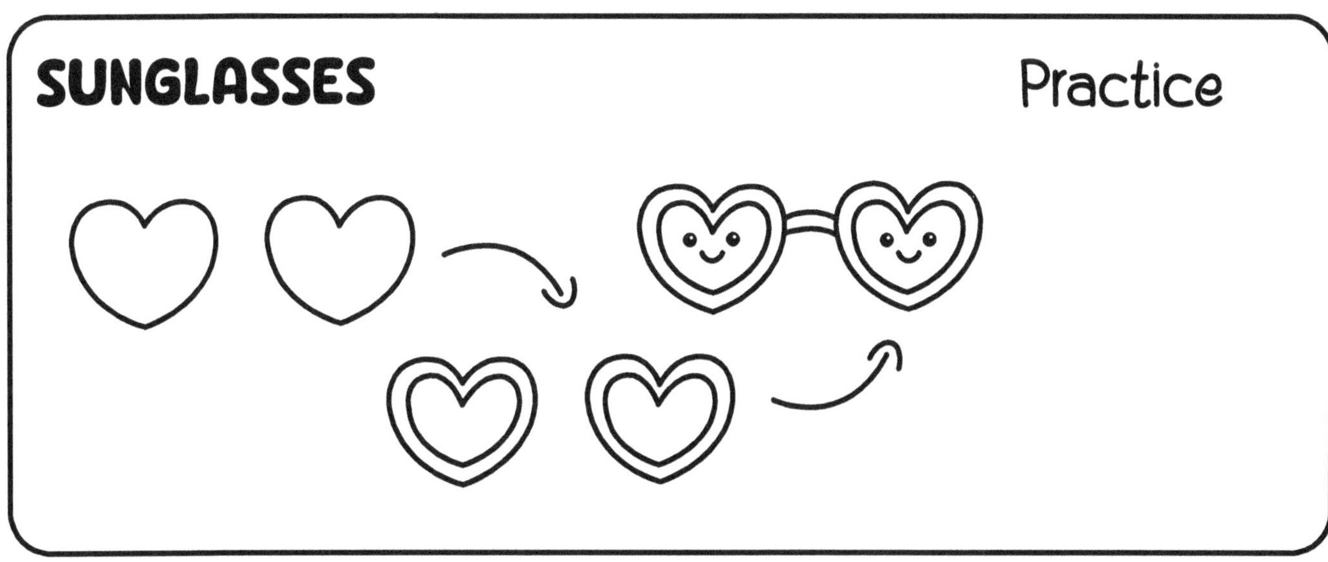

STATIONERY ITEMS

PENCIL

Practice:

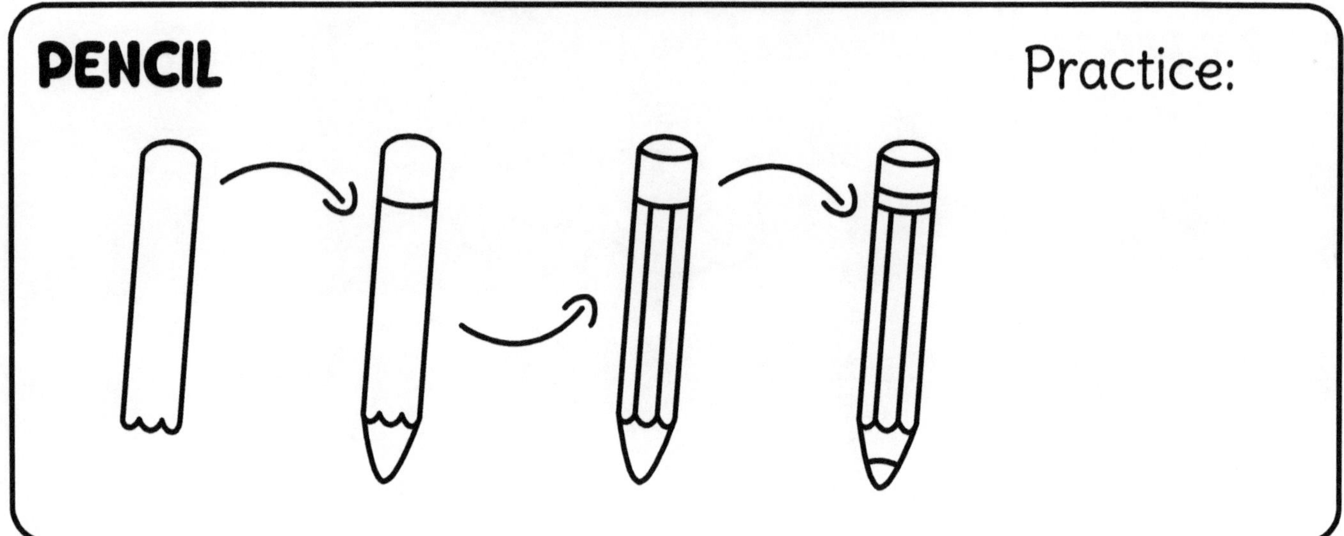

PEN

Practice:

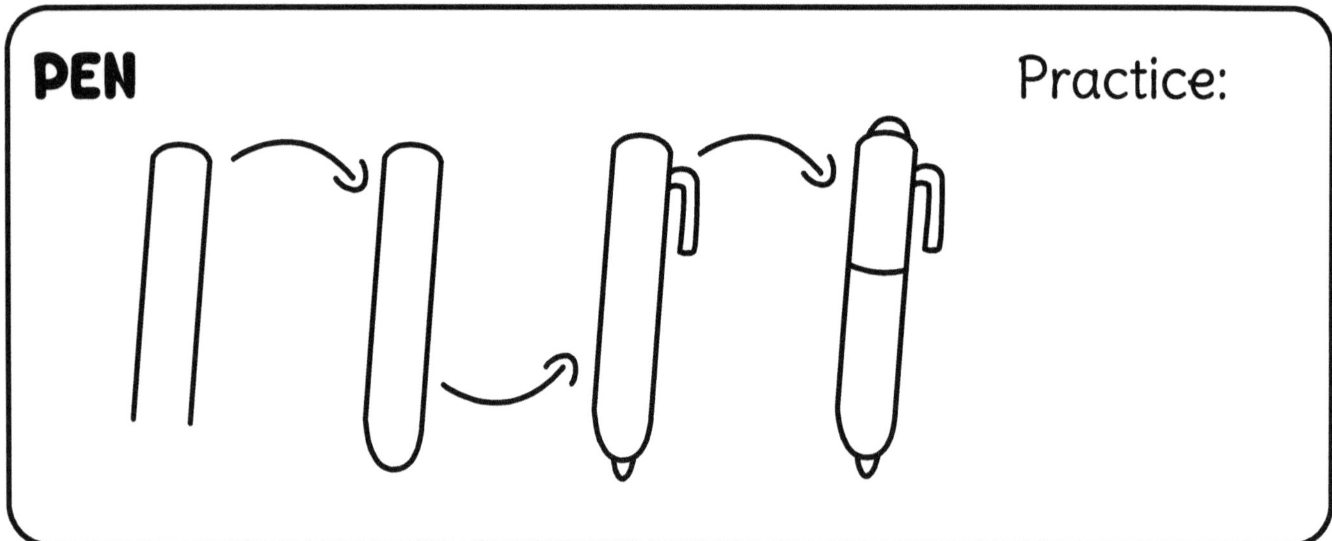

ERASER

Practice

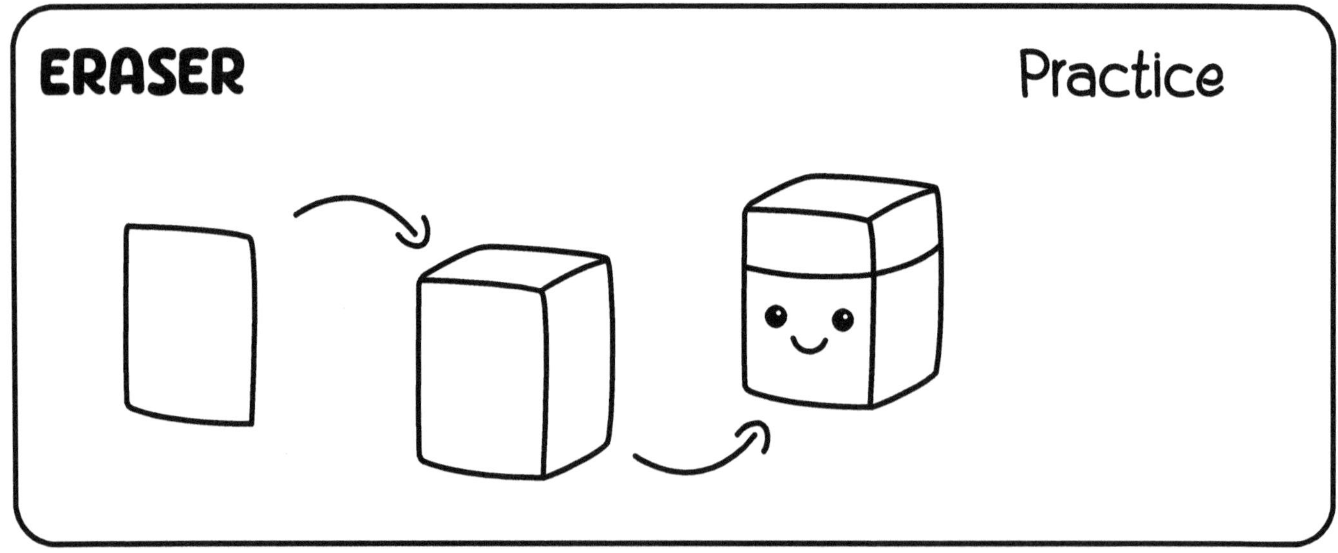

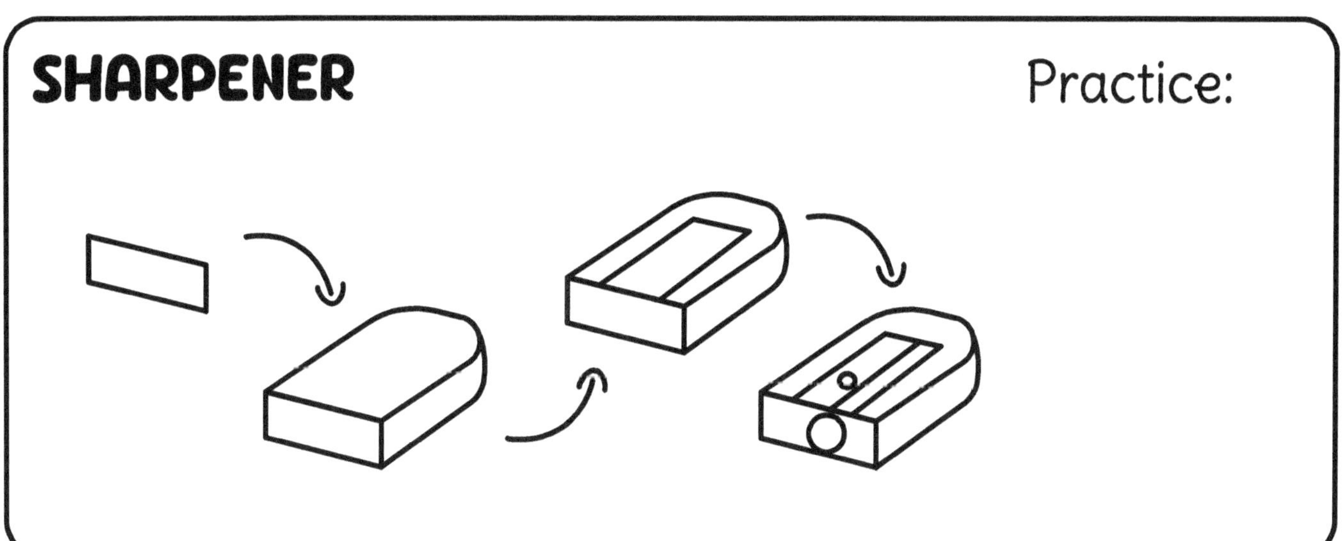

SHARPENER
Practice:

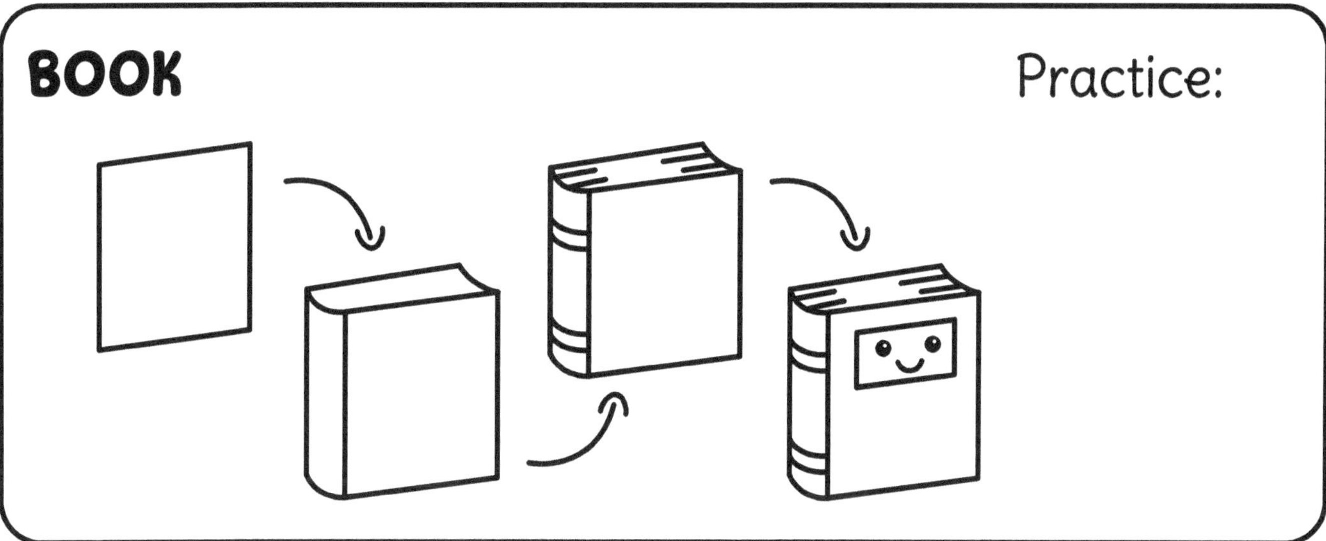

BOOK
Practice:

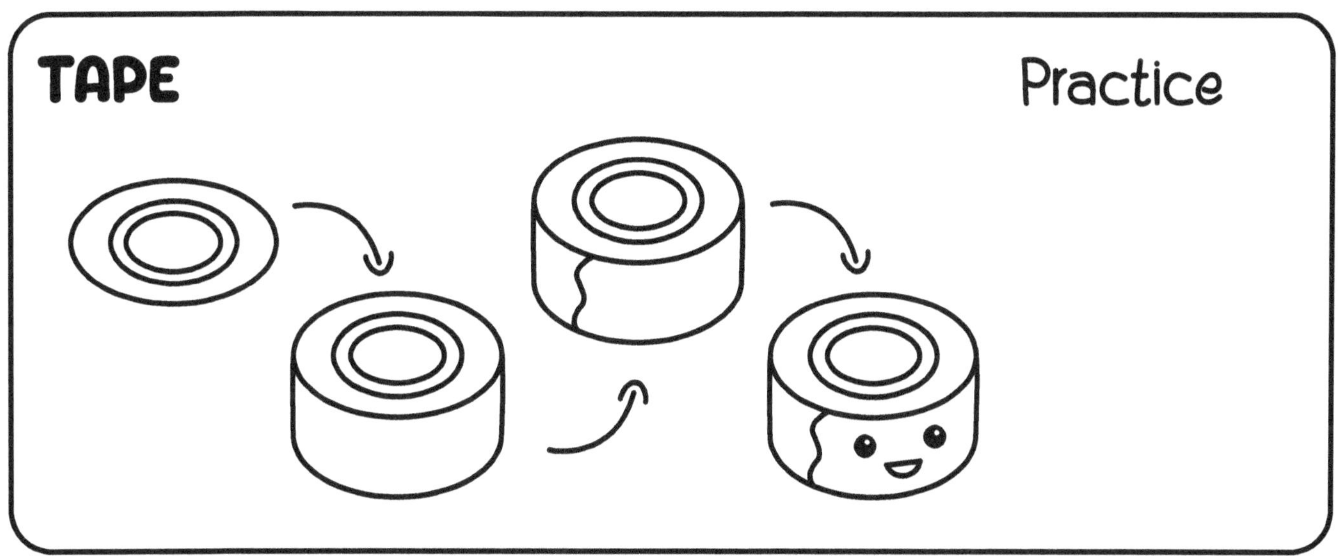

TAPE
Practice

SCISSORS

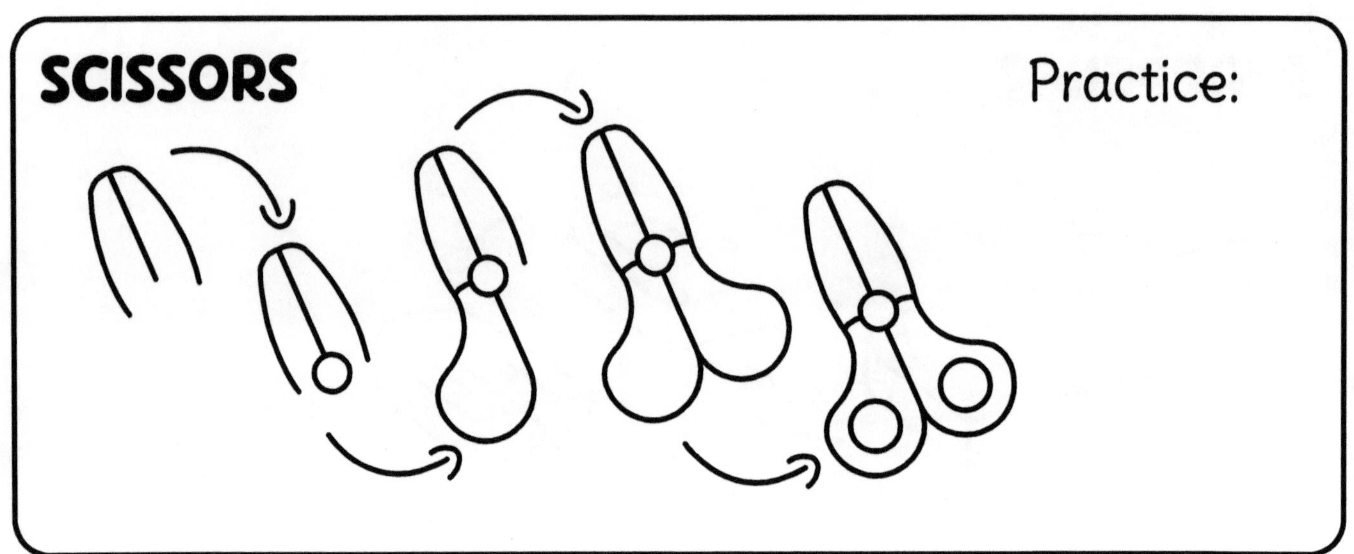

PENCIL CASE

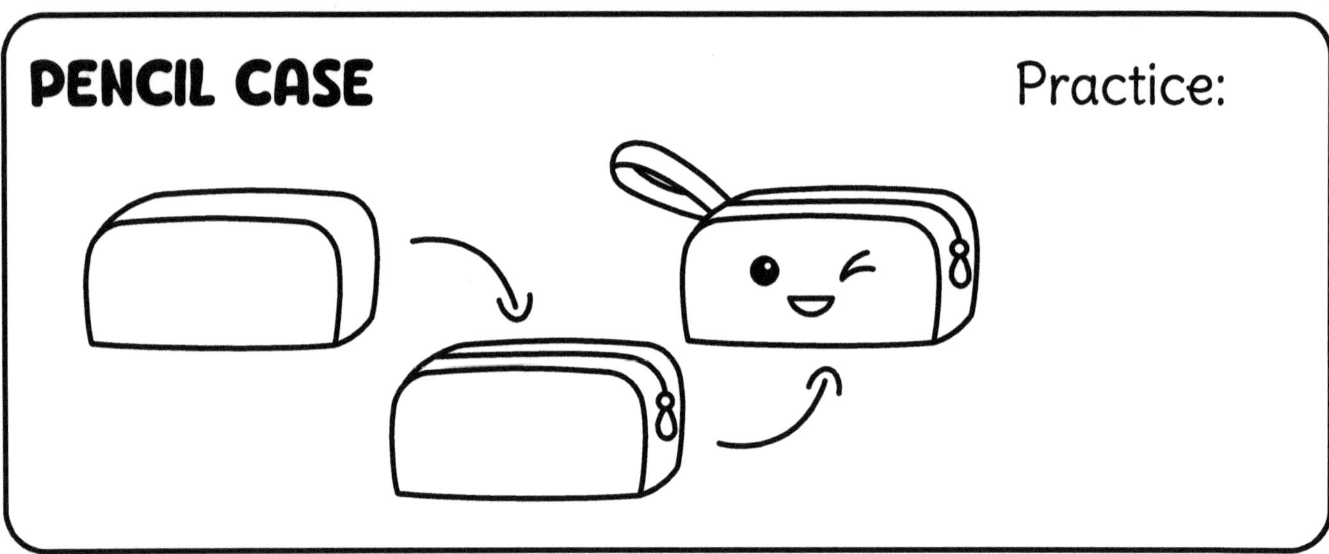

BACKPACK

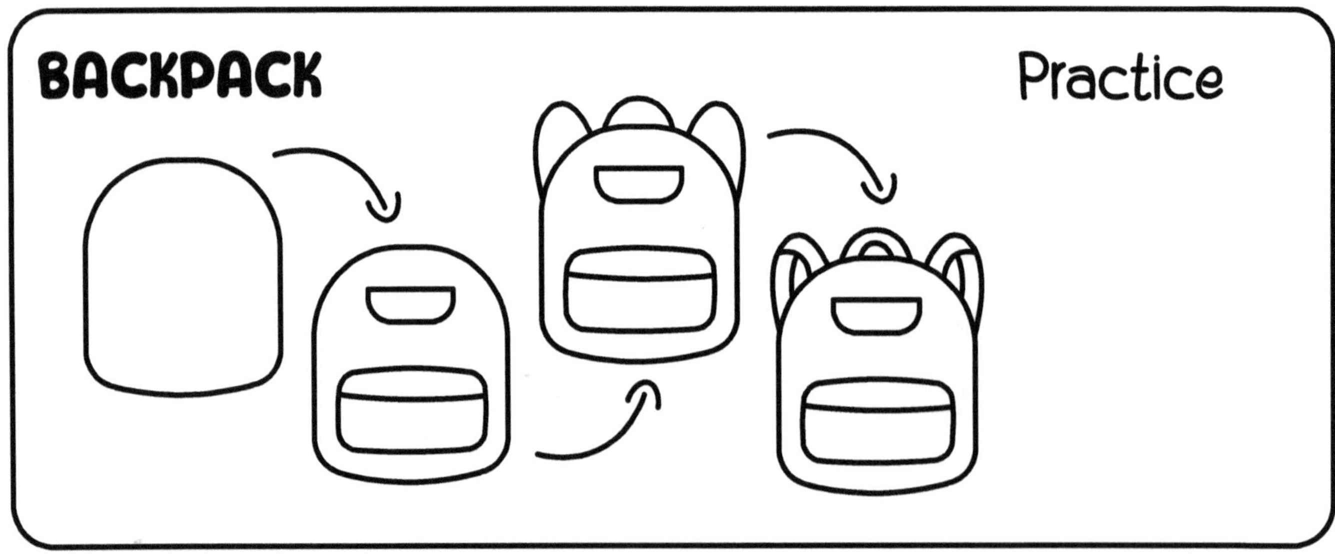

BATHROOM

TOILET PAPER
Practice:

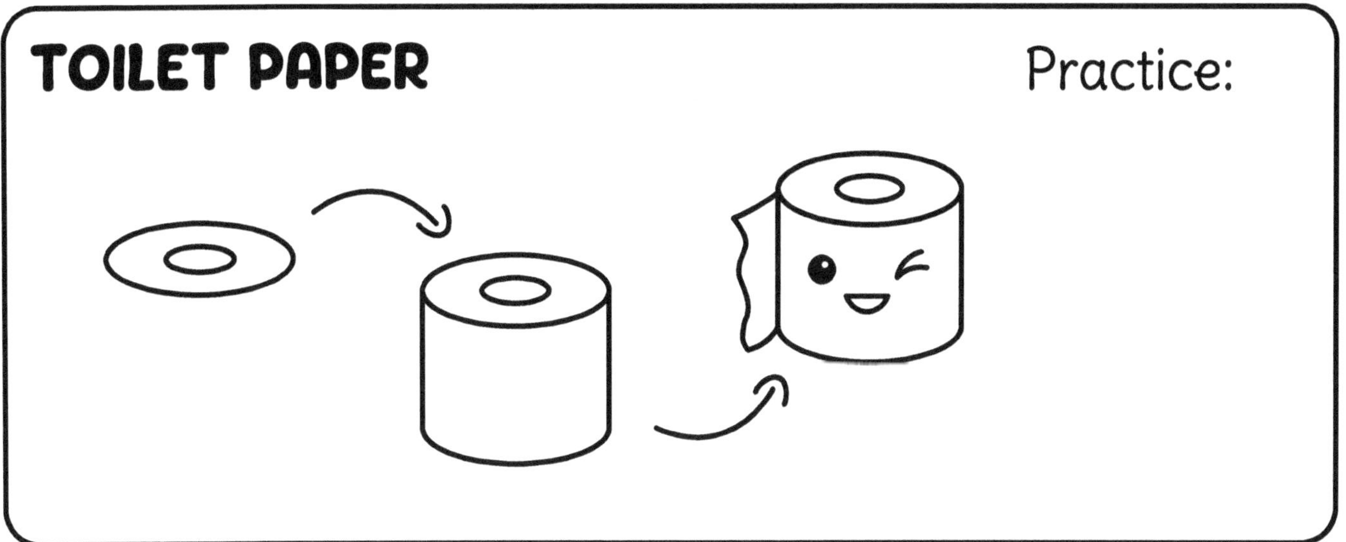

TOOTH BRUSH
Practice:

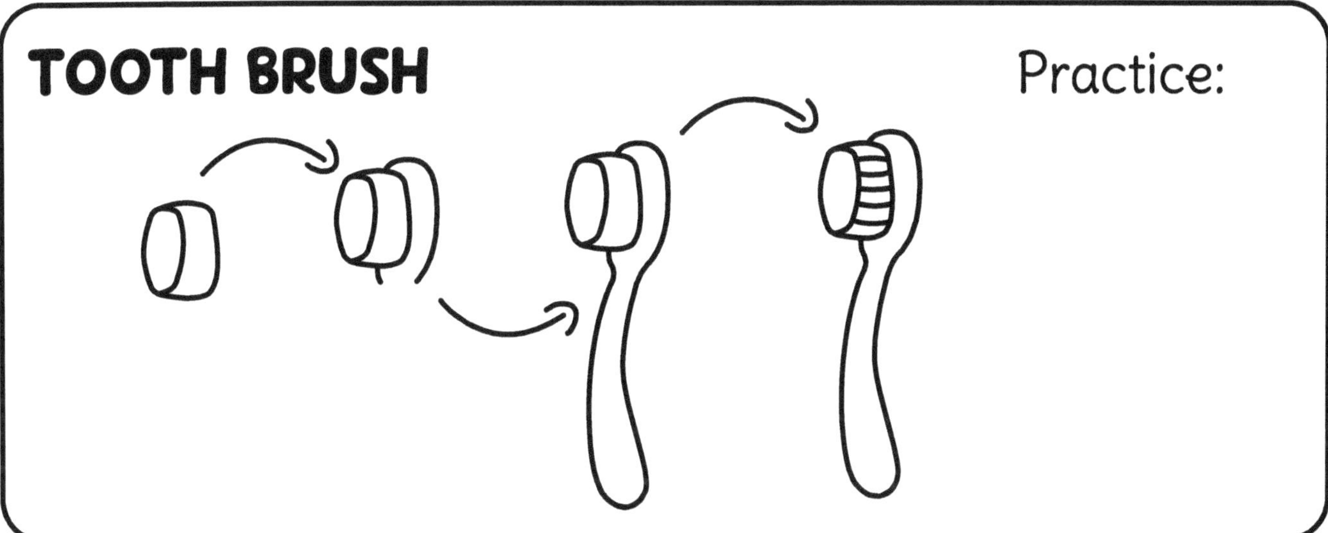

TOOTH PASTE
Practice

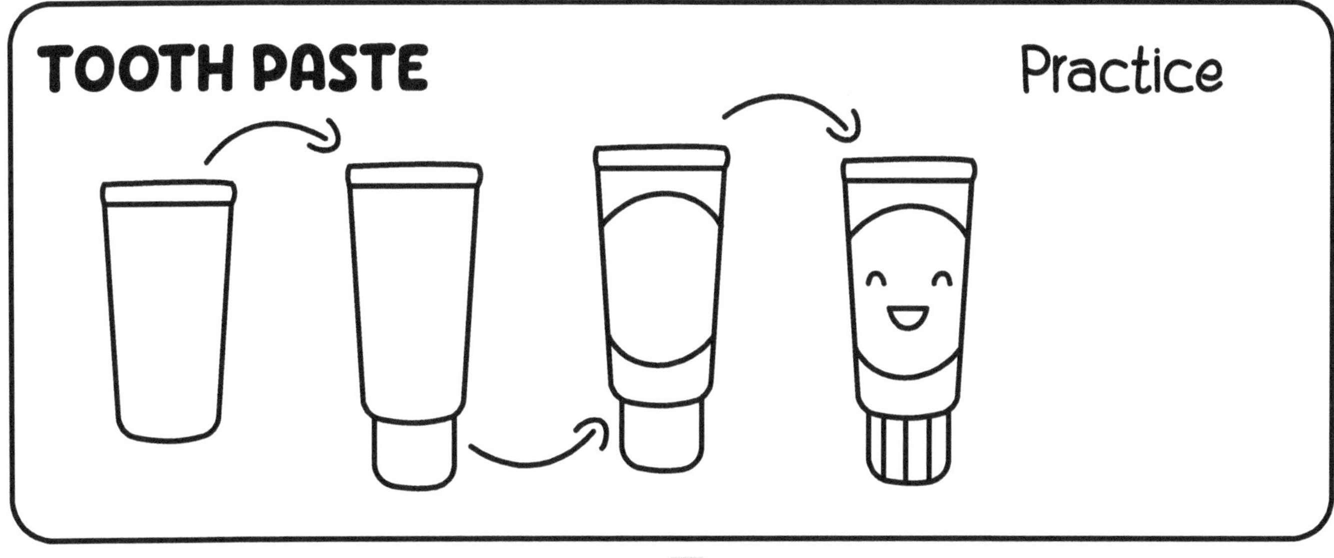

FACE WASH

Practice:

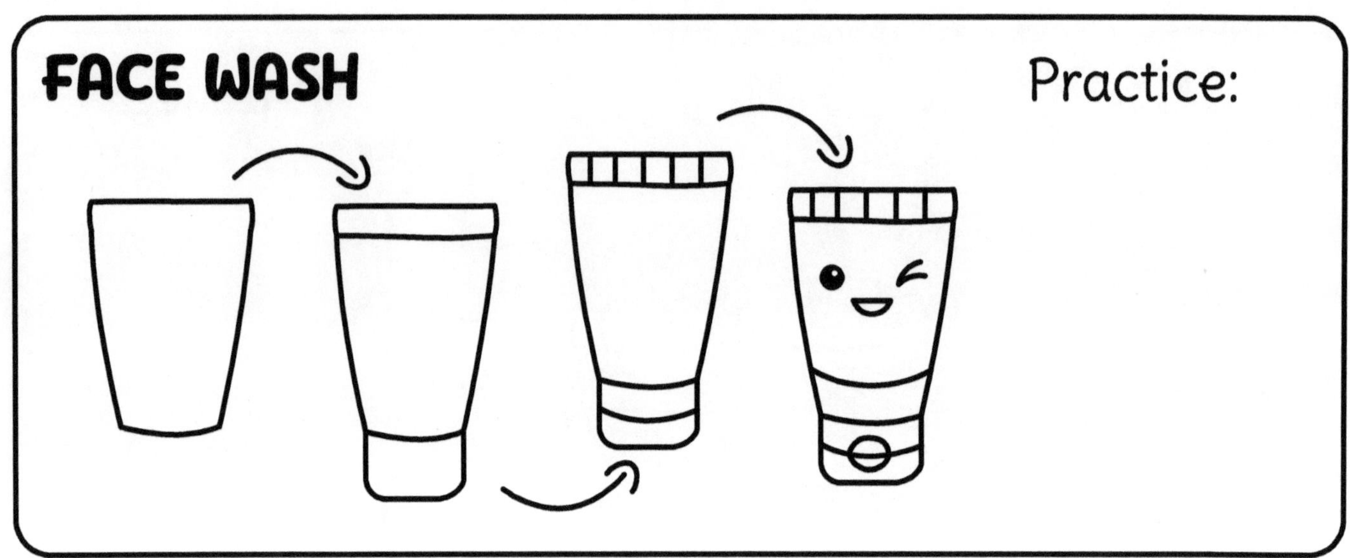

SHAMPOO

Practice:

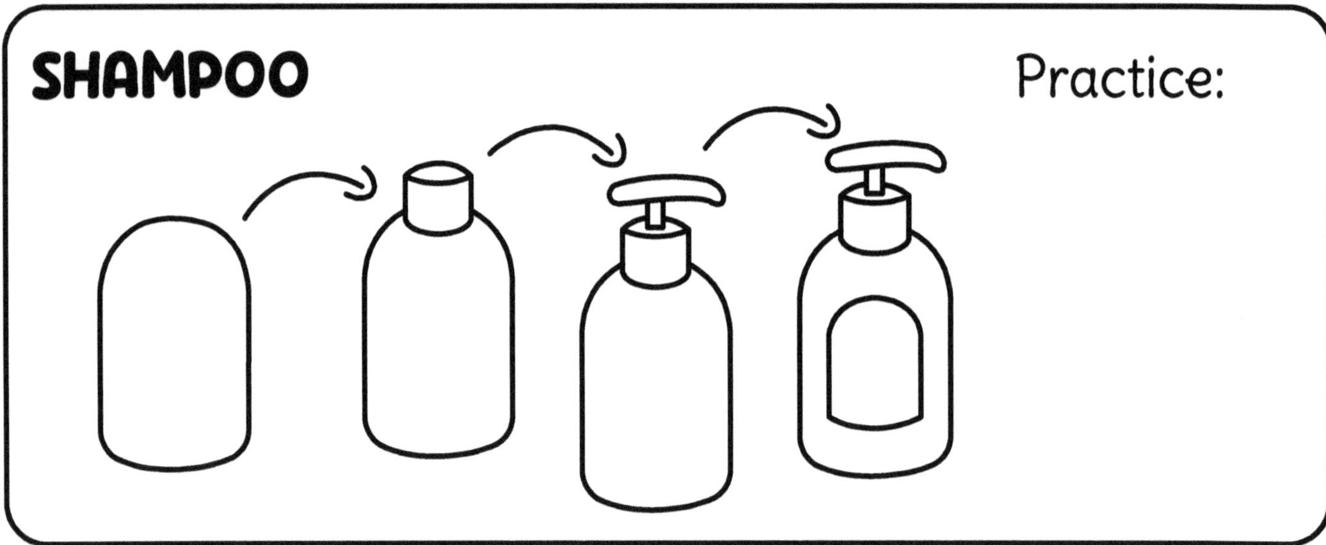

CREAM

Practice

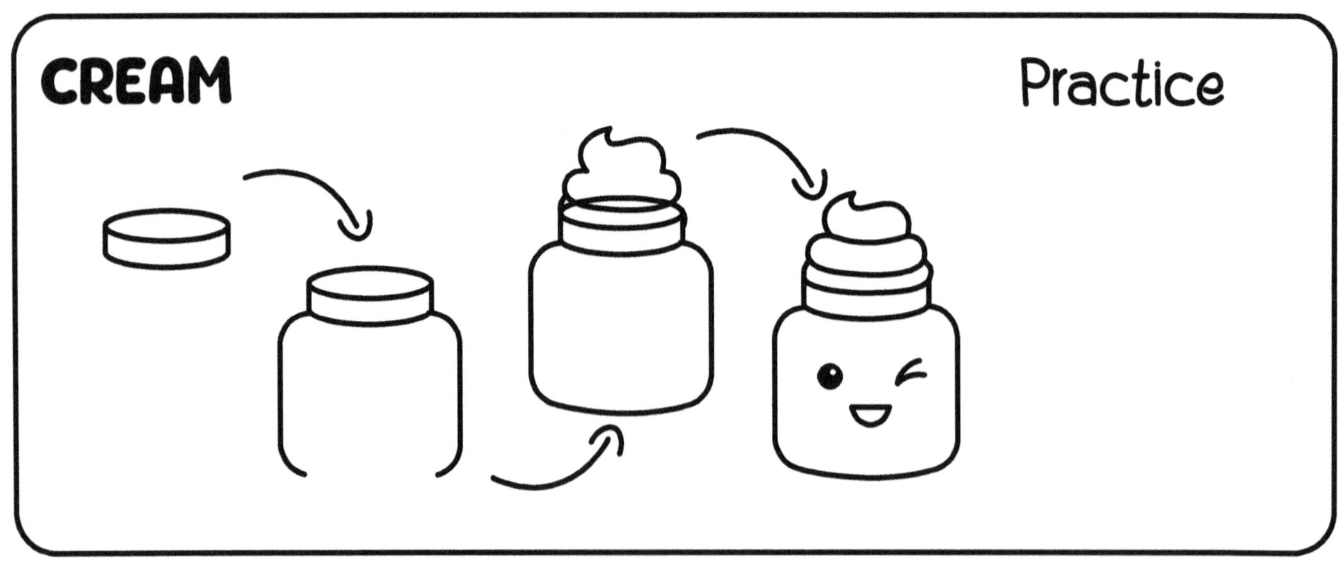

HAND MIRROR

Practice:

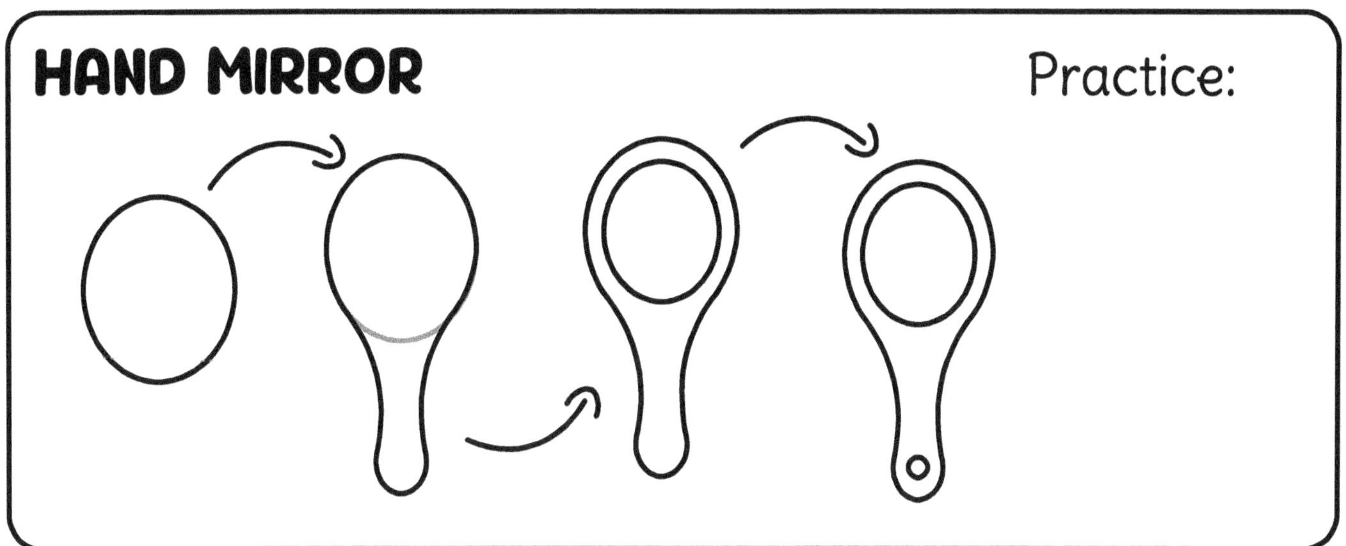

TOWEL

Practice:

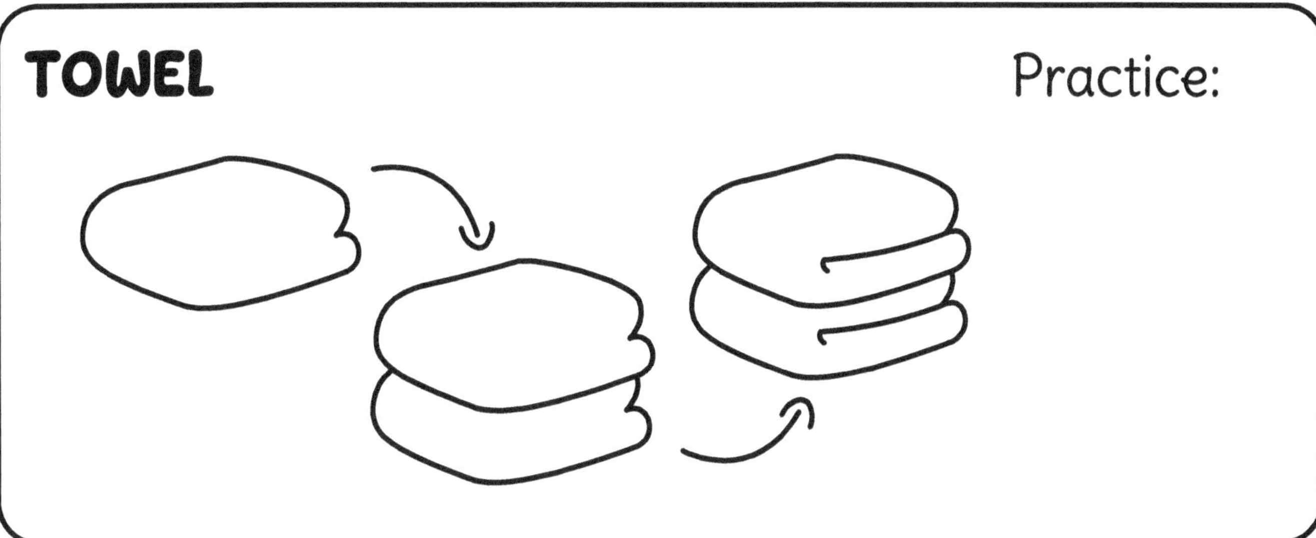

RUBBER DUCKY

Practice

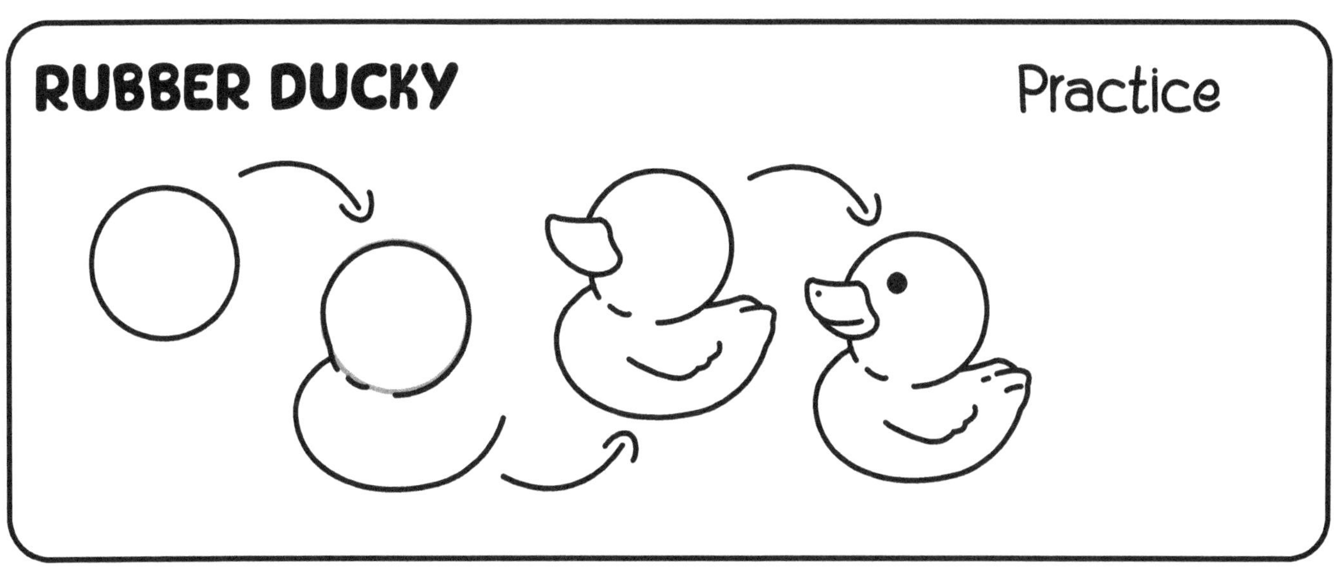

BASKET

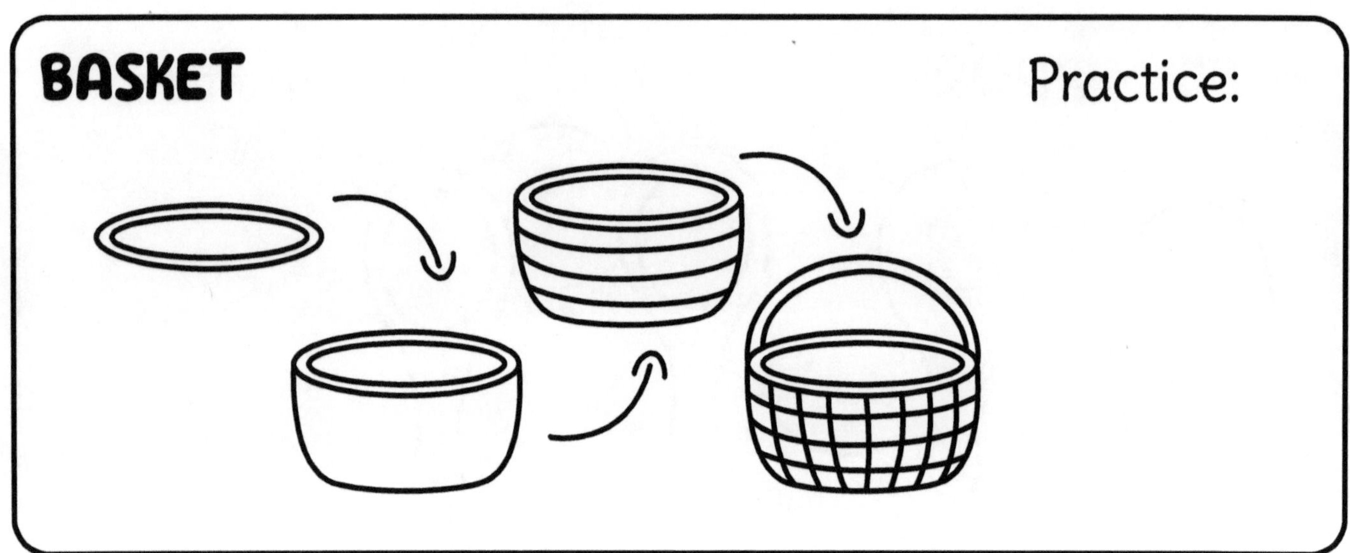

BUCKET

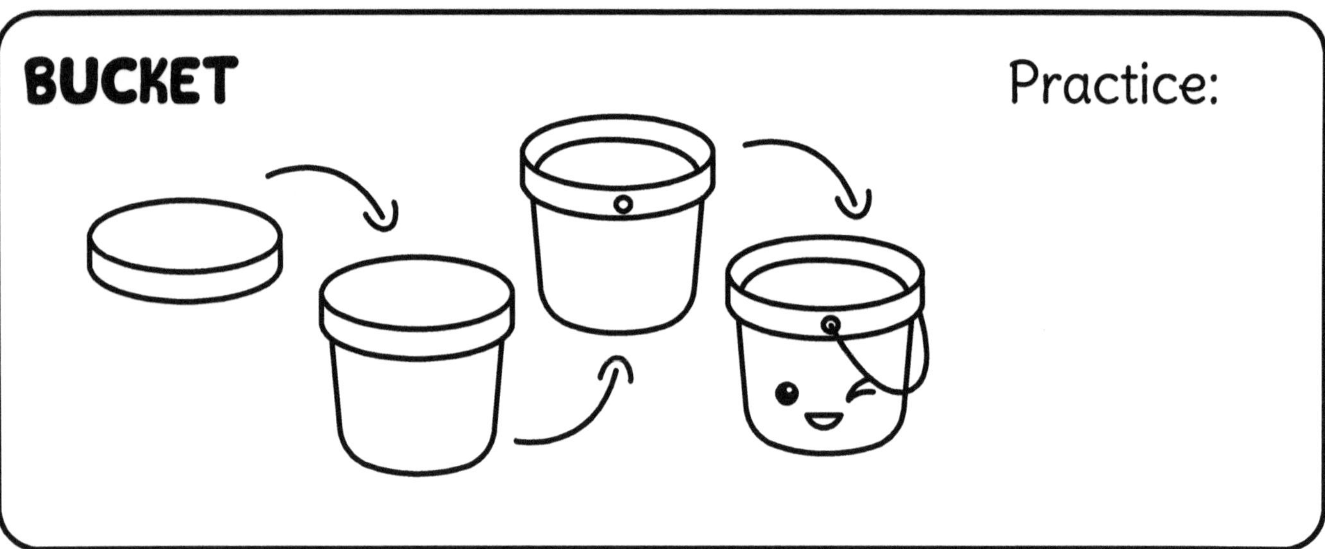

COMB

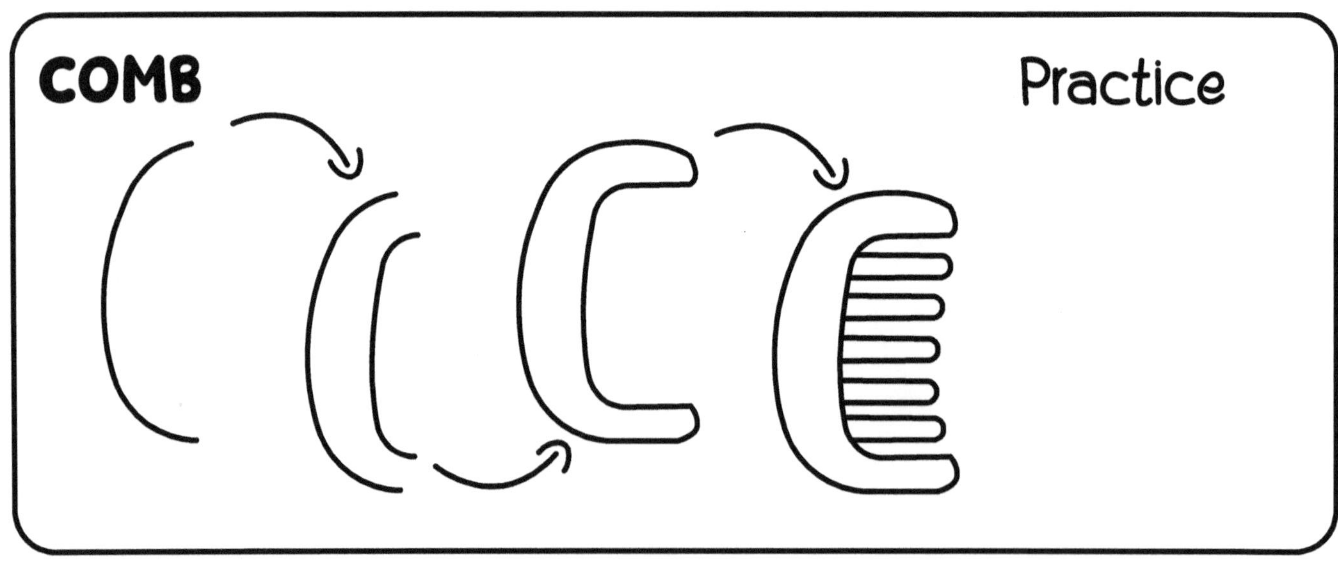

KITCHEN TOOLS

TEAPOT
Practice:

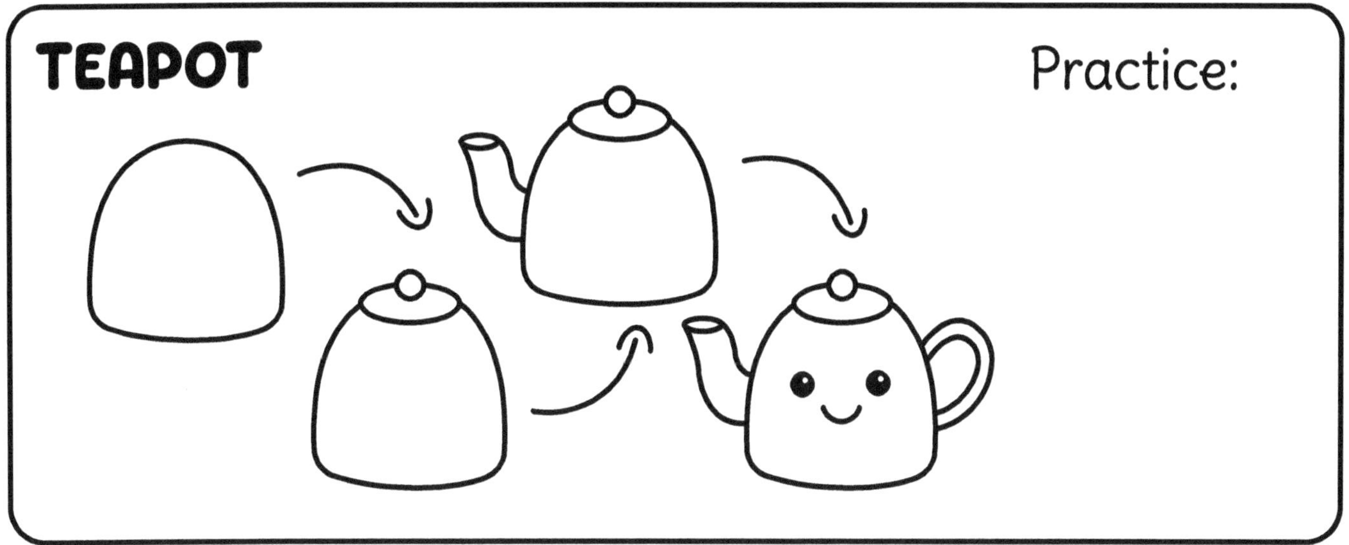

TEACUP
Practice:

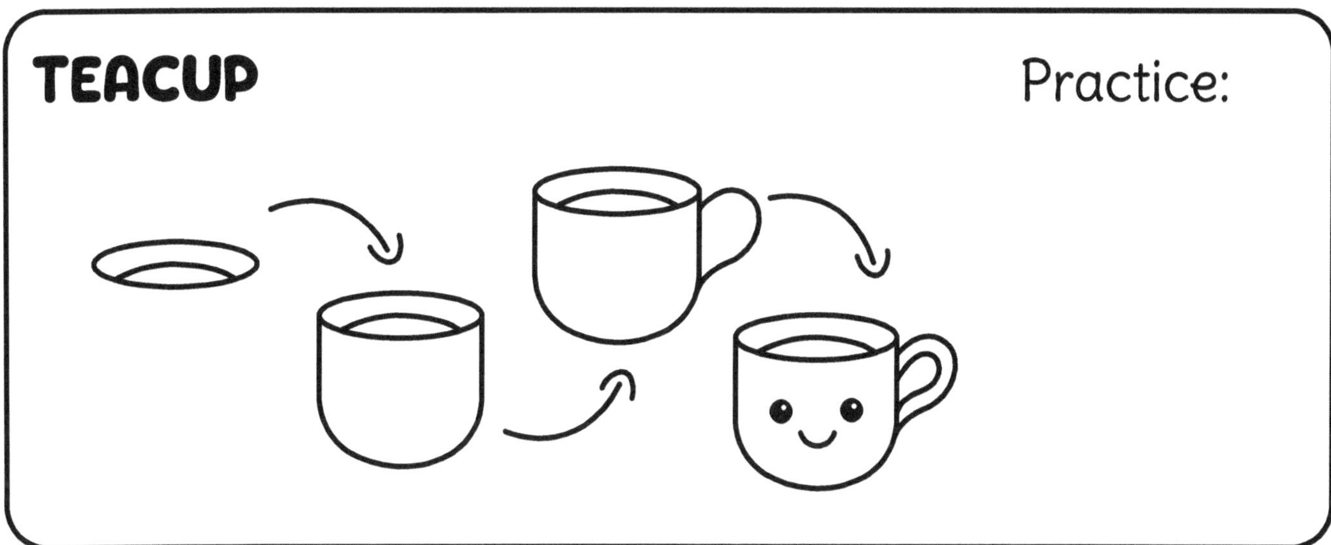

TEA BAG
Practice

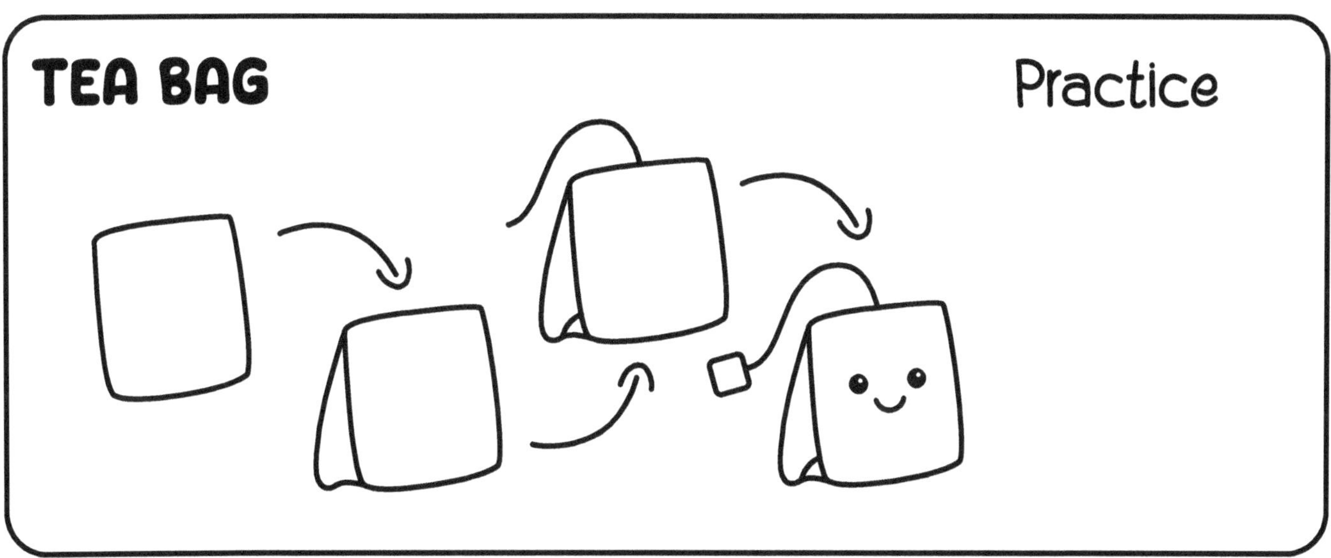

JUG

Practice:

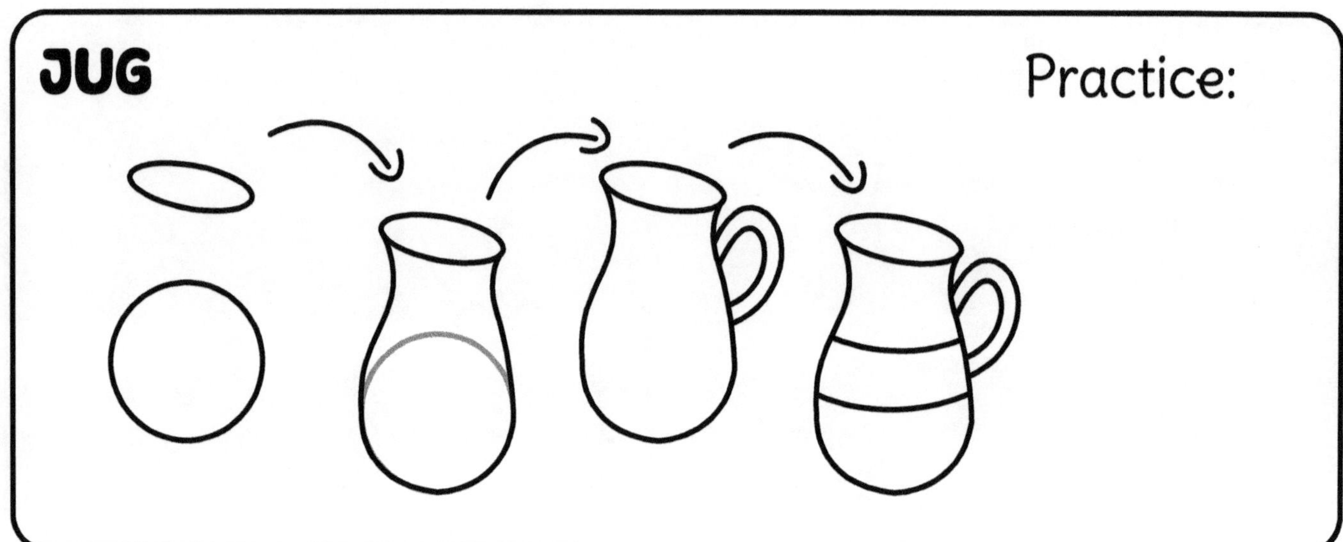

PLATES

Practice:

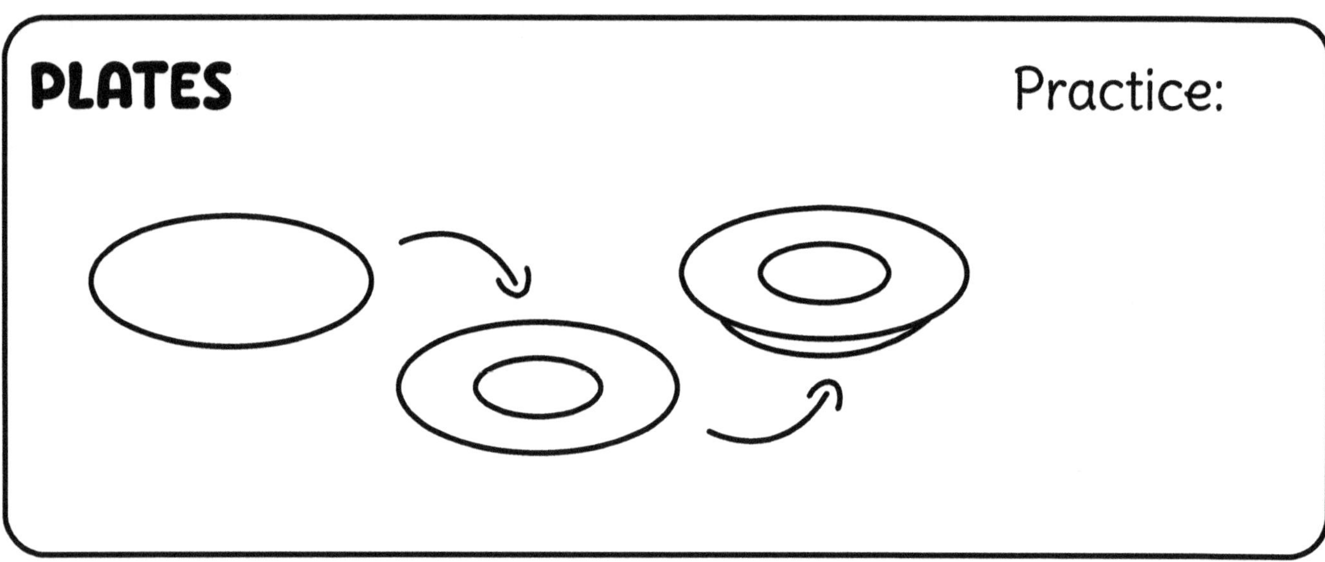

SPOON

Practice

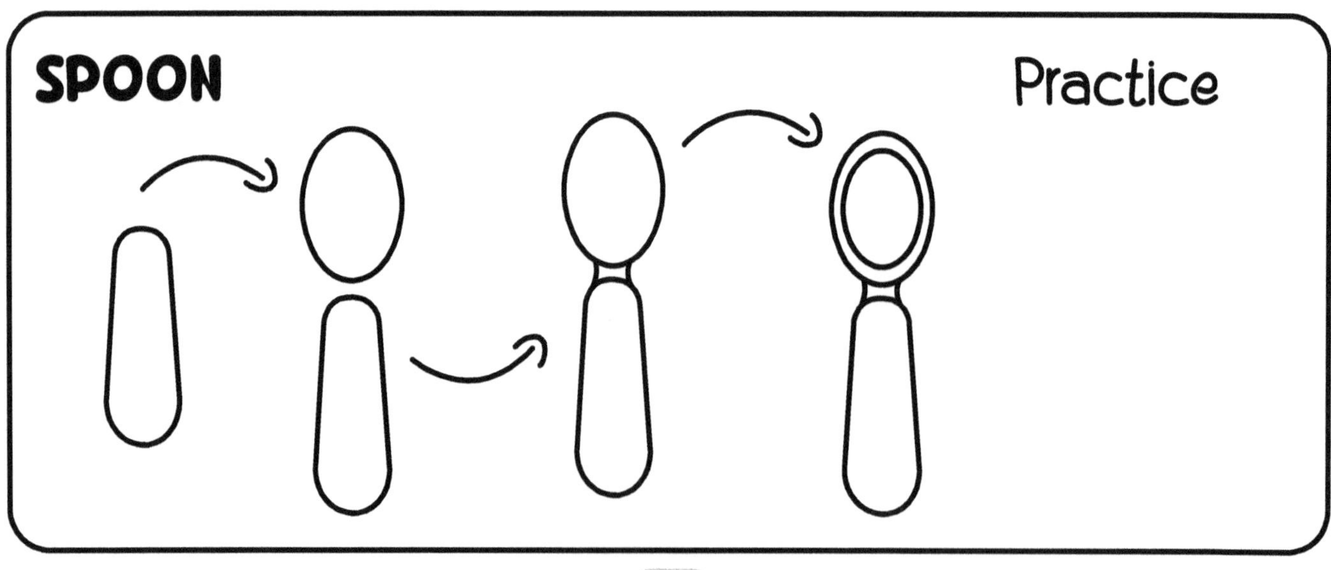

FORK

Practice:

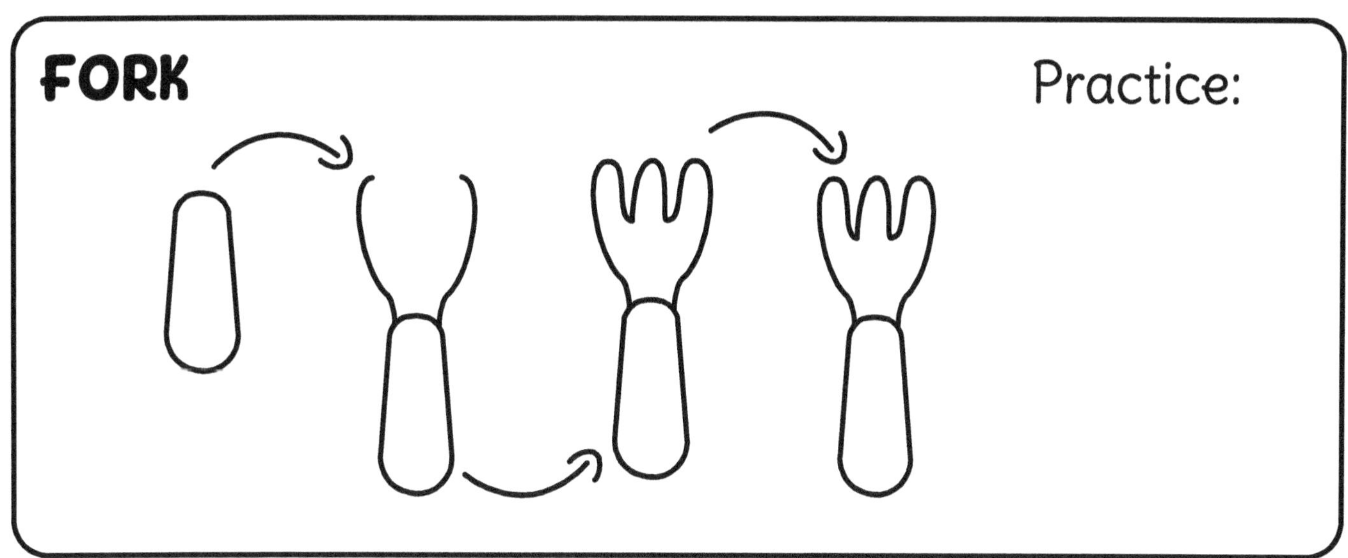

KNIFE

Practice:

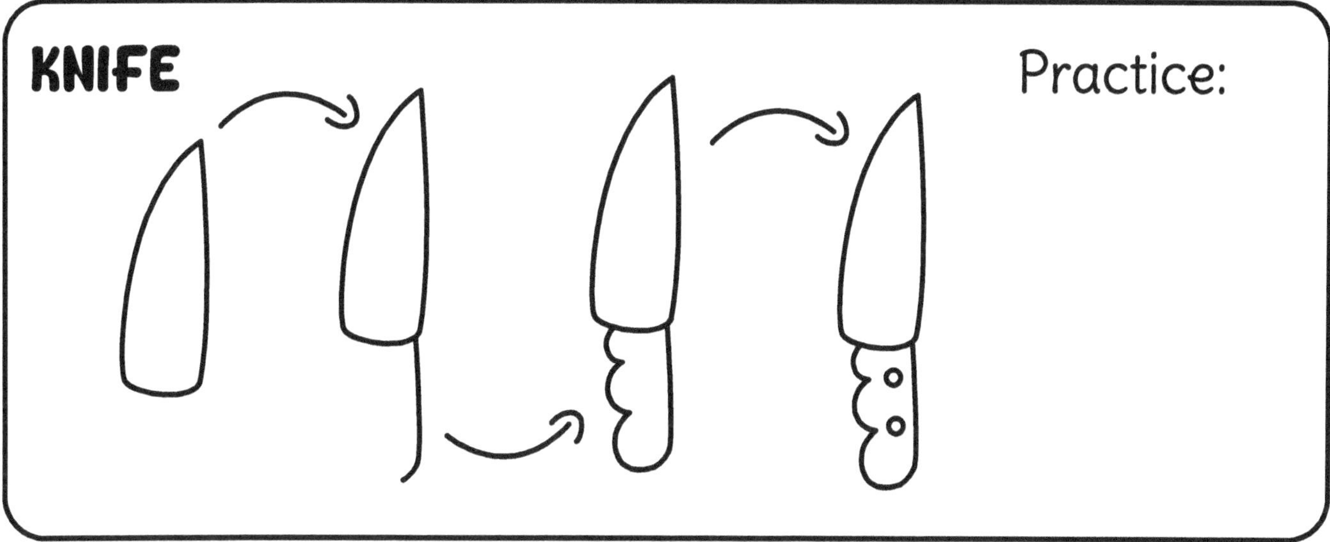

POT

Practice

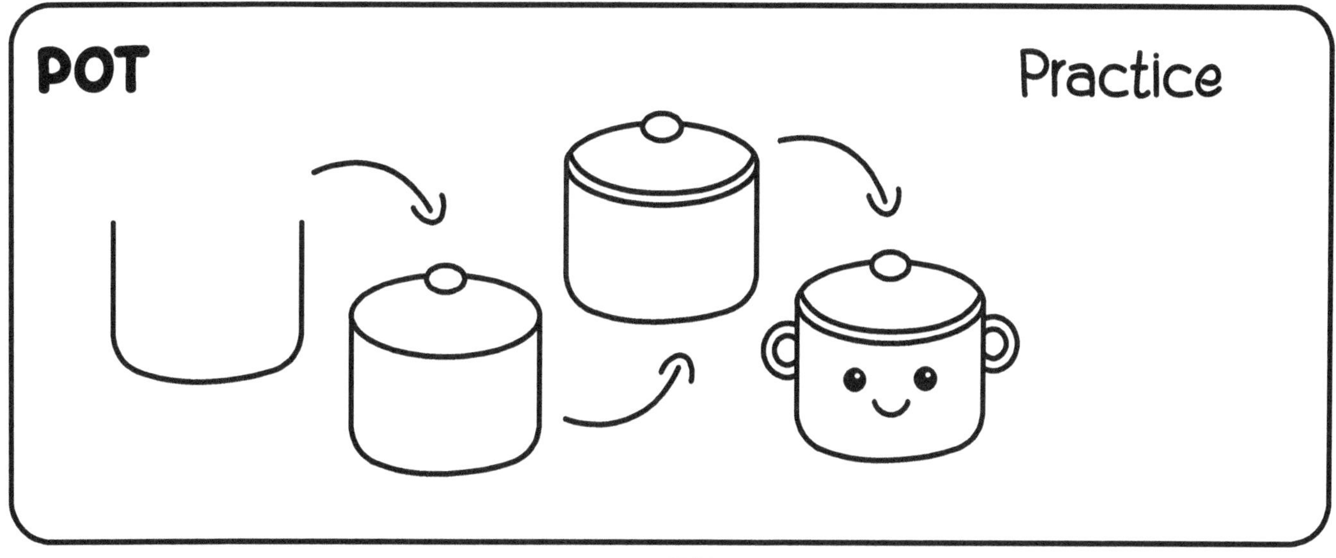

PAN

Practice:

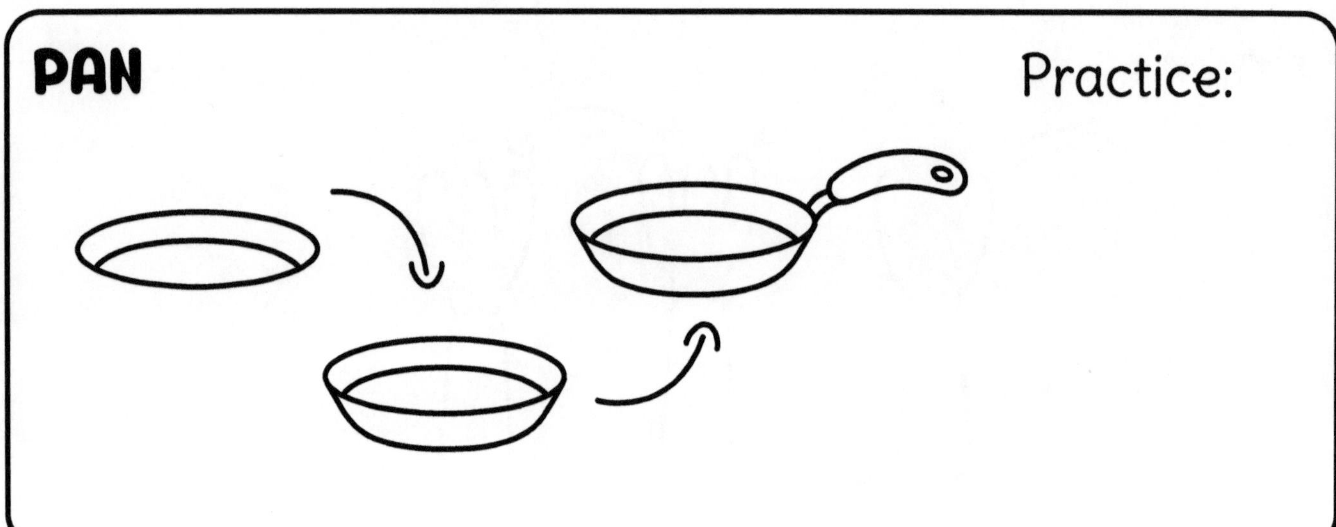

WATER BOTTLE

Practice:

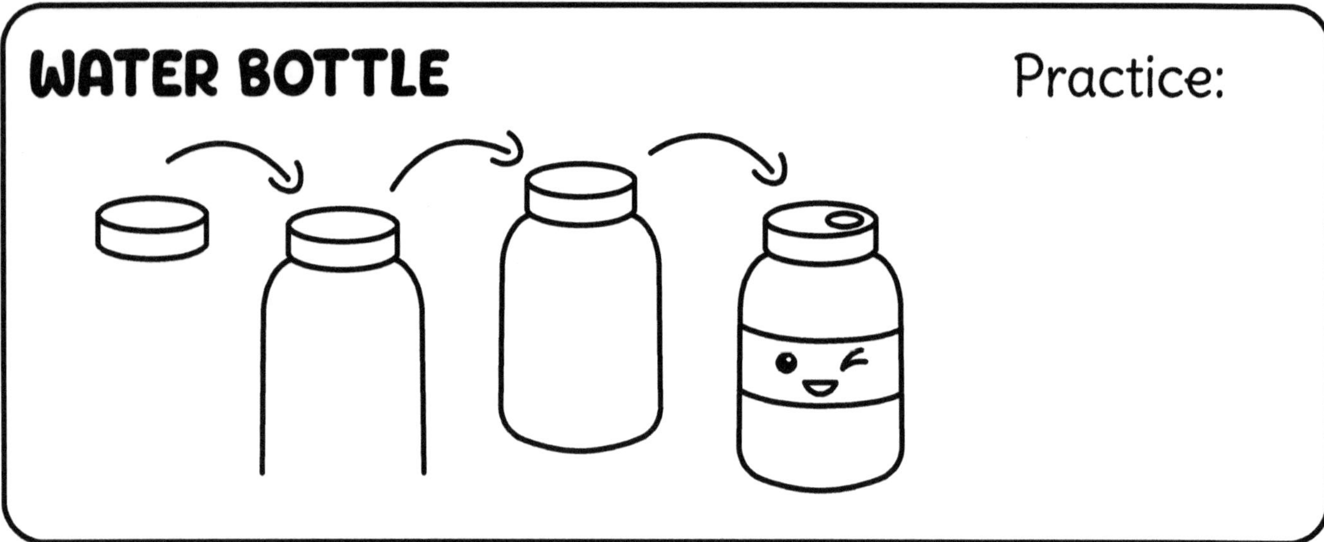

WHISK

Practice

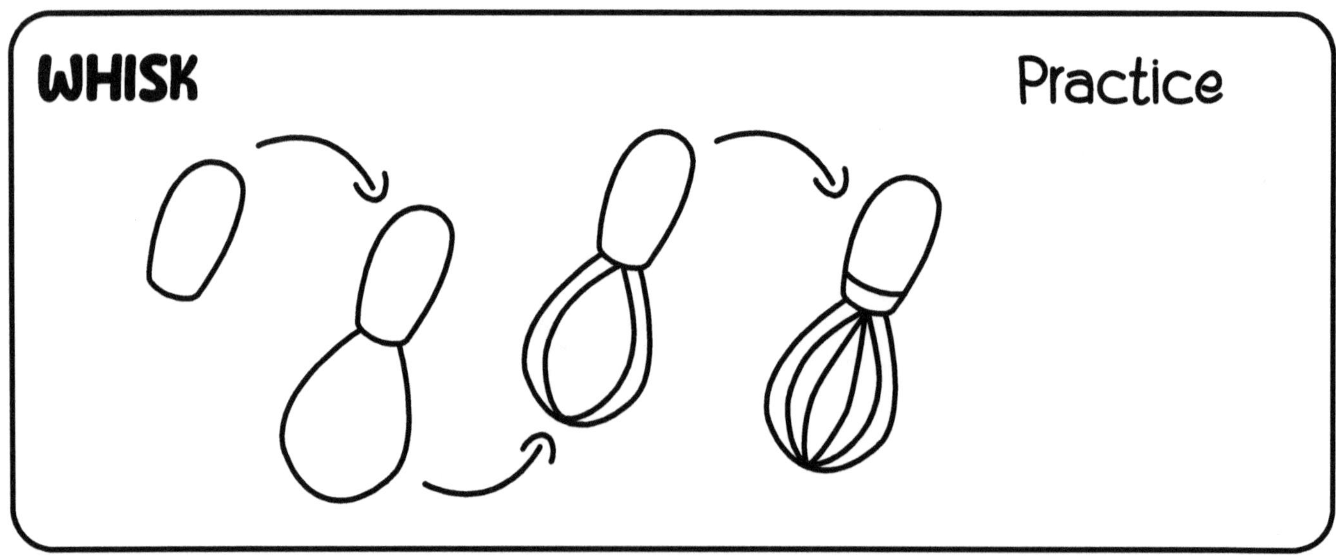

BOWL

Practice:

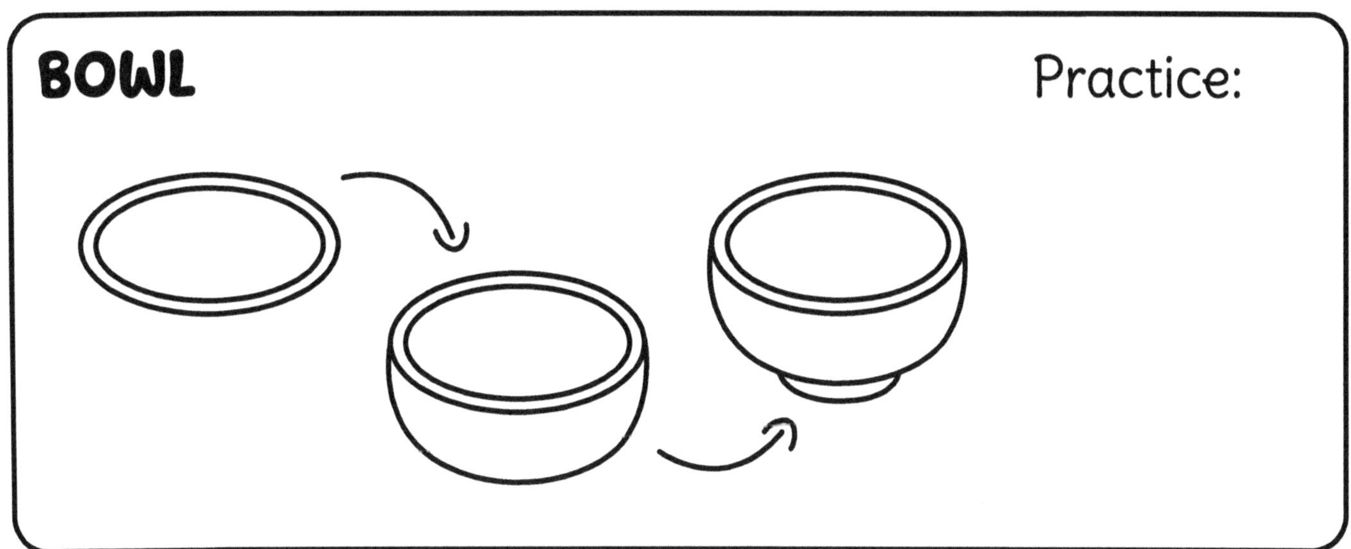

SALT SHAKER

Practice:

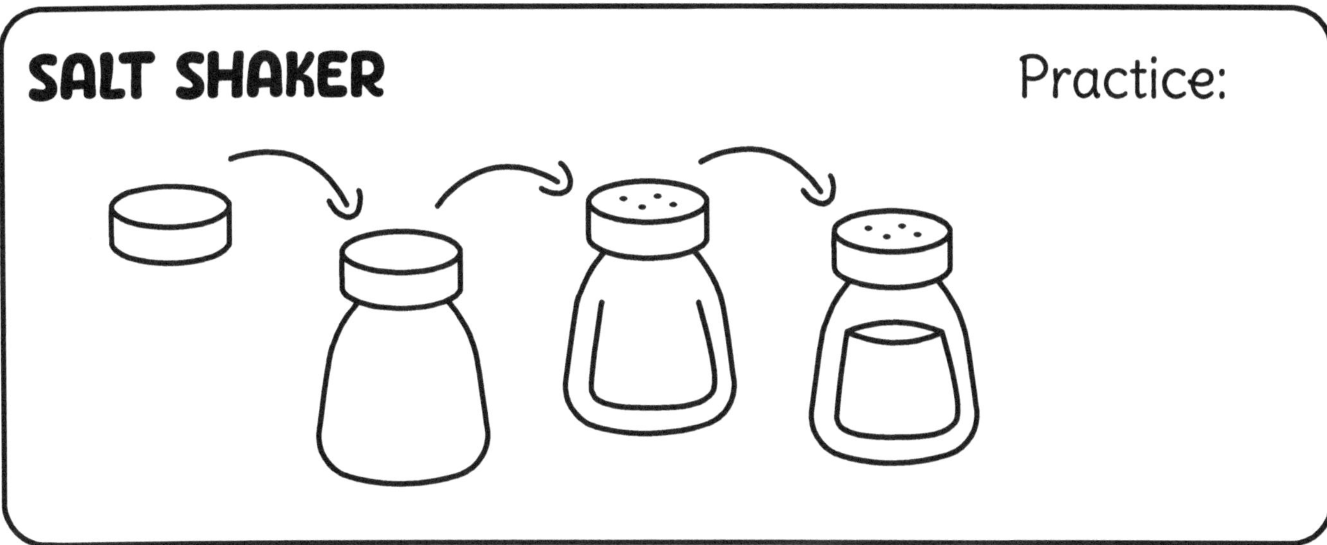

TOASTER

Practice

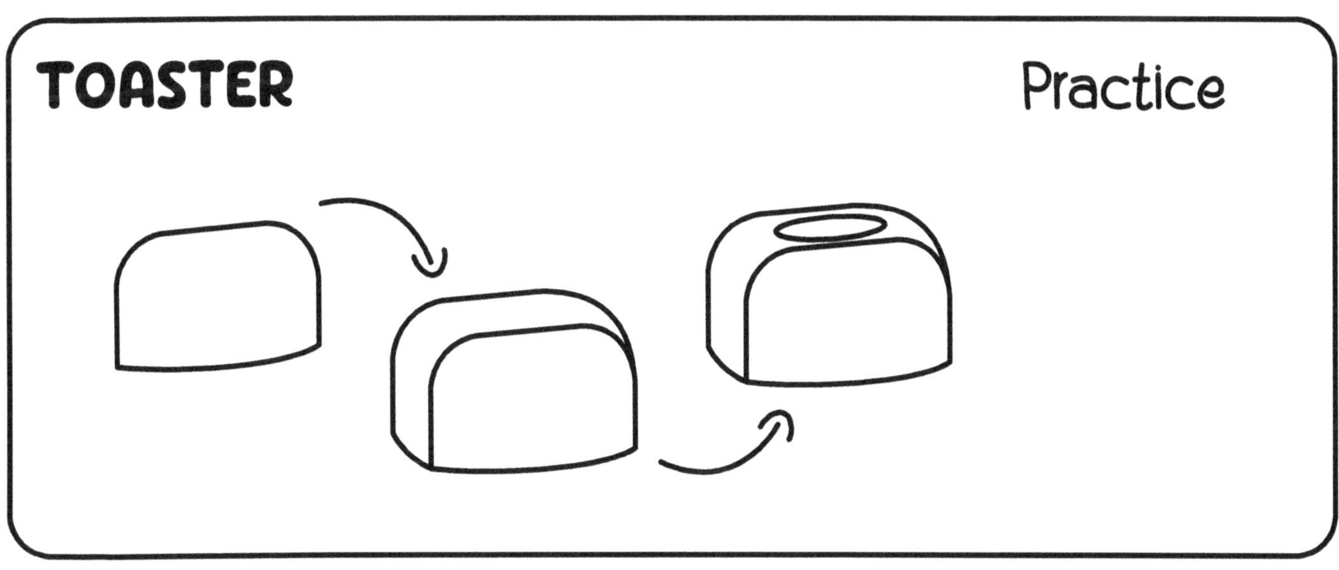

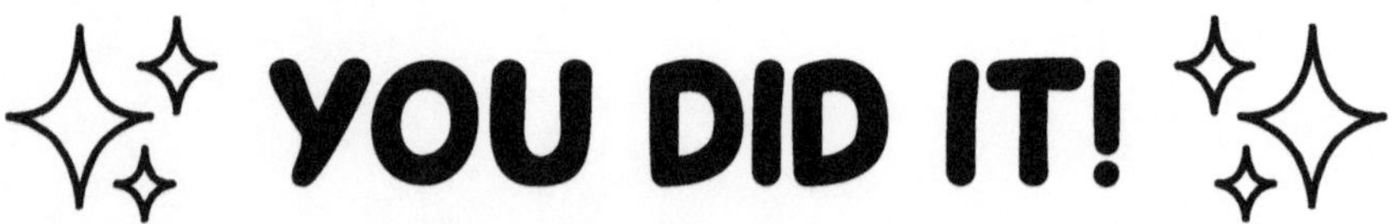

✨ YOU DID IT! ✨

YOU MADE IT TO THE VERY END—WOW!

You reached the very end of this book, and that's something to be proud of. Every page you completed helped you learn, grow, and become more confident at drawing.

This book is finished, but your learning journey is just getting started. Keep exploring, practicing, and believing in yourself!

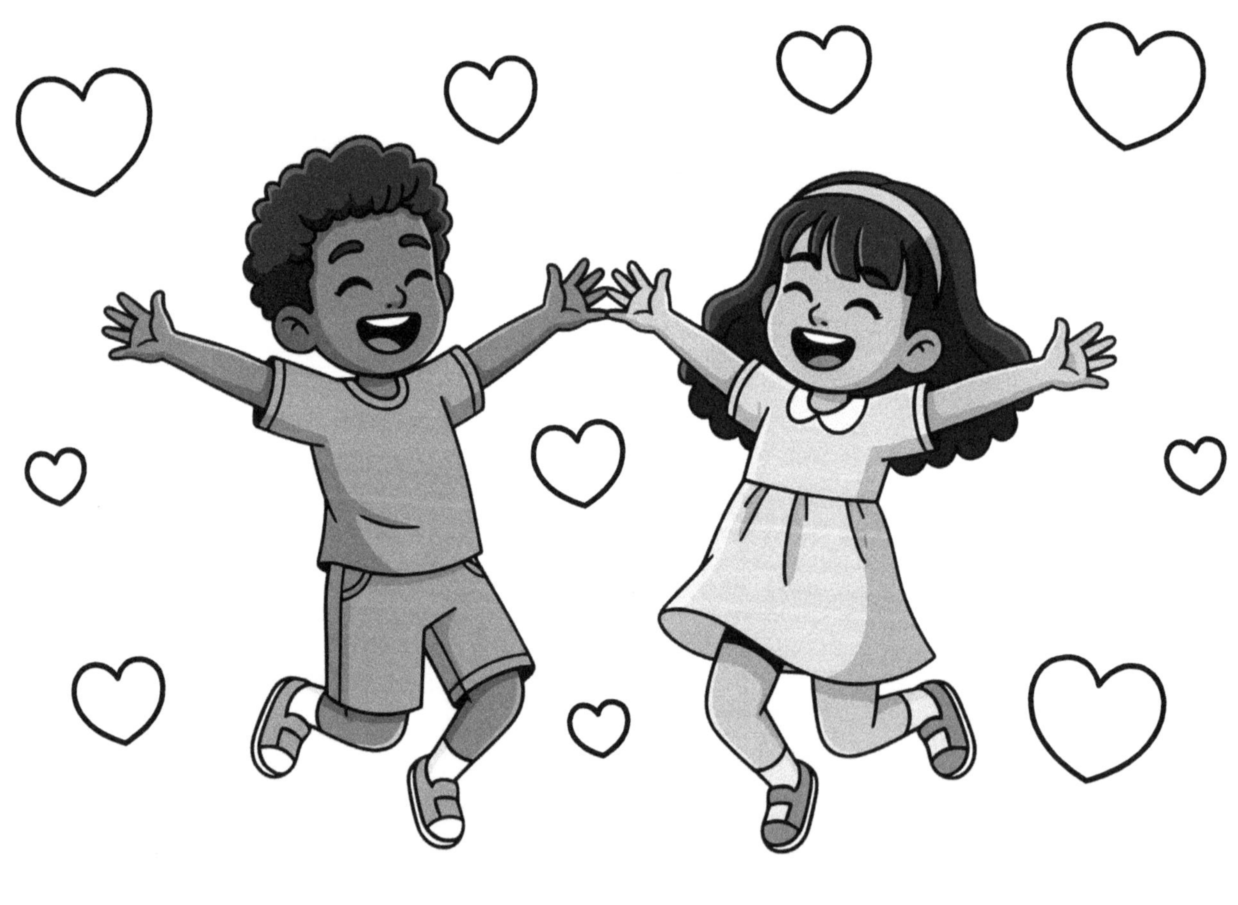